Gender, Countertransference and the Erotic Transfe

Gender, Countertransference and the Erotic Transference offers new insights into working with complex transference and countertransference phenomena. Including views from a wide spectrum of theoretical backgrounds, it makes a unique contribution to discourse on the themes of gender, sexuality and the erotic transference.

The contributors are highly experienced clinicians with international reputations as theorists in the fields of analytical psychology, psychoanalysis and psychoanalytic psychotherapy. Illustrated with closely observed clinical examples and detailed theoretical discussion, innovations in technique are introduced on themes including developmental mourning, female perversion, the meaning and purpose of the erotic transference, the dying patient, lesbian homoerotic transference and supervision of the erotic transference. Countertransference is vividly explored in chapters on sexual difference, the therapist's body and the challenging topic of perversion in the analyst. The book is divided into four parts:

- Gender and the Erotic Transference
- Erotic Transferences and the Symbolic Function
- Women Working With Women
- Historical Perspectives on Women Working with Men.

Gender, Countertransference and the Erotic Transference extends existing theory, highlighting the symbolic nature of the transference/countertransference dynamic. It will be compelling reading for experienced clinicians, students and trainees in the fields of psychoanalysis, analytical psychology and psychoanalytic psychotherapy, as well as counselling, the arts therapies and social work.

Joy Schaverien, PhD is a Jungian analyst in private practice, a Professional Member of the Society of Analytical Psychology in London, a Training Analyst and Supervisor of the British Association of Psychotherapists, and a member of the International Association for Analytical Psychology.

Gender, Countertransference and the Erotic Transference

Perspectives from analytical psychology and psychoanalysis

Edited by Joy Schaverien

Routledge
Taylor & Francis Group

LONDON AND NEW YORK

First published 2006 by Routledge
27 Church Road, Hove, East Sussex, BN3 2FA

Simultaneously published in the USA and Canada
by Routledge
270 Madison Avenue, New York, NY 10016

Routledge is an imprint of the Taylor & Francis Group, an informa business

© 2006 selection and editorial matter, Joy Schaverien; individual chapters, the copyright holders

Typeset in Sabon by BookEns Ltd, Royston, Herts.
Printed and bound in Great Britain by MPG Books Ltd, Bodmin, Cornwall
Paperback cover design by Hannah Armstrong

Cover picture: Nature Lesson III by Peter Wilson (1986). Woodcut in four colours.

This publication has been produced with paper manufactured to strict environmental standards and with pulp derived from sustainable forests.

British Library Cataloguing in Publication Data
A catalogue record for this book is available from the British Library

Library of Congress Cataloging in Publication Data
Gender, countertransference, and the erotic transference:
   perspectives from analytical psychology and psychoanalysis/edited by Joy
   Schaverien.
     p. cm.
   Includes bibliographical references and index.
   1. Psychotherapy–Erotic aspects.   2. Transference (Psychology)
3. Countertransference (Psychology)   4. Gender identity–Psychological
aspects.   5. Jungian psychology.   6. Psychoanalysis.
I. Schaverien, Joy,
   [DNLM: 1. Transference (Psychology)   2. Countertransference
(Psychology)   3. Sexuality–psychology.   4. Gender Identity.   5. Professional-
Patient Relations.   6. Psychoanalytic Therapy.   WM 62 G325
2006]
RC489.E75G46 2006
616.89'17–dc22

                                        2006007194

ISBN 13: 978-1-58391-763-3 (hbk)
ISBN 13: 978-1-58391-764-0 (pbk)

ISBN 10: 1-58391-763-2 (hbk)
ISBN 10: 1-58391-764-0 (pbk)

Contents

Acknowledgements

Many of the chapters in this book have been previously published and we would like to thank the following for their permission to publish them in this form.

Palgrave Macmillan for permission to publish Chapter 3, 'Supervising the Erotic Transference and Countertransference', which was first published in *Supervising and Being Supervised: A Practice in Search of a Theory*, (2003) edited by J. Wiener, R. Mizen and J. Duckham. Basingstoke and New York: Palgrave Macmillan.

Journal of Analytical Psychology for permission to reprint:

Covington, C. (1996) 'The purposive aspects of the erotic transference'. *Journal of Analytical Psychology* 41: 339–352.

Schaverien, J. (1999) 'The death of an analysand: transference, counter-transference and desire'. *Journal of Analytical Psychology* 44(1): 3–28.

Springer, A. (1995) 'Paying homage to the power of love: exceeding the bounds of professional practice'. *Journal of Analytical Psychology* 40: 41–61.

Springer, A. (1996) 'Female perversion: scenes and strategies in analysis and culture'. *Journal of Analytical Psychology* 41: 325–338.

International Journal of Psychoanalysis for permission to reprint:

Goldberger, M. and Evans, D. (1985) 'On transference manifestations in male patients with female analysts'. *International Journal of Psychoanalysis* 66: 295–309.

Karme, L. (1979) 'The analysis of a male patient by a female analyst: the problem of the negative Oedipal transference'. *International Journal of Psychoanalysis* 60: 253–261.

Kavaler-Adler, S. (1992) 'Mourning and erotic transference'. *International Journal of Psychoanalysis* 73: 527–539.

International Review of Psychoanalysis for permission to reprint:

Kulish, N. M. (1986) 'Gender and transference: the screen of the phallic mother'. *International Review of Psychoanalysis* 13: 393–404.

Journal of the American Academy of Psychoanalysis for permission to reprint:

Guttman, H. (1985) 'Sexual issues in the transference and countertransference between a female therapist and male patient'. *Journal of the American Academy of Psychoanalysis* 12(2): 187–197.

Psychoanalytic Psychology for permission to reprint:

Kavaler-Adler, S. (2003) 'Lesbian homoerotic transference in dialectic with developmental mourning: on the way to symbolism from the protosymbolic'. *Psychoanalytic Psychology* 20(1): 131–152.
Copyright © 2003 by the Educational Publishing Foundation. Reprinted with permission.

British Journal of Psychotherapy for permission to reprint:

Ellis, M. L. (1997) 'Who speaks? Who listens? Different voices different sexualities'. *British Journal of Psychotherapy* 13(3): 369–383.

Schaverien, J. (1997) 'Men who leave too soon: reflections on the erotic transference and countertransference'. *British Journal of Psychotherapy* 14(1): 3–16.

Williams, S. (1993) 'Women in search of women: clinical issues that underlie a woman's search for a female therapist'. *British Journal of Psychotherapy* 9(3): 291–300.

Attachment and Human Development for permission to reprint:

Orbach, S. (2004) 'What can we learn from the therapist's body?' *Attachment and Human Development* 6(2): 141–150.
http://www.tandf.co.uk/journals/titles/14616734.asp

Contributors

Coline Covington, PhD is a Training Analyst with the Society of Analytical Psychology and the British Association of Psychotherapists, Jungian section. She has co-edited with Barbara Wharton, *Sabina Spielrein: Forgotten Pioneer of Psychoanalysis* (Routledge 2003). She has also co-edited with Paul Williams, Jean Arundale and Jean Knox, *Terrorism and War: Unconscious Dynamics of Political Violence* (Karnac 2002). She has published numerous papers. She is in private practice in London.

Mary Lynne Ellis, BA Art, Dip. Art Therapy, MA Art Therapy, Dip. Psychoanalytic Psychotherapy UKCP, MA Modern European Philosophy is in private practice as a therapist and a supervisor in North London. She has also worked in the NHS and the voluntary sector. She has taught on a number of psychoanalytic and art psychotherapy trainings, including the Site for Contemporary Psychoanalysis, the Women's Therapy Centre and the University of Hertfordshire. She has lectured widely on psychoanalytic theory and practices. Her publications include *Lesbians, Gay Men and Psychoanalytic Training* (Free Association Books 1994) and 'Shifting the Ego Towards a Body Subject' in B. Seu (ed) *Who am I? The Ego and the Self in Psychoanalysis* (2000).

Marianne Goldberger, MD has been in the private practice of adult and child psychiatry and psychoanalysis since 1963. She is a training and supervising analyst at the Institute for Psychoanalysis at the NYU Medical Center, and is active there as a teacher and supervisor of candidates. She is a Clinical Professor of Psychiatry at the NYU College of Medicine. She has been on the editorial board of the *Psychoanalytic Quarterly* since 1989, and has contributed to the analytic literature on a variety of subjects, including two papers on transference manifestations in male patients with female analysts.

Herta A. Guttman, MD, FRCP(C) received her medical training at the University of Geneva, Switzerland and her psychiatric training at McGill University, Montreal, Quebec. She is Professor of Psychiatry, McGill University, and was director of the Allan Memorial Institute,

McGill University Health Centre, from 1989 to 1999. Her clinical interests and teaching were in individual and family therapy, women's issues and consultation-liaison psychiatry. She is the author of 50 articles, several book chapters and has presented widely on a variety of topics. She has retired from everything but her research into the family relationships of women with borderline personality disorder, having recently obtained a grant to study such women and their sisters.

Laila Karme is a Member of The New Center of Psychoanalysis (The Merger of The Southern California Psychoanalytic Society and Institute with the Los Angeles Psychoanalytic Institute). She is Clinical Associate Professor of Psychiatry and the Behavioral Sciences, University of Southern California.

Susan Kavaler-Adler, PhD, ABPP, is a New York psychologist and psycho-analyst in practice for 31 years. She is the Founder and Executive Director of the Object Relations Institute for Psychotherapy and Psychoanalysis, where she serves as a Training Analyst, Supervisor, and Faculty Member. Dr Kavaler-Adler is the author of 50 articles on psychoanalysis and object relations theory, and three books: *The Compulsion to Create: Women Writers and Their Demon Lovers* (Routledge 1993; Other Press 2000); *The Creative Mystique: From Red Shoes Frenzy to Love and Creativity* (Routledge 1996); *Mourning, Spirituality and Psychic Change: A New Object Relations View of Psychoanalysis* (Brunner-Routledge 2003), which won the 2004 National Gradiva Award from the National Association for the Advancement of Psychoanalysis. Dr Kavaler-Adler has won ten other awards for her writing in psychoanalysis from the Postgraduate Center for Mental Health and the National Institute for the Psychotherapies. She conducts special groups on writing and 'developmental mourning'.

Nancy Kulish, PhD is an Adjunct Professor of Psychology, University of Detroit/Mercy and Adjunct Assistant Professor, Department of Psychiatry, Wayne State Medical School and Training and Supervising Analyst at the Michigan Psychoanalytic Institute. She has been chosen as the National Woman Psychoanalytic Scholar for 2005 of the American Psychoanalytic Association. Currently she is on the Editorial Board of the *International Journal of Psychoanalysis* and an editorial reader of the *Psychoanalytic Quarterly*. She has published and presented on topics ranging from female sexuality, gender, transference/countertransference, adolescence to termination. With Deanna Holtzman, PhD she is the co-author of *Nevermore* (Jason Aronson 1996) about the loss of virginity.

Susie Orbach, PhD co-founded the Women's Therapy Centre in 1976 and the Women's Therapy Centre Institute, a training institute in New York in 1981. Her books include *Fat is a Feminist Issue, Hunger Strike, On Eating, What's Really Going on Here, Towards Emotional Literacy, Understanding Women, Between Women* and *What Do Women Want?* (both with Luise Eichenbaum) *The Impossibility of Sex* is a series of imagined tales from therapy told from the psychotherapist's point of view. She has a PhD from the psychoanalysis unit at UCL and is currently a Visiting Professor at the LSE. She is convenor of ANYBODY (working on body diversity) and a board member of the International Association for Relational Psychoanalysis and Psychotherapy.

Joy Schaverien, PhD is a Jungian Analyst in private practice in the East Midlands, UK. She is a Professional Member of the Society of Analytical Psychology in London, a Training Analyst and Supervisor for the British Association of Psychotherapists and Visiting Professor in Art Psychotherapy at the University of Sheffield. A member of the International Association for Analytical Psychology she teaches at the Jung Institute of Copenhagen and was co-organiser of the supervision programme in Moscow. Author of many articles on art and psychoanalysis and transference, her books include: *The Revealing Image* (Routledge 1991; Jessica Kingsley 1999), *Desire and the Female Therapist: Engendered Gazes in Psychotherapy and Art Therapy* (Routledge 1995) and *The Dying Patient in Psychotherapy: Desire, Dreams and Individuation* (Palgrave 2002).

Anne Springer is a Jungian psychoanalyst and psychologist in private practice in Berlin, Germany. She is a training analyst at the Institute for Psychotherapy and the C. G. Jung Institute of Berlin and former president of the DGAP (German Society for Analytical Psychology). Since 2003 she has been President of the DGPT (German Society for Psychoanalysis, Psychotherapy, Psychosomatic Medicine and Depth Psychology) and is a member of the editorial board of *Analytische Psychologie. Zeitschrift für Psychotherapie und Psychoanalyse* (Analytical Psychology. Journal for Psychotherapy and Psychoanalysis). Former publications have been on clinical issues and the history and politics of analytical psychology.

Sherly Williams is a Psychoanalytic Psychotherapist in private practice in Bedford, UK. She worked at the Birmingham Women's Counselling and Psychotherapy Centre for several years. She is a founding member of the Jungian analytical psychotherapy training at the West Midlands Institute of Psychotherapy and has taught and supervised psychotherapists in the Midlands since 1992. She has published several papers on clinical issues.

Introduction

Joy Schaverien

This book is intended to offer some new theoretical insights into working with complex transference and countertransference phenomena. Gender and the erotic transference have both been much debated in recent years but I hope that this book may offer a fresh contribution to that debate by considering both topics in tandem. The book follows on from an earlier publication *Desire and the Female Therapist* (Schaverien 1995). Since that book was published colleagues frequently ask for the references for the papers cited and so the idea emerged of a new book. However, this project developed a life of its own; it is a personal selection of chapters that make a contribution to the themes of gender, sexuality and/or the erotic transference. Rather than inviting contributions from a single analytic school the chapters have been chosen for their innovation in relation to these topics and so views from a wide spectrum of theoretical backgrounds are included. Most of the chapters have a strong clinical focus and in all of them theory is illustrated by case examples. The authors are from Britain, Canada, Germany and the USA. There are contributions from analytical psychology, psychoanalysis and psychoanalytic psychotherapy, and it is anticipated that the book will be of interest to colleagues from a similarly wide range of backgrounds.

Erotic transference

It is well known that Freud discovered the concept of transference as he observed a situation in which his colleague Breuer became the object of an erotic obsession by his patient Anna 'O' (Jones 1953–55: 1, 246). Breuer terminated the treatment but this led Freud to consider the symbolic aspect of their encounter. Freud noticed that female patients, in particular, seemed to fall in love with their doctors. This led him to consider that such powerful feelings may be evoked by unconscious transference of unresolved emotions, from childhood, into a present situation. Transference, fuelled by incestuous family dynamics, is evoked by libidinal impulses and so characterised by eros (Freud 1912, 1915). In order to better understand the symbolic nature of the transference, Szasz (1963) applies a metaphor. He reminds us that the flag of a nation stands for the nation, but it is not the nation. It is the ability to maintain the 'as if' that is important here. It is similar in analysis; the analyst may sometimes stand for emotions associated with another person in the patient's life, for example, the parent, or primary carer. However, this is a symbolic relationship and the analyst is not the parent. (See Schaverien 1991: 14–15 for a fuller discussion of this.) It is vital for the analyst to retain conscious awareness of the symbolic nature of the transference. This is even when the current emotions are live and present; it is the loss of the symbolic attitude that may lead to the impulse to act out. It will become evident in the chapters that follow, that the erotic transference is not some idealised or romantic notion but a complex and often compelling encounter with primal forces.

Freud and Jung collaborated from their first meeting in 1906 until 1914, when irreconcilable differences emerged. These differences were primarily over the meaning of sexuality in analysis. Jung marked his break from Freud with the publication of *Symbols of Transformation* (Jung 1916a) in which he developed his understanding of incest fantasy in analysis. Whilst Freud regarded transference regression as primarily related to infantile sexuality, Jung understood it to be regression with a purpose. This was not merely, as Freud proposed, to possess the mother and oust the father, in the Oedipal sense, but of returning to the parental shelter from whence to grow forward. Jung's contribution was to consider the meaning and purpose of incest fantasy as it emerged within analysis (see Covington Chapter 5). Later, writing of the transference Jung stated:

> The incest element involves ... an emotional complication of the therapeutic situation. It is the hiding place for all the most secret, painful, intense, delicate, shamefaced, timorous, grotesque, unmoral, and at the same time the most sacred feelings which go to make up the indescribable and inexplicable wealth of human relationships and give them their compelling power. Like the tentacles of an octopus they twine themselves invisibly round parents and children and, through the transference round doctor and patient.
>
> (Jung 1946: 15)

The contributors to this volume are engaging with just such material. They confront this secret, intense, compelling and often painful material in the clinical setting. The aim in writing about it is to contribute a little to understanding ways of working with such intense emotional demands whilst retaining the ability to think. Ultimately the intention is to facilitate the individuation process and free the client from outdated patterns of relating.

Gender

In the chapters that follow we will be considering some gender identity conflicts that emerge when an erotic transference is activated and so it is helpful to differentiate sex and gender. Stoller distinguishes gender from sex (Stoller 1968). He limits sex to biology, explaining that sex is determined by physical conditions, and the terms which apply to it are *male and female*. Conversely gender is psychological or cultural rather than biological and the terms for gender are *masculinity and femininity*. 'There are elements of both in many humans but the male has a preponderance of masculinity and the female has a preponderance of femininity' (Stoller 1968: 9). This is a view that has gained acceptance in psychological treatments. Furthermore Stoller distinguishes 'gender identity' and 'gender role' which are conditioned by both of the above and develop, beginning at birth, into a 'core gender identity' (Stoller 1968: 29–30). He argues, based on clinical evidence, that the reinforcement of the environment establishes gender identity, irrespective of abnormalities in biological development (Stoller 1968, 1975).

Problems encountered in analysis may arise when the client presents as very certain about their gender role, gender identity, or sexual orientation. Very often the underlying problem is a degree of psychological insecurity in the establishment of normal bisexuality. Whether predominantly male or female, homo or heterosexual, all of us carry the potential for the opposite. Samuels has written that despite the prevailing view that gender confusion is a problem, it may be the other way around. The problem may in fact be 'gender certainty' (Samuels 2000: 39–40.) He argues convincingly that 'gender certainty' can be a problem in culture, as well as the clinical setting. We will see from some of the chapters that follow how the analyst, by maintaining a symbolic attitude with regard to such transference phenomena, facilitates the client's experiments with their gender identity and role. Thus within the safe environment of the therapeutic relationship a more personally satisfying way of being in the world may be achieved. (See Covington Chapter 5, Ellis Chapter 7, Kavaler-Adler Chapters 6 and 9, and Springer Chapter 10 for clinical examples).

The symbolic attitude

Jung wrote in terms of symbols and found apposite imagery as metaphors for psychological processes. He was interested in the power of psychological opposites that become manifest in the transference (Jung 1928) and realised that any conscious attitude is compensated by an unconscious one. To elucidate he turned to the thermodynamic principle of entropy; explaining that energy is transformed as the result of the attraction and drawing together of opposite elements; for example, hot and cold. This sets up intense conflict, which, if overcome, gives way to equilibrium – a sense of security and calm, which is not easily disturbed (Jung 1928: 26). This is not always the outcome.

If the conflict of opposites is pacified prematurely there may be closure, a false resolution, which results in stasis (Jung 1928: 32). This has a psychological parallel in the transference–countertransference dynamic, where the intensity of the attraction and repulsion of opposites may draw the analyst into the patient's world. Sometimes the psychological process is static; then despite the patient's erotic endeavours, the analyst is left feeling cold. At other times the atmosphere in the consulting room heats up, producing an intense attraction, which may be hard to resist. The point is that, if these reactions are understood symbolically and mediated accordingly, the encounter becomes meaningful.

Jung's theory of contrasexuality is based on gendered opposites (Jung 1946). If the feminine element in a man, or the masculine element in a woman is unconscious it is likely to be projected and so attached to a figure of the opposite sex. This is often revealed in the transference where the incestuous dynamic may be experienced as very concrete reality. The purpose of understanding these opposites within the individual psyche is to develop a conscious attitude and integrate such projections within the personality (Jung 1916b: 20). It is the symbolic attitude, the transcendent function (Jung 1916b) which brings the unconscious to consciousness and so facilitates movement from a concrete psychological attitude. It is the 'as if' that permits space between the impulse and the act.

Racker, a Kleinian analyst, made a similar point but from a different theoretical base (Racker 1968). He refers to the talion law and argues that whatever the conscious transference manifestation, its opposite is also present but often unconscious. Thus when love is conscious in the therapeutic relationship its opposite, hate, is also present but split off. Similarly, when hate is the dominant theme, love may be present but unconscious. Frequently, the love and hate experienced in the transference is understood to be based in infantile experience and the corresponding countertransference is interpreted as maternal. This is especially the case with female analysts. However, this is only one facet of the dynamic and in all gender combinations some of the desire expressed in the transference and experienced in the countertransference is based in adult sexual feelings. This is what can be so confusing for the client and sometimes for the analyst too.

The long held differences between the schools of psychoanalysis, which were founded by Freud and Jung respectively, have continued in the psychoanalytic community. However, the differences may sometimes be bridged and there have been a number of moves in this direction, for example Wiener's (2004) review of the literature on transference and counter-transference. Colman (2005) gives a very comprehensive and up-to-date discussion of the similarities and differences between the analytic schools through discussion of sexuality and body metaphors. He contributes by clarifying the difference between what he calls 'interpreting *towards* sex and interpreting *away* from sex' (Colman 2005: 642). This is a very useful elucidation of metaphor and unconscious phantasy concluding that it is possible for 'widely divergent analytic approaches to have equal success'. He reminds us that we do not judge a metaphor in terms of whether it is 'correct' (Colman 2005: 658). There is not one right way of doing analysis.

Although they might not agree over some points I think that all the contributors to this volume would consider themselves to be working within a boundaried psychoanalytic frame and attempting to facilitate a symbolic attitude even if the metaphors and interpretations given might differ according to their theoretical allegiances.

The paternal function

The paternal function is an important symbol of the boundaried nature of the analytic enterprise. This is discussed in a number of the chapters that follow. Although the contributors do not quote Lacan I find him helpful in understanding this symbolic aspect of the transference and, in particular, the paternal function. With regard to the erotic transference it is relevant to consider his use of the term desire, which is often considered to be the province of Lacanian theorists. Developed from Freud's writings, this is rather different from the desire discussed by Freud and Jung, which is a form of eros related to sexuality in its biological and sensate form. For Lacan desire is a perpetual state of being that relates to language; it is not eros, or libido in the accepted sense, and it does not rest on physical sensation (Bowie 1991). Desire is the 'dynamo, everywhere in motion and nowhere at rest, that propels all acts of speech, all refusal to speak and all conscious and unconscious mental representations' (Bowie 1991: 122). I understand this as the move towards the other and so to community. In considering the paternal function it is this relation to speech that draws me to Lacan. In clinical work it is the inability to articulate and therefore symbolise some aspect of experience that is often at the root of the problem that brings people into analysis. The problem is unconscious and therefore cannot be articulated.

In Lacan's writings the 'lack' is a state of identification outside the symbolic order. A state that cannot be symbolised is unconscious as it lacks a social link. For Lacan therefore it is language which offers the way into community. The symbolic function is supported by 'the *name of the father* ... which since the dawn of history, has identified his person with the figure of the law' (Lacan 1977: 67). It is the phallic qualities which bring difference (Lacan 1977). These include boundary setting, law giving and the entry into language. If this is interpreted in gender-specific terms, as Lacan's language at first appears to indicate, it causes problems. However, Irigaray (1985) has argued that this is a misunderstanding; it is a psychic structure rather than biological 'given' that is intended. Therefore, if we comprehend the meaning, without necessarily adhering to the limits of gender specificity, the phallic is not necessarily literally, nor solely, the province of men. The phallic qualities associated with the law could then be related to the paternal function rather than the actual penis. In the chapters that follow there is much discussion of boundaries, as well as the paternal function in the female analyst, and therefore Lacan's work in this area is an important contribution.

Although drawing on very different theories, in this introduction my point is that the symbolic attitude is central in mediating the transference and countertransference relationship. In different ways and using different language and metaphors, each of the major theorists in the field of psychoanalysis seems to be attempting a similar project. The aim seems to be to find a way of articulating and negotiating the territory of human relatedness within a boundaried and therefore safe setting.

Countertransference and gender

Historically, countertransference was viewed as resistance, as unanalysed personal material in the analyst. Countertransference today includes this possibility, but it is also understood to be a tool: a guide to monitoring the transference. Women psychoanalysts were the first consider countertransference in this way (Heimann 1949; Little 1950; Tower 1956). However, it was not until the 1980s that the reality of the analyst's gender was systematically discussed (for example, Chasseguet-Smirgel 1984, 1986; Spector Person 1983, 1985, 1986). In 1984 Kulish published a literature review on the effects of the analyst's gender on the transference (Kulish 1984). Since then publications on countertransference experiences have proliferated and this has included attention to gender issues (Schaverien 1996). In 1993 there was a full issue of *Psychoanalytic Inquiry* devoted to 'The impact of gender on transference and countertransference' which included articles by three of the contributors to this volume; Goldberger and Evans Holmes (1993), Karme (1993) and Kulish (1993). *Psychoanalytic Dialogues* regularly addresses topics related to the erotic transference and countertransference (Messler Davies 1994, 1998, 2003). Therefore, it was surprising to read a comment from Bonasia (2001) who considered there to be little written by women in the psychoanalytic literature on the erotic countertransference (Bonasia 2001: 260). His courageous article on counter-transference was published in the same journal in which many of the papers included in this collection, as well as others on the topic, were originally published. This has led me to realise that many of the articles included here do not directly refer to countertransference in their titles. However, as counter-transference is a guide to understanding the transference, they are not easily separated; even when not stated, countertransference informs the analyst in the clinical setting and in writing about it. Therefore this volume is unquestionably about countertransference. The cases described all focus on either, or both, gender issues and the erotic transference, but the means of mediating understanding is through conscious attention to countertransference experiences.

Sexual and other forms of acting out can be a problem in professional practice. Therefore it is necessary to become conscious of the meaning of the sometimes complex countertransference experiences that the analyst may encounter. However, the confusing web of gender roles and sexual identities that the transference weaves may transfix and enthral. So what actually happens? Looking at this from outer reality it seems clear. Two people, each with their own history, gender and sexual orientation, meet alone in a private room for the purpose of one helping the other. But then the imaginal world begins to weave its spell. It is as if the transference plays tricks; it mixes reality with fantasy and engages both people in a dance where material certainty and the imaginal world may become confused. Gender, and other facets of reality too, may sometimes become confused.

For example, the importance of the reality of gender was acknowledged by feminist therapists who insisted on the importance of women working with women; women's therapy centres were founded on this premise (see Orbach Chapter 11 and Williams Chapter 8). Even so a female patient experiencing sexual arousal when working with a woman analyst may be alarmed; and the analyst may interpret such arousal in infantile terms, rather than admit the possibility of her own homosexual arousal. Open discussion of both possibilities is necessary. These issues are addressed by Schaverien in Chapter 3, Kavaler Adler in Chapter 9, Springer in Chapter 10.

Whilst the reality of gender may not preclude any material arising it might influence the order in which it becomes conscious. It is common for the male as well as female analyst to be viewed as maternal because the analytic setting engenders maternal qualities. Likewise the female analyst as well as the male may be experienced as paternal, setting boundaries and establishing the analytic frame. Analysts of both sexes may be experienced as a lover or brother, as well as mother, father, sister. The analyst may have a sense of their identity in the world yet, as the transference intensifies, it may seem as if this is challenged. Adult sexuality may not be the prime experience of the regressed client. However, even when the most conscious element of the material is infantile, adult sexuality may import a sexual dimension. This can impact on the analyst, evoking countertransference experiences contrary to perceived views of the embodied self and sexual orientation. Unfamiliar sexual or emotional arousals may threaten to shatter the self-concept of either or both parties. What is real for the person of the analyst may bear little resemblance to the client's experience of their analyst in the transference. A fluid psychological attitude is required.

There is not space here for a fully updated literature review but it is important to mention some of the more recent and influential publications on gender and the erotic transference and countertransference. These include Breen (1993), Samuels (1985, 1989, 1993, 2000), Gabbard (1989, 1994, 1996), Gabbard and Lester (1995), Wyre and Welles (1994), McDougall (1995), Maguire (1995), Raphael-Leff and Jozef Perelberg (1997), Spector Person (1999), Lester (1985, 1990), Denman (2004), Messler Davies (1998, 2003), Rutter (1989), Colman (1996, 2005), Mann (1997, 1999), Young-Eisendrath

(1999, 2004). This is far from an exclusive list and other articles that have influenced the contributors to this book are referenced individually at the end of their chapters.

Research

The authors in this book present observations from clinical practice and locate their theoretical contributions within the literature current at the time they were written. Therefore, it is relevant to briefly consider the question of research. The approach applied by most contributors here is discursive; it is both phenomenological and case study based. Throughout the history of psychoanalysis the case study has been an accepted research method and McLeod reminds that this started with Freud's own writing (McLeod 1994: 103). Roth and Fonagy suggest that the single case study could be seen as a form of evaluation or as small-scale research 'aimed at developing the theory and practice of the technique'. Their view is that ultimately this leads to a need for more stringent research (Roth and Fonagy 1996: 49). The chapters presented here all aim to develop theory and practice and so, whilst not explicitly research, each makes a contribution to understanding of either gender issues or the erotic transference, and in some cases both. It is important to establish that, in common with accepted practice, identities of clients have been disguised and, where appropriate, permission sought. (See Gabbard 2000; Wharton 1998, 2005 for discussion of publication of clinical material in the interest of research.)

The book

Finally I turn to the book. The book is divided into four parts; each begins with an introduction and rationale. There are three chapters in Part I, and four chapters in each of Parts II, III and IV. The book is most coherent if read in sequence, but it is presented so that the reader can select, beginning with the section that most interests them. There is a detailed introduction at the beginning of each section so here I give merely a brief preliminary outline of the shape of the book.

Part I, entitled 'Gender and the Erotic Transference', includes three chapters of my own, exploring erotic transference in the female analyst/male client pairing through detailed attention to countertransference phenomena. In Chapter 1 questions are raised about why some male patients leave analysis prematurely. Chapter 2 is about the dying patient in psychotherapy and Chapter 3 considers some gender and sexual identity issues encountered in supervision. In Part II, 'The Erotic Transference and the Symbolic Function', Springer, Covington, Kavaler-Adler and Ellis focus on the symbolic nature of the transference. Springer (Chapter 4) discusses the breach of boundaries by the analyst. Covington (Chapter 5) and Kavaler-Adler (Chapter 6) focus on the erotic transference when working with men. Covington's chapter is about its meaning and purpose and Kavaler-Adler considers developmental mourning. Lastly in this section, Ellis (Chapter 7) writes about difference. Although very diverse, each of these chapters vividly demonstrates the reason why maintaining analytic boundaries is so vital.

In Part III, 'Women Working with Women', Williams, Kavaler-Adler, Springer and Orbach develop aspects of the transference–countertransference dynamic when both members of the analysing pair are women. Williams (Chapter 8) questions why some women seek out a woman analyst. Kavaler-Adler (Chapter 9) further develops her idea of developmental mourning, this time focusing on a woman client. Springer (Chapter 10) discusses female perversion and Orbach (Chapter 11) considers what the body can contribute to understanding the mind. Part IV is entitled 'Historical Perspectives on Women Working with Men'. It offers chapters by Guttman, Kulish, Karme and Goldberger and Evans Holmes. These four chapters were selected for their historical significance. Each of the authors has written extensively on these related subjects since the early 1980s. Guttman (Chapter 12) discusses archetypal themes in the male patient/female analyst dyad, Kulish (Chapter 13) the phallic mother and paternal transferences, Karme (Chapter 14) the negative Oedipal transference and Goldberger and Evans Holmes (Chapter 15) discuss a variety of transference manifestations of male patients with female analysts. Since the early 1980s, when these four chapters were written, the field has expanded greatly. However, although the literature reviews may seem limited, the themes addressed in this section remain relevant today.

The chapters included address the issues discussed above without turning away from the challenges of monitoring and working with complex erotic transference phenomenon and countertransference experiences. The challenge for each of the authors has been to maintain understanding of the symbolic nature of the transference, whilst working in the imaginal field between two people. Each shows how there are times when such phenomena place analyst as well as patient under immense pressure to abandon thinking in favour of acting on the feelings engendered.

References

Bonasia, E. (2001) 'Countertransference: erotic, eroticised and perverse'. *International Journal of Psycho-Analysis* 82, Part 2: 249–262.

Bowie, M. (1991) *Lacan*. London: Fontana Modern Masters (HarperCollins).

Breen, D. (ed.) (1993) *The Gender Conundrum: Contemporary Psychoanalytic Perspectives on Femininity and Masculinity*. London and New York: Routledge.

Chasseguet-Smirgel, J. (1984) *Creativity and Perversion*. London: Free Association Books.

Chasseguet-Smirgel, J. (1986) *Sexuality and Mind*. London: Karnac.

Colman, W. (1996) 'Aspects of anima and animus in Oedipal development'. *Journal of Analytical Psychology* 41(1): 37–58.

Colman, W. (2005) 'Sexual metaphor and the language of unconscious phantasy'. *Journal of Analytical Psychology* 50(5): 641–660.

Denman, C. (2004) *Sexuality*. London: Palgrave Macmillan.

Freud, S. (1912) 'The dynamics of transference'. *Standard Edition* Vol. XII. London: Hogarth Press.

Freud, S. (1915) 'Observations on transference love'. *Standard Edition* Vol. XII. London: Hogarth Press.

Gabbard, G. O. (1989) *Sexual Exploitation in Professional Relationship*. Washington, DC: American Psychiatric Press.

Gabbard, G. O. (1994) 'Sexual excitement and countertransference love in the analyst'. *Journal of the American Psychoanalytic Association* 42: 1083–1106.

Gabbard, G. O. (1996) *Love and Hate in the Analytic Setting*. New Jersey: Jason Aronson.

Gabbard, G. O. (2000) 'Disguise or consent: problems and recommendations concerning the publication and presentation of clinical material'. *International Journal of Psycho-Analysis* 81: 1071–1086.

Gabbard, G. O. and Lester, E. P. (1995) *Boundaries and Boundary Violations in Psychoanalysis*. Washington, DC: American Psychiatric Press.

Goldberger, M. and Evans Holmes, D. (1993) 'Transferences in male patients with female analysts: an update'. *Psychoanalytic Inquiry* 13(2): 173–191.

Heimann, P. (1950) 'On countertransference'. *International Journal of Psycho-Analysis* 31: 81–84.

Irigaray, L. (1985) *The Speculum of the Other Woman*, trans. G. Bell. New York: Cornell University Press. (Original work published in French 1924.)

Jones, E. (1953–55) *Sigmund Freud: Life and Work*. London: Hogarth Press.

Jung, C. G. (1916a) *Symbols of Transformation*. CW Vol. 5. London: Routledge & Kegan Paul.

Jung, C. G. (1916b) 'The transcendent function'. CW Vol. 8. London: Routledge & Kegan Paul.

Jung, C. G. (1928) 'On psychic energy'. CW Vol. 8. London: Routledge & Kegan Paul.

Jung, C. G. (1946) 'The psychology of the transference'. CW Vol. 16. London: Routledge & Kegan Paul.

Karme, L. (1993) 'Male patients and female analysts: erotic and other psychoanalytic encounters'. *Psychoanalytic Inquiry* 13(2): 192–205.

Kulish, N. (1984) 'The effect of the sex of the analyst on the transference: a review of the literature'. *Bulletin of the Menninger Clinic* 48: 95–110.

Kulish, N. (1993) 'Gender-linked determinants of transference and countertransference in psychoanalytic psychotherapy'. *Psychoanalytic Inquiry* 13(2): 286–305.

Lacan, J. (1977) *Ecrits: A Selection*, trans. A. Sheridan. London: Routledge. (Original work published in French Editions du Seuil 1966.)

Lester, E. (1985) 'The female analyst and the eroticized transference'. *International Journal of Psycho-Analysis* 66: 283–293.

Lester, E. (1990) 'Gender and identity issues in the analytic process'. *International Journal of Psycho-Analysis* 71: 435–453.

Little, M. (1950) ' "R" The analyst's total response to his patient's needs'. In M. I. Little *Towards Basic Unity*. London: Free Association Books (1986) edition.

McDougall, J. (1995) *The Many Faces of Eros: A Psychoanalytic Exploration of Human Sexuality*. London: Free Association Books.

McLeod, J. (1994) *Doing Counselling Research*. London: Sage.

Messler Davies, J. (1994) 'Love in the afternoon'. *Psychoanalytic Dialogues* 4: 153–170.

Messler Davies, J. (1998) 'Between disclosure and foreclosure of erotic transference and countertransference: can psychoanalysis find a place for adult sexuality'. *Psychoanalytic Dialogues* 8(6): 747–766.

Messler Davies, J. (2003) 'Falling in love with love: Oedipal and post-Oedipal manifestations of idealization, mourning and erotic masochism'. *Psychoanalytic Dialogues* 13(1): 1–27.

Maguire, M. (1995) *Men and Women, Passion and Power*. London & New York: Routledge.

Mann, D. (1997) *Psychotherapy: An Erotic Relationship*. London & New York: Routledge.

Mann, D. (ed.) (1999) *Erotic Transference and Countertransference: Clinical Practice in Psychotherapy*. London & New York: Routledge.

Racker, H. (1968) *Transference and Countertransference*. London: Hogarth Press.

Raphael-Leff, J. and Josef Perelberg, R. (eds) (1997) *Female Experience: Three Generations of Women Psychoanalysts on Work with Women*. London & New York: Routledge.

Roth, A. and Fonagy, P (1996) *What Works for Whom? A Critical Review of Psychotherapy Research*. New York: Guilford Press.

Rutter, P. (1989) *Sex in the Forbidden Zone*. Los Angeles: Tarcher.

Samuels, A. (ed.) (1985) *The Father: Contemporary Jungian Perspectives*. London: Free Association Books.

Samuels, A. (1989) *The Plural Psyche: Personality, Morality and the Father*. London & New York: Routledge.

Samuels, A. (1993) *The Political Psyche*. London & New York: Routledge.

Samuels, A. (2000) *Politics on the Couch*. London: Profile Books.

Schaverien, J. (1991) *The Revealing Image*. London: Tavistock/Routledge.

Schaverien, J. (1995) *Desire and the Female Therapist: Engendered Gazes in Psychotherapy and Art Therapy*. London & New York: Routledge.

Schaverien, J. (1996) 'Desire and the female analyst'. *Journal of Analytical Psychology* 41(2): 261–287.

Spector Person, E. (1983) 'Women in therapy: therapist gender as variable'. *International Review of Psycho-Analysis* 10: 193–204.

Spector Person, E. (1985) 'The erotic transference in women and men: differences and consequences'. *Journal of the American Academy of Psychoanalysis* 13(2): 159–180.

Spector Person, E. (1986) 'Male sexuality and power'. *Journal of Columbia University Center for Psychoanalytic Training and Research, Psychoanalytic Inquiry* 6(1): 3–25.

Spector Person, E. (1999) *The Sexual Century*. New Haven & London: Yale University Press.

Stoller, R. J. (1968) *Sex and Gender*. London: Hogarth Press.

Stoller, R. J. (1975) *Sex and Gender*, Vol. 2: The Transsexual Experiment. London: Hogarth Press.

Szasz, T. (1963) 'The concept of transference'. *International Journal of Psycho-Analysis* 44: 432–443.

Tower, L. E. (1956) 'Countertransference'. *Journal of the American Psychoanalytic Association* 4: 224–255.

Wharton, B. (1998) 'What comes out of the consulting room? Reporting of clinical material'. *Journal of Analytical Psychology* 43: 205–223.

Wharton, B. (2005) 'Ethical issues in the publication of clinical material'. *Journal of Analytical Psychology* 50(1): 83–89.

Wiener, J. (2004) 'Transference and countertransference: contemporary Jungian perspectives' in J. Cambray and L. Carter (Eds), *Analytical Psychology: Contemporary Perspectives in Jungian Psychology*. Hove & New York: Brunner-Routledge.

Wyre, H. K. and Welles, J. K. (1994) *The Narration of Desire: Erotic Transferences and Countertransferences*. Hillsdale, NJ: Analytic Press.

Young-Eisendrath, P. (1999) *Women and Desire: Beyond Wanting to be Wanted*. London: Piatkus.

Young-Eisendrath, P. (2004) *Subject to Change: Jung, Gender and Subjectivity in Psychoanalysis*. Hove & New York: Brunner-Routledge.

Part I

Gender and the erotic transference

This section presents three of my own papers about gender and the erotic transference. I decided to include these at the beginning of the book because it gives a clear sense of my interest in the topic and my reason for choosing the other papers in the book. The focus in the first two chapters is the transference of the male patient and the countertransference of the female analyst. It begins with Chapter 1, 'Men Who Leave Too Soon', which acts as an introduction to the book. It is based on a paper originally published in 1997, which developed from reflecting on why certain men in analysis with women analysts tend to leave when the transference appears to become strongly erotic but before there is time to analyse it. The key to this problem may rest in reflection on countertransference experience. It is proposed that it is the desire for intimacy and the unconscious fear of it that leads the patient to leave. The analyst is then left with the feelings. Chapter 2, 'Individuation at the end of life', develops the same themes but from the point of view of someone who stayed in analysis. However, the erotic transference and reciprocal countertransference dynamic was with a patient nearing the end of life. This gives a particular meaning to 'men who leave too soon'. A powerful erotic transference became manifest from the beginning and then after three months the patient was diagnosed with a terminal illness. This case of a male patient working with a female analyst in some way reveals many of the technical issues that will emerge in the chapters which follow. There was, in the beginning, an undifferentiated state in which certain perverse elements were manifest (see Springer Chapter 10). Two forms of mourning were involved: first, the developmental mourning Kavaler-Adler describes in Chapters 6 and 9, where the patient first of all had to give up inner objects of infancy in order to move into the Oedipal phase. Relinquishing of these inner objects preceded, and made possible, the second type of mourning; the outer world mourning process, as the very real losses associated with his impending death, were worked through. Both a maternal and later paternal transference became manifest. Thus, the working through and resolution of the erotic transference was complicated by the very real physical situation. This intensified the erotic aspect of the transference and made very particular demands on the analyst.

Chapter 3 addresses the topic of supervising the erotic transference (or lack of it). Thus issues of gender and sexual orientation in supervision come to the fore as highly charged and significant factors. Through attention to gender issues, and assumptions that may be made about sexuality, the importance of considering the gender and sexual orientation of the pair in supervision is drawn out. The views of their own sexuality may influence both supervisor and supervisee. As will be discussed by Ellis in Chapter 7, we see how cultural norms and stereotypes enter into the unconscious transference dynamics. These three papers were originally published in (1997, 1999 and 2003 respectively). They trace my developing interest in this topic and I hope set the scene for the book as a whole.

Chapter 1

Men who leave too soon
Reflections on the erotic transference and countertransference

Joy Schaverien

It is observed that certain male patients in psychotherapy with female analysts end prematurely. Attention to common factors in the cases of the 'men who leave too soon' reveals what appears to be a pattern. Some leave to avoid intimacy, others to avoid consciousness of erotic/aggressive impulses in the transference where the feminine may be alternately idealised and denigrated. Unconscious collusion in traditional gender dynamics may contribute to avoidance of sexual feelings in the countertransference. This may sometimes result in interpretation of eros in infantile terms in denial of the adult, sexual dynamic.

This chapter is a development of one of the themes in my book *Desire and the Female Therapist* (Schaverien 1995). In questioning why it might be that there had been, until that time, relatively few reports of erotic transferences written by female analysts working with male patients I proposed that:

> 'It is possible that male patients terminate before, or when, the erotic transference begins. It also seems that female analysts may find it more acceptable to remain within the frame of the maternal rather than to confront the sexual transference.
>
> (Schaverien 1995: 24)

Beginning from the subjectivity of the female analyst, her countertransference, I identify a group of patients whom I will call 'men who leave too soon'. I will illustrate the theoretical discussion with two examples from clinical practice with the intention of attempting to understand some of the dynamics which constellate around sexual difference when the analyst is a woman and the client a man. This is an exploration of one facet of the influence of gender in the therapeutic relationship but it is not intended to offer an essentialist, or fixed, view of sexual difference. I give particular attention to the erotic transference/countertransference in an attempt to differentiate the adult/sexual from the infantile/erotic.

The gender and power imbalance of the female analyst/male patient dyad runs contrary to traditional cultural and social conventions of relations between women and men. Inevitably, whether conscious or unconscious, this influences the transference and the countertransference. In considering why it is that certain men, working with female analysts, end their psychotherapy 'prematurely', I have noticed a pattern. Some of 'the men who leave too soon' begin therapy by manifesting an evident desire for intimacy. They develop an intense, dependent and erotic transference and then terminate suddenly, and often without warning. This sudden end seems to occur after only a few months and in such a way that interpretation is prevented and the analyst is left feeling powerless.

The premise is that sexual difference makes a difference in psychotherapy. Whilst there are common factors which transcend gender difference, I consider that giving attention to this one pairing may highlight particular countertransference problems encountered by the female analyst and the difficulties some male patients experience in the transference. However, the chapter is not addressed solely to female analysts. There are implications here for all gender dyads and irrespective of sexual orientation.

It is common, since Freud first identified the transference (1912, 1915, 1917), to read accounts by male analysts of erotic transferences of female patients. In the past the countertransference, particularly if it was sexual arousal, was blamed on the seductiveness of the patient. In recent years this attitude has changed and some men have written openly about sexual arousals in the analytic situation, taking responsibility for their own countertransferences. They have openly discussed the problems of handling the impulse to act out sexually and the importance of understanding the meaning of such arousals (see Samuels 1985; Field 1989; Rutter 1989; Sedgwick 1994). The insight gained from resisting the impulse to act out, whilst permitting it to become conscious, is shown by all of them to be helpful. It deepens the transference and so the patient's relationship to herself.

In the past female analysts were less likely to write openly about long-term erotic transferences in their male patients. Indeed, it has been claimed that male patients rarely develop sustained erotic transferences and that female analysts rarely experience erotic countertransferences with female or male patients. Frequently, manifestations of eros are attributed to the infantile transference and its countertransference appeal. An implied consequence of this is that women analysts are less likely than male colleagues to act out sexually. However, research in Britain and the USA (Pope et al. 1993; Russell 1993; Garrett 1994; Jehu 1994) have shown that there is evidence that a percentage of female analysts do act out sexually with both male and female patients. There are times when this is a result of the maternal and sexual elements in the countertransference becoming mixed up and acted out. (See McNamara 1994 for a vivid account of such a case.)

The fact that I am discussing this topic owes much to feminism. Feminist therapists have demonstrated that there is much to be gained from attending to transference and countertransference issues specific to the female analyst/female patient pair, and especially the mother/daughter transference. The

Women's Therapy Centres in Britain and the USA were founded on this premise (Eichenbaum and Orbach 1983; Ernst and Maguire 1987). Elsewhere I have reviewed the literature on the topic of the erotic transference/counter-transference in clinical practice with particular reference to the female analyst/male patient pair (Schaverien 1995, 1996). I will not reiterate all of these references here but draw attention to certain key issues.

It seems to have been mainly (but not exclusively) female analysts (Heimann 1949; Little 1950) who were the first to write about the countertransference as a total response to the analytic situation. Tower (1956) was quoted by Searles in his seminal paper 'Oedipal love in the countertransference' (1959). It has been suggested by Guttman (see Chapter 12) that female analysts may be more likely to openly admit their countertransferences, whereas it seems that men may more readily focus on the transference.

In recent years papers on gender and sexuality written by women have included Meador (1983), O'Connor and Ryan (1993), Springer (1996, Chapter 4) who have discussed the erotic in the female/female dyad. Spector Person (1983, 1985, 1986) identifies specific transference and countertransference phenomena encountered by female analysts working with women and men respectively. Various aspects of the erotic transference, with women or men, have been discussed by Guttman (1985, Chapter 12), Lester (1985, 1990), Kavaler-Adler (1992, Chapter 6), Messler Davies (1994), Wrye and Welles (1994), Covington (1996, Chapter 5), among others. Maguire (1995) has traced the history and many of the clinical complexities of gender relations in psychotherapy. This is by no means a comprehensive list but it does seem to indicate that, having primarily concentrated on women working with women for many years, it is now possible to consider gender difference within psychotherapy from a feminist perspective.

Countertransference and men who leave too soon

In writing openly of sexual themes in the countertransference, there is a danger that one will be viewed as exhibitionist. Indeed, as Searles (1959) did so many years ago, I used to think it was my own unresolved Oedipal needs which dominated in situations where the erotic intensifies the countertransference. Now, after many years of analysis, discussion with colleagues and through supervising other analysts, I have come to realise that I am merely discussing a common and known aspect of the therapeutic process. Female therapists, just like their male colleagues, at times experience sexual arousals in the countertransference. Others admit to actively avoiding this by refusing to work with male patients. Thus, I am now convinced that, rather than merely airing my own problem in public, I am discussing what does in fact happen. The problem is in admitting it. The fear which prevents us speaking, or writing, of these arousals publicly, and sometimes prevents us taking them to supervision, may be some form of unspecified guilt: perhaps a fear of being blamed for causing arousal in the man, or of being seen as needy and seductive like the female patients of the early analysts. This inhibits open discussion. If, as women, we are fully to own our difference, we have to admit to our sexuality within the therapeutic relationship. This includes owning impulses towards acting on erotic countertransferences with male and female patients. It also means discussing these feelings in supervision in order to become conscious and to identify their meaning in the context of any particular therapeutic relationship. (This is discussed in more detail in Chapter 3.) We are no more immune from countertransference desires than are our male colleagues. Unless this is admitted, it remains split off and attributed as merely an aberration of the male and, most importantly, impairs our ability to work with all of the material which emerges in psychotherapy.

It has been argued convincingly by feminist writers that, as a result of social and cultural pressures, as well as the predominance of mothers in early development, men and women generally develop psychologically in different ways. In order to establish their difference, boys have to break with the primary identification with the mother and develop a separate masculine identity. As a result of this, intimacy may be feared as threatening their masculinity and drawing them back to the maternal realm. Girls too have to separate from the primary identity with the mother but then come to terms with it again. Their sameness means that they are more likely to fear separation (Chodorow 1978; Olivier 1980; Gilligan 1982; Eichenbaum and Orbach 1983). In connection with claims that there is an absence of the erotic element in their work with male patients by some female analysts, I am proposing that one reason for this may be that, in certain cases, the male patient leaves to avoid intimacy. Some men terminate before the erotic transference has fully developed. The female patient may be less worried about her attachment to the analyst. In considering this I have noticed a common crisis at the point at which eros and/or dependency become evident. At this point certain male patients leave therapy; these are the 'men who leave too soon' of the title of this chapter.

When I state that these men 'leave too soon' I have to question 'too soon' for whom? Clearly the patient does not consider that the ending is too soon or, presumably, he would not have left. Thus I am forced to admit that it is too soon for me – the analyst. So this is a countertransference experience. It has often been stated that the countertransference comes first. It is this, the analyst's desire, which ignites the transference. Without the countertransference there would be no therapy (Stein 1974; Hillman 1977; Lacan 1977). When a patient begins therapy he or she takes a risk to speak to a stranger about their most intimate thoughts and feelings. However, it may be less clear that the analyst also makes a significant investment in the process. If the patient leaves suddenly and without warning, the analyst is obliged to withdraw this investment. The parallel with sexual intercourse is evident in the language which I use – creative, fulfilling intercourse is prevented by the early termination.

I should make it clear that I am not discussing *all* who leave their therapy after a brief period. Many men – and women – end after a short time in a way which is appropriately worked through. For some a brief term of therapy relieves the problem and that is what they require. For others early termination may indicate a recognition, in the patient, that therapy is not right for them; for example, the patient may sense her or his propensity for a psychotic breakdown. There is sometimes a mutual understanding, at a conscious or even an unconscious level, that something was wrong – there was not a 'fit' between *this* analyst and *this* patient. In these cases an early end to the therapy is right. Thus I am not suggesting that *all* early endings are premature. The cases to which I refer are those where there seemed to be a 'fit', the therapy starts at depth, but nonetheless the patient leaves. The analyst experiences disappointment. The patient may be thought to have left out of some resistance to the process and the analyst may wonder if the resistance would have responded to the 'right' interpretation. In such cases the disappointment, experienced in the countertransference, is both a response in the analyst and also a reflection of the unconscious experience of the patient. However – as he has already left – there is no way of checking this and so the analyst is left with all the feelings. Therefore I consider that the 'men who leave too soon' merit closer attention than it at first appears.

My hypothesis is developed from understanding gained from experiences with men who have stayed. With them, despite the difficulties experienced during the therapy, a form of symbolic and creative intercourse eventually became possible. Many of them too reached a point of crisis where the intensity of their feelings made them consider terminating. On analysis, it emerged that they were leaving to avoid dependency or were confused by their feelings which were very often a mixture of undifferentiated sexual and aggressive impulses. As these feelings began to differentiate it became clear that they were characterised by infantile/erotic needs. However, this may only emerge once the adult/sexual feelings have been acknowledged and worked through. This crisis in therapy may be productive and lead to consciousness and so a deepening of the transference.

Archetypal themes

Archetypal themes in the transference are evoked by the individual's experience of the predominating culture of the wider society as well as the smaller culture of the family or institution in which she or he has grown to maturity (Jung 1959). The power imbalance of the therapeutic relationship evokes the memory of past relationships and, especially, those of early childhood. When the analyst is a woman and the patient a man, there is an apparent paradox. Women, as mothers, are powerful in the early years of a child's life. It is the mother, or primary caretaker, usually female, who is the first object of desire. She is the focus of all the ambivalent emotions associated with dependence. In the first years the child experiences a form of matriarchy. It may have been a struggle for the man to establish himself as separate from his mother and to achieve autonomy and so, when he enters therapy with a woman, conflicted feelings associated with gender and power dynamics may surface. Whilst unconsciously awed by the perceived power of the analyst, he may defend fiercely against any form of dependent transference.

In observing common factors in the therapy of the 'men who leave too soon', I have noticed two distinct archetypal patterns in the transference. These are neither exclusive nor finite but offered as examples of the types of situation I have encountered. First is the 'man of the world' with whom I sense an immediate struggle over who is dominant in the relationship. He is often the male breadwinner who feels it is his duty to provide for his family but is out of touch with his own needs (see Schaverien 1995: 28 for an example). In archetypal terms he is rather like the hero who is prepared to fight the dragon, rescue the princess and bring home the treasure. The split, which is in part culturally conditioned, is such that he in no way consciously identifies with the princess; or to put it another way, his own vulnerability is split off and attributed to the women and children in his family. When he begins psychotherapy with a woman he feels immense discomfort with the power imbalance. There are many ways he may attempt to cope with this. He may treat the analyst as a colleague, as if this is a business transaction, or he may associate the situation with visiting a prostitute. In the first example he denies his own neediness and in the second denigrates the authority of the analyst by turning her role into that of a 'woman' whom he merely pays for her services. His dependency needs evoke tremendous anxiety and many such men seem to terminate their therapy rather abruptly. In the countertransference it is often a struggle to maintain the analytic stance and not to collude with the denigration.

The second type is the man who enters into a dependent transference with a pronounced erotic atmosphere very early, often after the first session (see Schaverien 1995: 36). In archetypal terms he evokes the helpless male child in the grip of the archetypal 'Great Mother', with its capacity to engulf or destroy. The countertransference is an experience of being too powerful and this may cause the female analyst to deny her connection to the patient, fearing being experienced as seductive or as an engulfing maternal presence. This was the case with Ben.

Eroticised regression

When Ben referred himself for psychotherapy there was an urgency in his request. He felt he was not a good father to his three small children and did not wish to repeat his own childhood which he felt had been far from satisfactory. He was married and in his early thirties and he had been having an affair for the last year with a woman who he considered to be intelligent and because of this he found it hard to believe that she would bother with him. This was echoed in the transference when he admitted he had selected my name from a list of people in the area on the basis of gender, he wanted to see a woman, and also because I had a PhD. He aspired to academic qualifications but had left school with none and he felt trapped. On the one hand he knew that he was intelligent and had the ability to learn but he worked in an industry which demanded physical and organisational skills but not academic ones. He felt that he had wasted his time at school and that his adolescence had been grey, characterised by depression. He said he had been ugly with spots and he still felt a sense of low self-esteem.

The countertransference appeal was in his evident motivation and investment in the therapy. This was compounded early on when, in recounting his attendance at many of his friends' weddings, he said, 'I have never been anyone's best man.' At that point I understood that he hoped he could become my 'best man'. Ben was a big man, but early on he told me that he was really a little boy and his appearance belied his true feelings. He was worried that if he cried all I would see was a grown man looking stupid crying. I interpreted that he wanted to make sure I would see the boy and this relieved the anxiety and he visibly relaxed. (Thus here I interpreted his child/infantile needs.)

He told how, when he was a child, he felt terrified of his mother and recounted an incident when he was frightened by her when he was five. This became live in the transference and he felt as if he was actually telling his mother how angry he was with her. He found this confusing and disturbing. He wanted revenge on his mother and used to imagine hurting her. He told me he now had the power because he could withhold his children from her by not permitting them to visit. (Thus, in retrospect, it is possible to see that he told me how he would punish me. He would withhold his child.)

On several occasions he told me 'I am really committed to this process you know!' I correspondingly felt that I too was committed to the process. He could hardly wait to return between his two sessions in the week. There was a countertransference appeal in his evident motivation and eagerness to develop himself and I imagined him realising the considerable potential I felt I could recognise in him. I looked forward to his sessions.

One day, after about three months, the theme of the session was how he was unattractive to girls when he was adolescent. He could get on with women now and he realised that they seemed to find him attractive, but it was too late. He recounted an incident with a girl in a shop that week who seemed to find him attractive. Then, towards the end of the session, he said how, when he was a spotty adolescent, his mother used to say he had horrible little eyes and that she wished his eyes were attractive like those of his father. I again interpreted how he wanted me to see the little boy but this time I immediately felt it was not right – it did not reduce the anxiety. In retrospect, I realise that he wanted me to admire him and see him as an attractive man.

I think the problem was that I did. However, my attraction to him was affected by the fact that he could almost be my son. Thus I was unconsciously denying the incestuous attraction and I think my comment compounded the narcissistic damage. He probably experienced me as seeing him as his mother had. The Oedipal dynamic was evoked and, like his mother, I denied my attraction to him. Samuels (1993) in a development of Jung (1946) and Searles (1959) argues that a form of 'erotic playback' between the child and the parent of the opposite sex is essential for a healthy sense of sexual viability. It seems that Ben's mother had, appropriately enough, established that the father and not her son was her partner. However, in doing so she had denigrated him in comparison and, rather than admitting that he was desirable but that a sexual relationship was taboo, she diminished him by comparison. Unconsciously I did the same.

At the end of the session he said again, 'You know I am really committed to this process' and, in response, I felt a momentary flash of sexual arousal. It was the end of the session so, being careful to maintain the boundaries, I ended it there. I had in mind to interpret the Oedipal desire in the next session, but he did not come for his next session. I wrote my usual note acknowledging the missed session and confirming that I was expecting him next time. I wrote again when he did not arrive for his next session and received a short letter telling me that, due to family and business problems, it would be impossible for him to continue his therapy. He affirmed that it was no reflection on the therapy and would I please send the bill. I wrote reminding him that he had said how committed he was to the process and that, even if he had to stop, it seemed important to come for one session to discuss the decision. He did not reply, nor did he pay the outstanding bill. At first I felt a sense of loss, then anger – I was disappointed. I could not believe he could abandon the therapy so suddenly when it had clearly already come to mean so much to him. And me!

I think there were a number of issues which contributed to his leaving and his precarious financial situation may have been part of it. If money had become a problem this could have felt unbearably humiliating for him given his history. However, he left owing me money and refused my overtures to work it through. Thus, on a psychological level, it seems that he was angry and I suspect that, in the transference, I was the embodiment of the mother for whom he could never be the 'best man'. It seems that the narcissistic damage which had taken place in his childhood was repeated. He did not understand the purpose of the repetition in the transference and, as I neither interpreted nor acknowledged the transference desire, I think he felt confused. Thus his anger and revenge on his mother were acted out in his depriving me of his 'child'. It is also quite likely that the violence of his envious and aggressive feelings were such that he protected me by leaving, fearing that his fury would annihilate both of us.

As already stated, it has been observed by feminist analysts that men often fear intimacy, associating it with their early experience with their mothers (Chodorow 1978). I think that this may have been the case with Ben. He desired but also feared intimacy. The transference was predominantly infantile/erotic but with an adult element. I avoided becoming conscious of the sexual arousal between himself and me, as adults, and this was a repetition of his childhood experience at the Oedipal stage. In common with other male patients I think he may have felt embarrassed and confused at what he experienced as an inappropriate arousal in relation to a female authority figure. When I did not interpret it he perhaps took this as confirmation that it was taboo.

In this case I think the erotic transference was linked to the excitement at the hope he found in psychotherapy. This understanding is derived from the countertransference; I found him rewarding to work with because I anticipated his attaining what I saw as his 'true' potential. However, beneath this were some very disturbing dependency issues which originated in the early pre-Oedipal relationships. If he had stayed I think his immense rage at the injustices and humiliations he had suffered in his early life would have become manifest in the transference. Thus the sexual man/woman transference dynamic was linked to deeper material which would have needed to be addressed if he was to free himself from his psychological bonds.

When the transference resonates at an archetypal level, as in this case, there is a fascination which may hold patient and analyst in thrall and make it difficult for the analyst to think. The patient, like Ben, who leaves prematurely may do so because he experiences the analyst as an embodiment of the shadow of the conscious attitude. He leaves to avoid confronting this split off part of himself. This may be exacerbated by the reality of the gender of the pair and irrespective of the sexual orientation of patient or analyst. The transference is rarely fixed and as we move through different positions within the psyche the transference changes too. The erotic is one element in this but it is not always overtly sexual. All human relations are in some way bound by eros and the early mother/infant bond is the first erotic relationship. Sexual relationships are developed out of this early erotic bond. My argument is that because of this, and especially when the analyst is a woman, the erotic transference is often attributed to its infantile origins and the sexual reality of the man/woman dynamic in the present is given scant attention. This is because it may be more acceptable, to the self-image of the female analyst, to view her role in maternal terms rather than in those of a potential lover. However, this is often the first manifestation of the transference as we have seen with Ben.

Sexuality and violence

In 1932 Horney suggested that male fear of women, and particularly the vagina, was the source of much idealisation of the feminine. Chasseguet-Smirgel (1984) develops this and suggests that some of the difficulties that male patients experience in therapy with a woman are related to a deep and primitive fear for their survival. For the little boy, the realisation that the woman 'possesses an organ which allows access to her body' is terrifying. If his pre-genital impulses are projected, his desire for connection with the mother may be experienced as her desire. This evokes a terror that he will be sucked back into the womb, absorbed and so annihilated (Chasseguet-Smirgel 1984: 171). The impulse to leave may be associated with this. It may be an attempt to destroy the desired, and also feared, object or else to kill off the desire itself. This type of material brings the analyst's body into the subject matter of the session in a very intimate way and an understanding of the symbolic nature of the transference is helpful in mediating this. It can be a relief to the patient to realise that the origins of his interest in the analyst's body may be connected to early developmental phases. The analyst may also be relieved to understand it in this way. However, problems arise when such explanations are used to avoid acknowledgement of the present reality. Adult feelings need to be differentiated from infantile erotic ones. In the course of longer term therapy, as I shall show in the case of Colin, the infantile and adult aspects of the erotic transference become more fluid, conscious and often exchange places. First I need to discuss in a little detail some of the countertransference problems that emerge when confronted with a mix of sexuality and violence.

Within the transference the analyst is often experienced as the perpetrator of past failures and abuses; she may be viewed as all powerful, as persecutor, as well as object of love and much else besides. This may be problematic if she identifies with these images or if she finds it difficult to accept the powerful position in which the male patient's projections place her. Guttman (Chapter 12) identifies a number of issues particular to the female analyst/male patient dyad. She differentiates between asexual and sexual imagery, that is, maternal and sexual transferences. These, like other elements of the transference, may be present simultaneously or at different times. The analyst may be idealised or experienced as sexually desirable but this may shift quickly to the negative, sexual, image of vamp or whore (Guttman Chapter 12). Apparently maternal images, in the transference, often have a sexual element whilst overtly sexual images may, once they are understood, be related to the maternal. Thus the transference, in this as in any other manifestation, is fluid and always changing. No position is fixed. The transference may be like a dream or even a nightmare in which both people are temporarily immersed.

There may be unconscious taboos, for analyst as well as for patient, on articulating feelings associated with images relating to violence and sexuality (Guttman 1985). The analyst's body becomes central in the material when, in the grip of an archetypal constellation, she is experienced as terrifying, sexually powerful or tantalising. Admitting that he is experiencing such feelings directly to a woman may seem very dangerous to the male patient. It may be less inhibiting for him to discuss such negative female stereotypes with a man, as is the norm in social interaction. What is unusual in this therapeutic relationship is that the 'witness is a woman' and so 'the male patient will be careful in expressing his sexual feelings lest he be considered dangerous' (Guttman 1985: 191). Men commonly fear that they will be seen as potential rapists and there is often anxiety that expression of such impulses is tantamount to acting on them. When the male patient's Oedipal feelings are linked to images in which the woman is sexually degraded, it is quite possible that a negative countertransference will arise (Lester 1985). There may be a strong pressure to collude with the patient in resisting this type of transference. It is at this point that many men seem to find a reason to terminate their therapy and the analyst may be unconsciously relieved to let him go.

An extreme negative transference may affect the analyst's awareness of herself as a woman but a positive sexual transference may also be problematic because she may be afraid of being seen as provocative (Guttman 1985). The analyst may deal with her own discomfort by viewing the patient as a needy child. This may be more acceptable to her than confronting the sexual arousal which might follow acknowledgement that he is desirable as a man. The female analyst may unconsciously deny the patient's sexual wishes as well as her own erotic countertransference (as I did in the case of Ben). However, it is relatively easy for the analyst to react positively to a patient of the opposite sex who is clearly attracted to her: Guttman (Chapter 2 and 1985: 190) suggests that, even if it is not consciously admitted, much of the reciprocal countertransference will be communicated non-verbally in gestures and body language. If it is handled consciously and appropriately, such an attraction can have a positive effect on the patient. A well-handled attraction to the patient may actually facilitate his feelings of self-worth (Guttman 1985). Contrary to avoiding the erotic nature of the therapeutic situation then, it might be important to address the question: 'Why is this person not lovable?' or 'Why am I not aroused by this person?' (male or female). Asking this question may reveal the problem which has brought the person into analysis in the first place.

Some men are only too easily able to appeal to the opposite sex. Messler Davies (1994) gives a vivid example of the problems of this type of transference. Such a man may need to know that the analyst can resist his attempts at seduction. His feelings of self-worth may be developed through the analyst's ability to resist his charms, but this can only happen if the analyst is fully conscious of her own countertransference arousals. Problems arise when the analyst's need to be loved, the 'desire to feel special to another person, are unfulfilled. There can be a temptation to seek validation and acceptance through the power of being a therapist' (Sniderman 1980: 306). As in the male analyst/female patient dyad there is always the potential for abuse and the distinction must always be between observing the affect and acting upon it.

My second example is Colin who was in his mid-forties and described himself as auto-erotic. He was an isolated man who had been experiencing serious suicidal thoughts. He quickly became engaged with his therapy, seeming hardly to notice to whom he was talking for the first few months. My experience of him was of a ravenous infant who used every moment of the session, taking the maternal environment for granted. There was no separation, we were not two people; it felt as if the infant/mother feeding relationship was evoked. He talked very fast, recounting many times in his life when he had experienced abandonment. It was evident that his emotional hunger was linked to early deprivation. The first time he made a move to leave was during this early phase. He became very angry, shouted at me that I had misunderstood him in the previous session, and told me that he was not going to come back. He was amazed that I did not instantly reject him but helped him to tell me about what had so angered him, the anger modified and by the end of the session he had decided he would not leave. A period of positive transference followed.

The second time he threatened to leave was more difficult to mediate. He had been in psychotherapy twice a week for several months when he unexpectedly missed three sessions in succession. Each time I wrote acknowledging the missed session and confirming the next one. Eventually I decided he needed some help to return and I wrote interpreting his confusion and suggesting he could contact me by phone. He did so and, fortified with alcohol, admitted that he was unable to come to his sessions because he had begun to experience sexual arousal accompanied by violent fantasies. It became clear that he was confused and frightened by the intensity of his feelings. This is written about in more detail in Schaverien (2002) and also in Chapter 2.

When he returned he was able to confess that he feared that he might attack or rape me; he became very aware that we were alone in the building. He said simply 'What do you do if you fancy your analyst?' He felt first that this was inadmissable but second it meant that he had to do something about it. He became acutely aware of the limits of the boundaries of the therapy room – would they hold? He desired, but also feared, that I would permit a sexual relationship with him or else that he would lose control and rape me. (The idealisation had broken down and the previously repressed sexuality and violence now emerged.)

Once he could speak of this it could be symbolised and I was able to interpret the pre-Oedipal aspect of his feelings. This made sense to him and he linked it to his relationships with women where he would get close and then suddenly leave or withdraw emotionally. He said that he desired sexual relationships with women but he had always felt, when he was in bed with them, that he needed something first, without understanding what it might be. As we explored the nature of his sexual fantasies it began to become evident that he desired maternal holding. He could not experience himself as sexual in relationship because his strongest desire was for holding. Once he had admitted this he was able to contact his dependent, infantile/erotic feelings. These were mixed up with sadistic, sexual and violent fantasies. For a number of sessions these dominated. Then gradually, as he described these feelings and the images that accompanied them, they began to be less fearsome and overwhelming for him. He recognised them as merely one aspect of his inner world and ones that did not need concrete expression. As the violent feelings became assimilated, the erotic transference intensified, the relationship deepened and the symbolic element in the therapeutic relationship became accessible.

This is the purpose of the erotic connection; it deepens the patient's capacity for relatedness. Colin was frightened when he began to experience sexual fantasies associated with violent imagery. His first impulse was to leave to protect both of us from his violence. However, he was able to make contact and then to return and face the feelings. He was at first unable to separate the impulse from the act but, as the symbolic nature of the transference became established, he began to be able to differentiate the thought and the deed. We both survived his aggression and this transformed the feelings, admitted them to consciousness and, because his desire was no longer split off, the relationship deepened and became rewarding for us both. Thus Colin could have become one of the 'men who leave too soon' but he did not. Like Ben he became overwhelmed by the combined sexual and aggressive feelings and left in order to protect me, and himself, from the rapist in him. However, he managed to return and work through these violent feelings and permit them to consciousness and, because we were able to speak about them, they could be modified.

Colin was a grown man with adult sexual desires as well infantile feelings. Within the frame of the therapy room I was, over time, experienced by Colin as every woman (or aspect of woman) who had ever been important to him. Sometimes these were idealised and at others denigrated images of women. He came to understand much of this as originating in the incestuous desires associated with the dynamics of his family at both a pre-Oedipal and an Oedipal level.

In the countertransference I was deeply involved with Colin; from the beginning of his therapy he engaged with an intensity which was hard to resist. However much of the time the connection between us was denied by him. He would not easily give me anything of himself so I had to trust the countertransference as a means of understanding his communications. If, for example I felt a wish to hold him, I realised that it was likely that he was experiencing such a desire. I made interpretations based in such experiences which were usually confirmed by him at some later time. If, on the other hand, I felt disconnected, it was usually because he was angry or encountering some other intense emotion and so cutting himself off from me. This was similar to his taking himself away from the therapy when he began to be sexually aroused. The difference was that now he was able to stay in the room and only cut off emotionally. Eventually he needed to do that less and would recognise it in himself and comment on it.

The point is that the sexual element in the transference, which was a mixture of infantile impulses and adult desires, was openly discussed. With Colin it was possible to acknowledge his infantile needs and to link them to his sexuality. The attraction between us, and my affection for him, did, as Guttman (1985) proposes, have the effect of furthering his feelings of self-worth. Moreover, and most importantly, it was through the acknowledgement of the multitude of facets of the therapeutic relationship that he began to develop the capacity to communicate with his family and friends in a more appropriate way than he had previously. He no longer had to leave as soon as intimacy threatened his sense of autonomy. Colin was often difficult to be with and rejecting of me and yet, despite exasperation and other more extreme negative countertransference feelings, my work with him was always sustained by the affection I felt for him. This was communicated, non-verbally, and in such a way that he eventually became able to trust it and gradually learn to trust others.

Conclusion

In this chapter I have identified a group of patients as the 'men who leave too soon'. By concentrating on the countertransference experiences of the female analyst and the transference of the male patient I have attempted to address some particular dynamics in this gender dyad. I have proposed that a common theme in the premature ending by some male patients seems to be related to fear of intimacy; or of becoming trapped in a relationship from which he would be unable to extricate himself. Sometimes there is a projected anxiety that in some unclear way he would be expected to be more of a man for the analyst than he is prepared for. In other cases the fear of violent/sexual impulses may mean that the patient leaves to protect the analyst. These impulses are often linked to desires in the transference which are based in infantile and dependent feelings but are confused with the sexual, at an adult level.

There are a number of reasons why the analyst might unconsciously collude in the premature termination of the 'men who leave too soon'. One form of abuse of power in psychotherapy is fostering dependence rather than encouraging the patient to form relationships outside of the therapy. The female analyst may be aware of this and so experience guilt if she enjoys the patient. She may fear being viewed as seductive and so deny consciousness of her wish to keep the patient to herself. As a result, rather than interpreting the transference in a way which enables him to remain in therapy, she may rather easily let him go. Similarly, if she fears his sexuality or aggression, she may acquiesce when he makes a move to leave.

The transference is a reflection of other relationships in the patient's life.

Therefore, if he threatens to leave when intimacy or sexual aggression constellate in the transference, it may be possible to understand the problems he encounters in the outer world. However such insights are rather pointless if we have already lost the patient. Differentiation of the adult/sexual from the infantile/erotic aspects of the transference may relieve some of the confusion. This may be one significant element in enabling the patient to remain in psychotherapy and, when the time is right, make an appropriate ending.

References

Chasseguet-Smirgel, J. (1984) *Creativity and Perversion*. London: Free Association Books.

Chasseguet-Smirgel, J. (1986) *Sexuality and Mind*. London: Karnac (1989 edition).

Chodorow, N. (1978) *Reproduction of Mothering; Psychoanalysis and the Sociology of Gender*. Berkeley: University of California Press.

Covington, C. (1996) 'Purposive aspects of the erotic transference'. *Journal of Analytical Psychology* 42(3): 339–351.

Eichenbaum, L. and Orbach, S. (1983) *What Do Women Want?* London: Michael Joseph.

Ernst, S. and Maguire, M. (eds) (1987) *Living with the Sphinx: Papers from the Women's Therapy Centre*. London: Women's Press.

Field, N. (1989) 'Listening with the body'. *British Journal of Psychotherapy* 5(4): 512–522.

Freud, S. (1912) 'The dynamics of transference'. *Standard Edition* Vol. XII. London: Hogarth Press.

Freud, S. (1915) 'Observations on transference love'. *Standard Edition* Vol. XII. London: Hogarth Press.

Freud, S. (1917) 'Transference'. *Standard Edition* Vol. XVI. London: Hogarth Press.

Garrett, T. (1994) 'Sexual contact between psychotherapists and their patients'. In P. Clarkson and M. Pokorny (eds) *The Handbook of Psychotherapy*. London: Routledge.

Gilligan, C. (1982) *In A Different Voice: Psychological Theory and Women's Development*. Cambridge, MA: Harvard University Press (1993 edition).

Guttman, H. A. (1985) 'Sexual issues in the transference and countertransference between female therapist and male patient'. *Journal of the American Academy of Psychoanalysis* 12(4): 187–97.

Heimann, P. (1949) 'On countertransference'. *International Journal of Psycho-Analysis* 31: 81–84.

Hillman, J. (1977) *The Myth of Analysis*. New York: Harper.

Horney, K. (1932) 'The dread of woman'. *International Journal of Psycho-Analysis* 13: 348–360.

Jehu, D. (1994) *Patients as Victims*. Chichester: Wiley.

Jung, C. G. (1946) *The Psychology of the Transference*. CW Vol. 16. Princeton: Bollingen.

Jung, C. G. (1959)*The Archetypes and the Collective Unconscious*. CW Vol. 9, Pt 1. Princeton: Bollingen.

Kavaler-Adler, S. (1992) 'Mourning and the erotic transference'. *International Journal of Psycho-Analysis* 73: 527–539.

Lacan, J. (1977) *The Four Fundamental Concepts of Psychoanalysis*. Harmondsworth: Penguin.

Lester, E. P. (1985) 'The female analyst and the eroticised transference'. *International Journal of Psycho-Analysis* 66: 283–293.

Lester, E. P. (1990) 'Gender and identity issues in the analytic process'. *International Journal of Psycho-Analysis* 71: 435–453.

Little, M. (1950) 'The analyst's total response to his patient's needs'. In M. I. Little *Towards Basic Unity*. London: Free Association Books (1986 edition).

McNamara, E. (1994) *Breakdown: Sex, Suicide and the Harvard Psychiatrist*. New York: Simon & Schuster.

Maguire, M. (1995) *Men, Women, Passion and Power*. London & New York: Routledge.

Meador, B. (1983) 'Between woman analyst and wounded girl child'. In B. Meador *Uncursing the Dark*. Wilmette, IL: Chiron (1992 edition).

Messler Davies, J. (1994) 'Love in the afternoon: a relational reconsideration of desire and dread in the countertransference'. *Psychoanalytic Dialogues* 4(2): 153–170.

O'Connor, N. and Ryan, J. (1993) *Wild Desires and Mistaken Identities: Lesbianism and Psychoanalysis*. London: Virago.

Olivier, C. (1980) *Jocasta's Children: The Imprint of the Mother*, trans. G. Craig. London: Routledge (1989 edition).

Pope, K. et al. (1994) *Sexual Feelings in Psychotherapy: Explorations for Therapists and Therapists in Training*. Washington, DC: American Psychological Association.

Russell, J. (1993) *Out of Bounds: Sexual Exploitation in Counselling and Therapy*. London: Sage.

Rutter, P. (1989) *Sex in the Forbidden Zone*. Los Angeles: Tarcher.

Samuels, A. (1985) 'Symbolic dimensions of Eros in transference–countertransference: some clinical uses of Jung's alchemical metaphor'. *International Review of Psycho-Analysis* 12: 199.

Samuels, A. (1993) *The Political Psyche*. London and New York: Routledge.

Schaverien, J. (1995) *Desire and the Female Therapist: Engendered Gazes in Psychotherapy and Art Therapy*. London and New York: Routledge.

Schaverien, J. (1996) 'Desire and the female analyst'. *Journal of Analytical Psychology* 41(2): 261–287.

Schaverien, J. (2002) *The Dying Patient in Psychotherapy: Desire, Dreams and Individuation*. London: Palgrave Macmillan.

Searles, H. (1959) 'Oedipal love in the countertransference'. In H. Searles (ed.) *Collected Papers on Schizophrenia and Related Subjects*. London: Maresfield (1986 edition).

Sedgwick, D. (1994) *The Wounded Healer: Countertransference from a Jungian Perspective*. London: Routledge.

Sniderman, M. S. (1980) 'A countertransference problem: the sexualising patient'. *Canadian Journal of Psychiatry* 25: 303–307.

Spector Person, E. (1983) 'Women in therapy: therapist gender as variable'. *International Review of Psycho-Analysis* 10: 193–204.

Spector Person, E. (1985) 'The erotic transference in women and in men: differences and consequences'. *Journal of the American Academy of Psychoanalysis* 13(2): 159–180.

Spector Person, E. (1986) 'Male sexuality and power'. *Journal of Columbia University Center for Psychoanalytic Training and Research, Psychoanalytic Inquiry* 6(1): 3–25.

Springer, A. (1996) 'Female perversion: scenes and strategies in analysis and culture'. *Journal of Analytical Psychology* 41(3): 325–338.

Stein, R. (1974) *Incest and Human Love*. Baltimore: Penguin.

Tower, L. E. (1956) 'Countertransference'. *Journal of the American Psychoanalytic Association* 4: 224–255.

Wrye, H. K. and Welles, J. K. (1994) *Narration of Desire*. Hillsdale, NJ: Analytic Press.

Chapter 2

Individuation at the end of life
A study of erotic transference and countertransference

Joy Schaverien

This chapter is offered as an exploration of transference and counter-transference issues when, in the process of analysis, the analysand becomes terminally ill. Written from the point of view of the analyst, eros and boundary issues are discussed. It is proposed that those who are about to die may form particularly intense erotic attachments and that this is characteristic of a speeded up individuation process. The chapter is based on the case of a suicidally depressed man who formed an immediate, dependent and erotic transference. After three months, he was diagnosed as having an inoperable lung cancer. From then on the analytic frame was challenged by pressures to act out in a number of different ways. It is argued that gender difference and the heterosexual pairing facilitated the differentiation of adult, sexual and Oedipal feelings from infantile, pre-Oedipal ones. Maintenance of the analytic frame enabled the individuation process to continue to the end.

Introduction

As Henry lay dying he was in his house in a bright room surrounded by his plants and cared for by members of his family. At that time I wrote: Henry is housed. He is at home. He says: 'I am more alive now than I have ever been'. In some part he attributes this to the effects of analysis. The fact that he was housed reflects the successful outcome of one of the main themes in our work together. His body was at rest in a house – the spiritual parallel of this was that his soul too was housed.

Analysts and psychotherapists in private practice are, it seems, increasingly confronted with working with those affected by cancers and HIV-related illnesses. Although there are many common factors, this is different from working in an institution, such as a hospital or hospice, where the terminally ill are the client group. When an analytic relationship is already established the onset of a life-threatening illness may have a profound effect on the analyst, posing particular problems in maintaining the analytic vessel. Adaptations have to be made to accommodate the physical deterioration of the analysand. However, despite this the patient worked to maintain the boundaries and to ensure that the individuation process continued, at depth, up to the point of his death.

In this chapter I shall propose that when the threat of imminent death emerges in analysis, or psychotherapy, a particularly intense form of erotic transference and countertransference engagement may constellate. It is as if the powerful archetypal state which death evokes holds both analyst and analysand in thrall. Plants which are about to die throw off seeds as a last effort at regeneration. Perhaps it is similar in analysis; the individuation process becomes urgent and seems to speed up. Wharton writing about her work with an elderly patient states: 'I am impressed by the drive to truly live as death draws near' (Wharton 1996: 36). It is as if the unconscious responds to the urgency of the situation and the analyst may become unusually engaged. I am also proposing, following on from my previous work in this area (Schaverien 1995, 1996, 1997, Chapter 1 in this book) that the gender of the dyad may have an influence on this process. The case I will describe was a heterosexual pairing and, alongside considerable infantile regression, there was a powerful erotic bond which maintained the close involvement and interest of the analyst throughout what became a challenging encounter.

The erotic transference and countertransference is, as Jung makes clear, a very necessary and purposeful element in the opus (Jung 1946). It is eros transformed which leads to individuation. Covington (Chapter 5) shows how the 'analyst's warmth and analytic understanding', in response to the patient's demands for a loving relationship, can facilitate this. Individuation is described by Jung as 'a process of differentiation ... having for its goal the development of the individual personality' (Jung 1913: para 757). This is achieved through the development of a symbolic attitude whereby split off and disowned aspects of the personality are differentiated and a conscious attitude attained. It may be that the threat of imminent death intensifies this process and makes it more urgent. The deaths from cancer, at a relatively early age, of two of my patients have led me to consider this topic.

Love and death

When analysts and psychotherapists write about the experience of working with a dying patient the countertransference, although often understated, seems to be central. The analyst's own individuation process may become involved in such an encounter. Dying does not merely pose a technical problem, although it brings technical issues to the fore. Confronted with common humanity in the face of death the analyst may be led to question the analytic frame in many ways and this is intensified if there is an already established erotic transference. In order to convey this with authenticity a degree of self-exposure is inevitable in writing about such a process.

The wounded healer archetype is well recognised as an aspect of the analyst's motivation for the work (Samuels 1985; Sedgwick 1994) and the terminal illness of the analysand brings this sharply into focus. Perhaps this contributes to the 'special' status some such patients attain. I stress that it is not all who face death who involve the analyst in this way but certain people who need to compensate for unlived aspects of their lives draw the analyst into an intense and almost irresistible process. The analyst is obliged to confront her or his own fear of death. The glimpse of her or his own mortality may contribute to an intensified identification with the patient. This may lead to anxiety about being a good enough analyst or to denial of the potential loss of the patient. Above all, in this situation, the patient journeys physically and psychologically to a place where, no matter what depth of analysis the analyst has experienced, she or he has not yet travelled. This is accompanied by the certain knowledge that one day she or he will also travel this path. This may be awe inspiring and the power imbalance of the therapeutic relationship may subtly shift. Hubback (1996), writing about losses experienced in old age, warns against a form of idealisation which places the elderly analysand automatically in the place of a wise woman or man because of her or his advanced years. Younger people who are about to die may evoke similarly complex countertransference feelings and they too may be idealised or feared because of the power attributed to their 'special' status.

In the English language it is notable that there is only one word for love and this is applied to express its many facets. Lambert (1981), searching for the means to differentiate the forms of love which become manifest in analysis, turned to the Greek. Erao, phileo and agapeo express different types of love; 'sexual passion was associated with erao (eros) while warm domestic affection, the ties between master and servant and, in Homer, between gods and men were more associated with phileo' (Lambert 1981: 39). Agape was similar to this but with the additional notion of esteem and bonding (Lambert 1981: 39, 40). Lambert shows how analysis could be understood as an agapaic venture; it survives destructive attacks and often includes the erotic.

It is well known that Freud introduced the notion of transference (Freud 1912, 1915) in order to understand the intense forms of feeling, particularly love, which became manifest in the analytic relationship. In this context it might be helpful to differentiate the consitituents of this. Greenson (1967), following Freud, divides the analytic relationship into three parts: the real relationship, the therapeutic alliance and the transference. The *real relationship* is the real and genuine relationship between analyst and analysand. It enables a comparison of what is real in the analysand's experience and what is real in the analyst's. When the analysand is terminally ill this 'real relationship' may at times be brought to the fore by the reality of outer world concerns and not least by the deterioration of the body of the patient. The *therapeutic alliance* is the alliance the analysand makes with the analyst whereby there is an agreement (not always stated) to work together to observe the transference. This alliance is based on trust, non-sexual liking and mutual respect (Greenson 1967). It demands of the patient an ability to take a symbolic or an 'as if' position in relation to her or his own material. This draws on the 'agapaic' capacities of the analyst and it might include (phileo) fellow feeling and compassion for another's suffering. Greenson writes that the *transference* is characterised by ambivalence; it is both repetition and inappropriate in the present situation. It includes vestiges of all human relating including love and hate in their primitive forms. When the client is dying these too may be intensified.

It is evident that Haynes (1996) was confronting all these elements when she writes from the viewpoint of both analysand and analyst in her moving account of the sudden death of her own analyst. Her honest disclosure to one of her own analysands reveals how flexibility with regard to boundaries can be, simultaneously, an agapaic and analytic intervention. When the analyst becomes seriously ill, awareness of the proximity of death may give an opportunity to work through an ending. Feinsilver's (1998) courageous account addresses this from the point of view of the analyst. When Feinsilver's cancer recurred, he discussed it with his patients enabling them to work through their feelings about it with him. Ken Wilber's (1991) philosophical treatise recounts the story of the terminal illness and eventual death of his wife Treya Killam Wilber whose own words complement his throughout the text. Their meeting, marriage and life together, which was tragically brief, is recorded from the points of view of both partners. Although this book is not about a professional relationship, the honest account it gives of the intense emotions evoked in a relationship by the constant threat of imminent death has implications for analysis. Wheeler's (1996) counselling client's chronic illness entered a terminal phase during their work together. She raises the client's denial of her illness and envy of the counsellor's health. This factor may be missed; it is so painful that it may be unconsciously denied by both people.

A number of single case study books have been written on the topic of the dying patient. Perhaps part of the significance of these is that the writing of them seems to involve the analyst's own individuation process. Wheelwright (1981) recounts how she was asked by a colleague to work with a young married woman who had a terminal illness. In her sixties at the time, she admits that she was herself interested for professional and personal reasons (Wheelwright 1981: 9). In this case the diagnosis was already made and her purpose was to help the analysand 'with the process of individuation' (Wheelwright 1981: 8). Bosnak's (1989) account of the analysis of a man with AIDS discusses the dying of his patient when both men were in their thirties. Bosnak's openness reveals the powerful manner in which such a patient can involve the analyst.

In the case described by Ulanov (1994) the onset of the illness occurred when her analysand, who was in her late thirties, was about to finish a six-year analysis. When speech failed due to the effects of a brain tumour Nancy made pictures. The bond between the analyst and Nancy is vividly conveyed:

'Nancy was not my first experience of death as analyst ... Nonetheless, her circumstances pulled on me as few others, because of the long work we had done together and continued to do ... because of the person she was ...' (Ulanov 1994: 91). As well as conveying the love involved in these therapeutic interactions, these books by Jungian analysts address the genuine problems of boundary issues. These become significant when the analytic frame is disturbed by medical interventions, by the deterioration of the patient and meetings with the family. Ulanov and Wheelwright's cases were female analyst and female analysand pairings and, significantly, both patients were married and their husbands were centrally involved. This was different from the patient I will describe; he did not have a current partner and so the analytic partnership became central. The man/woman pairing added to an erotic transference in which infantile regression was at first undifferentiated from heterosexual passion.

A similar erotic intensity seems to have constellated in the case described by Lee (1996), a music therapist, who writes about his work with a musician with AIDS. This book is accompanied by a CD recording of the client's piano playing within the therapy. In some sessions therapist and client play together in duets and in others the client plays solo and the therapist listens. Clearly this is not an analytic encounter, but my point is that it is evident that the love which developed in this therapeutic relationship tested the boundaries to their limits. Like my patient Henry, this too was a single man whose life seemed to have lacked fulfilment. Lee describes how the imminent death of the patient intensified the process and the therapist relinquished the therapeutic stance and agreed to the client's request to befriend him. Thus, in response to the demands of the patient, the therapist could be understood to have acted out.

I am not intending to discuss the rights or wrongs of this but rather to use this case as an example of the tremendous conflicting emotions that may arise in the analyst when confronted with death. It highlights how the analyst may be drawn into an archetypally charged state where rational thinking is not easily maintained. With people who have not lived their lives to the full or those who are dying relatively young it is particularly distressing for the analyst. Further, when the client has no partner, added pressures are placed on the analyst and the impulse to act out may be difficult to resist. This raises serious questions regarding the nature of a therapeutic ending when the client is dying.

The analytic frame is discussed by Minerbo (1998) whose patient became too ill to travel for her analysis. She discusses the relative merits of maintaining analysis or offering supportive psychotherapy. In this case analysis was maintained in the last year of the patient's life through telephone sessions. McDougall (2000) also describes the use of the telephone as well as the fax machine for intermittent contact when her terminally ill patient was in hospital or unable to travel. Clearly there are no rules and each case has to be assessed at the time and in the full knowledge of the situation. It may be that in some cases to befriend the client is the most therapeutic solution whilst in others it may be appropriate for the analyst to withdraw when the work seems to be complete. In cases like that which I shall discuss below, it may be in the interest of the client to continue analysis to the end. This has to be a matter of judgement in each case.

Henry

Henry was referred by his GP because he was suicidally depressed. At 46 Henry was divorced and his ex-wife and three teenage children were living in another part of the country. Recently he had been unable to function at work due to intense anxiety. Employed at a senior level in a company where he was well respected, he had neglected a certain task and, fearing that his mismanagement would implicate the company in litigation, he had been unable to go to work. Seized with panic and psychologically paralysed he had taken to his bed and reverted to the depressed state which had haunted him intermittently for most of his adult life. He had returned to his parents' home where he had become totally isolated. Unable or unwilling to communicate, he avoided approaches from family or work colleagues, and so he spoke to no one.

When he was referred, although the cancer which was diagnosed three months later must have already been active in him, no one knew that Henry was terminally ill. It is of course evident that when we engage with someone in their analytic journey (McDougall 1995) we can never predict the direction that journey will take. Certainly neither he nor I could have predicted that Henry was to die two and a half years later.

The first contact was in December two weeks before my Christmas break. Henry's ambivalence to the process was evident in the first telephone conversation: 'Dr X suggested I contact you. Then (having arranged an appointment he became anxious) he said: I'm not sure if I can come because I don't know if I can drive on this medication nor if I could borrow my parents' car to get there. I'll phone the GP and check if it is OK to drive.' Five minutes later he phoned to say that he would come at the appointed time. After this interchange I expected a young man in his early twenties and was surprised to meet a tall thin man in his forties with large glasses, wearing jeans, and looking somewhat unkempt. His accent, which gave the impression of a public school education, belied his rather dishevelled appearance. At the end of the initial session he readily agreed to attend twice a week.

He began the following week. He sat in the chair, ignored the couch, and without looking at me he talked fast and his history poured out of him. By the time of my Christmas break, which was two weeks later, Henry had already engaged in analysis. His dependence was such that he was concerned about how he would manage in my absence. The countertransference engagement reflected this and I too was worried about how he would survive. At this stage my concern was a response to his expressed suicidal thoughts. Later, especially as he became progressively more ill, this became a constant theme of the breaks in therapy. As time passed I was increasingly faced with the questions: Would he survive? Would I see him again?

Boarding school

Henry's anxiety about the breaks echoed his early history of repeated separations. He was the third of six children, and the only son. His family had owned several grand houses and at the age of four he moved to live in one of these with his parents and elder sisters. It was here that he was now living in isolation.

The main trauma, as he presented it, was that he had been sent away to boarding school at the age of eight. He told me of this in the second session and from the way it was communicated it was clear that the wound was still fresh; it seemed as if he had been waiting to tell his story since that time. He recounted the excitement of the preparations, the packing and the journey. He was treated as special. As the only son in the family he was favoured by his mother and he was told he was chosen for this exciting event whilst his sisters were to stay at home. He was therefore unprepared for the appalling realisation, on his arrival, of utter loneliness. He described feeling homesick and crying secretly under the bedclothes. There was no one to witness his distress; no one knew how unhappy he was. From this time in his life there was never anyone to mediate his experience. In the first months of therapy it seemed that he responded to this aspect of the relationship, to having a witness. He said: 'This is what I have been looking for all my life but I did not know what it was.' At last there was someone to understand and give words to the loneliness which had haunted him.

An example will give a sense of his despair and is relevant with regard to a later incident within the analysis. Soon after starting at prep school he ran a race. He was a very small boy and all the other boys were bigger than him, but with supreme effort and against all the odds he won. Having won he looked around and realised that there was no one there to celebrate his victory. He desperately wanted his parents to have seen his triumph but they were not there. Immediately after the race he developed severe flu symptoms and was put to bed in the sanatorium of the school with a high temperature. His parents were contacted but told that it was not serious and so there was no need for them to come. As he recounted this he re-experienced the loneliness and despair he had felt and he became aware that, even at the time, he had realised that he was ill because he wanted his parents to come to him. When they did not come he felt truly abandoned and soon cut himself off from his feelings. Thus he learned not to cry.

His special role, as the only son in the family, was replaced by living as an insignificant boy in a vast male institution. A child in a boarding school is expected to conform to the collective values of the institution. Jung writes that: 'Individuation is a natural necessity ... its prevention by levelling down to collective standards is injurious to the vital activity of the individual ... any serious check to individuality, therefore is an artificial stunting' (Jung 1913: para 758). This seems to encapsulate his experience of boarding school; the child was no longer a special individual in a family, of girls, but a member of a collective – a group of boys and men. His emotional life was not valued and at such an early developmental stage this can, and did in this case, have catastrophic psychological consequences. When Henry returned home for vacations he was unable to communicate his suffering to his family and so he felt that no one really knew him.

The sense of betrayal and isolation which began at this time were to influence the rest of his life. He had never been able to communicate his distress at what he experienced as complete abandonment. He found out during the analysis that his mother had cried all the way home after leaving him but it seemed that she had never been able to communicate her sorrow to him. The boarding school experience seemed to replay an earlier separation from his mother when he was an infant. The combination of these events had left him with a deep yearning for his mother but also a vengeful anger. Very often boys who are sent to boarding school at an early age yearn for an idealised mother (see Schaverien 2004 for a fuller discussion of this). The separation was a rupture which came too early. Later, in adolescence, separation from the internalised mother (the maternal imago) is not possible because there has been too little actual closeness. From then on all women seem tantalising; offering the hope of the idealised love object but also the constant threat of abandonment. This contributes to a pattern where women are idealised and then denigrated – loved and hated. This was replayed in the transference in which I was sometimes experienced as the yearned for home/mother/lover, alternating in quick succession with the boarding school/rejecting mother. Boarding school could be understood as an object of negative transference – loveless and cold.

The house

This pattern remained active in Henry and he had never been able to settle anywhere. During the brief years of his marriage Henry had had a home but since his marriage had broken up several years previously he had not had a significant relationship nor a place of his own to live. He would stay with friends until they became fed up with him and then he would resentfully return to stay with his parents. This paralleled his psychological state. When he was in a relationship he had been housed and when that broke down he was unable to house himself. He explained that once married he had been 'joined by the hip' to his wife. This indicates the level of regressed dependence he experienced within that relationship and it also gives some sense of the pattern which was to emerge in the transference. It was as if he 'fell into the therapeutic relationship'; it seemed to offer the promise of a psychological home.

This was evident in one early session when he became very angry with me. I had given him my holiday dates in the previous session along with the bill. He shouted at me that he had always had doubts about analysis. Enraged, he said accusingly: ' I'm not coming back – I can do this myself – this is the most intimate relationship I have had in my life and you just sit there and tell me about holiday dates.' Thus the early dependence in analysis replayed his history. He had described several relationships with women where he had invested everything in the relationship and then withdrawn. He would unconsciously set himself up for rejection and then, when it happened, blame the other person. When his anger had subsided and I had not retaliated, he was amazed and relieved. I was able to acknowledge his anger and how difficult it must be for him, if this is the most intimate relationship he has had in his life, when I tell him I am going away. He agreed, relaxed and then said, 'I can talk about anything here – that's right isn't it?' He then told me how worried he was about his sexual fantasies and he described them to me. After this he seemed much relieved and a period of positive transference followed.

Henry had a real sensibility for the very fine houses where he had lived with his relatives at different times in his life. In some sense it was houses rather than people which seemed to symbolise intimacy in his inner world. Bachelard evokes this psychological aspect of the house when he writes: 'a house constitutes a body of images that give mankind proofs or illusions of stability. We are constantly re-imagining its reality' (Bachelard 1964: 17). People had failed Henry but what had remained constant were the houses of his childhood. The memory of these houses held for him a yearning, nostalgia and a sense of intimacy. One of the first memories analysis evoked in Henry was of when he was four. He remembered standing, looking down the lane from the house and wondering where it would lead; it seemed to stretch so far. At the time this memory seemed to be a metaphor for the beginning of the analytic journey as well as the beginning of his life's journey. In retrospect there is the added poignancy of the knowledge that this journey was moving to its conclusion.

He loved and hated with equal intensity the historic townhouse where his parents still lived. It had been in the family for generations and it was his understanding that it was in preparation for his inheriting it and the family business that he was sent away to boarding school. However, when he was 16 his father, assuming his son not to be interested, made the house over to a trust and sold the business. The parents would live in it for the duration of their lives but after that it would go out of the family. Henry was not consulted and he was devastated. He had lost the home to which he had planned to return and he was faced with having to consider earning his living for which he was totally unprepared. It seemed that his fury at this injustice had psychologically paralysed him and he had never stayed in a job, completed a course, nor lived in one place for any length of time since.

This insult to his self-esteem was further compounded by an incident which took place around the same time. A young woman who was employed by his parents had offered herself to him sexually; at 16 he was terrified, and frozen, had not responded. He returned to school and fantasised about this but when he next returned home his mother, greatly distressed, told him that his father was having an affair with this girl. Thus it seemed that at the point at which he was to move into the world he was dashed back to the maternal realm. A father's two important functions in introducing his son to the world might be understood to be to help him find a life role and to encourage his relationships with women (Samuels 1985; Perry 1991). At both these crucial points his father appeared to have intervened, barring the way. We might understand that his Oedipal strivings were not appropriately thwarted by his father, rather he was denigrated by his father's actions. His role in the family firm and his potential as a sexually viable man were negated. Furthermore his mother was left terrifyingly available to him. It was possible to understand his depression as masking the fury he felt at these injustices; he talked of revenge. He described himself as like the 'Count of Monte Cristo' returning after years of exile to wreak his revenge on those who had wronged him (Dumas 1990). This revenge was directed at his parents; he was now living in their large house but hardly speaking to them and refusing to eat their food.

Transference

The transference immediately plunged him into associations with his early relationship with his mother. There had clearly been an emotional bond and he was moved to tears when he remembered a certain piece of music his mother had sung to him when he was very little. He said sadly that she no longer sang. After this he went home and talked with her about his early years; the memory freed him a little. It was as if he had not felt held since this early time in his life but it was significant that there had been such a time.

Near the beginning of therapy Henry commented, as he left my room one day, on how effective my heater seemed to be. He thought it would be warm in here when it snowed. I noted this as it seemed to indicate that the transference was already active and the warmth he was feeling was generated in the therapeutic relationship. Soon after this it snowed heavily and most people cancelled because it was difficult to travel but Henry arrived on time; he commented that it was a challenge to get through. It emerged that when the family had moved into the house which was now his parents' home it was a very cold winter and the physical discomfort of the cold had been compounded by a feeling of emptiness. He remembered waking one night feeling alone and fearing that his parents would die. He called out in his distress but no one came to comfort him and he cried alone all night. Thus his comment about the snow seemed to be linked to a hope that he might find some respite from his lifelong sense of isolation and emotional coldness. The similarity to his boarding school experience was evident and seemed to indicate that this feeling of abandonment originated from an earlier developmental stage which was replayed at school.

As well as the early infantile dependence, which was clearly evoked, there was a sexual attraction which, I would argue, was operating at both an Oedipal and a reality level within the transference. This was confirmed much later when he told me that among his first impressions of me was that I reminded him of his first serious girlfriend. It seems that Henry's immediate transference was a regression to the early infantile relationship with his mother. This was evident when he stated that this was 'the most intimate relationship of his life'. However, this was not all; the association with his first girlfriend seems to have had a basis in reality. Thus the transference, which was infantile in origin, was complex; evocations of other early attachments being aroused by real similarities. It seems that when such real likenesses occur they add a dimension in the early phase of the analysis. If handled consciously this may be helpful in deepening understanding of transference material. This was evident in the analysand described by Covington (Chapter 5) whose erotic transference appears to have been fuelled, in the initial stages, by certain realities of resemblance between his analyst and his mother.

It seems that disparate elements of the psyche, which had been invested in different women during Henry's life, now seemed to constellate in the transference and to evoke a positive attraction and sense of belonging. This was significant because it was soon to become almost unbearable for Henry to stay in therapy and this attachment generated the impulse to leave but ultimately it enabled him to stay. The significance of the early remark about the snow resonated and, as time progressed, it became a symbol of commitment and the warmth that was to develop between us.

Countertransference

The type of intensity with which Henry told his story and the evident dependence was immediately appealing and there were two distinct but linked levels of interaction operating simultaneously. The first was infantile where I was experienced as a part object; a convenient breast or ear but not a person. Henry was controlling but this did not at first anger me. Perhaps it is rather like the way a mother feels about her child; she recognises and accepts the demands, for a time, even when they may seem to be unreasonable. Henry talked rapidly and without looking at me and I felt as if I was in the presence of a ravenous infant. An archetypal maternal environment constellated. Through the countertransference I recognised his tremendous need for nurturing and simultaneously his terror of me. This maternal counter-transference was a response to the evident early deprivation. However, the intense erotic atmosphere was not solely infantile. Searles (1959) writes of the Oedipal love experienced in the countertransference and it is clear that the

Oedipal transference was activating a reciprocal countertransference. However, there is also the 'real relationship' and I was aware of Henry as a man and of a mutual sexual attraction evoked by the awareness of the irrefutable fact that we were both adults in an intimate situation.

I hope that in this part of the chapter I have managed to convey the considerable erotic involvement; there was clearly a fit and the analysis started at depth. This attachment constituted a bond which helped to sustain the relationship later when it might have otherwise broken down. Furthermore the positive countertransference – the love I felt for him – came to serve an additional purpose once his terminal illness was diagnosed. It enabled me to accompany him in a way which might otherwise have proved more difficult.

Diagnosis

We had been meeting twice a week for three months when Henry described physical symptoms which troubled him. He consulted his GP who sent him for tests; he was very quickly recalled and lung cancer was diagnosed within the week. His session was due immediately after his hospital appointment and he arrived having been told that he had cancer and that the prognosis was poor. This information had been delivered unceremoniously by a junior hospital doctor. Henry arrived in my room reeling from the shock and unable to process the information. He was anxious about telling me and could not conceive of telling his family for fear of upsetting them. From that day until his death two years later he was rarely out of my mind.

He kept the diagnosis to himself that week. The following week, after some discussion and interpretation of his fear of contaminating others with his bad news, he decided to tell one of his sisters. Predictably she was upset and he found this almost overwhelming; he was barely able to contain his own feelings and those of other people terrified him. Eventually he was able to tell his parents and they offered him some support, but the sense I had was that they could not face the possibility that he would die and so did not want to discuss it.

The full process of the next two years cannot be encapsulated in this chapter and so I will describe the main boundary issues which emerged. Henry's suicidal feelings were immediately forgotten in his desire to beat the odds and live. He wanted to live for his children and so he gave up smoking from the day of diagnosis. A course of radiotherapy reduced the tumour in his lung. He often travelled the 50 miles to the hospital alone in a hospital car. Occasionally one of his sisters came from a distant town to keep him company but much of the time he went through the appointments and the treatment alone. He wanted me to go with him and there were times when he fantasised me accompanying him. However, he stated that he did not want me there as his psychoanalyst. Thus we had to work analytically with his desire for me as his ideal partner/mother at the same time as acknowledging the very real loneliness of his situation.

Although I encouraged his moves to involve his parents and interpreted his destructive attitude towards them, many of his attempts to make contact with them failed. He desperately needed someone with whom to share his hopes, fears, anxieties and the experience of the treatment; and that role fell to me. On the days when he had to go to the hospital he was never far from my mind and, although I did not physically accompany him, I did so in spirit. When he was waiting for a particularly difficult appointment or going for tests, the outcome of which would have implications for his life expectancy, I gave him permission to phone me. If I was away from home I gave him a phone number so that he could contact me. He never abused this and only phoned when he was desperate or when he needed to share particularly good or bad news. On one occasion he phoned to say that the tumour had reduced as a result of the radiotherapy, on another that the doctors were unable to do any more for him.

Henry spent a good deal of time in the library researching his particular form of cancer. He would discuss prognosis and possible outcomes. He made a decision not to accept chemotherapy, which he knew would make him feel very ill, after learning that it would not cure him. In some ways Henry feared death less than he feared life and the illness gave his life a focus and a meaning that it had previously lacked. At one point when he was in remission he became aware of the problems he would have to confront without the illness. He realised he would have to find a job and somewhere to live and this threw him into a panic.

The analysis continued at depth. He became dependent and stated that if he became too ill to make decisions for himself he would want me involved. I did not want to foster his dependence and so at every opportunity I encouraged his moves towards his family and friends. However, Henry's old pattern of getting close and then rejecting people was often played out with his relatives and friends during the course of his illness. I was really the only person who was constant and who could mediate his anxiety and this was because, despite impulses to do otherwise, I held to the analytic frame. The contract to meet for 50-minute sessions twice a week made me safe for Henry. It enabled me to observe and interpret his regular rejection of me.

Sexuality and violence

Henry raged at me, he envied me because I was well and he was ill; he found his need of me humiliating. At times he was in despair and he could not bear the fact that I would not travel with him to hospital. He spat out what I offered him telling me that there was no relationship between us and he attempted to abandon the therapy several times. On one of these occasions he became terrified of his sexual feelings. I have described this in Chapter 1 but it is relevant to mention it here as it contextualises the discussion and gives a sense of the conflicts he experienced in the analysis. Henry missed several sessions and I wrote acknowledging the missed sessions and confirming the next appointment. Eventually I sensed that he was in trouble and unable to return so I wrote interpreting his confusion and suggesting he make contact by phone. When he phoned he admitted that he was unable to come because he had begun to experience sexual arousal accompanied by violent fantasies.

He was evidently confused and frightened by the intensity of his feelings but the phone conversation made it possible for him to return. Having begun to discuss it in the telephone conversation he confessed that he feared he might attack or rape me. His awareness of the boundaries of the sessions became very important because he both desired but also feared that I would permit an 'incestuous' relationship with him. In this sexual transference he feared that I would permit a sexual relationship with him but also that he would lose control and rape me. The idealisation had broken down and the previously repressed sexuality and violence now emerged. He felt that having the feeling was the same as engaging in the act. There was no psychological separation – the thought and the deed were the same. This is a very early and concrete way of relating. However, speaking of it is the beginning of the ability to symbolise and now it had been spoken I was able to interpret the pre-Oedipal aspect of his feelings.

This made sense to him in terms of his relationships with women which went wrong because he would get close and then suddenly leave or withdraw emotionally. He desired sexual intimacy but he had always felt, when he was in bed with them, that he needed something first. He had been confused and unable to understand it but, as he opened up his sexual fantasies, it became evident that the vulnerable regressed child in him desired maternal holding before he could experience himself as sexual in relationship.

After talking about this his dependent, infantile erotic feelings came to the fore and these were mixed up with sadistic, sexual and violent fantasies. For a number of sessions these dominated. He told of his almost obsessive current interest in newspaper reports of men who had murdered their girlfriends. He worried about his potential to do the same, to murder me. During this phase he had dreams which revealed his envious and murderous impulses towards his mother and myself. As he expressed these feelings, they began to be less fearsome and overwhelming for him. He recognised the violent impulses as merely one aspect of his inner world and so they were gradually assimilated. This permitted the beginning of separation/differentiation and Oedipal material emerged. Now he began to see me as a person and to take an interest in who lived in my house. The erotic transference intensified and the relationship deepened. This is the purpose of the erotic connection; it deepens the patient's capacity for relatedness (Jung 1946).

The boundaries of the analytic relationship permitted Henry to safely experience transference feelings in which I would sometimes be idealised and at others denigrated. Every facet of his relationship with women was replayed. At the same time the connection between us was denied by him; he would not freely, nor openly, acknowledge that he was giving me anything of himself. I learned to trust the countertransference as a means of understanding his communications and made interpretations based in such experiences. These were usually confirmed by him at some later time. So if I felt disconnected, it was usually because he was angry or encountering some other intense emotion and so cutting himself off from me. This was similar to his taking himself away from the therapy when he began to be sexually aroused but he became able to stay in the room and merely cut off emotionally. Eventually he needed to do that less and would recognise it in himself and comment on it.

The fee

It has been pointed out by Haynes and Wiener (1996) that 'the three major taboo areas of our era are sex, death and money'; all three converged in this analysis. When someone is terminally ill during analysis or psychotherapy, the question of payment becomes an issue. This is one central difference from working in an agency. Ulanov (1994: 92) describes the significance of continuing to charge for sessions when her client, Nancy, was dying. She considers it was an acknowledgement of the analytic nature of the relationship. Wheelwright (1981), on the other hand, made allowances for the situation: 'I agreed to see Sally in her own home, and to charge a minimal fee or none at all ... it was important that Sally, so painfully aware of the financial burden to the family, not incur additional expenses' (Wheelwright 1981: 9–10). If the earning capacity of the analysand is reduced, the previous fee becomes an impossible additional demand adding to the stress of the illness. The analyst has the choice to adapt to the situation or the therapy has to terminate.

When Henry was reduced to living on state benefits some compromise had to be reached but this was not a simple interaction. Once again Henry did not come for his session. This time the reason was that he could no longer afford to pay. His employer, who clearly valued him, had continued to pay him for a year and half but he was now on state benefit. He was sure this was the end of the therapy and so, instead of telling me of his problem, he left. Again he could have become one of the 'men who leave too soon'. This was a repetition of the pattern whereby he had left all the significant women in his life when he felt that they had failed or misunderstood him. It reveals the inner world split whereby there is no sense of an internalised person with whom to negotiate. Unaware of the reason for his withdrawal, but fairly sure that he was angry, I wrote to him after the first missed session reminding him of the next one. He left a brief message on my answerphone saying he would not be coming. Before the next session he phoned from another part of the country saying that he could not come as he was staying there to help a relative. He missed several more sessions before he phoned to speak to me. It emerged that behind his apparent anger with me was the fact that he could not afford to pay my account. I made it clear that I would not discuss this on the phone but that if he returned we could think about the situation.

When he returned he was in considerable distress; vulnerable and regressed, he was able to acknowledge how dependent he felt. His hatred of me for having something he needed was intense. These two conflicting feelings were battling within him as they had done all his life but now they had come to the fore. He felt empty and humiliated; unable to give anything from himself, he needed to be able to pay me. When he found that he could not do so he felt angry and embarrassed so he just left. It seemed that the lack of money made him feel impotent. Once we were able to understand how it affected him it was possible to discuss the fee. A compromise was made. He would pay the outstanding bill in small amounts and then in future he would pay a sum which he could afford; this acknowledged the symbolic aspect of the fee. This arrangement worked until he became very ill and was hospitalised when I saw him without charging him. However, I emphasise that this did not alter the fact that this continued to be analysis until the very end.

Process

The snow theme recurred in the spring, a year after diagnosis. The radiotherapy had taken effect, the tumour was considerably reduced in size, and Henry felt physically much better. He was very positive and hopeful that this remission might last for a very long time. One day he brought photographs which he had taken of the spring flowers which were emerging everywhere. They delighted him and he felt that the renewed growth of spring echoed his state; he was pleased to be alive and optimistic about the future. He arrived one day carrying a small bunch of snowdrops which he gave to me. He was grateful and felt that the analysis was helping and that life now held some hope of a positive future. It seemed that the cold of winter had turned to spring both literally and also metaphorically. The snowdrops, like the heater in my room, seemed to symbolise the beginning of a sense of himself as a separate and viable person with something he could give.

Henry dreamed vividly and, in retrospect, his dreams can be understood as relating to particular phases in his illness. At its onset he dreamed of going on a journey and losing his travel documents. When he was having radiotherapy he had a waking dream image where he was chasing a burglar out of an upstairs room in his house; this he associated with the radiotherapy shrinking the tumour, which indeed it did. Once he dreamed a birth dream where he was emerging from a mountain; his head was out and then something crashed on top of him. It seemed that he was at last coming to life in the analysis only to be threatened with imminent death (the dreams are discussed in detail in Schaverien 2002).

Reflecting on this one day he said sadly, 'I am a nice sort of a chap and all this is wasted [indicating himself]. You would think someone would have wanted it – and it will now go into the ground – to nothing.' I was profoundly moved by this. There were tears in my eyes and I spoke from the heart when I said, 'I think you are a nice sort of a chap.' He sat in silence and it was unclear to me what he was feeling for the rest of that session. After this intervention I questioned myself, feeling that I had broken some taboo – that I had lost the analytic attitude – that this was a damaging comment. I feared that it had been seductive and that perhaps I had missed his aggression in the moment. However, when he returned for his next session he was able to tell me that this had had a profound effect on him. It was, he said, as if the ground had been swept from underneath him. He had been unable to speak because he was struggling with tears. He had realised that that was all he had needed someone to say to him when he was a little boy; he had always felt that he was seen as 'horrible'.

Thus my genuine affection for him helped; it communicated itself to him and enabled him to internalise an image of himself as lovable. The grief which was fully present in that session seemed to release him from the cycle of anger and depression. Such an intervention cannot be faked; at that moment I had been in touch with him. He had permitted himself to stay with the meeting in the moment and instead of withdrawing or running away Henry stayed with his grief. He permitted me to care. Nor did he reject me in the next session, which would have been his usual pattern. Thus something positive emerged from this intuitive and genuine response to the immense sadness of the situation.

It seems that the erotic transference and countertransference, which was active in this therapeutic relationship prior to diagnosis, was now especially poignant and intensified. We both knew he was dying and, as time went by, it became increasingly unlikely that he would move from the analysis into making more positive connections in the world; there was so little time left. In the beginning of the chapter I suggested that the imminent death of the analysand may intensify the erotic transference, making particular demands on the countertransference. I am aware that this could be seen as a way of denying death; an eroticisation (Blum 1973). However, Henry could work with the symbolic aspect of the transference and was not denying his death; rather he was coming to life in a new way within the transference. This included mourning all the losses that were imminent for him. It was this new-found freedom within himself which enabled him to relate, and it was this which deepened the feelings between us. Analysing whilst death approaches brings the reality of the frailty and humanity of both people to the fore. This may be the reason why in some cases, as described earlier in the chapter, there is a temptation to befriend rather than continue analysis to the end.

Henry found it almost impossible to cry and very often I found it almost impossible to restrain myself from crying. The emotion which was played out between us was very powerful and not least as the relentless progress of the disease claimed more and more of his body. As the tumour in lung cancer spreads it often puts pressure on the vocal cords. One day, two years after he first came to me, Henry's voice became hoarse; it was reduced to a whisper. He explained that the doctor had told him that it might not get better. It was a shocking realisation followed by tremendous grief. We both experienced the sadness but when Henry saw that I was moved he switched off his feelings. The feelings returned and then he asked: 'Will you miss me?' I nodded; I was well aware that I could have offered an interpretation. However, the authentic answer was that I would miss him and it seemed to me that any other response would have been a betrayal; it would have been dishonest. Henry was never again able to speak out loud, from then on he could only whisper. Thus each stage in his deterioration brought additional considerations into play.

Henry hated to see emotion in me; it terrified him and he would run away, if not physically, by withdrawing emotionally. However, there were by now occasions like this one when he could sit quietly and experience the grief. I became able to differentiate my own grief from his projected feelings and to understand that, when he was not owning his sadness, I would experience it as almost overwhelming. A major source of distress for him was his children; they were the most important people in his life. He discussed his conversations with them about his impending death and the grief in these sessions was almost overwhelming. He began to consider where he would be buried; he wanted to be in the family plot in the churchyard near his parents' house. It was only after working on this in analysis that he was able to tell them of his wishes. Once the grief was released he was able to risk the emotional impact of talking to his family. His fear of speaking about anything relating to his death was that either he would get upset or else that his parents would do so. This eased when he had permitted himself within the analysis to experience the depth of feeling associated with his potential losses.

It was not long after this that he moved out of his parents' house and rented a house for himself. It was a modest terrace house and not a grand style house as his family lived in but it was his own. He discussed every detail of the move with me and told me that he wanted plants like those I have in my room. He said, 'My mother keeps her plants in the dark and so they die; yours are live and very healthy.' The significance of this comment was not lost on me nor on him and it was clear that I was with him in his move. However, what was encouraging was that he began to contact friends he had not seen for years and to talk to his sisters. Thus it could be understood that the analysis was freeing him from old patterns of relating and he was beginning to make moves into the world.

Hospital and hospice visits

When a person is physically ill other professionals inevitably become involved. During admissions to hospital or hospices analytic boundaries have to be adapted. In anticipation of this we discussed his wishes. I needed to be clear whether he would want me to visit him if he had to go into hospital. He said that he would want me to visit but if possible to avoid meeting his family. He also said that if decisions had to be made on his behalf regarding medication he would want me to do this. I made it clear that if he wanted to maintain the analysis in this way then he would have to make provision for it; he would have to prepare the space within the hospital for such eventualities. By now such outer world considerations were having to be made alongside the interpretations of his dreams and understanding the transference.

It was nearly two years after the diagnosis that Henry phoned early one morning to tell me that he had called the doctor. He was living alone in his rented house and had awoken with difficulty breathing. The GP had seen him and immediately called an ambulance to take him to hospital. Henry phoned me as he waited for it to arrive; I sensed his anxiety and mediated it as best I could. An hour or two later he phoned and left a message for me to call him at the hospital. When I spoke to him he sounded faint and asked me to tell him where he was, i.e., what ward was it? His parents were going to visit him but he needed to speak to me; it was as if he needed to touch base. I was worried by his apparent confusion and concerned that if I left visiting him till I was free in the evening he might have died. (I phoned the ward sister to ask how he was and was reassured by her reply.) I reminded myself that his parents were with him and I had my other patients to see. It was important, because of his investment in the analysis, to maintain my position as his analyst and not rush to his side immediately. To do so would have been seductive; attempting to fulfil the role which he tried to place me in as his partner. Thus a distinction was made in my mind which maintained the analytic frame.

It was early March and the hospital was 18 miles away. By evening, when I was free to go to see him, it was snowing heavily and I was very anxious driving. It was so bad that halfway there I considered turning back but I continued with the journey. I found him alone in a side ward, feeling better and able to breathe. He was sitting up in bed in his pyjamas. This was a strange situation for both of us; for months he had tried different ways to get me out of my room. This had been interpreted until it had become relatively easy to acknowledge the desire. The erotic element in the transference was by now a conscious feature of the relationship and there was a clear understanding that however much he might want it we would not go to bed together. The humour of the situation was not lost on Henry and he said, 'Don't tell me that I did this just to get you out of your room.' He was conscious of that possibility as he noted that he had got me out of my room and I had, 'finally got him lying down'. This was a reference to the couch – which he would never use. He was also aware of the significance of me getting to see him through the snow. It seemed that the heater of the therapeutic relationship was surviving the snow. I stayed for 50 minutes and then I left. I visited him again later in the week at the hospital by arrangement. When I arrived Henry was surrounded by flowers and cards from his family and friends, many of whom had responded to his hospitalisation by coming from long distances to visit him. During this time his parents spent a good deal of time sitting with him and their affection for each other was acknowledged.

A week later he was discharged from hospital and returned to the pattern of living alone and coming to see me. His connection to me was changed by this hospital admission. In contrast to his previous life events he had experienced me as being there for him; when he phoned because he needed help I had responded. The significance of this was interpreted but the main effect was that it established for him that I cared enough to be there when he really needed me; he could trust me. It could be said that this broke a therapeutic boundary. However, he was never misled; he knew that he needed me to maintain the boundaries of the relationship even in the hospital. Thus the analytic process changed and adapted to the reality of his life; the inner world and the outer world were coming closer together.

It was as if the separation differentiation of the individuation process was speeding up. There was an urgency in the material he brought. He was beginning to feel a sense of himself as an agent in his life and this was reflected in the fact that he now had a place to live. Emotionally and also physically; he was 'housed'. Henry would still get angry because I would not be all that he wanted me to be for him and deny the connection between us. However, he would more quickly recognise this denial in himself.

Hospice and home

The day my two-week spring break began he arranged to go into a hospice. His physical condition was deteriorating and he was less able to look after himself. I was away from home for one week and gave him permission to phone me, when I returned, to make an appointment. When I visited him in the hospice he had told the nurses that I was his psychotherapist and he arranged with them that we should not be disturbed during the 50-minute session. Thus it was he who made sure that the boundaries were maintained. He was feeling very weak and was convinced that he would never leave the hospice. He had dreamed he was making a bed; it was a huge white round bed, it was like polythene and, in the dream, he knew this was his death bed. This dream was devastating in its simplicity; it seemed that he was becoming reconciled to the inevitability of his death.

On one occasion during this phase, which lasted a fortnight, he was feeling so ill that he was hardly able to speak. He had a fever and, after telling me how ill he felt, he lay down on his bed coughing and sweating profusely. I sat beside the bed in silence. He was wearing pyjamas and his feet were bare and he was apparently asleep. I had a strong sense that he was cold so I got up from my chair and covered him up without apparently disturbing him. He continued sleeping but occasionally he would open an eye and look at me. This reminded me of the way a baby who is apparently sleeping opens one eye – just to check you are still there. After 50 minutes he awoke; it was as if he was conscious of the time and had used the session in this way. Later we were able to process this experience. He felt it was in some ways a repetition of the time when he had run his race at boarding school and then become ill and no one came. It was different this time because I had witnessed how ill he was and had sat with him and then, later the same day, his parents and his sister had done the same. He admitted that this was very important to him and considered the possibility that this had contributed to him being ill in this particular way.

Henry was offered medication and he was refusing to take it. He asked me to speak to the hospice doctor on his behalf and I found that she was very concerned about him. She told me that they experienced him as hostile; they had offered him medication and counselling and he had refused both. The refusal of counselling was not surprising as he was already in analysis. However, it was something of a surprise to understand that the doctors were encountering him as such a hostile, isolated and defended character. It seems that the changes which were taking place within him had not extended to this situation. The transference here was to the boarding school; the hospice evoked regression to a dependent state within an institution.

The doctor saw no reason why he could not return home if he would accept the medication and she had told his family so. After this discussion I consulted an analyst colleague who is also a physician and she explained the potential positive effects of the medication he was being offered. On my next visit I was able to approach this topic from a practical as well as an inner world level. I explained how the medication might help him to feel better. However, I also interpreted his resistance to accepting help; pointing out that he was replaying his recent experience of living in his parents' house and refusing their food. Furthermore, his resentment of being looked after by strangers was replaying the boarding school experience. A part of him did not want to leave the hospice. To die there would have been a bit like suicide; it would have punished those who cared for him. Thus my role was dual. On the one hand I was offering practical information and on the other using my therapeutic knowledge of him to reduce his resistance. After this session he agreed to take the medication and very soon he felt significantly better. One of his sisters offered to move in with him and look after him in his house. She could not bear for him to die in the hospice. Thus he was able to return home.

After this I offered to visit him at home but Henry was determined to maintain the analysis in the context of my room as long as possible. He continued to struggle to do so when he hardly had the strength to walk from his car to my room. We discussed what he would want me to do when he could no longer come to me, i.e. would he want me to visit his home? He said it would be time enough for me to visit him when he could no longer get to me and he continued to come to me until two weeks before he died.

Eventually he became too disabled to travel and I visited him at his home. His body had deteriorated so there was little muscle tone and he could not move. He was given morphine to alleviate the pain. A week before he died he was bright and lively and it was then that he said that he felt 'more alive now than he had ever been'. He did not seem afraid to die and he knew that he had little time left. He found a renewed spiritual belief and turned to the God he had learned to trust when he had been a child. Many of his friends from the past came to visit him and he enjoyed their visits but he now found them exhausting. He cancelled a session that week as he was too exhausted to see me and so it was a week before I saw him again. When I did he was unable to speak and apparently unconscious. I sat with him for a while, talked a little with his sister and then left. His sister phoned me the next day to tell me that he had died three hours later.

The funeral

The funeral raises additional issues regarding analytic boundaries. The analyst works with the inner world and this is the territory of the family. However, when his sister phoned again to invite me to the funeral I was relieved; I needed to be there. I was aware that this was for me and not for Henry. I met members of his family who were aware of the role analysis had played in his life but I left immediately after the church service.

Conclusion

The tension between the inner and the outer world is held within the framed analytic vessel. The frame exists primarily for the benefit of the patient and when he or she becomes terminally ill it has to be reconsidered. As the progress of the illness takes its course and death approaches, the borders between inner and outer worlds are transformed. It seems that there is a point at which, if the process has been reasonably successful, the two are reconciled.

The purpose in writing this has been first of all an attempt to make sense of the complex erotic countertransference and transference engagement in this case. I hope that this may help others faced with the imminent death of a patient to consider the complex boundary issues which inevitably emerge. Sometimes it felt inhuman not to befriend Henry and travel to the hospital with him. However, it was clear that he needed me to maintain the boundaries so that he could come to trust the safety of the relationship. Much of my own engagement was generated by the transference. Even so it is evident that this relationship, fuelled by the erotic connection between us, contributed to my own development.

Acknowledgement

This chapter is dedicated to the memory of Henry who taught me so much. Although his identity must remain hidden I am grateful to him for giving me permission to write about his analysis. I am also indebted to my colleagues (they know who they are) who helped me in maintaining the boundaries when I so often felt like breaking them in one way or another.

References

Bachelard, G. (1964) *The Poetics of Space*, trans. M. Jolas. Boston: Beacon Press (1969 edition).

Bosnak, R. (1989) *Dreaming with an AIDS Patient*. Boston: Shambala.

Blum, H. P. (1973) 'The concept of the eroticised transference'. *Journal of the American Psychoanalytic Association* 21: 61–76.

Covington, C. (1996) 'Purposive aspects of the erotic transference'. *Journal of Analytical Psychology* 41(3): 339–352.

Dumas, A. (1990) *The Count of Monte Cristo*. Oxford: Oxford World: Classics.

Feinsilver, D. B. (1998) 'The therapist as a person facing death: the hardest of external realities and therapeutic action'. *International Journal of Psycho-Analysis* 79(6): 131–150.

Freud, S. (1912) 'The dynamics of the transference'. *Standard Edition* Vol. XII. London: Hogarth Press.

Freud, S. (1915) 'Observations on transference love'. *Standard Edition* Vol. XII. London: Hogarth Press.

Gordon, R. (1978) *Dying and Creating: A Search for Meaning*. London: Library of Analytical Psychology, Vol. 4.

Greenson, R. (1967) *The Technique and Practice of Psychoanalysis*. London: Hogarth Press.

Haynes, J. (1996) 'Death of the analyst: the end is where we start from'. *Harvest* 42(1): 27–44.

Haynes, J. and Wiener, J. (1996) 'The analyst in the counting house: money as symbol and reality in analysis'. *British Journal of Psychotherapy* 13(1): 14–25.

Hubback, J. (1996) 'The archetypal senex: an exploration of old age'. *Journal of Analytical Psychology* 41(11): 3–18.

Jung, C. G. (1935) 'The soul and death'. *CW* Vol. 8. (1989 edition). London: Routledge & Kegan Paul.

Jung, C. G. (1913) 'Psychological types'. *CW* Vol. 6 (1989 edition). London: Routledge & Kegan Paul.

Jung, C. G. (1946) 'The psychology of the transference'. *CW* Vol. 16. (1989 edition). London: Routledge & Kegan Paul.

Jung, C. G. (1955) 'Synchronicity: an acausal connecting principle'. *CW* Vol. 8. (1989 edition). London: Routledge & Kegan Paul.

Lambert, K. (1981) *Analysis, Repair and Individuation*. London: Society of Analytical Psychology and Academic Press.

Lee, C. (1996) *Music at the Edge: The Music Therapy Experiences of a Musician with AIDS*. London and New York: Routledge.

McDougall, J. (1995) *The Many Faces of Eros: A Psychoanalytic Exploration of Human Sexuality*. London: Free Association Books.

McDougall, J. (2000) 'Theatres of the psyche'. *Journal of Analytical Psychology* 45(1): 45–67.

Minerbo, V. (1998) 'The patient without a couch: an analysis of a patient with terminal cancer'. *International Journal of Psycho-Analysis* 79(1): 83–93.

Perry, C. (1991) *Listen to the Voice Within: A Jungian Approach to Pastoral Care*. London: SPCK.

Samuels, A. (1985) *Jung and the Post-Jungians*. London & New York: Routledge.

Schaverien, J. (1995) *Desire and the Female Therapist: Engendered Gazes in Psychotherapy and Art Therapy*. London and New York: Routledge.

Schaverien, J. (1996) 'Desire and the female analyst'. *Journal of Analytical Psychology* 41(2): 261–287.

Schaverien, J. (1997) 'Men who leave too soon'. *British Journal of Psychotherapy* 14(1): 3–16.

Schaverien, J. (2002) *The Dying Patient in Psychotherapy*. Basingstoke and New York: Palgrave Macmillan.

Schaverien, J. (2004) 'Boarding school: the trauma of the "privileged" child'. *Journal of Analytical Psychology* 49(5): 683–705.

Searles, H. (1959) 'Oedipal love in the countertransference'. In *Collected Papers on Schizophrenia and Related Subjects*. London: Maresfield (1986 edition).

Sedgwick, D. (1994) *The Wounded Healer: Countertransference from a Jungian Perspective*. London and New York: Routledge.

Ulanov, A. B. (1994) *The Wizard's Gate: Picturing Consciousness*. Einsiedeln: Daimon Verlag.

Wharton, B. (1996) 'In the last analysis: archetypal themes in the analysis of an elderly patient with early disintegrative trauma'. *Journal of Analytical Psychology* 41(1): 19–36.

Wheeler, S. (1996) 'Facing death with a client: confrontation or collusion, counter-transference or compassion?' *Psychodynamic Counselling* 2(2): 167–178.

Wheelwright, J. H. (1981) *The Death of a Woman: How a Life Became Complete*. New York: St Martin's Press.

Wilber, K. (1991) *Grace and Grit: Spirituality in the Life and Death of Treya Killam Wilber*. Dublin: Gill & Macmillan in association with Shambala: Boston.

Chapter 3

Supervising the erotic transference and countertransference

Joy Schaverien

In this chapter I will consider the frame of analysis in relation to the frame, form and structure of the supervisory relationship. It is not in question that the erotic transference is central in analysis. However, problems sometimes arise because the erotic transference and the associated countertransference may confront the analyst with the limits of the analytic frame. The erotic reveals much about the patient's way of being in the world but it may be difficult to introduce into supervision. This may be because it engages the analyst-as-person and so may, at times, challenge the analyst's self-concept and sense of professional identity. The supervisor's countertransference may be a way of accessing such material when it might otherwise be missed. This too is complex as it brings to the fore issues of gender and sexuality within the supervisory relationship. However, in a time of threats of litigation and awareness of ethical dilemmas, confronting this topic within supervisory practice is essential. I will give vignettes from supervision where the erotic was either very evident or notably absent. The question is also raised regarding the influence of gender of the analyst, supervisor and patient.

The erotic transference in analysis

Transference is at the very centre of the analytic enterprise. It was Freud who came to understand transference as a repetition of past patterns of relating when he noticed that his patients frequently seemed to fall in love with their psychoanalyst (Freud 1912, 1915). It was the case of Anna O, who was the patient of his colleague Breuer, that led him to realise that in psychoanalysis the undivided attention of the analyst, the confidentiality of the setting and its bounded nature led to the re-experiencing of past patterns of relating (Jones 1953). The analyst was unconsciously related to as if he were a parent or authority figure and so the transference was very often characterised by affect originating in childhood (Freud 1905). Freud (1912) wrote that the pattern for conducting erotic life is laid down in the early years of life and 'if the need for love has not been satisfied the person is bound to approach every new person he meets with libidinal anticipatory ideas' (Freud 1912:

100). Therefore he considered that neurosis could be traced back to infantile sexuality.

Jung's view was rather different from that of Freud and their disagreement over this was one facet of the break that eventually occurred between them (McGuire 1974). Jung considered Freud's view to be reductive. He proposed that incest fantasy had a meaning and purpose beyond regression to infantile sexuality. He agreed with Freud that regression in the transference was a return to an earlier state of being but he thought that its purpose was in order to grow forward anew (Jung 1956). Incest symbolism engaged the patient, and sometimes analyst, in an intense process, which drew the analyst into an atmosphere of familial intimacy (Jung 1946: 56). Jung writes: 'The patient, by bringing an activated unconscious content to bear upon the doctor, constellates the corresponding unconscious material in him' (Jung 1946: 12). Thus the analyst may become temporarily affected by the patient's material (Jung 1946). This involvement offers understanding that is beyond cognition and which, over time, facilitates the patient's separation from the initial undifferentiated state. The analyst is at once a participant and observer in this process.

Supervision helps to maintain the ability to observe and to think when the analyst is immersed in such intense material. The purpose of supervision is to focus on the patient and not the analyst and yet attention to the bodily responses, emotions and images experienced by the analyst is very often a key to understanding the transference. This 'counter'-transference is an analytic tool that needs to be honed and all experiences of the analyst, when with the patient, are potential material for supervision. However, the erotic transference and the associated countertransference can be a sensitive area that the analyst may be reticent to discuss, as it brings the analyst-as-person into the material of supervision. Awareness of bodily arousals, or lack of them, in the analyst may indicate the level of functioning of the patient at any particular time. For example, regression to an infantile state may evoke a maternal response or, conversely, a rejecting repulsion, whilst Oedipal demands may arouse a genital response in the analyst. This may be additionally confusing as such arousals may arise irrespective of the gender or conscious sexual orientation of the analyst or patient. These are not fixed and perceptions of them may alter, taking different priorities during the course of an analysis. As we have seen, eros is central in the individuation process but it is not merely one thing. The meaning of its insistent presence or persistent absence in any particular therapeutic relationship may reveal much about the patient's way of being in the world. Attention to the countertransference is often the key to the level of functioning of this particular patient at this particular time. There are many other countertransference responses that are less obviously demanding but this area needs to be given particular attention, as it can be embarrassing to approach in supervision.

Framing supervision

Like analysis, supervision is framed. The analytic vessel is metaphorically considered to be a sealed container. Jung likened it to the alchemist's alembic within which opposing elements are first attracted, come together and mix, and from the intense chemical reaction something new is produced (Jung 1928). In analysis, unconscious elements from patient and analyst come together in the transference in a similar way. Like the chemical elements there may be an attraction or repulsion, then a mixing, and finally a separating out of the diverse elements and a new conscious attitude is born (Jung 1928). The frame of the analytic vessel needs to be strong in order to withstand the pressure from the powerful reactions that take place within it.

Supervision might be viewed as contributing to this frame, but to report material from such a sealed container might be considered a breach of the sacrosanct nature of analysis. However, supervision too offers a sealed vessel that, at its best, is an extension of the frame of the analytic vessel. In considering this I turn to the wider culture of society and to one of the many framed spaces set apart from everyday life for a particular purpose (Schaverien 1991). The theatre is a well known metaphor for the psyche (McDougall 1986; Gordon 1989; Jenkyns 1996) but I will consider it in terms of its form and structure.

In the traditional theatre the proscenium arch frames the drama. The audience is admitted to the auditorium, the outer frame, but not to the stage, the inner frame. Actor and audience play their part in this imaginal enterprise; both know the rules. It is a cultural given that on entering the theatre the spectator is required to suspend disbelief. This is a symbolic enactment and to interpret it concretely would be to confuse the frames of reference. The action is imaginary; however, if the performance is good both player and spectator experience real emotions. Therefore tragedy may move the spectator to tears, whilst aggression may induce fear; the effect may be cathartic, evoked by empathy, or identification with the protagonist. There may be vicarious enjoyment in witnessing an intimate drama but removed from it (Aristotle 1965). Psychologically, members of the audience make a split that enables them to suspend disbelief.

There is a parallel here with the frames of analysis and supervision. Analysis is a drama that takes place between two people, the patient and the analyst (or in groupwork the group and the analyst). As if from the privileged position of the audience, the supervisor witnesses the drama, sometimes moved by what is observed. There is an attempt to help one of the actors de-role and to join the supervisor/spectator in observing the action from a critical distance. In order to do this the actor/analyst makes a psychological split that permits her to simultaneously stand beside the supervisor, as a spectator of this drama, as well as playing a part in it.

The therapeutic relationship

In order to examine these different psychological positions I turn to Greenson (1967), as discussed in the previous chapter. As we saw, Greenson, following Freud, differentiates facets of the therapeutic relationship:

- *The real relationship* is the *real* experience of patient and analyst together. This is like entering the theatre. It takes account of practicalities such as the setting up of the frame, financial arrangements, breaks and the limits of analysis.
- *The therapeutic alliance* begins in the assessment session whereby the analyst assesses if the patient has the capacity to think symbolically. Like the viewer in the theatre, a psychological split is required whereby a part of the patient maintains an alliance with the analyst to observe the drama of the transference. This therapeutic alliance mediates between the real and the imaginal and requires a symbolic mental attitude. A patient who thinks too concretely, such as someone who is in a psychotic state, would be unable to understand the symbolic nature of the transference.
- *The transference* is an imaginal enterprise whereby past patterns of relating become live in the present. Although it may feel very real, the transference is *symbolic*. In the moment it may seem '*as if*' the analyst is the parent but a part of the patient knows that this is not the case. Psychological transformation gradually develops as this re-experiencing of past patterns of relating brings insight that is gradually integrated (Freud 1912, 1915, 1917; Greenson 1967). Transference is present, although usually unconscious, in all relationships but in analysis it is given attention. There is not always an intense transference, as Peters (1991) has graphically demonstrated, and so a distinction needs to be made between the milder forms of transference and the intense forms of it. Intense transference engagements evoke powerful countertransference responses.

Supervisory relationship

If we extend Greenson's categories into the supervisory relationship we see that the same categories apply but with altered priority:

- *The real relationship in supervision* is a comparison of what is real between analyst and supervisor.
- *Transference in supervision* is treated differently than in analysis. The imaginal drama that is transference is enacted on the analytic stage and not the supervisory one. Transference will develop between analyst and supervisor, as it does in all relationships, but the difference here is that it is not interpreted unless it is inhibiting the process of supervision. This is because interpretation of the transference between analyst and supervisor would be a breach of the supervisory frame; it would place the analyst in

the position of patient. However, if the drama that develops between analyst and supervisor is monitored, it may be understood as parallel process; that is a reflection of the therapeutic relationship that is being discussed (Langs 1994).

- *The supervisory alliance* is central but it is a different form of alliance from that of the therapeutic alliance. It is an agreement, usually implicit, to observe the analysis as presented by the analyst. Like the actor who de-roles and stands beside the spectator to consider his performance, the analyst stands beside the supervisor to observe the patient/analyst interactions. For this to be effective there are certain requirements of the analyst:

(a) Giving an account of the patient's history.
(b) Writing up and reporting the facts of the interaction.
(c) Observing the transference.
(d) Observing the emotional impact of the interaction.
(e) Observing the countertransference including, at times, emotional and bodily sensations, images and fantasies generated in the analyst by the therapeutic relationship.

The supervisor's role will include:

1 *The supervisory countertransference.* Takes account of the whole supervisory relationship, its feeling tone and the attitude of the analyst, as well as the material presented.
2 *The supervisor as witness.* The witnessing function of the supervisor is significant given the confidential and sealed nature of the analytic vessel. For the analyst it may be a relief to have someone with whom it is permissible to discuss confidential material and express the feelings evoked within the analytic frame. This is important because it helps the analyst process and think about the analytic material.
3 *Reflections on the transference*, dreams and imaginal material.
4 *Listening to the unconscious* or underlying implications of the patient's communication as reported by the analyst.
5 *Practical help*, for example, discussion of boundary issues and decisions regarding assessment, fees and termination.

Thus in supervision the central framed area, the stage on which the drama is enacted, is the analysis. Supervision is like the auditorium in which analyst and supervisor together observe the images shaped by the feeling tone and content of the sessions. Rather than a breach of the sacrosanct nature of the analytic vessel, supervision is an extension of the frame and it benefits the patient by helping the analyst to think objectively.

The erotic transference in supervision

The erotic transference is sometimes difficult to access in supervision because, as already stated, the associated countertransference brings the analyst-as-person to the fore. The analyst may be reluctant to report erotic countertransference experiences for fear of disapproval. Yet observation of such countertransferences may be significant in unlocking areas that most distress the patient. Open discussion is often liberating, overriding the taboo on speaking of sexual feelings, whilst avoidance may repeat the secrecy of the incestuous dynamic of the patient's family. A distinction in the mind of the analyst, as well as patient, needs to be made between incest fantasy and acts of incest. It is incest fantasy that is evoked within the analytic frame. However, if there has been sexual abuse in the past, there may be an unconscious expectation that analysis will repeat this experience. This is a confusion of frames and so a distinction is needed within analysis between the symbolic, the 'as if', and the concrete. Like anger, the erotic, sometimes takes the analyst to the borders of the analytic frame but it may not be immediately evident in the reported material. In the following examples I will consider some of the many manifestations of the erotic transference with attention to gender and sexual orientation. The focus is the supervisory relationship and so the patient's material is not discussed in depth.

The erotic countertransference

Daisy had heard me speak about the erotic transference and counter-transference at a clinical meeting of her society and soon afterwards she made an appointment to consult me. She was working privately and, a year earlier, a professional man in a high-powered job had contacted her asking for analysis. She admitted that because of his social status she had been slightly in awe of him even before she met him. On meeting him face to face she had been immediately attracted to him; the analyst-as-person was then in conflict with the analyst-as-professional. Pope et al. (1993) discuss this type of situation and suggest that at this point there is a choice to be made; in taking the person on for therapy, the analyst makes the decision to forego any personal or sexual encounter. Daisy agreed to see this man, as a patient. She was curious about this attraction and what it might mean. As the therapy developed, his appeal became stronger and it became fairly evident from his material that the attraction was mutual. In analysis the task is to interpret any material that arises. Therefore understanding of the type of appeal of this patient would have been helpful (Samuels 1985; Rutter 1989).

However, because Daisy felt guilty about her own feelings she found it difficult to take this to supervision. After a few months, aware that she was confused, she plucked up courage to raise this sensitive topic with her supervisor. The supervisor seemed to ignore it and so Daisy did not mention it again. Soon after this, as part of a planned move unrelated to this incident, she changed supervisors. This offered her the opportunity to approach the subject afresh. Daisy waited a while before raising the topic with the second supervisor. This supervisor took the matter very seriously, advising Daisy to terminate the analysis as soon as possible. This response confirmed Daisy's doubts about her own practice; she felt humiliated, incompetent and as if she had committed some misdemeanour. Ashamed of her feelings, she ended the therapy without disclosing the reason to the patient. Now she came to consult me because she realised that perhaps there could have been another way. Indeed I do consider that there was another way and that this had been a lost opportunity for both patient and analyst.

First, let us consider the analyst. Daisy's story is far from unique as such arousals are a rather ordinary aspect of the work. The point is that there was a confusion of frames here; the transference and the real relationship had become mixed up. The feelings in Daisy arose out of a two-person relationship but she felt responsible for them. In such situations it is common for women analysts to blame themselves for causing the arousal in the man (Guttman Chapter 12; Schaverien 1995 and Chapter 1). This was compounded in supervision when the feelings were not treated as part of the symbolic enactment of the drama that is transference, but as real and inappropriate. In order to differentiate her own personal feelings from those of the patient, some discussion of Daisy's personal state was needed in supervision but this did not happen. As we discussed this now, a year later, it emerged that Daisy had been personally vulnerable as her marriage had recently broken up. This does not necessarily indicate a need for further analysis but the analyst's personal support network might be discussed and if the supervisor does consider that some unanalysed element in the analyst is a problem, this too might be offered for consideration. This is all a part of supervision because it is only when the problems that are inhibiting the analyst's work have been discussed that the patient's material can be fully addressed.

If we knew more about this patient it is likely that his part in this dynamic would become clear. I would have wanted to know more about the nature of the attraction. Did she want to go to bed with him? What were her fantasies? Was this appeal for maternal holding or sexual contact? Was this similar to other dynamics in the patient's life? It would be important to consider what it was about this patient that was so irresistible and what purpose the attraction served. Reflection on his history and the presenting problem might have revealed much about the patient as it is likely that this was a reflection of similar problems elsewhere in his life. The premature termination of analysis is the patient's loss and he may feel confirmed in the sense that he is dangerous, too much for others, or that he is unlovable.

The supervisors should be considered, as it would be too easy for them to be split off as bad object/supervisors. It is likely that many of us have been in the position of these supervisors, the first seemingly hoping that, if the topic were not discussed, it would go away; the second possibly worried about sexual acting out and consequent litigation. Concerned about the extent or limits of their responsibility, the supervisor may be tempted to cling too rigidly to the perceived rules. Neither of these supervisors held to their witnessing role. The first appeared not to have heard and so was like the 'other' parent in cases of sexual abuse who, when told, is unable to accept the truth and turns away; thus refusing to be a witness. The second supervisor relinquished the witnessing role by advising termination of the analysis. There may be good reason for doing this in certain rare cases. There are other possible reasons for turning away from the erotic transference. For example, it can be pleasurable to work with someone to whom one is attracted, and this can induce guilt in the analyst and envy in the supervisor. As witness to this particular type of human drama, the supervisor may fear being gratified in a voyeuristic manner. This merits attention as part of the supervisory countertransference, as it is likely that this too is a reflection of the therapeutic interaction under discussion indicating a need for thought and discussion rather than action.

This analyst seemed to be faced with two options, both of which involved action that would breach the analytic frame. To go to bed with the patient, even if the patient seems to want it, would be an abuse of the analyst's power and so unethical. However, to terminate the analysis with no valid explanation to the patient is also potentially damaging and this too might be considered to be unethical. Instead of action, the aim would be to permit full expression of the feelings: first, in supervision, where it would be possible to reflect on their potential meaning in the context of this therapeutic relationship; then in analysis where, if the topic were opened out, it is likely that the patient would contribute to understanding of the meaning and purpose of the arousal. I am not suggesting disclosing to the patient, but rather finding a way of listening to his material and questioning it in such a way that the topic is permitted. The problem is that it is personally exposing to present this type of material in analysis and in supervision. In supervision it confronts the supervisor with her own sexuality and this may contribute to the difficulty in openly discussing the material. It takes the analysis to the edge of the frame and exposes the analyst-as-person. In order to reinstate the frame, the boundaries between analysis and supervision need to be clearly delineated in the supervisor's mind, with the patient as the central focus of supervision.

The hidden erotic transference – the gift

The reality of the gender and sexual orientation of the dyad in supervision, as well as in analysis, may influence the erotic transference. Gender and sexual orientation are central to our ways of being in the world. Unconscious allegiances or differences may be evoked around issues of gender and inhibit discussion of sensitive material. In the case I will now discuss the analyst and supervisor were both women and the patient a man. This may have contributed to the fact that the erotic transference was initially unnoticed.

However there are times when the erotic transference is impossible to detect until some comment or action of the patient takes the analyst by surprise. The presentation of a gift to the analyst is such an act and one that reveals much about frames. The patient may confuse the therapeutic relationship with a potential love affair. This can be especially confusing for the male patient working with a female analyst, as he may be troubled by his arousal in relation to a female authority figure, and so find it impossible to broach the subject. It may be difficult for the analyst to pick up signals that would indicate the emergence of an erotic transference and, if it remains hidden, the analyst may miss the erotic until it is too late (Schaverien Chapter 1).

Jess, an analyst in her mid-thirties, had been seeing Trevor, a man of a similar age, weekly for a year and a half. Trevor had discussed his early life experiences with a belittling father and a dominant but loving mother who died when he was in his early twenties. His feelings of inadequacy with women came to the fore when, soon after beginning analysis, his relationship with his woman friend broke up. His failed relationships with women then dominated the sessions. He knew that women found him attractive but this present rejection evoked the memory of his first girlfriend and he wondered why she had left him. Frequently Trevor would recount how he had fallen in love with both these women, throwing all of himself into the relationship. He was devastated when in each case the woman had found it too much and withdrawn. He felt hopeless but as he recounted this there was apparently little real emotion. Jess tried to help him to understand the link between these losses and his mother's death. She interpreted his feelings of inadequacy in relation to earlier elements of his history. She attempted to make links with his dependency and the infantile elements of the transference. It seemed that, throughout this time, she was treated as a convenient listener but Trevor did not seem to relate to her as a person.

In supervision each week Jess would report the latest session or two and we would discuss the material in terms of Trevor's early experiences. I usually ask for a written account of the sessions but I do not always insist on a verbatim report, except when the analyst is in training. Writing up sessions is an important discipline. It keeps the actual material of the session, and so the patient, in focus. It also distances the supervisor from the analyst and maintains the focus on the patient. This is a non-verbal statement of boundaries and it reiterates the purpose of the work. Reflecting on my own experience in this supervision, the supervisory countertransference, I realised I was getting little sense of the transference and so I asked Jess to record the sessions in detail. The most evident manifestation of the transference was the way that Jess seemed to be treated rather like the mother who provided for him but who knew best; it seemed that he was in awe of her perceived power.

Jess described Trevor's appearance as designed to appeal to women but there seemed to be very little fire in this therapeutic relationship and so I asked

Jess whether she found him attractive. She thought about this and then said that he was attractive, in a 'medallion man' sort of way, but despite his rather confident, macho presentation he left her unmoved. This seemed quite odd considering the amount of material that was about women who were apparently attracted to him. It seemed that either Jess was denying his appeal or Trevor was splitting off his sexuality in the analytic context. He was not appealing to her as a man but neither was he drawing her into his world at an infantile erotic level. This suggests that there might be a secret split-off aspect to his sexuality that was played out in masturbatory fantasy but did not translate into the reality of interpersonal relating.

It was when Trevor went alone on a two-week summer holiday to a European resort, returning with a suntan and a gift of a necklace for his analyst, that the erotic transference became available to be understood. The necklace was a simple beaded one, of the sort quite typical of the resort; it was not expensive, but pretty. Jess had accepted it despite feeling uncomfortable and rather embarrassed about it. She wanted to discuss this as she felt that the gift was inappropriate. When questioned she said that she had accepted it because she did not want to hurt Trevor's feelings but now she had a problem. As she reflected on what to do with it, she realised that she could not wear it and that taking it home would be quite wrong. It would be taking something into her personal life that did not belong there. It became clear that she could not accept it because it was not meant for her personally. This gift was for Trevor's analyst/lover, a part fantasy figure evoked by the transference, with little real relationship to who Jess really was. Clearly to wear the necklace would be inappropriate.

Until this time the erotic transference had been hidden. Jess had been unclear about what Trevor's feelings for her might be and so had been unable to interpret them. The effect of this lack of comment on the nature of the relationship was that Trevor's expectations had been raised. The presentation of the gift brought all this out into the open. The problem was its substantial existence. The symbolic had been misinterpreted as real and the necklace was a concrete manifestation of the confusion of frames. Even though he had given no prior cues to this, it was now evident that Trevor was thinking of Jess as a potential lover. Denying the reality of the limits of their relationship he had convinced himself this might be possible without checking it out. It became clear that Jess could now relate to her task; it was imperative to interpret the multiple levels of the transference.

After discussing, in supervision, how she might return the gift in a manner that would help Trevor, she took the necklace back to him. In supervision this was an incident where, as well as considering the transference, practical help was necessary in thinking about how to approach it. Returning the gift was a tough thing to do but it was also a form of kindness. It brought out into the light that which was previously hidden in the shadow. Jess explained to Trevor that she recognised his feelings for her but that the task in the analysis was to develop an understanding of how his relationships went wrong. At first he was understandably angry, then hurt, but gradually over several sessions he came to understand that this was typical of the way in which he related to women. Trevor admitted that he was attracted to his analyst and came to realise that this was neither something to be denied nor ashamed of. Moreover he realised that this sort of thing often happened in his relationships with women. He did not check out their feelings first, but went ahead and fell for them, only later realising that they did not reciprocate. By making it possible for him to discuss the meaning of the gift and interpreting his desire for her to be his woman, a whole area of past sadness became available to him. At last he could truly grieve for his losses rather than, as before, repeating them but in a split-off manner. He became sad and the inflated macho image gave way to a much younger, rejected child aspect of his personality. Once its meaning had been understood it became possible for him to take back the gift.

This supervision was characterised by my knowledge of Jess, an analyst who was well able to use her own feelings in relation to her patients. Thus, as her supervisor, I knew that this case was different from others she had brought in the past. The supervisory countertransference takes account of the aliveness of the presentation as well as the material that is presented. In this case I sensed that there was something unstated but neither Jess nor I could pinpoint it until the presentation of this gift. Once the necklace appeared, the main thread of the drama that is analysis was exposed. The analysis was, like the action on the stage, the inner frame of this process; it was the central action. Supervision was at one remove, the outer frame, with analyst and supervisor like the audience observing the action; this is the supervisory alliance. The protagonists in this drama were Trevor and Jess. However, the emotional responses of the supervisor, like those of the audience of a theatrical production, are significant. At first as witness to this drama I was not engaged because it was not engaging Jess. This changed when the erotic became live within the analysis. The relationship was then available for mediation and the unconscious could begin to become conscious. The point is that a variety of emotional and intellectual responses are demanded of the supervisor as spectator and attention to these very often reveals the parallel process. However, it also raises the question of whether a male supervisor might have picked up the erotic transference earlier than I did. A man might have been more able intuitively to sense the sexuality in the relationship. Did the fact that Jess and her supervisor were both women mean that there was an unconscious collusion in discussing this male patient's rather macho presentation? There are no clear answers to such a retrospective question but in terms of supervisory practice it merits consideration.

Sexual orientation and erotic transference

The final point in this chapter is the way in which too fixed an idea of the sexual orientation of analyst or patient can limit the progress of analysis and prevent the deepening of the transference. This leads to an implicit question regarding the influence of gender and sexuality in supervision. Problems of the erotic transference arising in same sex pairings may inhibit the full emergence of the meaning of homosexual material. Holly was working with a woman, Carol, who had been married for ten years. Initially the patient appeared to be quite happy in her marriage. Her presenting problem related to other areas in her life. However, several months into the analysis she began to speculate about whether or not she might after all be lesbian. As far as Holly knew, her patient did not know that Holly was herself lesbian. The patient had become aware of her feelings about other women and reported fantasies about their bodies. This puzzled her and she was worried that it might affect her marriage.

In supervision Holly discussed her concern that the analysis was evoking something that was not previously there in her patient. When asked she said that she was not aware of being attracted to her patient but was worried that she might be unconsciously influencing her. Thus the analyst-as-person was inhibiting the performance of analyst-as-professional. Concerned that if Carol explored this she would be taking on something that would radically affect her life, Holly veered away from discussion of the topic. In supervision she suggested that perhaps it was time to end the therapy before it damaged this patient's marriage. In this situation the supervisor needs to listen carefully to the reports of the sessions to attempt to elicit what is really going on.

I asked Holly to recount the previous two sessions, in detail, reading from the written reports. This is where writing up is so important. I listened to the material without commenting and a pattern seemed to emerge. Beneath the overt dialogue were oblique references to the body of the analyst. Carol talked of leaving her session and seeing a woman walking along the street. The idea came into her mind that she felt attracted to this stranger. It seemed that this was linked with the material of the session that she had just left. In the next session the nature of the erotic fantasies were developed and it became evident that she had been drawn to the woman's breasts. We speculated that it was possible that indeed Carol's interest in other women's bodies related to her desire for closeness with her analyst's body, but perhaps this was primarily a desire for maternal closeness.

The problem here was that the analyst had too fixed an idea of her own and the patient's sexual orientation. Holly's anxiety about influencing Carol, and so affecting her life adversely, meant that she avoided the material that would deepen the transference. The nature of any desire needs to be fully explored and after that the patient may need to deal with any potential consequences in the outer world. This arousal may or may not have led to a lesbian lifestyle, but at the time it was merely the erotic aspect of the therapeutic relationship that was being aroused by the deep, intimate relating of the analysis. Here again is a confusion of frames; this time the analyst was confusing the real and the imaginal. The imaginal enterprise that is transference needed to be fully explored before its affects in the outer world were addressed. It is also possible that Carol may have sensed, in some unconscious way, that her analyst was lesbian. However, what is important for the analysis was that Carol's own homosexuality was now coming to the fore and that was part of the material she needed to explore.

Analyst and supervisor were both women and so were the patient and analyst. It is possible that in a same-sex pair unconscious identification may inhibit awareness of the erotic transference. In the example that follows the patient and analyst were both men. This may contribute to an unconscious perception in the female supervisor of otherness, which may inhibit confrontation of the erotic transference.

Erotic transference as defence

Philip, a rather formally attired doctor, came for weekly psychotherapy supervision as part of his psychiatric training. The patient, Jack, was completely the opposite of Philip in every way. He was an artist, flamboyantly attired, overtly gay and it seemed that he spent a good deal of each session describing his sex life in detail. As this continued it seemed that he was attempting to tantalise Philip with descriptions of one-night stands and exciting but dangerous encounters with strangers. Philip had a rather fixed idea of his own heterosexuality and Jack's behaviour seemed to him to be wild and unbounded. As the therapy progressed Jack made more blatantly obvious moves towards his analyst. He teased in a way that began to feel intrusive and presented dream material incorporating sexual fantasies of being together with Philip.

Philip's discomfort was evident as he recounted this material. It seemed that this was in part because his own homosexuality was unfamiliar to him and therefore he saw Jack as completely 'other'. Whilst he was interested in the descriptions of this different lifestyle, he could not identify with it. As we explored this, it became evident that Philip was meeting elements of himself with which he was unfamiliar. This is a delicate matter because a supervisor who attempts to set the agenda for his supervisee's analysis is intruding and yet to gently point the way is sometimes necessary. It was a relief when Philip volunteered that he was working on this in his own analysis. Here again the analyst-as-person was inhibiting the use of the countertransference as a means of understanding the communications from the patient.

Once Philip's discomfort had been acknowledged in supervision, he relaxed. It was then possible to focus on the meaning of Jack's seductive behaviour. It gradually emerged that Jack's sexual behaviour was a distraction from the pain of relating. He was terrified of really relating to his analyst and so having to admit his vulnerability and dependency. His overt sexual behaviour was defensive. It was interpreted and over a few weeks began to be assimilated. Then it emerged that Jack was afraid of getting in touch with the pain of the rejection by his military father that had been compounded by his admission of his sexuality. The accounts of his exciting life had distracted his analyst in rather the same way as he distracted himself from the pain of this rejection. The sexual interest in Philip was not erotic in a relational sense; it was a means of keeping at bay the pain that would follow if he permitted Philip to witness his distress. When the sexual issues were laid aside, the flamboyant Jack was able to reveal a sad, shadowy figure overwhelmed by grief. A phase of mourning then followed in which he permitted Philip to accompany him.

In this case the erotic transference was at first a defence against being in touch with unhappiness. Initially both analyst and patient had been arrested in their understanding, each by his fixed idea of his own sexual orientation. Philip was sure of his heterosexuality and Jack was rebelliously claiming his identification as a gay man. Until this was mediated and they could each move towards the other, the analysis was stuck. There was much drama in this supervision but it was a drama at first distant from the analytic relationship.

This was a male analyst/male patient pair and the supervisor, as a woman, was admitted to a male domain with the potential for feeling like a voyeur. In this case this would be in part the real relationship, in part the supervisory countertransference, but also the parallel process.

Conclusion

In analytic case discussions and supervision it is still important to be alert to the presence or absence of loving or sexual feelings just as we are alert to anger, envy or aggression. Perhaps these emotions engage the analyst-as-a-person more than any other aspect of analysis. In this chapter I hope to have shown how the role of the supervisor can facilitate presentation of this sensitive material. The supervisor, as witness, uses the supervisory counter-transference as a guide to the nature the analytic dyad. When the analyst is able openly to discuss this very sensitive material the psychological engagement is deepened.

References

Aristotle (1965) *On the Art of Poetry*, trans. T. S. Dorsch. Harmondsworth: Penguin.

Freud, S. (1905) 'Three essays on the theory of sexuality'. *Standard Edition* Vol. VII. London: Hogarth Press.

Freud, S. (1912) 'The dynamics of transference'. *Standard Edition* Vol. XII. London: Hogarth Press (1963 edition).

Freud, S. (1915) 'Observations on transference love'. *Standard Edition* Vol. XII. London: Hogarth Press.

Freud, S. (1917) 'Transference'. *Standard Edition* Vol. XVI. London: Hogarth Press.

Gordon, R. (1989) 'The psychic roots of drama'. In A. Gilroy and T. Dalley (eds) *Pictures at an Exhibition*. London: Tavistock/Routledge.

Greenson, R. (1967) *The Technique and Practice of Psychoanalysis*. London: Hogarth Press.

Guttman, H. (1984) 'Sexual issues in the transference and countertransference between female therapist and male patient'. *Journal of the American Academy of Psychoanalysis* 12(4): 187–197.

Jenkyns, M. (1996) *The Play's the Thing*. London & New York: Routledge.

Jones, E. (1953) *Sigmund Freud: Life and Work*. London: Hogarth Press (1980 edition).

Jung, C. G. (1928) 'On psychic energy'. CW Vol. 8. London: Routledge and Kegan Paul.

Jung, C. G. (1946) 'The psychology of the transference'. CW Vol. 16. Princeton: Bollingen (1954 edition).

Jung, C. G. (1956) 'Symbols of transformation'. CW Vol. 5. Princeton: Bollingen (1976 edition).

Langs, R. (1994) *Doing Supervision and Being Supervised*. London: Karnac.

McDougall, J. (1986) *Theatres of the Mind: Illusion and Truth on the Psychoanalytic Stage*. London: Free Association Books.

McGuire, W. (1974) *The Freud/Jung Letters*. London: Hogarth Press.

Peters, R. (1991) 'The therapist's expectations of the transference'. *Journal of Analytical Psychology* 36(1): 77–92.

Pope, K. S., Sonne, J. L., Holroyd, J. (1993) *Sexual Feelings in Psychotherapy*. London and Washington: American Psychological Association and Princeton Academic Press.

Rutter, P. (1989) *Sex in the Forbidden Zone*. Los Angeles: Tarcher.

Samuels, A. (1985) 'Symbolic dimensions of Eros in transference–countertransference: some clinical uses of Jung's alchemical metaphor'. *International Review of Psycho-Analysis* 12: 199.

Schaverien, J. (1991) *The Revealing Image: Analytical Art Psychotherapy in Theory and Practice*. London and Philadelphia: Jessica Kingsley Publishers.

Schaverien, J. (1995) *Desire and the Female Therapist: Engendered Gazes in Psychotherapy and Art Therapy*. London and New York: Routledge.

Schaverien, J. (1997) 'Men who leave too soon: reflections on the erotic transference and countertransference'. *British Journal of Psychotherapy* 14(1): 3–16.

Schaverien, J. (2002) *The Dying Patient in Psychotherapy: Desire, Dreams and Individuation*. London: Palgrave Macmillan.

Part II

Erotic transferences and the symbolic function

The four chapters in this section are theoretically innovative, developing understanding of the symbolic nature of the transference. Anne Springer (Chapter 4) approaches this through the highly charged topic of boundary violations by the analyst. She opens a debate of great relevance for this book by drawing attention to 'incest on the couch'. By so naming it she places the topic of sexual violations by analysts into the area of the repetition of familial trauma. In Jungian terms she describes this as a breakdown of the symbolic function. She points out that although members of ethics committees get to hear about incidences of 'incest on the couch' they are shrouded in secrecy due to the confidential nature of the very process of investigation. This fuels the fantasies of the rest of the analytic community about what actually goes on in these situations. Therefore her interest is to investigate the psychological state of the analyst at the point when he breaches the bounds of professional practice. Her view is that the analyst is perverse in the sense that such violation is non-relational – he is relating to his own inner object rather than his patient. The breakdown of the symbolic function leads to concretising what should have remained symbolic. She links this to eroticised hate.

Covington (Chapter 5) and Kavaler-Adler (Chapter 6) continue the theme, started in Part I, of women analysts working with male patients. Both give vivid accounts of the depth analysis that facilitates transformation in the state of the patient. Both develop understanding of the importance of the analyst's ability to maintain the symbolic position and to continue to think, despite intense pressures from the patient to act. In Chapter 5, Coline Covington gives a brief contextualisation of the origins of the erotic transference from Freud and Jung. Following Jung, her single case study demonstrates both the meaning and purpose of the erotic transference. She traces different phases in the analysis of a man with whom there was a strong pressure to act out sexually. Covington monitors her countertransference and describes how it was at first not possible to respond lovingly to the patient's erotic feelings. She makes it clear that the dangers at this point are that the analyst fails to meet the patient's desire with understanding or else fails to frustrate this desire. It is only when the erotic component begins to differentiate, and the patient is able to experience the analyst as a separate person, that loving feelings can be reciprocated by the analyst. Her emphasis is on the importance of the female analyst recognising the paternal transference as well as the negative Oedipal transference (see Karme Chapter 14).

Susan Kavaler-Adler (Chapter 6) begins with the Kleinian view of mourning of the depressive position and extends this into what she calls developmental mourning. Her single case example of a male patient traces in great detail the developmental mourning process as it evolves through a deeply erotic transference, proposing that mourning is 'a critical factor in modifying the erotic transference from a major resistance into ... a positive force'. She demonstrates that the erotic transference is as primary with men with women analysts, as it is with women in analysis with men.

Mary Lynne Ellis (Chapter 7) is critical of psychoanalytic theories that consider homosexuality as causally, biologically determined. She draws on the work of Foucault and two vivid clinical examples to consider the wider social context. Whilst not overtly about the erotic transference, this chapter is included because of the complex social and cultural issues that it raises with regard to transference when working with difference. This leads on to the next section of the book where same sex erotic transferences are discussed in depth. Ellis focuses on race, gender and sexual orientation and clearly shows how assumptions of cultural and social norms, from both patient and analyst, impact on the therapeutic relationship. Once again the need for the analyst to understand the symbolic nature of the transference is evident.

Chapter 4

Paying homage to the power of love

Exceeding the bounds of professional practice[1]

Anne Springer

I should like to present a number of thoughts on the subject of the violation of professional ethics in analytical practice. I shall consider an occurrence that has now come to be termed descriptively and analogously 'incest on the couch', but which in my view is – as I hope to be able to validate – the expression of a particular pathological state. Further, this pathological state is doubtless to be found potentially in all of us in different degrees, and in some individuals it becomes manifest in the extreme form of sexual acting out in the countertransference.

Introduction

Violation of professional ethics is to be understood first of all as the narcissistic abuse of a male or female patient with the intention of satisfying the male or female analyst's own needs for recognition and power and in order to ward off anxiety, depression, hate and pain. With the aim of drawing up a possible clinical classification of such occurrences and improprieties, which destroy the analysis as a constructive process of relationship, I will attempt to develop a hypothesis. *Sex in the Forbidden Zone*, as Rutter (1991), an American Jungian analyst, called his study of the abuse of dependent relationships, is apparently a more frequent occurrence than we all, with our analytic ego-ideals, would like to acknowledge.

Statistics

In a number of comprehensive studies carried out in the USA, the average figure given for psychotherapies in which such violations occur is roughly 10 per cent (Reimer 1991: 215). One of these studies (Bouhoutsos et al. 1983, in Reimer 1991: 217–18) shows that in more than 90 per cent of such cases (from

---

1 This is a revised version of a lecture given at the DGAP Conference in March 1992.

a total of 559 cases) the violation involved a male therapist and a female patient. The Bouhoutsos study shows that, in comparison, cases in which a female therapist enters into a sexual relationship with a male client are extremely rare and that the therapist is on average 40 to 50 years old.

In most of these cases the acting out began in the consulting room of a private practice. In at least one-third of the cases the impropriety was repeated with other female patients, some estimates being as high as 80 per cent. As far as it was possible to establish, a large number of therapists involved were going through phases of personal crisis in both their lives and their relationships, which might imply inner conflicts.

Apart from a limited survey carried out in France (Füchtner 1987), there have been no specific investigations into the frequency of breaking the rules of 'abstinence' in the sense of sexual intimacy with regard to male and female analysts. In 1977 Butler and Zelen (Reimer 1991: 221) interviewed 20 male psychiatrists and psychologists who had been sexually intimate with female patients and whose training had either been psychodynamic-psychoanalytic or humanistic-psychological in orientation. The average age of the therapists in this study was 51 years, with consulting experience lying between five and thirty years. Eighty per cent of these therapists could not remember the exact events which had led to sexual contact. Almost all of them reported that during the period in which sexual intimacy had taken place they had felt hypersensitive, in need of affection and lonely as a result of unhappy marriages, recent separations or divorces. Fifty-five per cent of these therapists said that they feared close relationships. Over half the therapists spoke of erotic feelings towards the female patients they had been intimate with when the latter had begun to talk about themselves during therapy and to speak about their feelings, i.e. as soon as a closer relationship had begun to develop towards the therapist.

In the limited study of the analytic setting carried out in 1975 in France and related by Füchtner, 30 patients and former patients, 15 of them male and 15 female, were interviewed quite extensively. Of the fifteen women interviewed, four reported that sexual intercourse had taken place during their analysis. The analysts involved had been prominent and experienced.

Non-sexual abuse in the analyst/patient relationship

It is, of course, virtually impossible to give a quantitative estimate of the more subtle and less spectacular violations of professional ethics in analyses and therapies, violations of which the purpose is the satisfaction of the male or female consultant's desire for recognition and power. One can assume, however, that the frequency of these cases is immensely high, and it is impossible to link frequency to the gender of the consultant.

I would maintain that an inherent connection exists between narcissistic abuse, revealed in the verbal activity of the male or female analyst (wanting to have the last word in attempting to interpret and understand the patient's actions, avoiding conflicts in order to preserve idealizing transferences, personal remarks about aspects of the patient's persona, voicing unreflected value judgements about the patient's conduct and appearance) and manifest sexual abuse.

Activities like these may be seen as part of a narcissistic transference/ countertransference style (see Wolstein 1988) and may well be found in the initial stages of the analysis before subsequent sexual activity, but this does not mean to say that such a style inevitably leads to sexual activity. I would like to concentrate my attention above all on the male analyst who commits sexual acts, since I assume that, despite the basic continuity in the abuse of the female patient, something decisive occurs within the analyst at the point where manifest sexual activity begins. It is this which I shall attempt to explain.

Acting out sexuality in analysis: historical aspects

Psychodynamic considerations of the issue of the violation of professional ethics in psychoanalysis and psychotherapy are of limited value because there are so few published cases which would make public discussion possible. There is very little to be found, considering the 100-year-old history of psychoanalysis.

The relationship between Jung and Sabina Spielrein has been well documented by Carotenuto (1991) and Covington and Wharton (2003). We know quite a lot about Elma Palos and Sandor Ferenczi. We also have access to the memoirs recorded by Hilda Doolittle of her analysis with Freud: The circumstances surrounding the temptations of an analyst are narrated in Rutter's book mentioned above: There is the self-portrayal of an American analyst, written under a pseudonym and retold in the guise of a novel, which I shall examine in more detail later (Wheelis 1988) and recently there has been the anonymous publication of *Verführung auf der Couch* (1988), the first account ever to be published in the history of psychoanalysis from the point of view of a female analysand during the analyst's training. Most recently, a second case history has appeared, relating the experiences of a female patient in France (Augerolles 1991). Apart from these, the literature includes a number of interviews with female patients, which for our purposes however are of limited value in formulating a hypothesis, and a few short case studies.

Violations of abstinence are on the other hand an open secret in associations of psychotherapists and psychoanalysts. They are talked about when colleagues come together in small groups and are passed on in the form of rumours. If the subject is brought up in subsequent perhaps even successful analyses of female patients to whom this has happened, or in reports to social insurance assessors, they are subject to professional secrecy. The result is that something remains in the dark which both hurts and dismays us all, and about which we all keep fantasizing. Only during recent years have societies and training institutes established procedures and investigating committees.

I shall now turn to the history of the violations of abstinence. The first beginnings of our profession are marked by the alarm caused by the possibility of the eruption of emotions and feelings in the therapeutic relationship. In 1892 Breuer is appalled and breaks off the treatment of Berta Pappenheim ('Anna O') when she reveals to him her fantasy of bearing his child – three months after Breuer's wife has given birth to a baby daughter. Breuer's wife rebels against the close relationship between the patient/rival and her husband. He sees his marriage in jeopardy, breaks off all contact with the patient, who is subsequently admitted to hospital, and withdraws from psychoanalysis.

Ida Bauer, the 'Dora' of Freud's 'Fragment of an Analysis of a Case of Hysteria' goes to see Freud for the first time in 1898 when she is 16 years old. She is urged to do so by her father, whom Freud has previously treated medically for the after-affects of a syphilitic infection. Ida has learned of her father's affair with a married woman, to whom in turn Ida has a highly idealizing relationship. It is hoped that Freud will be able to talk her out of this 'idea', or at least this is her father's intention in sending his daughter to see him. Two years later Freud's analysis of Ida begins but she breaks it off after 11 weeks. In these 11 weeks a very close relationship developed, 'one long conversation about love, sexuality and their fates' (Wellendorf 1987: 70–84). When one reads the Dora text again today, one is aware of how insistent Freud becomes, particularly in the last sessions before the analysis is broken off, and how vigorously he asserts the correctness of his interpretations. He desires acknowledgement; he wishes to be recognised as a researcher and therapist, and most probably as a man too. From today's point of view Freud's behaviour falls short of good analytical practice and contravenes the principle of abstinence.

In 1904 Jung begins his treatment of Sabina Spielrein in the psychiatric clinic in Zurich. The treatment is so successful that after she is discharged from the clinic in 1907 she resumes her study of medicine. She continues to consult Jung privately. In 1906, at the very beginning of his correspondence with Freud, Jung writes about her in his second letter to him. After expressing his doubts about Freud's theory of sexuality, he describes his patient's infantile neurosis, which included the handling of faeces, and her pleasurable feelings related to scenes of fighting between her father and brother. He then asks Freud to give his comments on this case. Four days later Freud replies:

> Perhaps you remember my contention in my *Theory of Sexuality* that even infants derive pleasure from the retention of faeces. The third to fourth year is the most significant period for those sexual activities which later belong to the pathogenic ones (ibid). The sight of a brother being spanked arouses a memory trace from the first to second year, or a fantasy transposed into that period. It is not unusual for babies to soil the hands of those who are carrying them. Why should that not have happened in her case? And this awakens a memory of her father's caresses during her

infancy. Infantile fixation of the libido on the father – the typical choice of object; anal autoeroticism. The position she has chosen can be broken down into its components, for it seems to have still other factors added to it. Which factors? It must be possible, by the symptoms and even by the character, to recognize anal excitation as a motivation. Such people often show typical combinations of character traits. They are extremely neat, stingy and obstinate, traits which are in a manner of speaking the sublimation of anal eroticism. Cases like this based on repressed perversion can be analysed very satisfactorily.

(McGuire 1974: 5F, 27 October 1906)

First of all it must be noted that Freud talks of 'perversion'; I will return to this point later. It must also be noted that he talks of a regression into the third and fourth years of life which reaches back into even earlier years; and that only the father is mentioned, not the mother. Subsequently, in 1908 and 1909 while the analysis continues, an affair develops between Jung and Sabina Spielrein, a romantic love affair beyond the bounds of everyday life which involves among other things the fantasy of a child – the heroic child Siegfried, who is perhaps supposed to reconcile the incongruence of a Jewish woman and a Christian man, in an attempt symbolically to eliminate the destructive element in the relationship. Emma Jung intervenes and contacts Sabina's mother and a furore ensues. Writing to Freud, Jung describes himself as the seduced party, and Freud replies:

> I myself have never been taken in quite so badly, but I have come very close to it a number of times and had a *narrow escape*. I believe that only grim necessities weighing on my work, and the fact that I was ten years older than yourself when I came to Ψ A., have saved me from similar experiences. But no lasting harm is done. They help us to develop the thick skin we need and to dominate 'counter-transference', which is after all a permanent problem for us; they teach us to displace our own affects to best advantage.
>
> (McGuire 1947: 145F, 7 June 1909)

The term 'counter-transference' is coined. From now on countertransference is for Freud the obstacle that the practising analyst has to overcome; and along with it – intended as a defence – appears the term 'abstinence'. In 1915, six years after the first appearance of the term 'counter-transference', Freud writes in his 'Observations on Transference-Love':

> I have already let it be understood that analytic technique requires of the physician that he should deny to the patient who is craving for love the satisfaction she demands. The treatment must be carried out in abstinence. By this I do not mean physical abstinence alone, nor yet the

deprivation of everything that the patient desires, for perhaps no sick person could tolerate this. Instead, I shall state it as a fundamental principle that the patient's need and longing should be allowed to persist in her, in order that they may serve as forces impelling her to do work and to make changes, and that we must beware of appeasing those forces by means of surrogates. And what we could offer would never be anything else than a surrogate, for the patient's condition is such that, until her repressions are removed, she is incapable of getting real satisfaction.

(Freud 1915: 164–5)

Abstinence thus means privation which is imposed above all for the benefit of the female patient, in order not to destroy the productive (in the sense of leading her out of her inner predicament) process of analysis to which she is entitled. Only the female patient is described as 'in need of love'. When Freud talks of the longings and the inner life of the analyst, he is talking of the analyst as the defensive party:

Again, when a woman sues for love, to reject and refuse is a distressing part for a man to play ... It is rather, perhaps, a woman's subtler and aim-inhibited wishes which bring with them the danger of making a man forget his technique and his medical task for the sake of a fine experience.

(Freud 1915: 170)

The intention is to protect the female patient, but underneath she is feared as a potent(ial) dangerous attacker.

As to Jung, in 1946 at the age of 71 Jung publishes his reflections on 'The Psychology of the Transference'. It is perhaps worth reading this study as a response to Freud's thoughts on transference love published 31 years previously. In his accounts of the events of transference and counter-transference and his attempts to systematize them, the following points strike me as being relevant to our present topic:

1 Here, too as elsewhere in Jung's writing, there are to be found contradictory evaluations of the transference as an important driving force of analysis.

2 In this study Jung's comments on sexual strivings and eroticizations on the part of both patient and analyst are marked by a certain tendency to demonize them, especially as far as female sexuality is concerned. It is quite apparent from these passages that, in the course of his career as an analyst, Jung has learnt to be extremely cautious with regard to sexuality and eroticism during therapy.

3 A factor of special significance in our discussion is the stress which Jung places on the 'unconscious identity of doctor and patient' and the intensity of the countertransference:

The transference, however, alters the psychological stature of the doctor, though this is at first imperceptible to him. He too becomes affected, and has as much difficulty in distinguishing between the patient and what has taken possession of him as has the patient himself. This leads both of them to a direct confrontation with the daemonic forces lurking in the darkness. The resultant paradoxical blend of positive and negative, of trust and fear, of hope and doubt, of attraction and repulsion, is characteristic of the initial relationship. It is the (hate and love) of the elements, which the alchemists likened to the primeval chaos.

(Jung 1946: para 375)

4   On account of the intensive participation of the analyst in the analytical process, Jung demands that a training analysis be made a part of professional training.

In the development of analytical psychology and in clear contrast to Freud, it can perhaps be said that although Jung repeatedly refers to the drive aspect, to sexuality and aggression, he emphasizes the aspect of meaning (the German word 'Sinn'). Blomeyer has expressed this in the following terms:

Jung's concepts refer less to the object, or that which is tangible to us, but rather to images which signify the world, above all inner images that often attain a high degree of abstraction. For Jung 'grasping' things is achieved not by touch but by mental conception. Sexuality and aggression, however, have to do with physical contact. Mental conceptions keep one at a distance

(Blomeyer 1991: 5)

Are Jungians protecting themselves from the physical contact of sexuality by hiding behind theory? Guggenbühl-Craig writes:

Every analyst is more or less aware that the constellation of sexuality harbours many dangers. Destructive sexuality works like an infectious disease. An anxious Jungian analyst, concerned only for his own welfare, often side-steps the dangers of sexuality by immediately pointing to the transcendental aspect as soon as any sexual feelings crop up. He gives careful attention neither to his own fantasies nor to those of his patient, but instead takes instant refuge in the deeper symbolism of the sexual phenomenon. This gives him a certain immunity against the dangers raised by an aroused sexuality. But it also destroys certain possibilities of relationship and spoils an opportunity of dealing with possible destructive tendencies in himself and his patients ... Though sexuality is ultimately a symbol, it can only be a living symbol if it is truly experienced.

(Guggenbühl-Craig 1982: 65)

It is possible that the fear of the dangers of countertransference can lead analysts to construct a defence based on overemphasizing the transcendental aspect and meaning. It is doubtful, however, whether sexual forms of acting out in the countertransference can actually be prevented by such a defence.

The genetic background of perversion

In contrast with Freud, the model of analytical psychology seeks to play down the theory of infantile sexuality, particularly with regard to the concept of polymorphous-perverse sexuality. Referring to Freud's concept of polymorphous-perverse sexuality, Jung writes in 1913, after taking his stand with the public critics of psychoanalysis with regard to the term 'perverse', so bitterly attacked by our critics':

> Perversions are disturbed products of a developed sexuality. They are never the initial stages of sexuality ... It is of the essence of normal sexuality that all those early infantile tendencies which are not yet sexual should be sloughed off as much as possible. The less this is so, the more perverse will sexuality become. Here the expression 'perverse' is altogether appropriate. The basic conditioning factor in perversion, therefore, is an infantile, insufficiently developed state of sexuality.
>
> (Jung 1913: para 293)

In 1928 he writes:

> If now, by means of a reductive procedure, we uncover the infantile stages of adult psyche, we find as its ultimate basis germs containing on the one hand the later sexual being in *statu nascendi* and on the other all those complicated preconditions of the civilized being. This is reflected most beautifully in children's dreams.
>
> (Jung 1928: para 98)

In the first Seminar on Children's Dreams, Jung talks of the bisexuality of human beings and describes this as an archetypal condition, saying:

> Under certain conditions, the active presence of such archetypes, and of similar ones, in the child's unconscious can give rise to 'perversions'. Then the children do strange, disgusting things which do nevertheless have symbolic meaning. Namely they show behaviour that at one moment is too clean, and at another too dirty. For example, a nine-year-old boy eats toads because he has a horror of them; a four-year-old child picks up excrements in the fields. A country child would never do that. Only very well brought up city children do such things. It is the unconscious search for original unity which gives rise to such behaviours. They should really

not be called perversions but rather faults in upbringing which are later mostly compensated for. That original, primitive image therefore leads not only to the most strange, painful, disgusting satisfaction, but also acts as a defence, for example, in people who pick their nose or have oral 'coitus' with a fountain-pen. Such activities are needed as a protection: in effect people form a circle with themselves. In fertilizing themselves they demonstrate that they are completely self-sufficient, the completely *circular original being* (the 'sphairos' of Empedocles). In that state nothing can touch them.

(Jung 1987: 47–8)

Jung's idea of perversion as a defence finds a counterpart in current psychoanalytical thinking on the subject of perversions. Morgenthaler (1987) understands perversion as a seal against the danger of disintegration through the return of split-off hate and rage. The perverse person badly needs the illusion that he can be powerful enough to keep the seal from breaking. To sustain this illusion he manipulates his object into a sadomasochistic prison-like relationship. The aim is to establish a state of feeling 'round' – independent and strong.

From a genetic point of view the disturbed area of a person with perverted structural elements belongs to that stage of child development in which the self and the boundaries of both body and ego crystallize and establish themselves through the mother's care and attention. During the course of its early development the child experiences its two parents, including their bodies, and forms an inner concept of the pair, a pair imago, an image of the primal scene. The internalized parents, as a pair, are the makers of new life – of babies, dead and alive, loved and tormented. The inner pair makes plans, has ideas and destroys them. It is both creative and destructive. If the child experiences and assimilates its observations of its real parents as locked in struggle, in the eternal masochistic struggle, then this will shape the child's inner ideas of creativity, and of the destruction, in hate, of its products; it will also shape the relationship between these two elements in the child's mind. The child experiences itself as part of different pairs, of the mother–child pair and of the father–child pair. Its ideas of the parent-pair and the fantasies of the parents also form images of the mother–child and father–child relationships. If the parent-pair acts sadomasochistically, the child will be bound in both love and hate, especially to the mother, who can neither let the child stay in safe proximity to her nor let it go and establish new, creative distance – on to the next generation or to the opposite sex.

Neither father nor mother can allow the child, as someone new and distinct, to imagine the world anew. Thus the child sometimes has to rely on some particular form of survival technique in order to accommodate love and hate in one relationship:

The capacity to create the emotional climate in which another person volunteers to participate is one of the few real talents of the pervert. This invitation to surrender to the pervert's logic of body-intimacies demands of the object a suspension of discriminations and resistance at all levels of guilt, shame and separateness. A make-believe situation is offered in which two individuals temporarily renounce their separate identities and boundaries and attempt to create a heightened maximal body-intimacy of orgiastic nature. There is always, however, one proviso. The pervert himself cannot surrender to the experience and retains a split-off, dissociated and manipulative ego-control of the situation. This is both his achievement and failure in the intimate situation. It is this failure that supplies the compulsion to repeat the process again and again ... Hence, instead of instinctual gratification or object-cathexis, the pervert remains a deprived person whose only satisfaction has been a pleasurable discharge and intensified ego-interest. In his subjectivity the pervert is *un homme manqué*.

(Khan 1979: 22)

Like Khan I assume that for the pervert, i.e. for the analyst whose acting out in the countertransference takes on a perverted form, the female patient has essentially the same object value as that of the 'transitional object' in Winnicott's sense of the term. According to Winnicott the child is free to handle the transitional object either affectionately or destructively. Only the child is allowed to change the transitional object. The transitional object must survive libidinal love and libidinal hate. It appears to the child as if it has its own reality; for the child it comes neither from inside nor from outside. According to Winnicott the transitional object serves to create an intermediate space and, in the normal course of development, is of help to the child in its separation from the mother, i.e. in the generation change. If development is pathological, however, the transitional object keeps its significance and continues to be used permanently as a protection against the inner and intense perception of separation, and of the hate, fear and pain connected with separation. In that sense it is a manic defence against feelings of depression and against the contents of fantasies relating to a depressive state.

In order to avoid the crisis of separation the pervert makes use of the 'technique of intimacy' in an eroticised flight into external reality and towards an external object. Khan gives a very impressive description of how the inner dilemma turns into a dilemma for the external object. The partner who has been chosen as an accomplice (in the case of an analysis this is the female patient) fends off the criticism of the conscience by his or her participation. Accompanied by fantasized scenes of mutual activities, the enactment, i.e. the sexual violation of the patient, alleviates the freezing of the inner world of the analyst by the acting out of his perversion.

Khan offers an impressive account of how the pervert acts out his dream and even implicates another person in its realization; of how he stages his dreams and fulfils them in certain points with the help of a real person. Because of the partial fulfilment of his dreams it can be assumed that the pervert, which includes the analyst who acts out in a perverted way, will not be able to arrive at any deep wish for change. As a result of a perverted part of the personality being activated, power and powerlessness are reversed and the reality of separation from the mother and from the parents, which constitutes the generation change, is preserved, but on the other hand denied. The desire for the fear of a symbolic fusion with the early mother are split off from one another and remain distinct, side by side.

The dynamics of sexual acting out by the analyst: an hypothesis

Let us now try to relate these notions to the sexual violation of professional ethics in psychoanalysis. It is my hypothesis that this sexual violation is an acting out in the countertransference which, both in its enactment and in its consequences, stages the arrangement of perversion as a specific style of forming and shaping the relationship.

What actually occurs at the moment of sexual acting out in the analytical relationship and what happens subsequently? Trusting in the integrity of the male analyst, of which she is assured in the terms of the contract she enters at the commencement of treatment, the female patient allows her sexual longings to be activated in the transference towards the analyst with the complete mixture of love and hate which this implies. The analyst, who in the preliminary stages of this development has already narcissistically expressed his erotic attraction either verbally or by means of posture, mimicry or gesturing, acts. It all looks very much like two people falling in love; and perhaps that is exactly what it sometimes is at this moment.

In actual fact, however – and not in the imagination – destruction is taking place. The analytical process is being destroyed and a sadomasochistic pattern of relationship is developing between analyst and analysand. At the therapeutic level the analyst plays the sadistic role while the female patient plays the masochistic role. A destructive (i.e. unfruitful and hopeless) relationship is established between them both, characterised by the gratuitous behaviour of the analyst and addictive feelings of being at his mercy on the part of the patient. If we examine this course of events (that is, as far as the accounts of actual cases allow us), it becomes evident that, in the sexual violation of professional ethics, what takes place is an act in which hate is eroticised and sexualised. This is the decisive clinical characteristic of perversion. As far as is known to me, there is only one passage in the literature dealing with the sexual violation of professional ethics in psycho-analysis and psychotherapy in which the question whether this phenomenon might not also be 'an expression of a perverse symptom-formation' is raised (Reimer 1991). I believe that there is enough evidence to suggest, however, that such incidents are the effect of a perverted segment of the personality which has congealed to become a character trait.

The analyst's perversion

Let us look at an abusing analyst in the process of reflecting on himself. The following assemblage of texts is taken from the fictional report of an analyst who, in his own interests, has quite evidently encouraged a female patient of his to fall in love with him and who at the very last minute recoils from the temptation of actually exceeding the bounds of professional practice, (Wheelis 1988). First of all an account is given of the last session before a three-week break:

> 'I beg your pardon?' Dr Melville says.
> 'I was mumbling,' Lori says ... because it's ... hard to say.'
> 'And what were you mumbling?'
> 'That I will miss you.'
> 'And why is it so hard to tell me that?' His voice is soft and encouraging.
> 'I don't know. Dependence, I guess ... I'm so afraid of ... leaning on you.'
> 'Does missing someone have to imply leaning?'
> 'Perhaps.'
> 'Would it be equally hard,' he asks gently, 'for you to say ...' he pauses, '... "I love you"?'
> She is silent for a full minute. 'That would be quite impossible!'
> How devious I am, he thinks ruefully. My question would have her believe I am measuring a degree of difficulty, but I'm not measuring anything, am not asking a question at all. I want to say: 'I love you', and that pause, separating the declaration from the perfunctorily framing question, leaves it on its own. I want her to hear it that way, yet to believe it to be but her fantasy that it might have been so meant, encouraging her thereby to such sentiments of her own.
> Ah, well, psychoanalysts too need to need to be loved. (pp. 28–29)

> This longing, he thinks, measures a lost oneness. The wound is covered over, with the salves and ointments of whatever relationships one can manage, but never heals. Certain faces evoke that primal wholeness; suggest it can be regained, that it's possible, that with luck it might just happen. The dagger of longing slithers through one's heart. But they are lost, these faces. They smile with that hint of promise, then disappear down that hall, that stairway, into elevators, airplanes, are lost in crowds – and the pain of that first severance comes back, sharp as ever; the wound is open, never heals. (pp. 105–106)

What tempted him in her ... what sweeps him away, is the prospect that his love of her may enable her to think well of herself. So that's the way it is, he thinks. She is no other, she is I. In loving her I love myself, in rescuing her I redeem a part of myself – weak, frightened, feminine – of which otherwise I must be ashamed. (p. 112)

I go through life seeking some extraordinary good, ignoring those goods commonly available in the give-and-take of human relations. Not the standard currency of human exchange but the pure gold of unconditional love. Absolute selfless adoration, that's what I want. Only that would heal the wound at the center. (p. 144)

Violation is part of my desire, the dark underside. Might be better not to know. But I do know. The garden must be secret, guarded, mysterious. Access must be hidden or difficult or denied. I seek to enter where, though I be desired, I'm not altogether welcome. Resistance must be overcome. Some advantage, not entirely fair or honorable, must be taken. The veiled face. That's the archetype. It signals both resistance and invitation, the one as important as the other. Of course that veil has been displaced upward. It's really the genital that is veiled, and the veil is to be rent. Not the open, smiling face. (pp. 158–159)

I'm not talking about rape. It's no good unless the woman wants it too, at least a little. I'm talking about something subtle and insidious ... Without violation nothing would happen. Life would stop. Someone must move close, invade the intimate space of another ... She must come to love me, including – and this is central – that part of me which wants to violate her. She must love me entire. This is the transforming acceptance. I am reborn, become, that rare thing, both whole and innocent. (p. 160)

Could it be that the wish to violate a woman issues from that part of self that was split off because it once entailed the loss of one's mother's love? If so, the wish would be aiming to recover and affirm this lost part of self. And if the woman, suffering the violation, still loves the violator, then that lost part of self need not be repressed, but may be reclaimed, restored ... A fearless woman is without attraction. Admirable perhaps ... but for that magic that pulls us on, sucks our hearts out, she must be vulnerable. (p. 165)

Keeping that fictional analyst's thoughts and feelings in mind, it seems reasonable to assume that an analyst who is in actual danger of abusing the patient or who has become guilty of sexual abuse and who sees and uses his female patient as a victim has experienced powerlessness and deep humiliation in relationships of dependency in his childhood. Unconsciously this evokes not only fantasies of revenge but also the fantasy that he might possibly be saved.

In the enactment during the analysis, the roles of victim and aggressor are reversed. The original victim becomes the aggressor, the avenger, the victor.

The original victim frees himself from his childhood powerlessness and triumphs over both humiliation he has experienced and the originally dangerous woman-mother. She now becomes the victim: the once humiliated son becomes, in an illusory fit of mistaken judgment, a powerful man. The greater the early traumatization, in the sense of humiliation with regard to his own sexual identity through a mother who did not consent to appropriate separation and who offered herself for idealization, and a father who existed only in the shadows, the higher the potential of the individual analyst to fight and humiliate the unconsciously hated mother with the aim of finally being accepted by her as man.

In analysis the hated (and beloved) mother is impersonated then by the weakened and dependent female patient, who offers herself in her desire for love and in her wish to be allowed also to hate. (Wheelis's patient loved *and* hated her analyst; he could not stand her/his love *and* hate.)

At the same time this scenario is designed in such a way that the attempt must fail, that the deep pain caused by the perception of inner reality is again eluded. Hate is set free, manifesting itself in the sadomasochistic arrangement which, according to all the published case reports, follows the first seduction on the couch. The probability of the analysis in which such a violation occurs is even greater when the female analysand, as is often the case with women who start analysis today, has already experienced sexual abuse in her life in the form of actual incestuous molestation and thus has introjected an element of perversion. The analyst's consulting room cannot accommodate the massive hate directed at the mothers which is acted out in the violation and which is warded off through eroticization and sexualization. By encapsulating pain and destructivity, the perverted part of the personality thus serves, as Morgenthaler has illustrated (1987), as a seal against the danger of disintegration. This seal closes the cavity produced by a narcissistic development which has gone off course. The female patient abused by the male analyst is supposed on the one hand to cure him by surviving unscathed both his hate, which is masked as love, and his love, which turns into hate. On the other hand she must not set anything in motion in this particular area of the analyst's inner world, since he would otherwise be confronted with depression and the pain of separation. Because of this the process must never be allowed to end and addictive repetition is the result. The patient is cheated of both her love and her hate. At this point, because of the staging in external reality of the personal character pathology of the analyst, who entices his patient into complicity, the analysis breaks down; the capacity of the analyst to imagine this relationship and himself within it fails.

This also implies, however, the breakdown of the transcendent function, which drives the analytical process forward and which describes the analyst's activity, i.e. the process of continuous symbolization in the relationship. The analyst is no longer able to 'think' the analytic relationship in Bion's sense of the word. It is no longer possible for him to be the container of the relationship. His task of being 'guided by thinking' is defeated by non-transformable physical sensations and unconscious fantasies, what Bion calls non-imaginable beta elements. This points to a failure of what Bion calls alpha function in the analyst (Bion 1983), which in turn suggests an absence in the analyst's early development of the kind of mothering that performs this function, turning physical discomfort into recognized and labeled and imagined experience. In sexual acting out, the analyst turns to the patient to perform this vital mothering function, which she is able to provide fully only when she identifies his physical behavior, later, as intrusive and violating.

Conclusions

First let me make just one comment on morals and ethics in our profession. To my understanding there is no question but that psychoanalysts, with their professional associations, should make a written declaration and draw up an official (i.e. citable and suable before a court of law) code of ethics to reinforce the imperative of abstinence – a Hippocratic Oath in a renewed and revised form. However, although laws, as dictates of conscience which imply certain ego-ideals, formulate attitudes of a society towards good and evil and make inquiry and judgment from case to case possible and thus contribute ideally to a humanization of society, the fact that we impose laws upon ourselves does not relieve us of the necessity to reflect upon the psychodynamics of the forbidden.

We clearly need a code of abstinence not only to be visible from an ethical standpoint but because of the permanent necessity of finding our identity as analysts in the transference/countertransference process. We need to define abstinence in a positive constructive way: abstinence signifies that the analyst is identified with his ability to imagine himself, the patient and the analytical process (Plaut 1966). He or she would then be identified with the mother imago in the stage of reverie: this is the mother who makes separation possible, who shares with the child the burden of the hate and separation as well as sharing eroticism and desire as experience. The early mother in the state of reverie is not thinkable to a Jungian analyst without rethinking Jungian theory. Neglecting infantile sexuality and overstressing transcendental aspects are part of the heritage of Jung's breaking up with Freud and the unsatisfactory working through of the separation, especially on Jung's side. Today we cannot reverse this process without a negative regression into primitive imitation but we can try to learn again as part of an ongoing mourning and separation process.

As an important part of this learning process in our training, everything should be done to establish conditions which make it possible to deal with early childhood material in the analytical process in the transference/countertransference process. This is difficult because of the structure of training analysis. Training analysts are identified not only with the patient/ trainee. Inside themselves and in their outside activities they want to care for the trainees, for their trainee's patients and for their (parental) institutes. Sometimes in their personal history and in their training analysis and in their own institutional history, separation processes have been complicated and insufficient. Our construction of training analysis sometimes tends to hinder the experience of the pains and wounds of separation, i.e. the experience of crossing the border towards a sense of being on one's own and belonging to the next generation.

To quote an observation made by Jung in conversation with von Franz when he was an old man: 'The problem of love is so complicated that you can be glad if you can say at the end of your life you have never been the cause of someone's ruin' (von Franz 1980: p 217).

References

Anonyma (1988) *Verführung auf der Couch* [Seduction on the couch]. Freiburg: Kore Verlag.

Augerolles, J. (1991) *Mein Analytiker und ich: Tagebuch einer verhängnisvollen Beziehung* [My analyst and I: Diary of a fateful relationship]. Frankfurt-am-Main: Fischer.

Bion, W. R. (1983) *Learning from Experience*. Northvale, NJ: Jason Aronson.

Blomeyer, R. (1991) 'Sexualitätat und Aggression in Konzepten der Analytischen Psychologie' [Sexuality and aggression in analytical psychology]. *Analytische Psychologie* 22: 1.

Carotenuto, A. (1991) *A Secret Symmetry: Sabina Spielrein between Jung and Freud*, trans. A. Pomerans, J. Shepley and K. Winston. New York: Pantheon Books.

Covington, C. and Wharton, B. (eds) (2003) *Sabina Spielrein: Forgotten Pioneer of Psycho-Analysis*. Hove & New York: Brunner Routledge.

Freud, S. (1905). 'Fragment of an analysis of a case hysteria'. *Standard Edition* Vol. V. London: Hogarth Press.

Freud, S. (1915), 'Observations on transference love'. *Standard Edition* Vol. XII. London: Hogarth Press.

Füchtner, H. (1987) Freud und Leid in der französischen Psychoanalyse' [Joy and pain of psychoanalysis in France]. *Psyche* 11: 1034–40.

Guggenbühl-Craig, A. (1982) *Power in the Helping Professions*. Dallas, TX: Spring Publications.

Jung, C. G. (1913) 'The theory of psychoanalysis'. *CW* Vol. 4. London: Routledge & Kegan Paul.

Jung, C. G. (1928) 'On psychic energy'. *CW* Vol. 8. London: Routledge & Kegan Paul.

Jung, C. G. (1946) 'The psychology of the transference'. *CW* Vol. 16. London: Routledge & Kegan Paul.

Jung, C. G. (1987) 'Seminar on children's dreams'. 1st series. Olten: Walter Verlag.

Khan, M. M. R. (1979) 'Intimacy, complicity and mutuality'. In M. M. R. Khan *Alienation in Perversions*. London: Hogarth Press.

McGuire, W. (ed.) (1974) *The Freud/Jung Letters*. London: Hogarth Press and Routledge & Kegan Paul/Princeton: Princeton University Press.

Morgenthaler, F. (1987) *Homosexualität/Heterosexualität/Perversion* [Homosexuality/ heterosexuality/perversion]. Frankfurt-am-Main: Fischer.

Plaut, A. (1966). 'Reflections about not being able to imagine'. *Journal of Analytical Psychology* 11: 2.

Reimer, C. (1991) *Uber Missbrauch von Abhängigkeit in der Psychotherapie. Die Ethik der Psychotherapie* [The abuse of dependency in psychotherapy. The ethics of psychotherapy]. Berlin: Springer.

Rutter, P. (1991) *Sex in the Forbidden Zone*. New York: Fawcett Crest.

von Franz, M.-L. (1980) 'Uber einige Aspekte der Ubertragung'. In H. Dieckmann *Ubertragung und Gegenübertragung* [Some aspects of transference]. In H. Dieckmann (ed.) *Transference and Countertransference*. Hildeschein: Gerstenberg.

Wellendorf, F. (1987) *Der Fall Dora: eine Mesalliance in Belgrad: Zur Idee einer psychoanalytischen Sozialforschung* [The Dora Case: a misalliance in Belgrade: Reflecting about psychoanalytic research on social topics]. Frankfurt-am-Main: Fischer.

Wheelis, A. (1988) *The Doctor of Desire*. New York: Norton.

Wolstein, B. (1988) 'Observations of countertransference'. In B. Wolstein (ed.) *Essential Papers on Countertransference*. New York: New York University Press.

Chapter 5

Purposive aspects of the erotic transference

Coline Covington

This chapter illustrates the erotic transference of a male patient towards his female analyst and the pressures and resistances within the transference and countertransference to act out sexually. The patient's desire to act out sexually is seen both as a form of repetition compulsion within the transference and, in its purposive aspect, as an expression of the patient's need to find a loving breast and an empathic father. The patient's confused sexual identity is seen as a narcissistic defence against the experience of unbearable frustration in the pre-Oedipal stage. Through internalizing a new primal scene, the patient is able to separate from his past and to work through the Oedipus complex within the transference.

Introduction

Neither Jung or Freud had the benefit of an analysis, but both discovered early on in their work with female 'hysterics' the intensity of the erotic transference and the dangers of their own erotic countertransference. In a letter to Jung dated 7 June 1909, Freud writes:

> Dear friend,
> Since I know you take a personal interest in the Sp. matter I am informing you of developments. Of course there is no need for you to answer this.
>   I understood your telegram correctly, your explanation confirmed my guess. Well, after receiving your wire I wrote Fraulein Sp. a letter in which I affected ignorance, pretending to think her suggestion was that of an over-zealous enthusiast. I said that since the matter on which she wished to see me was of interest chiefly to myself, I could not take the responsibility of encouraging her to take such a trip and failed to see why she should put herself out in this way. It therefore seemed preferable that she should first acquaint me with the nature of her business. I have not yet received an answer.
>   Such experiences, though painful, are necessary and hard to avoid. Without them we cannot really know life and what we are dealing with. I

myself have never been taken in quite so badly, but I have come very close to it a number of times and had a narrow escape. I believe that only grim necessities weighing on my work, and the fact that I was ten years older than yourself when I came to A, have saved me from similar experiences. But no lasting harm is done. They help us to develop the thick skin we need to dominate 'countertransference', which is after all a permanent problem for us; they teach us to displace our own affects to best advantage. They are a 'blessing in disguise'.

The way these women manage to charm us with every conceivable psychic perfection until they have attained their purpose is one of nature's greatest spectacles. Once that has been done or the contrary has become a certainty, the constellation changes amazingly.

(McGuire 1974: 145F)

Jung replies (12 June 1909):

Dear Professor Freud,
Many thanks for your letter. I had to tell myself that if a friend or colleague of mine had been in the same difficult situation I would have written in the same vein. I had to tell myself this because my father-complex kept on insinuating that you would not take it as you did but would give me a dressing-down more or less disguised in the mantle of brotherly love. For actually it is too stupid that I of all people, your 'son and heir', should squander your heritage so heedlessly, as though I had known nothing of all these things. What you say about intellectual overvaluation is right on every point, and to cap it I still have the absurd idea of some kind of moral obligation. All that is too stupid, but useful.

Not a word from Adler. From Frl. E————, who has started coming for treatment again, I heard that he is moving away from you and going off on his own, in the opposite direction to you, even. Is there any truth in it?

(McGuire 1974: 146J)

Here we see the seeds of Jung's break from Freud. While Jung expresses his gratitude to Freud for his reply, he points to his father-complex and goes on to write about squandering Freud's heritage and overvaluing his own intellect. In these passages Jung reveals his own wish to destroy the father. This is borne out when Jung continues in his letter to speak of Adler's move away from Freud, thereby anticipating his own renunciation of Freud.

It is not surprising, given Jung's 'father complex' and what we know about his relationship with his mother, that he was so powerfully drawn to women and particularly to some of his female patients, most notably Sabina Spielrein. However, unlike Freud, Jung seemed less afraid of his superego and it was perhaps this that led to his dangerous entanglements. He confesses his vulnerability in a letter to Spielrein dated 4 December 1908, in which he writes in a state of desperation, begging her not to revenge herself on him:

> I am looking for a person who can love without punishing, imprisoning and draining the other person ... Return to me, in this moment of my need, some of the love and guilt and altruism which I was able to give you at the time of your illness. Now it is I who am ill.
>
> (Kerr 1994: 205)

Through his own illness, through his search for a loving mother, Jung was able to realize some of his most important theoretical ideas – his discovery of the anima and countertransference, his work on alchemy and symbolization.

The desire for sexual intimacy and its meaning in the transference was of fundamental importance to the formation and history of psychoanalysis, and indeed remains so today. Through their different struggles with their father-complex, both Jung and Freud came to recognize the vital importance of the incest barrier in promoting psychological growth. Starting with Freud's and Jung's first experience of working with female patients, of their 'narrow escapes', a certain amount of attention has been given to the subject of the erotic transference in relation to male analysts; much less attention has been given to this subject in the case of female analysts. This chapter is an attempt to look at the pressures and resistances within the erotic transference and countertransference to act out sexually and what these mean from the perspective of my own clinical experience.

Case

John was 44 when he started his analysis with me. He had had a previous analysis with a man when he was in his twenties that had lasted three years and he had seen a psychiatrist intermittently since that time. John was a very successful businessman and was at a crucial point in his career where he was being considered for a substantial promotion. The last time he had received a promotion, he told me he had had a breakdown and it was the anxiety of another breakdown that had brought him to me. He handled his first session as a seasoned patient, giving me a full historical synopsis of his life, making links between himself and his father, who had also been a powerful businessman but who had always been a remote figure within the family. The only point at which John revealed any feeling was when he told me that his mother had been American (he assumed I was) and that, as he put it, she too had been beautiful. Both parents were portrayed as powerful and distant figures. He then abruptly returned to the subject of his career and his anxieties about losing his promotion. I was aware of how for a brief moment when he had been describing his mother, John had shown some warmth towards me, smiling at me in a slightly seductive way, and then it felt as if he had just as suddenly poured cold water on me. I thought he was telling me about his anxieties about being potent, and, specifically, about his anxiety that if he was promoted to his father's powerful position he would be punished. He wanted to discover he was attractive as a man and at the same time he equated being attractive with being punished. What became clear was how John had constructed a very competent false self behind which his real self was trapped in a nightmare world of seduction followed by the threat of castration.

In the second session, John recounted a recurring dream in which he had committed a murder and could not find anywhere to hide the body. The body was that of a woman. John linked this dream with his sexuality and said in a tantalizing way that he had a secret which he was always trying to hide. John told me that he secretly saw himself as a woman. We could then see that it was his passive, homosexual identity that he was failing to conceal and to bury in the dream. He confessed to having a compulsive fantasy of watching a little girl sticking the handle of a spoon up her bottom and then being hosed with cold water by a punitive mother. The fantasy took different forms, but always with these basic ingredients, consisting of some act of anal penetration accompanied by a punitive, phallic mother. It was clear that John was afraid that his mother would punish him for wanting to be a woman, yet he felt he could only be attractive if he was a woman. Since his twenties, John had regularly sought prostitutes who would enact his fantasy for him. He explained that he did not want sexual intercourse with them, what excited him was having them put their fingers up his anus. His search to find a phallic mother in these prostitutes had become an addiction that had enabled him to carry on with his version of reality, i.e. to continue being his mother's homosexual lover and in this way to avoid competing with his powerful father. John's fear of feeling desire for his mother was so great that it could only be circumvented in his mind by becoming a girl. This defence was beginning to break down, however, as he was becoming increasingly anxious about being caught. At the same time, John admitted he also wanted to be caught and, finally, allowed to be a man.

John made it clear to me in the beginning that he expected me to make sense of these things for him and to provide him with a manual, as he so aptly put it, which he could follow. In the countertransference I felt John was asking me to penetrate him, like the prostitutes. He wanted to find in me that phallic mother who would make him feel safe when he was under her control. His technique of seduction was to try to make me feel very powerful, so that he could continue to hide his masculinity and thereby keep us both as the bisexual couple in his inner world. In this way he was able to transform the failure of oral and phallic erotism into anal erotism and to remain fixated to that position.

John's erotic transference to me, hinted at in the first session, began to unfold. He appeared at my door promptly, usually panting from his exertions to arrive on time and also from excitement. He would then lie on the couch and stretch out, his hands nearly touching me as I sat at his side. I remained where I was, being careful not to move away from John, which he would certainly have taken as a sign of rejection. John needed to know that I would not be frightened and try to escape, as he felt his mother had, from his desire to touch me and to be touched by me. He soon began telling me that his sessions were the only times in his week which felt constructive, how much he looked forward to them and, in fact, how his wife was convinced he had fallen in love with me. I became his idealized, beautiful and cruel mother from whom he expected the cold water treatment. His intense fascination with, and hatred of, his beautiful mother was tangible. He would stare at me with icy, penetrating eyes, behind which I could sense his anxiety about feeling any warmth with me. Whenever he was able to accept warmth from me, he would immediately put me to the test and become insistent on knowing what my thoughts and feelings were about him. He became obsessively controlling of me. At times, when he felt particularly frustrated by my failure to respond in the way he wanted me to, he would refuse to speak or he would tell me there was no point to anything and the only real solution was suicide. The moment John felt unwanted by me in his mind, he would in effect threaten to bugger me and to destroy the analysis, as he put it; then we would both be 'in the shit together'. I felt blackmailed whenever he did not get his way with me and imagined he had been subjected to this kind of treatment from his mother. Rather than interpreting John's behaviour as an attack against me, which would have only served to reinforce his expectation of being seen as bad by me, I spoke about his fear of allowing himself to receive warmth from me and his fear of what this might lead to, as this was a new experience for him.

As John was able to feel increasingly dependent on me, what emerged was his need to find a responsive mother who would accept his desire for her and recognize him as desirable. What also became apparent was his identification with this sadistic, controlling mother whom he had internalized, who had herself severely punished John when he had gone against her wishes or had shown signs of independence. John's continual pressure on me to allow him to touch me threatened to repeat or re-enact his mother's rejection of him and turn me into the cold, unresponsive mother of his desire, thereby confirming his belief in himself as essentially unlovable and attributing this to his having a bad penis (i.e. to his failed masculinity). This also meant that John could remain, in secret, his mother's emasculated love object and sustain his fantasy that mother preferred him over father. No parental intercourse was allowed to take place in his mind. This also enabled John to maintain an illusion of being in complete control over me and over the primal scene. As a consequence, he did not know he could arouse someone else's desire, or love, he only knew how to control, seduce and manipulate and to be unlovable. John wanted to convince me of his nastiness so that he could stay with me forever as my 'hopeless case', while harbouring the fantasy that by sacrificing himself (i.e.

his gender identity) to me fully he would one day win me over. The pressure John put on me to allow him to touch me came not only from his need to control me but also from his intense need to internalize me, to internalize a living and different mother who could then continue to exist inside him, in other words, to achieve object constancy.

The degree of control which John had been subjected to and to which he subjected others had left him in a lifeless and essentially empty world, around which he had had to construct an elaborate narcissistic shell as a means of surviving. While he could present a good show – he was an impressive actor – it also belied his constant need to impress himself on others because he was hardly there, and to use others as a mirror to reassure himself of his existence. Like a magician, he would pull his glittering tricks out of his hat, out of an empty, mindless space, out of his anus. Here John appeared as the trickster in his most frightening, unrelated aspect. In the transference, John felt he needed to perform for me. Because he was not powerful, he had tried to present a pretty show for his mother; he had wanted to give her a glittering penis in order to make her feel that she had a vagina and to enhance her power. Off-stage, John lived in solitary confinement, in a place which he described as his ice tower, surrounded by glittering mirrors where he had grown to despise the ever present sight of himself. John's principal technique for avoiding or denying this inner reality was to keep as many balls in the air as possible, taking on more and more projects at work, and mentally creating an endless stream of sexual fantasies, in which in one way or another he was always the onlooker identifying with a woman who was being tantalized or tortured sexually by another woman, or being the naughty little girl who must be punished for her misbehaviour. In this way he could remain in his mind a man and a woman at the same time.

This compulsive fantasizing enabled John to maintain his illusion of bisexuality and to deny his psychic reality. By their very nature, these fantasies could never evolve or lead anywhere. John used them within the analysis to entertain me, in a masturbatory way, as a defence against revealing his real feelings and desires. When this happens in analysis, a kind of anti-narrative is established which is both boring and static. If the patient's desire for relationship is not recognized in some way, this can also lead to an intensification of symptoms, like the uroboros who eats his own tail and can never be satisfied. In John's case, his need to excite me and seduce me also derived from his need to create some sense of life, to make me come alive in his mind and to ensure I would stay with him. Inevitably, this felt not only very demanding and draining but utterly devoid of feeling, so at the end of one of his discourses, no matter how brilliantly delivered, we would both be in the ice tower, frozen in time.

This repetitive and inauthentic narrative was what had been constructed in John's previous analysis. John and his analyst had evolved an account of his life which was close enough to his persona that he could then add it to his repertoire of mental devices. In his need to be bright and brilliant for his mother, he seemed able to remember and reproduce his analyst's interpretations almost verbatim. While they may have been correct theoretically, they had not had a transmutative effect. He had remained in his ice tower, untouched. I imagined that John's previous analyst had been unable to assume a passive, feminine role in relation to John with the result that he had continued to act as John's powerful father with whom he was still frightened to compete and whom he could only imitate. In retrospect, perhaps the most promising feature of John's first session with me was the flicker of passion he showed when he referred to his beautiful mother, associating me with her. Here was the possibility of something igniting between us which might lead to melting his icy encasement. My difficulty was how to touch him with words, because he had no mind yet with which he could receive and assimilate words. Words were more like narcissistic objects for John, which were used defensively to simulate relating. Initially, I found I could touch John and give him warmth concretely through the tone of my voice and the expression in my eyes.

John emphasized that the only way the analysis could proceed and be fruitful would be for us to be on equal terms. He told me all of his thoughts and secrets; it therefore followed that I should tell him mine. Above all what he demanded was reciprocity and it was only by means of this reciprocity that John could ever, he would argue, believe he could be cared for. John wanted me to play the role of his beautiful mother with whom he had felt on equal terms, who had been there exclusively for him. Just as his desire for there to be no difference between him and his mother meant that no parents could exist in his inner world, similarly, he wanted to eradicate the distinction between us and to destroy the analysis. He wanted not only to be close to me, but to control and possess me, in as concrete a way as possible, so that he would have access to my body and my mind at all times. The intensity of John's demands on me revealed both the strength of his hatred and destructiveness, but also the extent to which his oral needs had been frustrated. I felt that John had hardly any experience of a loving breast; instead he had felt his mother's desire for him as coming from her need to feel excited in order to feel alive.

In the countertransference I felt *at this point* no desire for John; I felt numb. John seemed to want me to be his prostitute. Either I had to be without feelings and a mind or John had to be the mindless one. We could not both have feelings at the same time. When I said this to John, he recalled having been held once by his previous analyst when he had broken down in tears and how he had only felt uncomfortable and frightened at the time. He then linked this to a memory of caressing his mother affectionately when she had been in tears and of his sudden fear that she would require him to become her lover and allow him to take his father's place. His attempts to give or receive affection had either been frustrated or had become eroticized. He could not transfer his need to give and receive affection onto someone else because all his libidinal desires remained cathected onto this seductive and rejecting internal mother. His way of defending himself had been to dissociate himself, going numb. As a result, there was no link between true affection and sexual desire with a differentiated object in John's mind.

After several months, John was coming to see me five times a week and would have seen me on weekends if I had agreed. He described me as the centre of his world, every act of his being directed towards me, towards gaining my recognition. He wanted to regress more and more, not in order to progress, but to fuse with me in a symbiotic state. It was not, in Balint's words, a benign regression, but a malignant one. When he was not with me, especially over weekends, he would torture himself with the fact that because I did not tell him about my life this meant he was unwanted, turning me once again into his rejecting mother in a masochistic attempt to control me. His sexual fantasies at this point had largely stopped, and only occasionally reappeared on weekends and breaks. In their place, John was beginning to fantasize about being touched by me and touching me, which he would describe in great detail, looking at me longingly. I had the sense that, as with his requests for me to see him on weekends, his desire was a bottomless pit and that nothing would suffice except total possession of me. John also made me feel like the beautiful mother in the narcissistic transference who had seduced her child so he would not grow, colluding with his wish to take revenge against his father. John wanted to make me have loving feelings towards him not only so that he could then control and frustrate me in the way he had felt controlled and frustrated by his mother but, more importantly, he needed to elicit from me a loving mother whom he could establish as a good and potentially enduring internal object and who made him feel like a desirable man. He was in search of a mother who could relate to him, enjoy him and help him to grow.

As John was able to differentiate more and more within the transference between a controlling mother and a receptive one, he could experience feeling wanted as a man for the first time. With the discovery that I was different from his mother, John could also begin to desire me as a separate object, not a narcissistic one, and to ask for love. He had only known what it was like to be wanted as a selfobject for his mother, as a narcissistic extension of her. What he had been familiar with was facing a mother in whose reflection he could see only emptiness. There was no mother to receive his desire, there was no breast wanting to be desired, he had never experienced this primary potency. He had to develop a pseudo-thinking, as was manifest in his sexual fantasies in which he would always identify with the woman. He could never allow himself to be the man and to develop his own mind. I think this was also indicative of his early identification with his mother, an adhesive identification that had formed in the place of ordinary projective and introjective processes. His call for a reciprocal relationship was correct insofar as this was what he had failed to receive at this most basic level. Initially, in his need to feel he could get inside me, John became a detective and not only spied on me and on my house, especially over weekends when he was excluded, but he also pieced together a biography of me. In a similar way he had had to be a detective in relation to his mother who remained largely inaccessible to him. He also wanted to know about my private life so that he could take the position of my partner, thereby breaking the boundary between us and eliminating father, with the ultimate aim of reducing us to a single entity.

The pressure I felt to respond to John's needs, and specifically to his depression, was also his way of communicating to me the pressure I thought he had felt as a child to alleviate his mother's depression, as well as the futility that whatever he could have done or tried to do would never be enough. Try as he might, he could never fill in for his absent father whom he saw as the source of his mother's depression. If I had been depressed, as his mother had been, it might have led to a destructive re-enactment of their relationship. As it was, in my neurotic countertransference, John represented that depressive father whom I had wanted to rescue, the depressive parent that I believe we all know and have within us. Had I not been so aware of this, my countertransference feelings might also have led me to act out with John and to have become in the end the phallic mother he wanted me to be for him, who could not bear for him to be separate and to grow.

As John fell more intensely in love with me in the transference, he put increasing pressure on me to demonstrate my feelings towards him, to gratify him, and to break the boundary of analysis. He continued to beg me to allow him to touch me and especially to kiss me. I was increasingly drawn to him, towards my internal image of a depressed father that I saw in him and my desire to make him feel potent. I also understood John's desire to touch and to be touched as not simply relating to a primitive level of need, which was clearly manifest, but as indicative of his need to find a responsive and spontaneous mother, who could demonstrate to him that she was not afraid of his feelings. This meant that rather than responding in a concrete way to John's requests, I found that, when I could respond spontaneously in words, John was able to feel touched by me and to feel less frightened of his loving feelings. I am sure that part of the aim of the erotic transference is to elicit the spontaneous response from the analyst in order to experience this in safety and to be able to feel that it is possible to express loving feelings safely. Without this, there can be no freedom to think or to symbolize because fantasy has to be continually blocked and controlled.

There was a delicate balance nevertheless in the level of frustration that John could bear. If I remained silent for too long John would feel pushed away; I would revert back to his icy mother in his mind, and he would once again become the rejected little boy who felt sadistic contempt for women and who also expected to be controlled by them. Then he would start to attack me, as his defence against feeling totally annihilated. Only by my interpreting John's attacks as his defence against his need to express loving feelings towards me was he able to come out of hiding again. After some time it became increasingly difficult to resist John's demands to touch me and to be touched. He made me feel that I was cruelly depriving him; a part of me longed both to mitigate his suffering and to expel this cruel mother from the transference. I also knew that I had to contain for us both these feelings of frustration, longing and hatred that were so unbearable for John. I imagined that John's mother had felt deeply frustrated and angry with John's often absent and aloof father and could not bear to feel close to John, particularly as he grew older. John's experience was of a sadistic frustration that denied his needs, not of a loving recognition. By gradually being able to identify this controlling part of him, which would push people away and leave him more isolated and rejected than ever, John was able to gain increasing control over his destructive and omnipotent impulses and to bear frustrations while being able to hold onto his loving feelings at the same time.

It was important to recognize that the sexual tension within the transference and countertransference came about when John tried to resolve his need for affection through sexuality. In this respect the erotic transference manifested John's need to be close to a mother and father, as well as his wish to repair the primal scene that was lacking and to find his own sexuality. His aggression resulted from his need to be held and accepted by a mother who could recognize him as different from herself. When John could see his need for affection, he was able to change.

At this point John had a series of dreams that seemed to indicate a significant shift in his inner world, towards the establishment of a good internal object with which he could relate. The dreams depicted John becoming closer and closer to me sexually, until we were on the brink of making love. These dreams were so highly charged that John said he was left with the sense they had not been dreams at all, but had actually happened. Because John felt he could elicit this response from me, albeit in his dreams, and that I too could have romantic feelings towards him without pushing him away, he was able not only to bear the frustration he felt when he was with me that he could not actually seduce me but also allow himself to be more potent outside the analytic relationship. He then had the following dream:

> I was walking down the street at night and a man in drag was following me. He was dressed like an old queen. I kept telling him to go away and he wouldn't until I got frightened and hailed a taxi and left. I was then at a party and I was talking to an actress. She was very self-conscious and was looking at everyone else in the room to see if they noticed her. I told her she should be careful not to do the same part all the time and to get type cast and said she should try doing different parts, that this would be better for her career. Then I was in another taxi seated in between an older woman on my right and my father on my left. I was stroking the woman's thighs and felt very affectionate towards her. We then went into a

restaurant, my father left the room, I then embraced the woman and said good-bye to her and went into a large room where I was soon joined by a younger woman. I don't remember what she looked like, I knew she was going to become my wife.

This dream seemed to chart the stages of John's analysis and of his anima development – from his original identification with a phallic mother (the drag queen), to a more narcissistic persona who was reminiscent of the magician, to finding himself in between his parents, able to express openly his sexual and loving feelings towards his mother without being rebuked and without triumphing over father, and finally about to embark on a new marriage.

This dream marked the final stage in John's romance during which he had to relinquish the fantasy of being in constant contact with me. This was the period of weaning which John had never experienced. His behaviour towards me also changed markedly. As he felt increasingly active and potent, he could for the first time imagine making love to me differently, this time as himself, as a man.

Discussion

When patients such as John want to act out sexually within the transference, they are demonstrating their need to find first of all a loving breast and second a warm, empathic father. For John, there was a failure at both the pre-Oedipal and Oedipal stages of development. Failure to meet these needs results in a narcissistic defence that aims to prevent the child from the possibility of being able to think, or to have a mind; in other words, to know about what he is missing. In John's case, to know about his unresponsive mother, who could not help him to develop and grow, and his absent father, who could not help him to separate from mother and become a man, would have been unbearable. This could only be known when he was able to find and internalize a different relationship within which he could be himself and have a mind.

Initially, John's coldness and his attempts to control me were his way of maintaining his gender confusion and his narcissistic defence. Although I have not described this process in the case of female patients, it is in my experience very similar. These women also want to convince the analyst of their unlovability and to turn the analyst into a phallic mother or a cold, rejecting father. In these cases it is especially important for the female analyst to recognize the paternal transference and the negative Oedipal transference. Failure to recognize the former may reinforce in the patient the sense of being rejected for having sexual desires and push the patient into homosexual retreat, whereby the only way of remaining close to father is through homosexual identification with him. On the other hand, failure to recognize the negative Oedipal transference may promote a malignant narcissistic attachment in which the female patient is never able to become a woman in her mind because she cannot separate from mother and allow the parents to be together in the primal scene.

While the erotic transference stems from a failure to resolve the Oedipal conflicts, I think the failure more often than not goes back to the early relationship with the mother in which her own feelings, particularly her own infantile needs for a responsive mother, make her frightened or overwhelmed by her baby's needs so that she is unable to receive his projections and to differentiate these from her own. If this process goes wrong, then there is never a strong enough attachment that can support separation. In effect, weaning becomes impossible and there is no safe container for imagination and thought to unfold. The mixed or negative messages the child receives at this early stage of development lead to feelings of worthlessness and to confusion of sexual identity which in turn lead to the perpetual attempt to deny reality, to deny desire and loss, just as the parents have done. To protect himself from this unbearable frustration, the male child turns himself into a girl in his mind and feels castrated, becoming in adulthood the lesbian lover of a phallic woman. In a similar way the female child turns herself into a boy in her mind because she cannot accept being castrated, and becomes in adulthood the homosexual lover of a passive man. Both deny they are men and women as part of a system of denial of psychic reality, as a defence against unbearable frustration. This homosexual identification later serves as a defence against the recognition that the child cannot marry mother or father. Oedipal frustration cannot be breached when the child's earlier experience of desire has been frustrated and denied. Such a defence inevitably blocks off the possibility of thought and symbolic process because there can be no inner space – the need and desire for the other is denied when it has been unmet. This is the task of the analyst: both to meet the desire with words and to frustrate its enactment.

For both male and female analysts there are two danger areas in treating patients who manifest erotic transferences. The first is the failure on the part of the analyst to meet the patient's desire with understanding. The second is, if there is no such understanding, to fail to frustrate this desire. In the first instance, the analyst can only contain and hold the patient when the ego is not ready to understand; the second instance refers to what the analyst must do when the patient's ego is ready to understand. If the analyst fails to be receptive to the patient's desire and, like the patient's parent, denies these needs in herself, the patient, if he is healthy enough, may in some cases terminate the treatment. But it is also likely, since this is a familiar scenario for the patient, that the treatment will continue and the analysis will become interminable, with both the analyst and patient locked in a sadomasochistic relationship. The patient in this situation is also likely to develop a stronger false self as a protection against the realization that his primitive needs are still not being recognized, much less met, and are experienced as being overwhelming. From the analyst's viewpoint, the fact that the patient is not changing, and continues to suffer, serves as a constant reminder of the analyst's uselessness and thereby acts to assuage her guilt about failing to provide the recognition and empathy which the analyst may never have received herself, either from parents or within analysis. As in the case of John, this is often apparent with patients who have had many years of previous analysis during which very little seems to have significantly changed, due to resistance on the part of the analyst to recognize the erotic transference. If the analyst responds in a defensive, frightened way to the patient, it will only send the patient into an anal sadistic or oral sadistic state. Then the patient will stop the erotic transference through guilt and not through understanding. The ego can only understand what is happening by working it through in the transference. In John's case, for example, he wanted to touch me in order to discover the difference between anal intrusion and sexual penetration. When this could be talked about, it could be discovered and worked through.

One feature these patients have in common, in my experience, is their failure to have experienced or to have been able to express any closeness or attachment to their previous analysts. As one patient said, 'I always thought it was against the rules for analysts to have any feelings for their patients.' What also commonly occurs in this instance is that the failure to recognize and analyse the early dependency needs of the patient drives the patient into a homosexual solution (or reinforces this solution) as a narcissistic defence. The patient's history is then re-enacted within the analytic relationship and the analyst takes on the role of the parent whom the patient can only hate, because loving feelings are too frightening, and so the patient cannot then separate to form new loving attachments.

In the case of the analyst who is able to respond to the patient's desire but is unable to frustrate the patient and is actually seduced, I would argue that the analyst is caught in a parental countertransference to the patient. The analyst who has an abusive image of a primal scene or who has not resolved the depressive position, and remains within a two-person state of mind, will find it difficult to resist acting out sexually within the transference and counter-transference. In this case the repressed desire to marry or remain exclusively with mother or father is fulfilled along with the destruction (in fantasy) of the parents who have only been experienced as cruelly frustrating or rejecting. This is the fate of Oedipus.

If we imagine Oedipus in analysis, he would most certainly have developed an erotic transference; it would also be clear that his search for a loving mother was due to his own early abandonment. If Jocasta had been Oedipus' analyst, she might well have been tempted to rescue him and to respond to his desire for her. Oedipus might prove irresistible in analysis, if Jocasta's own pre-Oedipal needs had not been met. Her own longing to feel wanted would conceivably make it too difficult for her to frustrate Oedipus in his desires. In this way, analyst and patient may also re-enact the patient's history of having been sexually abused by a parent. It is understandable that Freud would have come to this conclusion in his treatment of hysterical women.

The strength and virulence of the erotic transference stems from this primitive need of the infant to feel wanted. This is the cry of the patient who says, 'For analysis to work, I have to fall in love with you and you have to fall in love with me.' My version of this statement would be slightly different. In such a case, for analysis to work, the patient does have to fall in love with the analyst. In turn, the analyst has to allow herself to be the object of her patient's love and to respond with warmth and analytic understanding. By these means she can provide an experience of empathic frustration within which the patient's self can emerge and grow.

References

Kerr, J. (1994) *A most Dangerous Method*. London: Sinclair-Stevenson.
McGuire, W. (ed.) (1974) *The Freud/Jung Letters*. London: Hogarth Press and Routledge & Kegan Paul.

Chapter 6

Mourning and erotic transference

Susan Kavaler-Adler

In 'Observations on Transference Love' (1915), Sigmund Freud speaks of the erotic transference as both a resistance and as a conduit for the deepest unconscious desires and conflicts to emerge. The two disparate courses that the erotic transference can take oppose one another. To the degree that the erotic transference is a resistance, it fails to be a conduit for unconscious desires. When the erotic transference is a conduit for unconscious desires, it allows those desires to be understood within the course of psychoanalytic treatment, reducing all forms of resistance.

Freud credits the attitude of the analyst: 'keeping firm hold of the transference' (1915: 166), but not succumbing to it, as well as the educative work done on the analytic process, as the two main factors in containing the resistance aspects of 'transference love'; so that the infantile aspects of the love can emerge and be analyzed. Yet, his comments throughout the essay emphasize the continuing difficulty, and sometimes the impossibility, of modifying the resistance so that treatment can proceed, as in the case of 'women of elemental passions' (Freud 1915: 166). He sees it as likely that a woman will retaliate for the unrequited nature of her love by withdrawing all co-operation from treatment.

Perhaps Freud would have been more optimistic about the facility to use transference love, by terms of containing and transforming the resistance aspects of it, if he had taken another factor into account. I propose a third and I believe a critical factor, in modifying the erotic transference from a major transference resistance into an ongoing positive force in the treatment process. Mourning as a clinical process is the third factor that I propose (for references related to mourning as a clinical process, which I call developmental mourning Kavaler-Adler 1993a, 1993b, 1995, 1996, 1998, 2000, 2003a, 2003b, 2004, 2005a, 2005b, 2006a, 2006b). Mourning was first acknowledged as a primary emotional process in Freud's 'Mourning and Melancholia' (1917). However, it was Melanie Klein who first saw mourning as the primary affective process underlying both developmental growth and clinical psychotherapeutic treatment. Klein's papers on the 'depressive position' dynamics, such as 'Mourning and its Relation to Manic Depressive States' (1940), highlighted the potential clinical acumen to be gained by understanding the mourning process.

In the following case, I demonstrate how an attunement to object-related contact, within the course of psychoanalysis, allows a natural mourning process to unfold, thus contributing to an ongoing positive evolution of the use of the erotic transference in treatment. The case also illustrates male transference love in relation to a female analyst, which was never discussed by Freud. My case is a case in point not only in demonstrating the role of mourning as a primary clinical phenomenon that affects the course of the erotic transference, but also in demonstrating that the erotic transference is as primary in men with women analysts as it is with women analysands of male analysts.

My case study also returns to the notion of erotic transference as a primarily object-related phenomenon, as compared to the changed definition of the erotic transference offered by self-psychologists, such as Trop (1988). Trop refers to erotic transference as the emergence of a developmentally 'curtailed' need for 'mirroring of the sexual self' (Trop 1988: 281).

In the case I am presenting it can clearly be seen that the erotic transference was based on object-related yearnings that motivated the expression of repressed areas in the analysand's personality. It was this expression of the repressed phenomena, connected to the object-related yearnings, which allowed the analysand to become a sexual being. As the analyst, I did not mirror this man's sexuality, but merely received and understood his feelings.

The case of Mr L

Mr L came to analysis in his late twenties, after many disappointing relationships with women. He was working in a mediocre job, and was frustrated in his wishes to be an artist. He had friends, but was generally detached emotionally. His main reason for seeking out treatment was to understand why he could not successfully relate to women, particularly on a romantic basis. He tended to become involved with distant and rejecting women, who at first were sexually seductive.

Mr L's disconnection from all his feelings, and in particular from his sexual feelings, made him unable to initiate sexual involvement. Therefore, he was drawn to women who actively seduced him, but all relationships with such women were short-lived. Once he was conquered, the women he chose tended to withdraw from him, even though he would try to hold on by attempting to please them in various ways, cancelling out his actual reactions. Many other women, who he associated with as good friends, would not entertain the idea of dating him or seeing him as a boyfriend. They did not view him as a sexual man, and he was deeply discouraged by this, although he remained detached from his pain until he became engaged in his psychoanalysis.

Mr L was interested in working with a woman analyst, and this seems related to his motivation to seek treatment as a way of dealing with his lack of sustained romantic relationships. He began treatment on a twice-a-week basis, but quickly moved into three-times-a-week, and then into four-times-a-week treatment. The course of his analysis extended over a seven-year period.

The mourning process

Mr L's analysis involved many stages of mourning. I will outline the overall movement from mourning of a pre-Oedipal object, to the capacity to allow a latent erotic transference to emerge. I will then outline the mourning of the Oedipal object that took place with the blossoming of the erotic transference. Next I will discuss the mourning process that allowed the erotic transference to become a transitional vehicle towards erotic relations with an available external object, as the erotic desires for the analyst were resolved. I will comment on the potential resistance aspects of the erotic transference that were resolved through varying stages of mourning. I will also comment on the need for conscious mourning of object loss, as opposed to a compensatory mode of narcissistic mirroring that can be used as a defence against feeling such loss. I will highlight how the mourning of the pre-Oedipal object allows the erotic transference to be tolerated, and used as a mode of exploration, rather than being resistantly manipulated by the analysand.

Mourning of the pre-Oedipal object

Early on in Mr L's treatment, his yearning for a pre-Oedipal mother was first felt by me and by Mr L himself, as it appeared both in memories and in the transference. One memory of a painful separation from a male friend at latency appeared to be both a screen memory of early yearnings towards the pre-Oedipal mother, as well as being a poignant object attachment and object loss in its own right. Mr L remembered lying in a dug-out hole in the dirt of the wilderness at the time when he lived in Nebraska. He and his friend, Richard, would fantasize together that the remains of a building they found in their private wilderness was the foot of a giant castle. This was their land of enchantment. It was a romantic world where friendship and adolescent homosexual love could bloom. The height of their mutual enthrallment arose one quiet summer afternoon, when they lay side by side, and also half on top of one another, inside their dug-out hole, a hole dug out of the dirt and the leaves. They didn't speak. They were blissfully at peace. Perhaps at that moment Mr L felt a sublime feeling that he had always yearned for, a sublime feeling that he may never have quite attained in infancy, with a mother who was full of tension and depression. His mother was remembered as hard. Although Mr L's warm, soft, and tender body contact with his male friend could have had aspects of some early breast that was more yielding than the remembered mother, it is also likely that his tranquil contact with his friend could have been the fulfilment of a yearning that had long been aroused and frustrated by his early mother. The relationship between the two boys can also be seen as a normal homosexual love that is a developmental move towards adolescence. However, in terms of the building of psychic structure it is most helpful to see it in terms of the tender attachment to a pre-Oedipal object that precedes the attachment to an erotically desired object, the latter object being generally classified in terms of psychic structure formation as an Oedipal object.

Mr L's earliest memories of his childhood involved frustrating scenes between himself and his parents. He remembered his parents telling him as soon as he learned to talk that he must stop, hold his breath, and not say anything unless what he wished to express was truly important. Such directives threw Mr L, still a toddler, into a tailspin. His urge to speak felt like a gasp that was pushed back into him. His words got all contorted inside. All spontaneous gestures and voice felt arrested. He was stunned and stuck. His excitement to convey his feelings was crushed. He felt as if he was forced literally to swallow his words. Deep body tensions were set up at this time that made withdrawal backward and inward into himself a reflexive reaction.

Given all this tension about expressing himself in words, it is no wonder that the happiest time of his life was remembered by Mr L as this time of tranquil silence as he lay comfortably, in body contact with his best friend. When he was then forced away from his friend by the same parents who forced his voice away from him, he felt internally desecrated. His parents were having trouble in their marriage and with an abrupt attempt at resolution they decided to leave town and move to New York. There was no discussion with the children. Before Mr L knew what was happening, he was sitting in the back of his family car, peering mournfully out of the back window. He had never said goodbye. The last time he and his friend Richard were together they hadn't discussed it. Nobody said anything. They got into some ridiculous fight over nothing. Now he might never see him again. Nor would Mr L see the other friends that he had made in California. He felt depleted, defeated, dead inside.

Only later in his analysis did Mr L mourn the loss of his friend Richard, and the loss of the kind of quiet contentment that he had so treasured during those few precious moments, those few and precious days. As his grief-laden sadness emerged, alternating with the angry protest against his parents that he had never made at that childhood time, his potential tenderness was born, and it touched his analyst. He embroidered his memories with the feeling of tender love felt belatedly now in the present. Although on the couch, Mr L let me know that tears arose, tears formerly blocked and suffocated. I felt him in his tender tear-filled sadness, and he felt me feeling him, so that a Winnicottian (1971) atmosphere of holding was engendered from which mourning could continue, as so many poignant times in his childhood were yet to be remembered.

Mourning his friend, who galvanized psychic yearnings for a good pre-Oedipal object, was just the beginning of Mr L's mourning in treatment. It was this mourning, and the need for the analyst which it opened up, that helped Mr L to reveal repressed memories of childhood shame. Mr L also mourned for parts of himself, child parts of him that had been injured and left behind. He remembered shame-ridden experiences of paternal castration. One memory of being punished and spanked particularly stood out. There was another memory of his father going into a rage and slapping him across the face. Both memories brought back to him his sense of despair about ever being understood. His father was not interested in hearing what he had to say.

His father would never have listened nor understood that he stole some quarters from their next-door neighbours in New York because it was his only way of expressing his misery, as well as his wish to retaliate against the parents who tore him away from his friend Richard, and from all the other friends in California. His parents united in their wish to punish him. He was seen as immoral, as a thief! He was forced to apologize to his neighbours in his parents' words. He couldn't even use his own words. He went through what felt like his trial and conviction in a numbed out state–dejected, passively obedient. He saw himself as a piece of shit, as a cast out turd.

He waited in his room as he was commanded by his father, not knowing what would happen next. Centuries seemed to go by. Then his father entered his room and commanded him to 'drop your pants!' His father spanked him on his bare behind, and never once looked him in the face. He submitted, and his self-hatred drowned out awareness of his hatred for his father. Later he would act out this hatred, and would do everything possible to disown his aggression since he associated his father with aggression. However, unconsciously he would identify with his father's detachment. Mr L commented on how, even at the height of his father's aggression toward him, in the midst of his own humiliation, his father seemed detached and uninvolved, seemingly doing what he thought he had to do. Mr L felt that he didn't even get the dignity of his father's personal sense of anger.

Mr L had repressed his reactions, not being able to tolerate the awareness of how lonely and unimportant he felt in the midst of his humiliating castration. In treatment, his hatred towards his parents, and particularly towards his father, came alive. So did his shame. He asked out loud the questions and protests that he could never have expressed at the time to his father. His secret superiority emerged as well, his belief that his father was contemptible. Yet he had always treated himself with contempt, repeating his father's behaviour towards him.

He had dreams in which another man split off from him, or came inside of him. Sometimes he held dialogues with this other man. He realized that this other man was a part of him, another half. He had his father inside him, and there was nothing he could do about it. All he could do was make peace with his father, by understanding his father's pain and grieving now for both of them. His rage at his father spent, his feelings of shame and humiliation beginning to heal with the expression of his inner wounds and the expressions of his shit-flawed self-image, he could now make amends. Moving from the paranoid-schizoid to the depressive position, he was able to realize how much pain his father must have been in to have been so numbed out himself, to have been so frequently filled with rage, so indifferent to anything his son said or thought.

Forgiveness came as he felt empathy for the lonely soul within his father. He could see a whole picture now too, one that had eluded him as a child. He could see how his father was both emotionally rejected and dictated to by his mother. He could begin to see his mother's pain too, for she was jealous and lonely with a husband who was in love only with his work, and who frequently had affairs with his secretaries. The whole picture began to come together, and Mr L began to have two whole parents. Only in this way could his own self become whole.

Mr L was freed by his capacity to feel the chain of affects, from his anger to the narcissistic hurt within his shame, and to the loss within his sense of loneliness as he separated from his internal bad part-object parents. Grief followed anger and hurt. He could then feel his parents' pain within his own pain, without the threat of losing his own separate perspective. He would never get to communicate to them what he had felt, and his grief was partly for that. There would always be a rift between them.

Yet, as he communicated his pain to me, his analyst, he psychically healed the rift with his parents and grew to empathize with their pain. He grieved the loss of what they could never be to each other. Through grief he allowed a tender sadness to emerge within him that was the route to contact with others. He could know and touch others now, and they could know and touch him. His painting became more tactile. The colour of rebirth from his despair emerged. His barriers with me were analysed and resolved, as he could let me feel him and could feel me in turn.

Dreams, as well as memories, revealed Mr L's need to reconnect with good objects within him that had been blocked out of awareness by fears of feeling their loss, and by relations with dead and depriving internal objects that had been held on to when his good objects had been repressed. His sense of self had been depleted by the loss of these objects, and his attachment to 'bad' objects, which seemed representative of his parents' detachment from his needs, prevented him from allowing good object contact in the present. In one dream, which manifested during the fourth year of treatment:

> Mr L emerged from a hut in the wilderness to find old friends who he had missed for many years. In relating the dream, he explained that he was warm and cosy in his hut, but he was all alone. It was as if he had found a cocoon in which to heal himself, as he was healing himself in treatment, but the cocoon could become not only a solitary place for recuperation, but also a place to hide, which might isolate him from others.

> In the dream, I, his analyst, appear as a messenger to bring him out of his cocoon and into the forest where his lost friends are still waiting for him, after many years. There is snow all around. He sees trees that are cold and bare. He is blocked by one tree, and tries to bang on it. He hits it again and again, but there is no response. Instead of moving on to find his

friends he gets caught up in trying to get this cold, dark tree to respond. The tree and others around are made of petrified wood. He finally gives up, concluding that 'You can't get blood from a stone!'. Having been caught up so long in trying to get a response from this stone tree, it has gotten darker and colder. There is snow all around.

Finally, he finds a bench in the wilderness on which all his friends lie piled up together under a blanket. In the dream, he realizes that he almost came too late. They might have frozen to death. He might have lost them. But he discovers them just in time. He lifts the blanket off them, and his friends greet him. They have kept warm by holding on to each other. He feels their warmth. Once having found them they are free to go. He lets them leave, grateful for the contact, and no longer holding them back from moving on with their lives. As they leave, a bed appears where the bench was, and a female friend of Mr L's appears on the bed. He wishes for her affection and feels his attraction to her.

In Mr L's associations to this dream, he says that at the point when he let his friends go, feeling the contact with them, and keeping their warmth within him, he felt his penis 'strengthen'. He related this strengthening of himself, within his penis, to an overall strengthening of his sense of self, but also particularly to his sexual self. His associations indicated that he connected his ability to let go of his friends, which allowed the discovery of a woman, to the strengthening of his penis. He understood that he was in danger of freezing his friends and killing them, which would have meant losing them forever, because he had frozen them in a moment of time within his memory in order to avoid losing them. He had put them under a blanket, or blanketed them with repression, because he wanted to hold on to them for ever.

He remembered later that within the dream he had felt as if they had been pulled away from him, when they had earlier left the hut he was in to find 'greener pastures'. This is how it had felt to him in his life. He never wanted to leave his childhood friends. They had left him to move on with their separate lives, and he had tried to hold on to them by repressing the memory of them, and of their warmth, and trying to keep them frozen in time, behind a blanketing wall of repression. In this way he remained alone, and he was not yet then ready to move on into a psychic place of sexual adequacy where he could relate to a woman.

This dream was a dream of significant mourning. It occurred a month after other dreams in which Mr L appeared furious at women who made him feel impotent. It occurred after incidents in life with women in which he felt that his penis could only stay hard if he was filled with cold rage. If he felt affectionate he felt impotent. With this episode of mourning, just as with the episode of mourning his childhood male friend, his sense of self changed. Again he allowed good internalizations to form within him by reuniting with warm friends from the past, no longer excluding their sense of warmth and love from his consciousness, nor any longer splitting them off in a seclusion that would turn them into cold 'petrified trees'.

He gave up on getting warmth from cold trees that seemed to represent a depriving early mother, as well as the distant women whom he had been drawn to, seemingly as a compulsive re-enactment in relation to such a mother. He came to terms with the loss of his friends in his life, and in this way felt the sadness which emerged with his associations to the dream. This sadness helped him get past his anger, past his fury at women, and past the cold rage that had more recently opened up into such fury. The sadness helped him assimilate his memories and his good internal objects, and this allowed him in turn to open up to feelings towards his analyst that had been frozen in time as well.

Just as he found a woman on the bed in his dream, so too in his analysis he began to find the analyst as an Oedipal level sexual object, now that his pre-Oedipal connections had been restored. Although, from early on in treatment, Mr L could experience erotic feelings towards women in his life, he had kept these feelings split off from contact with the analyst. He had alluded to wishes to be seen as attractive to the analyst, and had feared being repulsive, but he had never felt the force of his own erotic passion. Earlier, he had strengthened his sense of self by restoring his childhood friend Richard to his consciousness, facing the never before faced grief of saying goodbye.

This made Mr L more capable of containing his feelings, and he opened up to his feelings of shame and of anger. Now, his ability to say goodbye to friends of his later (college) years – friends who, like Rich, also represented pre-Oedipal needs for basic nurturance and affectionate contact – enabled him to acquire a strengthening of his 'penis', i.e. of his basic sexual identity. This allowed him to contain erotic feelings, and to open up an erotic transference that had formerly remained latent. The girl he discovered on the bed in his dream became associated with his female analyst.

Erotic transference

Up until the time of the mourning process described, Mr L's erotic desires were fixated in sadomasochistic fantasies of being tied down by a woman, and of being made to submit to all kinds of sexually arousing tortures. His fantasies echoed Mr L's passive submission to women in his life and to his female analyst. These fantasies were used for masturbation, which became a ritual of re-enacting an enslaved position that Mr L inhabited in relation to his mother. His enslaved position in relation to his mother was most chiefly characterized by his inability to say no every evening when his mother asked him to go into the kitchen and get her 'her' ice cream. One dream highlighted the deeper level of his humiliation. He dreamt that:

He was forced to sit naked at the dinner table by his mother. He shivered from the cold, felt mortified as others sat at the table for dinner, and when someone offered him a blanket to cover himself his mother flew into a rage.

Mr L's associations revealed that he thought his mother was getting sexual stimulation from his nakedness, and that he felt exploited by her and uncared for. This view of himself as a sexual victim pressed for re-enactment, and could have become a resistance to opening up to contact with his analyst, and with his unconscious Oedipal erotic desires, if significant mourning had not already allowed him to feel that he was strong enough, and sexual enough, to reveal his fantasies to me rather than to pull me into a covert form of acting out.

Generally, Mr L had eroticized his rage towards his mother, and had developed certain characterological patterns. He inverted himself into the role of the victim, and controlled others by being controlled. His sexual fantasies, which he cherished and nurtured during his secret masturbation rituals, were filled with this role of erotic victimization. Sometimes one woman tied him up, sometimes three at a time. One dream revealed his transference to me as one of these women who intimidated him and even terrified him:

> The woman in his dream was huge compared to him. He was forced to please her in all kinds of ways that substituted for any kind of sexual intercourse, since his penis was too small.

The dream revealed his secret terror. When he consciously constructed and controlled his sexual fantasies and sex play, he could turn the terror into erotic thrills. In his dream he didn't have that control, and much of his emotional withdrawal from me in the clinical situation could be understood in the light of his terrified inhibition and his hidden erotic longings.

With the mourning process proceeding, however, Mr L began to emerge from his guilt and shame ridden cocoon by sharing his masturbation fantasies and dreams with me. As he did so his dimensions in relation to mine became more proportionate in his fantasies and associations. His dreams began to reveal all kinds of phallic explosions, and often these dreams were wet dreams. *In one dream, there was a tidal wave of emotion coming in at both of us from the outside.* It was clear that Mr L saw both of us as threatened by the breadth of his passion. His emotional longings had to be experienced full force, just like his phallic eruptions, in order that the two could come together. Mr L spoke of standing up to the tidal wave and facing the fear. He would face his passion now that he had me by his side.

As Mr L's tidal wave of passion came out into the open, leaving the ocean of the unconscious and coming out into the light of day, he wooed me fiercely. He constantly thought of 'lines' to say to me as he entered my office, which he revealed with some degree of embarrassment, testing the waters. Over time, his shame diminished and his awakening sense of humour became more predominant.

Also, during this period Mr L would constantly observe what I wore, waiting to see if I would wear a red dress. If I did, he hoped I wore it specially for him. He found everything I wore exciting. With his secret attraction to me no longer concealed, he opened up all the Oedipal erotic desires that seemed to have been rebuffed during his childhood by his 'cold tree' mother. His wish for me to wear a red dress, which he considered 'sexy', became an ongoing motif in his daily speculations about whether I had dressed that morning with him in mind. Former dreams of being in a bed with a strange woman now turned into dreams of feeling loving and close, feeling that we were becoming integrated with one another.

This period brought dreams and fantasies of my lying beside him in bed, or of me suddenly appearing at his doorstep and coming inside his home to make love to him. He described waking in the morning and imagining me beside him. He wanted to feel the pressure of my body, our tenderness, our caressing. He imagined us sharing our secret flaws together, bonding through the sharing of our shame, revealing the awkward areas in our bodies, evolving an exquisite attunement to each other's entire body surfaces.

The erotic feelings came up directly in our sessions. He exclaimed that he felt a full feeling coming up from his 'gut and through his penis' while being with me in a session. When we discussed his coming four times a week to work with all the dreams and fantasies that were opening up, he felt a kind of sexual ecstasy, believing then that I really wanted him.

Mr L wanted me to yearn as intensely for him as he yearned for me. Once, upon meeting a young woman he was attracted to, he vividly described to me his pursuit of her, painting a scene for me which culminated in a sweet, sensual, and prolonged kiss. Not receiving the reaction he expected, he burst out in an uncharacteristic exclamation, which felt as if it was accompanied by the stamping of a foot: 'God damn it, I want you to be jealous!' His mother always had been jealous of any girl that he showed interest in. In fact, she would have tantrum-like rages, stamping her feet. He resented this, as it had made him feel overwhelmed with guilt, but now he realized that he wanted me to be jealous.

Mourning the Oedipal object

Since I had become so vividly painted as Mr L's Oedipal love, only disappointment and mourning could bring his transition into finding a true love who could be his own. A critical time of growth arrived during my summer vacation, leading to his last year of treatment, his sixth year. Mr L reported to me that after my departure he had woken up in the mornings with the weight of grief that he had never known before. He felt a heavy sadness and wept. His sadness brought the full impact of his realization that I was never going to come to his home, to his bed. I would never be his.

Surrendering to this truth, he emerged from his cocoon in a radical new way. He felt a newfound sense of determination, a willingness to take risks. He joined a dating service, made a video of himself, and within three dates he had met the woman who would become his bride. As he began to date her and to know her, his painting showed his erotic joy, and the mournful colours of his past brightened. His romantic fantasies were replaced by romantic realities that were better than any fantasies could have predicted. His courtship with his fiancée was filled with surprises, gifts, and tender concern and caring.

On Valentine's Day, Mr L cancelled one of his analytic sessions (for which he paid) to take his fiancée to a well-known elegant restaurant. In his words, he was determined 'to give her royal treatment'. It became clear that I had served as a transitional love object, who could be relinquished as I was internalized within him. When Mr L left treatment he said, 'You will be deep inside of me for the rest of my life!', but he also said, 'You're no longer the focus of my erotic longings'. As his treatment drew to a close his fiancée was the one who empowered the female figures both in his fantasies and in his artwork. He was now working in an executive-level position and was also expressing himself in art. Primarily, at that time, he was preparing for a wedding and marriage. His mourning of his analyst was the last stage in an overall mourning process. This mourning process allowed him to open up the full force of his erotic feelings and fantasies, without being held back by shame, repressed anger, and despair as he had once been. It allowed him to feel more whole so that he might face his fear and contain his feelings.

In this way he could collaborate in analysis in order to understand his feelings, rather than being compelled to re-enact his childhood Oedipal wishes without self-reflection in treatment. He no longer needed to try to please me or play out the part of a sex slave, with the sexual aspects of the drama hidden. His 'transference love' became a real love, in which he appreciated the real aspects of the relationship with the analyst. By being open to contact with the analyst as he mourned his losses and opened to formerly blocked-off feelings, he could integrate her into a loving core within him, where he already had installed his childhood friends.

At one point in treatment, Mr L had resisted engaging in new relationships with women, as he wished to remain in an exclusive erotic relation with me, his analyst. However, he voluntarily brought this up for discussion in his analytic sessions and was able to prepare to mourn me by facing his resistance and letting go. When I left for my summer vacation, in Mr L's sixth year of treatment, the grief he felt about having to say goodbye to me as an erotic love object came with the growing realization that I could become an internal object within him that could make him more secure, but I could not be a real external lover. This gradually enlarging awareness allowed him to let go of me, as he had of his childhood friends, and to move towards a woman who could truly be available to him as a lover and as a wife.

Because Mr L had been able to use his analyst as a transitional object, he could choose a wife who was warm, loving, caring, and related in a way that his former girlfriends had never been. As he mourned childhood friends, let go of negative internal parents, and grieved for the parents who had hurt him, he could take in more good internalizations of the analyst. Then, in time, he became able to grieve for the loss of his fantasy wishes towards the analyst. This allowed him to open up to a new relationship with a woman that could truly fulfill his needs as an adult man.

As Freud first said in his 'Observations on Transference-Love' (1915), it is possible for the erotic transference to become the major mobilizing force in favour of this psychoanalytic treatment. However, Mr L's willingness to enter the erotic transference in an overt way, and his later willingness to surrender to it, were both facilitated by the mourning of object loss and object disappointment. Without such mourning, Mr L might have ended up sitting for ever in the 'transference glow'. In a case reported by Gould (1989) just such a situation was described:

> While some of his good feeling may be a reality-based reaction to feeling good and gratitude for the improvements in his life, the uncritical glow I think, also bespeaks, in addition, a transferential halo. I suspect that his current transference resistance may be in his pleasure of basking in the limited intimacy of the therapeutic situation. He can enjoy psychological and emotional closeness that is time-limited each session and in which concurrent physical intimacy with its attendant anxieties is not possible.
>
> (Gould 1989)

In a discussion of Gould's case, I (Kavaler-Adler 1989) point out how Gould's analysand's resistance was related to a failure to mourn the regrets of his past. I speculate that his transference resistance, which was also an erotic transference resistance, was reinforced by defences against the feelings of grief related to the guilt of his own rejections of intimacy with women in his life, with roots in the original mother–son situation.

Gould's analysand's resistance to grieving can be contrasted with that of Mr L, who was able consciously to confront his resistance to giving up the fantasy of an exclusive bond with the analyst as he was able to feel the grief of regret related to his rejections and distancing in relation to women in his past. This allowed him to tolerate the attendant anxieties of intimacy in his life, which Gould states her analysand, Mr M, still could not do. In Mr L's case, his developing capacity to grieve in his treatment, beginning with his grieving the pre-Oedipal object, allowed him to remember and grieve each former relationship with women in his life. Mr L mourned his own part in creating distance with women who aroused erotic desires in him, after he experienced the anger towards these women for their own distancing. Both the anger and the sadness of regret were parts of his mourning process.

Gould's (1989) analysand had not yet mourned and faced his losses, many of which had been promoted by his own aggression. He was, therefore, not able to say goodbye and to accept the limits of reality that dictated that he needed to move on to a real erotic relationship with an available woman. Gould's analysand's perpetuation of the erotic transference tie to his female analyst seems to be a good example of what Freud cautioned about in relation to the resistance aspects of the 'transference love'. The analyst's abstinence alone did not dissolve Mr L's resistances. The analysand's mourning was essential, and I, as the analyst, needed to be aware of the defences against this mourning, particularly defences that served to deny guilt and regret.

In Mr L's case, guilt and regret were faced and felt at many times during the course of his treatment. He felt regret about never having said goodbye to Richard. He felt guilt and regret about his fight with Richard before he left. He felt guilt and regret about not having been able to let go of his friends, and not having respected their needs and their freedom. He felt guilt about all the times he had held back from women and from me, his analyst. He felt regret about all the times he had held back in retaliation against his parents, even though he knew that they had hurt him. He got past such retaliation by grieving the losses that came with his hostile behavior, and at one point said, 'Just because my father doesn't call me for my birthday doesn't mean I have to hold back from him. I don't have to continue to act like he does'.

The mourning of one's own aggression, and the specific mourning of the Oedipal object within the depressive position, is a basic developmental understanding within Kleinian theory. Mr L's feeling of regret is an essential aspect of mourning, related to the owning of aggression as part of the process that leads to the healing power of tolerated loss, and to the self-integration process that comes through mourning within the context of the holding aspect of the transference (Modell 1976). Feeling regret is essential in Kleinian theory in order that reparation to the object can be made, to both the internal and external object. The mourning of loss, in terms of grieving regret for times when potential love and connection were destroyed by distancing behaviors, is critical for resolving neurotic longings for an incestuous object.

The negative transference and Mr L's aggression

The analysand's destructiveness was expressed in a passive aggressive manner, as withholding himself from contact with the analyst. This was dealt with on a continuing, session by session basis, in terms of resistance to connection. The destructiveness also appeared in fantasy form, rather than in enactment. The analysand's sexual fantasies were of a sadomasochistic nature in which he controlled the sadist through masochistic submission. All this was related to a relationship with an internal mother within him. Through the avenue of confronting resistance to contact and connection, interpretations could be made about the sadomasochistic scenes being played out, and about both the aggressive and erotic nature of the wishes behind them. With this neurotic patient, the object-related strivings were always in preconscious if not conscious awareness, and the resistance interpretations were enough to make Mr L aware of his desires and of his fears of his desires. His sense of shame was resolved through his connection with early memories so that he did not block resistance interpretations due to shame.

The mourning that took place in the treatment allowed Mr L to resolve his aggression into healthy self-assertion, which was expressed increasingly within the therapeutic object relationship, and also in other relationships in his life. During the course of the analysis, I, as the analyst, would experience the withheld negative transference and its underlying aggression in terms of feeling sleepy. However, when I confronted Mr L with the point at which he had pulled back he was able to respond in a manner that was reparative to object connection and facilitative to the analysis.

Object relations versus self-psychology

Erotic transference is primarily an object-related phenomenon. It is the transferential expression of the most intense mode of desire for the object. It is a psychophysical state of desire, as shown in the case of Mr L who needed to feel like a full sexual subject, the owner of sexual passions. In its full form, the erotic transference expresses the most passionate combination of genital cravings for the other, combined with deep longings for tenderness and for the reparative gift of love. A separate other is its prime target, and psychic fantasy charts the route to that target.

Yet, in 1988, Jeffrey L. Trop redefined the erotic transference in terms of his self-psychological view of development and of psychic structure. In an article entitled 'Erotic and Eroticized Transference: A Self-Psychological Perspective', he writes: 'I describe this as an erotic transference in that the developmental need is for mirroring of the sexual self' (1988: 281). His definition places the patient he addresses in that paper in the role of a sexual object, not of a sexual subject. Also, he speaks about a need for an Oedipal self-object arising in the transference, totally negating the desired object as a separate other. His definition of the erotic transference seems to limit his treatment, and to set up a schema that opposes the full-blown emergence of unconscious erotic desire.

In his 1988 article, Trop writes of a female patient in terms of his definition, stating that her erotic attraction to men in her life is related to the revival of a 'developmental longing for a protective, involved, and alive father to compensate and protect her from her undermining experience with her mother' (1988: 277). Trop believes that, due to a mother who always stole her father's attention from her, this woman's healthy desire to exhibit herself, and to feel that she was attractive to a man, had been cut off and defended against. Trop writes: 'What she had not acquired during her development was confidence in her own capacity to elicit aliveness and responsiveness in others' (1988: 278).

Up to this point in his article, Trop has dealt with his patient more as a sexual object than as a sexual subject. According to Trop's definition of erotic transference as the need for mirroring of the sexual self, a self-psychologist might actually attempt to provide a positive mirroring reflection for such a patient, which would keep the patient in the position of the object of the mirror, denying her as a sexual subject with passions of her own.

Worse, using his definition, a self-psychologist might use such mirroring as a narcissistic compensation that would block the erotic passion from emerging. To offer mirroring of the self in the face of sealed-off erotic desire only creates a narcissistic compensation that never can replace the kind of object-related eroticism that one feels when the sadness of object loss opens up renewed love and desire. Such narcissistic compensation defends against object loss, and thus defends against the very fundamental object-related growth process that can only come through mourning.

However, Trop himself does not succumb to any such facile notion of mirroring, and he appropriately deals with his patient's shame. He helps his patient to see that she finds exhibition of herself shameful due to the early injury following her father's repeated attraction to her. He does not, however, deal with the repressed exhibitionistic wishes behind the inhibition concerning self-exhibition. Further, he does not deal with any conflicts over repressed sexual passions, passions which may have gone underground when the patient's father hurt her by turning away from her to attend to her mother. He deals with the narcissistic aspect of the patient's view of herself in her father's eyes, without delving into the fantasy level of her expectation of a man's lack of response to her.

Nor does Trop deal with his patient's conflicts about successfully arousing men, as opposed to the perhaps safer consequences of being rejected. He is appropriately related to his patient's concerns as he addresses his patient's shame about exhibition of herself, but he is not yet dealing with her conflicts over her erotic desires. Trop's definition of the erotic transference seems to be restraining him as he then moves gingerly into the area of erotic desire. Trop writes (1988) that when he interpreted his patient's inhibitions in relation to self-exhibitionism to the father's past behaviour, as well as attributing to both parents' behaviour the related problems she had in primarily attracting pseudo-confident men – interpreting that she was too inhibited to initiate interaction – his patient began to develop sexual feelings for him, her analyst (1988: 279). This could be the emergence of a potentially powerful erotic transference as a major conduit for the deepest unconscious desires, but then Trop interprets:

> The therapist conceptualized the patient's erotic feelings as being fueled by a revived need to consolidate her own femininity by evoking a mirroring response from him. This constellation of hopes for a responsive man had been repeatedly fractured by her father's withdrawal from her.
> (Trop 1988: 279)

Trop thus isolates a self issue, and neglects all the object-related conflicts concerning wishes for the most intense mode of object connection, the erotic connection:

> The therapist communicated to her that her fantasies about him helped her delineate a vision for herself as a woman with a responsive and admiring man. It helped her to consolidate a feeling that a man would be able to appreciate her and that she would be capable of pleasing a man.
>
> (Trop 1988: 279)

This leads to the patient talking about her fear of exposure in a social situation, but then the beginning-to-bud erotic transference seems to be averted:

> She began to go to social events and dances and gained more confidence. She still felt attracted to the therapist, but said that she knew her life had to continue and preferred to keep these feelings to the side.
>
> (Trop 1988: 279)

Reading this, it appears that the erotic transference never flowered with Trop's exclusive focus on the self, and the patient therefore never mourned the loss of the therapist as a fantasy love. It appears that she merely displaced her feelings onto others, putting a whole erotic part of herself aside, i.e. splitting it off, in order to put feelings for the therapist aside. How much self-integration was actually achieved in this case then becomes questionable.

Trop's definition of erotic transference, as related to the wish to have the self mirrored, neglected the patient as a sexual subject with deep erotic passion, and his treatment minimizes the patient as a sexual subject, although some discussion of sexual fantasies in the transference is alluded to. Explicitly, he refers only to the female patient's wishes to have warm interludes with the therapist and to hold hands (p. 279). This leaves the reader in the dark as to how deep a level of erotic desire was reached in the treatment situation. One could conclude that the emergence of explicit eroticism was minimal, and that this accounts for the patient's relative lack of difficulty in turning away from erotic desires in the transference to external sexual relations. The lack of difficulty suggests displacement rather than the kind of resolution that can come from grief and mourning in which a deeply erotic part of the self becomes integrated into the central self, and thus becomes interpersonally connected to others.

The lack of such in-depth resolution is also suggested by the patient's choice of a future sexual companion or date. The chosen male is noted by Trop to be different from past object choices in terms of being shy and kind, rather than being pseudo-confident. Although this choice may indeed be a change for the better as Trop suggests, the choice of a shy and kind man may also imply that the patient backs off from initiating a sexual relationship with a man who is less shy and possibly more erotic and passionate. One might even conjecture that the new object choice is in line with choosing a male similar to the analyst for whom the erotic transference was aborted by displacement, rather than being fully developed and thus necessarily mourned. This could be another form of living in the transference glow as in the case of Gould (1989).

At the end of his 1988 paper, Trop expresses the opinion that the Oedipal wishes described in the transference need not be renounced (1988: 282–3). He states that they can be 'consolidated and integrated' (1988: 283) without renouncing them. He then goes on to add that these erotic wishes for the Oedipal object can be 'reality tested and mourned but will not necessarily dissolve at the end of therapy' (1988: 283). This is the first time Trop mentions mourning, and his belief that the wishes need not be renounced suggests that he does not seriously consider mourning. To mourn is to feel object loss, even if only of a fantasy object, and there is renunciation necessarily involved.

In the case of Mr L, addressed in this chapter, it is clear that Mr L did renounce the analyst as an erotic Oedipal object in order to open up to a full erotic relationship with another woman. However, he did not need to renounce me as a real internalized object, someone who had been with him for six years, and had emotionally held him and related to him. He renounced the Oedipal erotic parent aspect of me, the fantasy part of me, the transferential part of me, but not me as a real object. This explains why the renunciation could be tolerated. It was not traumatic. The evidence of this is that Mr L felt deeply sad about letting go of me as a fantasy lover, rather than feeling enraged, paranoid, empty, or fragmented.

It is not comprehensible to me how Trop can assume that mourning of the Oedipal transference object takes place without any renunciation. Perhaps it is the impossibility of such a mode of mourning that explains why Trop only mentions the word 'mourning', and does not indicate any of the mourning process as actually having occurred in his case example of treatment.

Perhaps Trop intends to say that mourning involves the sustaining of a fantasy of the analyst as an erotic love object in one's internal world, even once the fantasy is finally recognized as a fantasy. Such a fantasy may continue to enrich the inner life of the patient once treatment ends, even if the disillusionment of recognizing that the fantasy cannot become a reality is acknowledged with grief. However, in the case of Mr L it can be seen that the patient was able to have a rich and passionate fantasy life that accompanied his real sexual life at the end of treatment, and this fantasy life was totally focused on his fiancée at this point, not on the analyst. If Mr L had needed to continue to fantasize about the analyst while sexually relating to his fiancée, his erotic life may have been attenuated.

Overall, Trop's case represents the work with an analysand who is still in the paranoid-schizoid position. As Ogden (1986) has pointed out, within the paranoid-schizoid position the self lacks a sense of subjectivity, and is experienced as an object. Trop's treatment reflects his regard for his analysand as an object, not as a sexual subject. He never moves into the depressive position. In order to do so, he would need to go through the negative reaction to his mirroring, not just assume that mirroring has only positive effects. The threat of being possessed by the mirror always leads to negative transference, and it is only through the negotiation of this negative transference that the subjectivity of the self in the depressive position can be reached. Trop's use of mirroring can defend against the negative reaction to the object, and thus can defend against the emergence of the self through the unsealing of unconscious erotic passions.

Summary

This chapter proposes that the clinical mourning process is a critical factor in transforming an aggressively laden erotic transference, and its potential for use as resistance, into a conscious erotic transference that progressively mobilizes the psychoanalytic treatment process. A psychoanalytic case is used to illustrate that the mourning of the pre-Oedipal object allows an erotic transference to emerge into consciousness in treatment. The case also demonstrates that the erotic transference takes the form not only of desiring but also of mourning the Oedipal level object. The case serves as a case in point in illustrating that erotic transference appears in cases in which female analysts treat male analysands. Further, it illustrates that erotic transference remains a primarily object-related phenomenon as opposed to being a merely narcissistic phenomenon. Finally, it illustrates the course of working through the erotic transference in an analytic treatment in which the therapeutic object relationship facilitates mourning.

References

Freud, S. (1915) 'Observations on transference-love. Further recommendations on the technique of psycho-analysis'. *Standard Edition* Vol. XXII. London: Hogarth Press.
Freud, S. (1917) 'Mourning and melancholia'. *Standard Edition* Vol. XIV. London: Hogarth Press.
Gould, E. (1989) 'Perspectives on transference'. *Psychoanalysis and Psychotherapy* 7: 62–73.
Kavaler-Adler, S. (1989) 'Discussion of "Perspectives on transference"'. *Psychoanalysis and Psychotherapy* 7: 80–84.
Kavaler-Adler, S. (1993a). *The Compulsion to Create: a Psychoanalytic Study of Women Artists*. London and New York: Routledge. Reprinted in 2000 by Other Press.
Kavaler-Adler, S. (1993b). 'Object relations issues in the treatment of the preoedipal character'. *American Journal of Psychoanalysis* 53(1): 19–34.
Kavaler-Adler, S. (1995). 'Opening up blocked mourning in the preoedipal character'. *American Journal of Psychoanalysis* 55(2): 145–68.

Kavaler-Adler, S. (1996). *The Creative Mystique: from Red Shoes Frenzy to Love and Creativity*. London and New York: Routledge.

Kavaler-Adler, S. (1998). 'Vaginal core or vampire mouth: a visceral manifestation of envy in women: the protosymbolic politics of object relations,' chapter 13, in N. Burke (ed.), *Gender and Envy*. London and New York: Routledge.

Kavaler-Adler, S. (2000). *The Compulsion to Create: Women Writers and their Demon Lovers*. New York: Other Press.

Kavaler-Adler, S. (2003a). *Mourning, Spirituality and Psychic Change: a New Object Relations View of Psychoanalysis*. New York and London: Brunner-Routledge.

Kavaler-Adler, S. (2003b). 'Lesbian homoerotic transference in dialectic with developmental mourning'. *Pychoanalytic Psychology* 20(1): 131–152.

Kavaler-Adler, S. (2004). 'Anatomy of regret: a developmental view of the depressive position and a critical turn toward love and creativity in the transforming schizoid personality'. *American Journal of Psychoanalysis* 64(1): 39–76.

Kavaler-Adler, S. (2005a). 'From benign mirror to demon lover: an object relations view of compulsion versus desire'. *American Journal of Psychoanalysis* 65(1): 31–92.

Kavaler-Adler, S. (2005b). 'The case of David: on the couch for sixty minutes, nine years of once-a-week treatment'. *American Journal of Psychoanalysis* 65(2): 103–134.

Kavaler-Adler, S. (2006a). 'Pivotal moments of surrender in mourning the parental internal object'. *Psychoanalysis and Psychotherapy*, in press.

Kavaler-Adler, S. (2006b). 'My graduation is my mother's funeral: transformation from the paranoid-schizoid to the depressive position in fear of success, and the role of the internal saboteur'. *International Forum of Psychoanalysis* 15: 117–130.

Klein, M. (1940) 'Mourning and its relation to manic-depressive states'. In M. Klein *Love, Guilt and Reparation and Other Works 1921–1945*. London: Hogarth Press (1975 edition, pp. 344–369).

Modell, A. (1976) 'The holding environment' and the therapeutic action of psychoanalysis'. *Journal of the American Psychoanalytical Association* 24: 285–308.

Ogden, T. (1986) *The Matrix of the Mind*. Northvale, NJ: Jason Aronson.

Trop, J. L. (1988) 'Erotic and eroticized transference: a self-psychological perspective'. *Psychoanalytic Psychology* 5: 269–284.

Winnicott, D. W. (1971) *Playing and Reality*. Harmondsworth: Penguin.

Chapter 7

Who speaks? Who listens?

Different voices and different sexualities

Mary Lynne Ellis

In this chapter I want to consider how, as psychoanalytic psychotherapists, we can respond more sensitively to questions of sexuality and sexual identity that are raised for us by our clients. Psychoanalytic theories of homosexuality have been restricted to interpretations regarding the internal world where, for example, pre-Oedipal fixations or Oedipal conflicts are regarded as the 'cause' of homosexuality. Such interpretations arise from a view of the truth of the individual's world (the unconscious) as being located outside or beyond the wider social context. The individual subject of psychoanalysis is ahistorical and acultural. In excluding a recognition of cultural constructions of sexuality psychoanalytic theorizing contradicts itself: in claiming that sexual identity is only partial and fragmentary it nevertheless holds to a normative view of sexuality in which heterosexual identity is equated with maturity. Even though it is claimed that heterosexuality must itself be subject to analysis (in the same way as homosexuality), a secure heterosexual identity is still, paradoxically, what is required if the analysis is to be successful.

Noreen O'Connor and Joanna Ryan, in their original and comprehensive study of psychoanalytic theories of lesbianism, *Wild Desires and Mistaken Identities: Lesbianism and Psychoanalysis* (1993), have challenged the extensive claims within psychoanalytic theorizing that lesbianism is, for example, a symptom of arrested sexual development, a narcissistic condition, a defence against separation anxiety, psychosis or the dread of mutilation and disintegration. Central to their work is a critique of the notion of the Oedipus complex as being universal, emphasizing instead the cultural specificity of sexual identity. They highlight the crucial importance of drawing from other disciplines outside psychoanalysis to enable us to address the complexities of sexualities and notions of identity, and to be more open to the individual and constantly shifting meanings that sex and sexuality hold for our clients. They show how the writings of Foucault, Merleau-Ponty, Derrida, Butler and others in the postmodern tradition can contribute to our developing a psychoanalytic practice that is truly concerned with the speech of our patients, with complexities of transference and the uniqueness of every psychoanalytic encounter. O'Connor and Ryan's work is informed by their recognition that questions of sexual identity have a historical relativity (1993: 19). However, they acknowledge:

> An understanding of the interconnections between what is expressed psychoanalytically and what is expressed socially, in legislation and in other practices or attitudes, would require an extensive study in its own right.
> (O'Connor and Ryan 1993: 25)

The question of the connection between the intra-psychic and the wider social and political context has, in the past 25 to 30 years, increasingly preoccupied psychoanalytic psychotherapists. It is striking that, in Britain, the work of the philosopher Michel Foucault has, with the exception of O'Connor and Ryan's book, been largely excluded from debates in this area. The reason may lie in the tendency of psychoanalytic psychotherapists in Britain to assume an already existing division between the psychic and the socio-political. Foucault claims, in contrast, that this division has itself arisen out of particular discourses that are socially and culturally specific.

In this chapter I begin by drawing on Foucault's analysis to highlight the socio-historical specificity of lesbian and gay identities. I show how these identities have been constituted out of complex webs of ecclesiastical, moral, legal, political and economic discourses and practices that are constantly shifting. Second, I discuss aspects of Audre Lorde's (1982) novel *Zami*, and show how this offers some particularly valuable insights into the question of identity in relation to both race and sexuality and the diversity of lesbian experiences. Lastly, I reflect on the relevance of these considerations to psychoanalytic theorizing and practice. As illustrations I present two case studies, one of a black lesbian and one of a white, male, married patient. My aim in these case studies is to show how a Foucauldian approach can be combined with a psychoanalytic approach to enable a more sensitive understanding of issues regarding identity and sexual orientation as well as race.

In *The History of Sexuality* (1984) Foucault's central claim is that the body cannot be seen purely as a material or biological 'fact'. It does not exist outside discourse; what is designated as normal or abnormal, natural or unnatural depends on the power of institutions such as the church, medicine or law, that is bought to bear on the body. His position challenges Freud's claim that the repression of sexuality has underpinned the development of bourgeois culture. Foucault argues that sexuality itself is constructed through various mechanisms and regimes of power ('polymorphous techniques of power') that permeate discourses on sexuality and both control and incite sexual pleasure (1978: 11). He claims, for example, that the meticulous surveillance of sexual practices within the bourgeois family in the nineteenth century paradoxically:

> acted by multiplication of singular sexualities. It did not set boundaries for sexuality; it extended the various forms of sexuality, pursuing them

according to lines of indefinite penetration . . . It did not set up a barrier; it provided places of maximum saturation. It produced and determined the sexual mosaic.

(Foucault 1978: 47)

Foucault identifies the eighteenth century as marking the beginning of a multiplication of discourses on sex. Within Christianity, the confession and self-examination, particularly in relation to sexuality, increased in importance. Every thought, desire, fantasy and action had to be meticulously observed and confessed. The focus of eighteenth-century ecclesiastical laws and rules governing sexual practices concerned matrimonial relations. Sexual activities that took place outside marriage, such as adultery, rape, sodomy and incest, were regarded as extreme infringements of the law, but it was only later that these came under scrutiny.

Gradually, according to Foucault, as heterosexual monogamy became increasingly established with its strictly regularized sexuality, attention shifted towards the sexuality of children, of so-called mad men and women, criminals, and those engaged in same-sex relationships. These people, previously hardly noticed, were called upon to confess what they were. They were viewed as belonging to an almost separate dimension, that of 'unnatural sexuality'. Jeffrey Weeks (1979: 27, 89) suggests that this focus on so-called sexual aberration and the search for its origins within the individual was influenced by the impact of Darwinism and the claim that survival depended on sexual selection – the ultimate test of biological success lying in reproduction.

It was within this context, as Foucault points out, that Krafft-Ebing's (1886) *Psychopathia Sexualis*, the compendium of case studies of perversions, was published. Krafft-Ebing was explicit in his moral judgements, condemning sexual practices other than heterosexual intercourse as being morally degenerate whilst, at the same time, viewing them as symptoms of illness. He regarded homosexuality as both acquired (particularly associated with masturbation) and congenital. His book was followed by numerous other publications that attempted detailed classifications of sexual pathologies (see Ellenberger 1970: 291–303).

Foucault (1984) cites Westphal's (1870) article on 'contrary sexual sensations' as constituting the birth of the medical category of homosexuality. This article contained the origins of the notion that gender identity and sexual identity are necessarily linked through the naturalness of heterosexual object choice. For the first time the homosexual became:

a personage, a past, a case history, and a childhood . . . Nothing that went into his total composition was unaffected by his sexuality. It was everywhere present in him: at the root of all his actions because it was their insidious and indefinitely active principle.

(Foucault 1978: 43)

The continuing debates as to whether homosexuality was innate or acquired had important consequences regarding legal penalties. It was claimed that, if it was acquired, homosexual behaviour should be deemed a criminal offence. This view was becoming increasingly prevalent and psychotherapeutic treatment was advocated as a method of treating homosexuality. It was from within this context that psychoanalytic theory developed. In *Three Essays on Sexuality* (1905) Freud makes many references to Krafft-Ebing (amongst others) as important sources for some of his theorizing.

Many of the significant developments in feminist, gender, and lesbian and gay studies over the past two decades have been influenced by Foucault's theorizing, emphasizing the socio-cultural and historical specificity of sexual identity and sexual practices. In their article, 'On "Compulsory Heterosexuality and Lesbian Existence": Defining the Issues', Ferguson et al. (1982) argue that the possibilities for lesbianism emerged as a consequence of women's economic independence from men. The growth of urban areas enabled women to leave the confines of small patriarchal farming communities and to free themselves increasingly from their emotional and sexual dependence on men. In her paper, 'Identity Crises: Who is a Lesbian Anyway?', the sociologist Vera Whisman (1993) offers a succinct and thoughtful history of lesbian identity – from the 'true invert', the masculine lesbian, Stephen Gordon from Radclyffe Hall's novel *The Well of Loneliness*, to the 'variant' of the 1950s, so defined by the founders of the first lesbian organization Daughters of Bilitis who discouraged butch–femme identifications and emphasized 'sexual preference'. It was the 1960s that gave birth to the notion of 'sexual orientation', lesbianism being a female version of homosexuality. This was supplanted in the 1970s with the equation of lesbianism with feminism and 'woman-identified experience' which did not depend on genital desire for another woman. In the 1990s 'queer politics' emerged – gender-bending, lesbian queers who see themselves more like gay men, and lesbians who have sex with men. Whisman concludes:

> In the end, a lesbian must simply be any woman who calls herself one, understanding that we place ourselves within that category, drawing and redrawing the boundaries in ever-shifting ways.
>
> (Whisman 1993: 60)

Her paper very usefully highlights the limitations of any theory that offers a definitive account or aetiology of 'the lesbian'. In psychoanalytic theorizing there is no distinction between the same-sex sexuality between, for example, two upper-class married white women such as Virginia Woolf and Vita Sackville-West in the 1920s and that of a black working-class woman who identifies as a lesbian queer in the 1990s. Where distinctions are made, these are in relation to different types of unconscious defence. For example, Limentani (1989) specifies three groups of homosexual individuals: those engaged in a flight from the opposite sex; those whose homosexuality serves as a defence against psychotic anxieties; and lastly the 'truly bisexual individuals' whose male and female aspects are dissociated and in whose personalities splitting and multiple identifications are dominant (Limentani 1989: 109).

Foucault's account of the complex interweaving of moral, legal, medical and psychoanalytic discourses and their roles as powerful mechanisms in the construction of sexuality as normal or abnormal continues to be relevant. Psychoanalysts have played a powerful role in the maintenance of laws and restrictions (see Note) in relation to homosexuality with their very public pronouncements that it is a pathology. For example, Ismond Rosen from the Institute of Psychoanalysis spoke publicly and on television in support of Clause 28 (passed as Section 28 in 1988) when it was being debated in parliament. Hannah Segal, who is well known for her left-wing affiliations and anti-nuclear campaigning, is explicit about her view of lesbian parenting, exclaiming about a baby adopted by a lesbian: 'What the hell is going to happen to this boy when he reaches adolescence?' (Segal 1990: 211). For Segal, homosexuality and lesbianism represent an attack on the heterosexual parental couple. Charles Socarides, the American psychoanalyst was invited in 1995 by the influential Association of Psychoanalytic Psychotherapy, to deliver its annual lecture. Their members work in the British National Health Service and their aim is to advance and promote the provision of psychoanalytic psychotherapy within it. Socarides publicly campaigned for homosexuality to be reinstated as a pathology by the American Psychiatric Association. In his view (1994), homosexuality 'cannot make a society or keep one going for very long. It operates against the cohesive elements of society. It drives the sexes in opposite directions, and no society can long endure when either the child is neglected or the sexes war with each other'.

These contemporary examples illustrate how psychoanalytic theory, while claiming to be value-free and based on 'observation' is, instead, a conflation of medical, legal and moral discourses. A proliferation of psychoanalytic theories has been generated which seeks to explain the aetiology of homosexuality but they all rest on the conviction, except in rare cases, that homosexuality can never be fulfilling, satisfying or mature. They also rest on the assumption that sexual identity can be viewed in isolation from the social context. Such a view does not take into account the diversity of forms of homosexual sex, identities, or relationships. It is in the dimension of sexuality that psychoanalytic theory emerges as so very impoverished. I would emphasize that this impoverishment extends also to accounts of heterosexuality. It is for this reason that it is particularly important for psychoanalytic therapists to look to other sources to extend our own possibilities of thinking about sexuality, to be open to the multiplicity of metaphors that point to the uniqueness of sexual experience and its constantly shifting nature. Philosophical texts are, as I have shown, one important source and another is literature.

In 1982 the black lesbian writer Audre Lorde (novelist, feminist theorist and poet) published her novel *Zami*. It tells the story of a black woman growing up in Harlem in the 1930s and her later life as a black lesbian in the 1950s during the McCarthy era. 'Zami', writes Lorde, is a Carriacou name for 'women who work together as friends and lovers' (Lorde 1982: 255). Lorde's writing is vivid and sensuous and is a testimony to the complexity and diversity of lesbian sexualities. It highlights how same-sex love does not necessarily imply sameness in roles, identities, experiences or cultures. For Lorde, it is 'difference' that is always at play. As black, white, butch, femme, young, old, as an oppressed group looking for a place of recognition, pressure on lesbians to form a group identity was strong but, she writes:

> Each of us had our own needs and pursuits, and many different alliances. Self-preservation warned some of us that we could not afford to settle for one easy definition ... It was a while before we came to realize that our place was the very house of difference rather than the security of any one particular difference.
>
> (Lorde 1982: 226)

The book contains many moving descriptions of lovemaking between women. For Lorde, sexuality is not confined to Oedipal configurations, flowing instead between many different shores:

> I have felt the age-old triangle of mother, father and child, with the 'I' at its eternal core, elongate and flatten into the elegantly strong triad of grandmother mother daughter, with the 'I' moving back and forth, flowing in either or both directions.
>
> (Lorde 1982: 7)

None of her descriptions can be exhaustively interpreted within a developmental schema. To attempt to do so would be to miss the complex interplay of positions that are exchanged and shift between the lovers. In the following passage it could be interpreted that there are moments that resonate with the pre-Oedipal of psychoanalytic theorizing: there is reference to need, to hunger, and to oral pleasure. But such an interpretation does not take account of the mutual exchange between the lovers, the simultaneity of giving and receiving pleasure, the shifting of power back and forth, the pleasure in the 'otherness' of the other lover:

> I dove beneath her wetness, her fragrance, the silky insistence of her body's rhythms, illuminating my own hungers ... Her body answered the quest of my fingers my tongue my desire to know another woman, again and again, until she arched like a rainbow, and shaken, I slid back through our heat coming to rest upon her thighs. I surfaced dizzy and blessed with her rich myrrh taste in my mouth.
>
> (Lorde 1982: 139)

Lorde's importance to us as psychotherapists lies in her acute sensitivity to the specificity of each of her characters' experience, which includes a recognition of the social context and the way in which discourses on gender, race, class and sexuality shape this experience. At no point can their experience be pinned down, assumed or generalized:

> Being women together was not enough. We were different. Being gay-girls together was not enough. We were different. Being Black together was not enough. We were different. Being Black women together was not enough. We were different. Being Black dykes together was not enough. We were different.
>
> (Lorde 1982: 226)

Gloria

In the following case presentation I will show how my struggle to be open to my patient's uniqueness and difference whilst recognizing her position(s) within the socio-historical context was crucial in our work. My relationship with this patient whom I shall call Gloria was particularly challenging as she herself longed so much to find an identity or a theory that would name her, explain her, complete her and to which she would 'belong'. Gloria's own search for explanations and her belief that the achievement of a particular identity would bring her happiness mirror the rigidity of psychoanalytic theorizing that equates maturity with the taking up of a heterosexual identity. For the purposes of this chapter the presentation is highly condensed, and I will restrict my focus to the aspect of the work that concerned Gloria's preoccupation with her identity.

Gloria was a 29-year-old mixed race woman. She had been born to a white English mother and a Nigerian father who died when she was 18. He was a soldier in the British army and Gloria's early life was spent moving between countries before her family settled in Britain where they moved several more times. Gloria had one older and one younger brother and a younger sister who, she said, was sexually abused by her father. She herself had wondered if she too was an incest survivor. Gloria stormed her way into therapy in a counselling centre in which I was working. She wanted to join a therapy group I was running and, since one of the group members knew her, I felt unable to accept her into the group. She responded to my decision with fury, crying and accusing me of being a 'fucking white racist', of shutting her out. She said that the other group member 'had everything' and that, as a mixed race lesbian, there was never a place for her. As her rage grew, so did my anxiety that she might smash me or my consulting room up. However, I also felt intrigued by the relentlessness of her demand and I warmed to her fighting spirit. She responded to my offer of a place in individual therapy with guilt – and amazement that the enormity of her fury had failed to drive me to reject her outright. Gloria also said that she had idealized me (since attending a one-day workshop I had run), and this was one aspect of her disappointment in me. She had just failed her degree in nursing. I was her fourth therapist and I saw her once a week in free therapy for just over three years.

Gloria's quest for her identity concerned her both as a lesbian and as a mixed race woman in white British culture. She often spoke of a highly significant moment in her life: her first memory of being subjected to racism. Aged ten and starting at a new school, she was taunted and stared at, called 'wog' and 'chocolate drop'. She could see the children's lips moving but it was 'like a television set with the sound turned down'. She could not hear and she could not speak. At home she barricaded herself in her room and, for a whole year after that, she hardly ever went to school. This was Gloria's most vivid memory of direct racism. However, she also expressed a desperation about the lack of recognition she received from her mother who, she felt, was unable to accept her with her dark skin colour, darker than her sister's. Her father's inability to feel any pride in being black and his rejection of his own culture, including his Catholicism, to integrate himself into white English culture were a frequent source of resentment to her.

From the first session when Gloria called me a 'fucking white racist', I was acutely aware of my position as a white therapist. In one session in which she was expressing her fury at white people's treatment of her as a black woman, I commented that she was also identifying with how these people saw her. She responded by saying this was because she had no self, she was 'nothing'. In the following session she admitted that she had been furious with me. She felt that I had implied that she should not fight racism, and that she was 'acting like a victim'. She ascertained that this was because I was white and therefore could have no understanding of her. At times, in the transference, Gloria assumed I was Jewish in an attempt, I think, to make an alliance with me on the basis that we both must have experienced racism.

That racism can have profound effects on an individual's world (conscious and unconscious) is often dismissed by psychoanalysts and psychoanalytic psychotherapists. Interpretations that acknowledge an individual's experience of racism are deemed to be 'a collapse into the sociological'. It is claimed that the 'deeper level' of the individual's suffering is located within early familial relationships, and it is assumed that such relationships occur in isolation from our racist culture. A Foucauldian analysis, in contrast, recognizes how powerfully racist discourses have penetrated and saturated interpersonal relationships. The main components of racism, those of hostility, devaluation and envy, can operate to create a persecutory world that is severely undermining and may even threaten complete annihilation.

Gloria often said 'I don't exist', 'I have no self', 'I am nothing'. Her frantic search to find what she called her 'real identity' led her to join black women's groups, lesbian groups, incest survivors' groups, Alcoholics Anonymous, Sex and Love Addicts Anonymous, Substance Abusers Anonymous, Compulsive

Eaters Anonymous, and an organization for dyslexic people. Each of these groups would disappoint and enrage her as she could never totally belong: in each of them she felt that her other identities were not sufficiently recognized; they did not recognise her black identity or her lesbian identity or her disability as dyslexic. The more she searched to belong, the more obliterated she would feel: 'It's like fading into the wall. I become as yellow as the wall.'

It was crucial that I acknowledge the extent of Gloria's despair and also the specificity of its form: her quest for an identity. It was an important moment in Gloria's therapy when she was able to laugh with recognition at my comment that, even if she did find a mixed race, black lesbian, incest survivors group for drug, eating and alcohol addicts with dyslexia, there would still be something missing. In searching for her identity Gloria sought sameness and totality. This must be distinguished from the taking up of an identity that signifies difference, thus enabling the articulation of the specificity of what may have been denied individually and institutionally by the dominant culture. For Gloria, as yet, to acknowledge her difference was to risk annihilation: 'I was like someone being bayoneted', she said of her experience of racism.

Gloria's search to belong was frantic, driving her in a relentless thirst for possession: 'I could destroy myself to get what I want'; 'I thought I was caring, but I don't give a toss about people'; 'I need Janet (her lover) as a life-support machine'. This was reflected in the transference. In a session after a holiday break early on in her therapy, Gloria declared to me that she was a 'batterer' and that she could have killed Janet when she had held her captive in her flat. I asked her whether, in her violence, she also felt angry towards me. She said her 'mind had gone blank' and then that she did not want to hurt me. She went on to talk of being obsessed with sex, following a woman on a train whom she wanted to 'fuck'. She felt she could smash up the therapy room kill someone or hurt herself; she didn't know where it would end. Gloria's fragility and desperation were compelling her to want to consume me in every possible way, including through sex and through destruction. It was important that I acknowledged the acute intensity of her feelings of vulnerability and powerlessness in my break. However, what emerged as being even more crucial was my statement that I was prepared to work very hard with her to explore the source of her violent feelings, but that if she was violent I would stop working with her. She looked visibly relieved and said to me that it was important to her that I was tough like that since, otherwise, she could not move forward. For Gloria it was vital that I acknowledge her violence as a real possibility, not only a fantasy and that it concerned me. It was also important that I insisted on a limit to her fantasies of power and domination, opening out the possibility of reflecting on and moving beyond her violence.

For many months Gloria spoke endlessly, of possession, of wanting to belong, of wanting to find her identity. Her speech was permeated with explanations and interpretations of her behaviour: 'That's the needy child, isn't it? That's the need for a mother, isn't it?' I was left feeling unmoved, objectified or non-existent as her words streamed over me, limitlessly. She would describe herself as 'being all over the place', 'mad', 'schizophrenic' and 'rambling'. My interpretations regarding her desire for possession, the all or nothing quality of her demand, and her experience of gaps and, separation as devastation and rejection were met with agreement followed by explanations and justifications in relation to her past: images of her father, as controlling, manipulative, possessive, evil and mad, and of her mother, as cold and calculating appeared. But it was as if my interpretations and her connections became yet more objects to add to her collection of explanations. At times I would say to her, 'And how do all these explanations help?' She would admit, sometimes tearfully, that she needed these to assuage the depth of her despair, yet her search was futile: 'It's all labels, isn't it? I've nothing inside ... it's like going into a hole and finding another hole ... there's no substance ... I'm like one of those dolls on a production line without eyes or features.' For Gloria necessity or limitation was associated with annihilation. She described this as being 'alone, totally alone, in the Antarctic with no clothes and no food, with the wind driving over me, and the cold sea'. Her survival was under threat.

After nearly a year in therapy Gloria began a new relationship with a woman, Paula. This was at a point in her therapy when she was exploring the distance between us. My experiences of being bored and non-existent in her presence were becoming much less frequent: I felt more space for my own spontaneity. When I had laughed with her in one session, she told me a few weeks later that she had realized that I was not only cold and authoritarian, as she had thought, but that I could be warm too. She associated this coldness with her mother's rejection of her, contrasting it with her father's possessiveness and eroticization of his relationship with her.

This relationship with Paula was very precious to Gloria. It marked a shift in her ability to reflect on her thirst for totality without being driven to violence. Shortly after it began she talked of being very self-destructive, getting into debt and not turning up at college. She wept saying, 'It's to do with my father, I feel I should have done more to keep him alive'. He had died when Gloria was 19 at a time when she was in trouble owing to drug abuse. She described seeing his dead body on the mortuary slab and of giving him her St Christopher, 'my own safekeeping for my own journey'. She felt now he was 'like a carcass' on her back and she returned to his grave where she burnt photographs of him in an effort to make him die. Instead, his presence as a tantalizing Don Juan figure with access to power and women came to life in the therapy.

Gloria grew terrified that Paula would leave her for a relationship with a man. She would say that she could never really 'have' women in the way that men do: she wanted to 'have Paula, open her up, get through to her, penetrate her, fuck her, thrust her way into her'. She began to wonder at this point too whether she really was an incest survivor as she could not remember any actual sexual contact with her father. She did, however, recall finding his pornographic magazines and his condoms. She also remembered standing at the top of the stairs provoking her father to be angry, knowing that her mother had forbidden him to hit her and experiencing, as she described it, an erotic excitement in tantalizing him.

In the transference Gloria would, at times, respond to my interpretations with almost masochistic excitement which she connected with her memory of provoking her father. She would also often flatter me, telling me how good I was as a therapist. 'I need to possess to feel real', she would say. During this period, in her efforts to control me, she would miss sessions before and after holiday breaks and wait for me to initiate contact with her.

As Gloria's anger towards men increased she fantasized about shooting them with a machine-gun, since they had the power she craved, including the power to take Paula from her and to exploit her as a woman as well. When a man jostled her on the tube she felt she was losing control. She was fighting for her life: 'There is no oxygen, it's like swimming and never reaching the shore or nearly getting there and the oxygen supply is taken off your back.' Images of her mother as suffocating emerged: 'My mother plays mind games, I used to think she was a witch, she messes things up and she's destructive. It's because of her I feel so insecure.' She expressed disappointment that even her father's death did not bring her closer to her.

Gradually, in the third year of her therapy, Gloria was realizing the limits of her quest. Periods of fury were interspersed with moving sessions in which Gloria wept, admitting feeling 'battle-worn', recognizing how for so long her fighting had protected her from her terror of annihilation, of being reduced to nothing. At times her distress at the racism she experienced on the graphics diploma course she embarked on 15 months into her therapy threatened to destroy her: 'It's like an endless spiral towards death'; she felt 'like an ant that is going to be crushed' in the face of another student, but she managed to continue. Her relationship with Paula, although turbulent, also survived and they managed to move into a new home together.

Gloria was able to acknowledge how she was changing and to look back at the enormity of her aggression at how she 'would grow huge and ugly, my shoulders would grow big and my words would come out of a sewer'. She felt, as a result of the therapy, that something different was emerging, 'but I don't know how to be that yet'. 'As if you don't have a language?' I asked her. 'Yes, that's exactly it, I don't have the words.' When she began therapy Gloria would say 'words have no meaning, they don't permeate my brain', and that it was as if other people were 'speaking a foreign language'. Eighteen months into her therapy she said that in speaking to me she was now beginning to 'feel real'. She said, 'It's like the Channel Tunnel, a channel of communication, and you're opening out the other end of it.'

In my work with Gloria I learned how crucial it was that I didn't subscribe to simplistic notions of identity and collude with her belief that she would be able to find her real identity. Instead, it was crucial that I saw how this search constrained her and served as a defence against her overwhelming fears of annihilation. It was only as she was able to realize the contingency of identity that she began to find her own voice from within her many different positions of difference. In not being as compelled to possess she was able to begin to find an intimacy that could allow for the other's difference.

My work with Gloria highlights how the significance of particular identities, such as being lesbian, being black, being a woman, or being working class can be constantly shifting and are often intertwined. Gloria's search for her 'real' identity arose from a desperate need to defend herself against her terror of annihilation. However, the way in which her identities as black and lesbian found articulation is also historically specific. It is hard to imagine a patient speaking of herself in such a way even as recently as 20 years ago.

A Foucauldian analysis allows for an interpretation which does not presuppose a split between the psychic and the socio-political. Such an approach contrasts with a traditional psychoanalytic approach: here the concern would be with Gloria's violence and depression as acultural and ahistorical and as 'underlying' her defensive search for her identity. A recognition of the historical specificity of Gloria's search and the identities she took up extends our understanding of her struggle: the conscious and unconscious impact of racism on her, the dynamics of desire between her father and herself and her relation to her mother as a girl/woman within the context of white patriarchal culture, her search as a lesbian for intimacy with a woman which could allow for mutuality and difference. Her terror of annihilation was rooted within the interplay of these various socio-cultural factors.

Derek

My next case illustration is an account of psychoanalytic psychotherapy with a very different client, a white, married man whom I shall call Derek. As in my work with Gloria, I was not concerned with an analysis of the 'causes' of his homosexuality in terms of intra-psychic dynamics, with a view to his moving towards a more stable heterosexual identity. Instead, I aimed to be attentive to the particular conscious and unconscious meanings his body and his sexuality had for him within the wider social context, the discourses of his family, his class background, Christianity, medicine, and contemporary gay culture. As with my account of my work with Gloria, I will show the importance of an approach that does not presuppose a split between the psychic and the social.

Derek was in his late forties. When he arrived at his first therapy session he had a grey, almost mechanical demeanour. He was immaculately dressed in a city suit, a conventional persona that masked an enormous conflict that pervaded his life. Derek lived in Berkshire with his wife Sally and their teenage daughter. Sally was a housewife who also did some voluntary work for a local charity. Derek was a stockbroker who did regular workouts in the gym. Sally's mother lived near them and was closely involved with their lives.

In the past year Derek had been in a private psychiatric unit for two short spells and had been prescribed antidepressants which he had recently stopped taking. What had preoccupied Derek and caused him terrible anguish, he shared with me with obvious trepidation, was that he was gay. He had known this, he said, since he was about 11. At 20 he had had a brief relationship with a man and, a few years later, he had got married in the hope of putting his homosexuality well behind him. After some years he began to cottage (have sex in public toilets) occasionally in his lunch hours. For the past two years he had had a relationship with a man, Peter, of which his wife was unaware. Three years before, he and Sally had attended marriage guidance counselling for a short time offered by a Christian organization (Derek was a committed Catholic), but Derek hadn't felt sufficiently understood by the counsellor. After that they had tried what he termed a 'compromise solution', making an agreement that, two evenings a week, he would be allowed to go out to gay bars. This had not lasted very long because Derek could not bear to see the distress he felt that he was causing Sally. Sally now thought things were 'back to normal' and that Derek's depression was a medical condition.

In this first session Derek wanted reassurance that I was not someone who would try to change him, that I didn't think that his being gay meant that there was something wrong with him. A psychiatrist at the hospital had told him that it was 'all to do with his relationship with his mother'. He had once talked to a priest who was reputed to be gay and had been told that his being gay need not stop him from being a Christian, but Derek was unsure about this.

In the first sessions Derek was very tentative when he talked about his sexuality, yet simultaneously he conveyed a desperate need to do so. He would return again and again to the effect of his homosexuality on his wife, terrified that she would be, as he said, 'destroyed' or become ill with distress. Derek's mother had died from cancer when he was 14 and he felt that he had never really mourned her. He felt that his father's and younger brother's grief had taken precedence. Derek recognized that there was a connection between his fears about Sally and his relationship to his mother. As the therapy unfolded he realized how much he had longed to please his mother, how he had always felt that she favoured his younger brother.

Gradually Derek began to talk about his feelings about his own body, the birthmark on his back, his shoulders being 'at a tilt' (which was not visible to me). His mother had been ill when he was born; he thought that she had nearly died and that his birth had caused it. Memories emerged of his being in the bath, of the acute pain when his mother would pull back his foreskin (which was too tight) to keep him clean, her obsession with his cleanliness making him sure there was something 'wrong' with his body. I suggested that his workouts in the gym were a way of trying to make his body his own. He said that he thought there was something in that; after a workout he would feel momentarily relaxed and good about himself.

In the transference it seemed that I represented an accepting mother, but this was threatening too. On one occasion I had to change his appointment to a later time and there was to be a gap between his leaving work and his appointment with me. He realized that he would probably spend this time in a gay bar and his guilt about coming to therapy surfaced. He felt that being in therapy was to indulge himself, that if I could accept him what on earth would that lead to. He felt that the therapy was a betrayal of Sally, that, although not secret, it was not having the effect that she hoped for: namely that he would be cured of his depression and so would no longer need to fantasize that being gay would be a way out. Their marriage could be saved.

Derek would often refer to his 'wild side'. It was then that the greyness would momentarily leave his face, his eyes would shine and he would laugh, turning his face away in embarrassment. I interpreted to him that, however terrifying it was that Sally might be destroyed, he also needed her as a way of constraining the wildness he feared. My interpretations regarding his fury with her were met with resistance. It was hard for him to recognize the aggression he directed towards Sally through his dramatic depressions and allusions to suicide, martyring himself to tell her 'look what you are doing to me'. His suicidal thoughts were very real to him. He would examine different ways of dying in detail; most of all he wished he could just go to sleep and never wake up. These feelings were heightened in the weeks leading up to the family holiday, but they were also a response to his beginning to face the strength of his own desire. I was extremely concerned about him and very aware of his precariousness. How could he live if to live was to destroy the other? His birth had nearly killed his mother, and her death when he was 14 had provided evidence that she could not survive his growing independence from her.

In one session he experimented with an alternative solution. He came into the session and threw himself into the chair, his head bent and his arm covering his face: 'I'm throwing in the towel', he said dramatically. He had contacted a Christian organization that would offer him counselling to help him be free of his homosexuality. I suggested to him that in taking flight from his conflict he was also attacking himself, that he was depriving himself of the possibility of desire or pleasure in his life. In this session more images of his mother emerged, particularly of her exhaustion and his fear that she would literally wear out. At home the atmosphere had been grey, void of any fun or spontaneity, with his father's depression always 'down on things'. This was just how life was, but Derek could see it was different in other families. Derek's parents were working class and they lived on an estate that bordered a middle-class area. Derek always felt that he could never be as smart as the middle-class children. He was very much inscribed in a discourse in which, as a working-class child, he was designated as inferior, as not having, of being deprived and unworthy of what other, financially better off people had access to. Alongside other aspects, Derek's position within discourses on class played an important role in relation to the question of his entitlement to his own desires.

Derek often spoke of Catholicism and perhaps for me, as a non-Christian, it was here that my own openness to difference was especially challenged. It was crucial that I allow Derek to find his own way in trying to integrate his homosexuality with his faith. Since Derek had been raised as a Catholic, those Christian discourses that designated homosexuality as a sin had been very influential in shaping his sexuality. Similarly, his decision to marry had arisen from his exposure to Christian discourses that hold marriage to be sacrosanct, a commitment before God, for life. To be homosexual was to be lured by the devil and he would describe horrifying fantasies of being in the devil's grip. The Christian notion of heaven was also a strong feature in his fears of change: over a number of sessions in which he talked about his mother's death, he realized how he had been saving himself for his mother in the after life. Ever since she died he had comforted himself with the thought that they would see each other again. He had therefore tried to preserve himself as the son she would have wanted, suspending his own life. For Derek, to live was to be for another.

Six months after Derek began therapy, a place came up for him and Sally at Relate. Derek would report on every session, puzzled by how much the counsellor would focus on Sally as if she, or at least her difficulty in accepting Derek's homosexuality, was the problem. He was amazed that, although she was extremely upset, she was not 'destroyed'. He battled with his wish for her permission in order to legitimize his own feelings. Each session he would risk more, being able to tell her finally that he had to follow his feelings. Together they decided that he should go out one night a week and see how that worked. The marriage counsellor was sceptical but Derek felt positive. Unlike the previous 'compromise solution' this arrangement represented a real turning point. Derek was able to tell Sally that there was no going back.

It became clear that Derek was already much more involved in the gay scene than he was able to tell me at the beginning, albeit restricted to the daytime. He had several longstanding phone contacts and a special contact address for gay men he was in correspondence with. He felt a particular affinity with gay prisoners, identifying with their experience of imprisonment, forming a particularly intense postal relationship with a convicted murderer who was gay. As well as seeing Peter, he would have other encounters with gay men who would respond to his ads; 'Married city gent seeks wild time with leather gays/skinheads'. He spoke with great fondness of a young skinhead with whom he would occasionally have sex. He was a biker who lived in a darkened room lit with discotheque lights and packed with disco equipment. We talked of his attraction to what he longed to express himself that was associated with toughness, spontaneity, wildness.

It was only after about eight months in therapy that Derek was able to talk more freely about a crucial aspect of this 'wildness'. He warned me that there was something important that he had yet to tell me, but it was very embarrassing. Also, he was afraid that in talking about it the excitement of it would disappear. It was a story that began in his childhood when he was seven years old. At school he was terrified of the boys' toilets with their rushing water and bad smells. He would rarely use them, managing to hold on until he got home at lunchtime or after school. One day, in a school assembly, he was desperate to go to the toilet. Too terrified to go he weighed up that it would be less terrible just to wet himself there and then: others hadn't been severely told off for their 'accidents'. However, when he got up, leaving the wet puddle, the consequences were enormous. He was publicly reprimanded by the head-mistress and his mother was furious with him when he returned home. He felt utterly humiliated. Up until she died his mother would keep reminding him when to go to the toilet.

When Derek started to masturbate he would recall this event in detail in a way that would arouse him, urinating in the family bathroom to achieve climax. He would recalculate endlessly just how much urine had been left on the floor at school and what it would have looked like. This fantasy had continued to dominate his adult sexual life, and he would masturbate in the same way when his wife and daughter were out. He admitted that he was very attracted to the notion of 'watersports' (sex with urination) with another man. This was the wildness that really terrified him and he felt that if he allowed full pleasure in his homosexuality this would have to include watersports. At the same time, he mused tentatively, could it be that there wasn't anything wrong with this if he could meet someone who was, as he said, 'like-minded'. He had confided in the skinhead but this man had not experienced anything similar.

It was crucial in this session that I just listened quietly. It seemed at the beginning that at any moment he might stop, delaying his revelation for another time. To speak of this aspect of his sexuality was such an enormous leap of faith and I was touched by the combination of terror and urgency in his voice. My openness to witnessing every detail of his story was absolutely vital and, in particular, my openness to its personal meaning for him. I made no effort in this session to make connections, to make it all understandable, to risk tidying it all up. It was important that this long-hidden story could just stand between us and be witnessed by us both.

In the next session and in later sessions we talked of how this fantasy had been a way of reworking his humiliating experience, of finding a way of being in control, his pleasure assuaging his feelings of humiliation, his finding potency in the face of these. It was essential that I was able to suspend notions of normality and pathology, to allow the uniqueness of Derek's experience to speak. My interpretations and connections were not made with a view to defusing the fantasy, to return him to a kind of mature homosexuality. Rather they were to flesh out the less conscious meaning that the fantasy had for him, allowing him to choose.

Several months after Derek's disclosure, his relationship with Peter ended. Shortly after, he formed a relationship with a young man, John, who was involved with someone else. For the first months they were sexually involved, but after a particularly intense and intimate sexual experience, John decided he could no longer be disloyal to his partner. Derek was very sad and disappointed about this but continued to enjoy and to be deeply committed to their friendship. John was a literary theorist and opened up a new world for Derek. He described his wife's puzzlement at the living-room table being piled high with poetry books and plays from the library. Derek also started to write his own poetry and occasionally brought them to sessions.

John was then appointed to a job outside London but they made plans for their friendship to continue. The emotional intimacy that Derek enjoyed with John was very new to him. There was an honesty and aliveness in it that Derek did not share with his wife. We discussed how it was no coincidence that John was not available to him sexually. This would be too risky, partly because such a situation would mean having to take a decision about leaving his wife, a decision that would take him a long time to find the courage to do. It might also mean he would be vulnerable to being again enslaved to the demands of another. Now, in the transference, it was the therapy that was making these demands, taking up too much time, making his week's schedule too tight. However, Derek's mechanical demeanour was being shed: his face and body had become more alive and expressive as he began to find a way to expand and move without constantly fearing the destruction of his mother.

From time to time Derek would think about the possibility of experimenting with watersports with other gay men, but with a relaxed thoughtfulness, none of the compulsiveness, and much less shame. In listening to him I was very aware that a traditional analytic view would hold firmly to the view that Derek's desires to participate in watersports, however consensual, must be pathological in every aspect. Such a perspective forecloses on possibilities of sexuality that are not related to sexual reproduction. In contrast, within contemporary gay culture, watersports and many other sexual practices are regarded as acceptable, provided they are consensual and pleasurable. From a Foucauldian viewpoint such practices are culturally specific; they do not arise out of a repressed sexuality that is located outside culture. In my work with Derek it was important that I held both positions simultaneously. Derek's pleasure had connections with his past experience of urinating publicly as a child, yet I also was concerned to hold open the possibility of watersports as a sexual practice that does not in itself have to be a symptom of psychopathology. Why, for example, should watersports be regarded as a symptom whilst other practices, such as oral sex, are regarded as being within the range of 'normal' sexual practices for heterosexuals within the west? In the nineteenth century arguments were waged within psychiatry and medicine as to whether masturbation was a symptom of disturbance or disease. What informs our views on what is normal or healthy, and what is abnormal and deviant?

Conclusion

My aim in this chapter has been to raise questions regarding the way in which we as psychoanalytic psychotherapists attend to the specificity of our patients' experience. What are the values that we bring to our listening? Is it necessary to presuppose a split between the psychic and the social? In showing how a Foucauldian perspective can be combined with a psychoanalytic approach, I have demonstrated how this can increase our sensitivity to the cultural specificity of our patients' speech. I have shown how questions of identity in relation to sexual orientation are intertwined with those of race and class. They also arise out of a multiplicity of shifting discourses including the legal, religious, medical and the colonial. I have emphasized that to truly engage with the complexity of our patients' experience in its conscious and unconscious aspects we must have the courage to suspend any temptation to simplify, to universalize and to colonize. As Gayatri Spivak, the cultural theorist, points out:

> For me, the question 'Who should speak?' is less crucial than 'Who will listen?' 'I will speak for myself as a Third World person' is an important position for political mobilization today. But the real demand is that, when I speak from that position, I should be listened to seriously; not with that kind of benevolent imperialism, really, which simply says that because I happen to be an Indian or whatever ... When they want to hear an Indian speaking as an Indian. ... they cover over the fact of the ignorance that they are allowed to possess, into a kind of homogenization.
> (Spivak 1990: 59–60)

Note

Such restrictions have included a differing age of consent for gay men (as compared with heterosexuals), the threat to lesbian mothers of the loss of the custody of their children, and restricted access to artificial insemination for lesbians because it has been supposed that they cannot offer an emotionally healthy upbringing for their children. This has changed considerably in the UK, reflected in the passing of the Civil Partnership Act 2004, but it is only as recently as 2000 that the age of consent for gay men was lowered to 16 in line with heterosexuals.

Section 28 was a bill passed in 1988 prohibiting the 'promotion' of homosexuality and the teaching of the acceptability of homosexuality as a 'pretended family relationship'. This law was eventually, after a long campaign, repealed in 2003.

References

Ellenberger, H. F. (1970) *The Discovery of the Unconscious*. New York: Basic Books.

Ferguson, A., Zita, J. N. and Addelson, K. P. (1982) 'On "Compulsory heterosexuality and lesbian existence": defining the issues'. In N. Keohane, M. Z. Rosaldo and B. C. Gelpi (eds) *Feminist Theory, A Critique of Ideology*. Brighton: Harvester Press.

Foucault, M. (1978) *The History of Sexuality*. London: Peregrine Books. 1984 Edition.

Freud, S. (1905) *Three Essays on the Theory of Sexuality*. Harmondsworth: Pelican (1983 edition).

Limentani, A. (1989) 'Clinical types of homosexuality'. In A. Limentani *Between Freud and Klein: The Psychoanalytic Quest for Knowledge and Truth*. London: Free Association Books.

Lorde, A. (1982) *Zami*. London: Sheba.

O'Connor, N. and Ryan, J. (1993) *Wild Desires and Mistaken Identities: Lesbianism and Psychoanalysis*. London: Virago (New London: Karnac 2003).

Segal, H. (1990) 'Jacqueline Rose interview'. *Women: A Cultural Review*, pp. 198–214.

Socarides, C. (1994) Article in *Washington Times*, 5 July.

Spivak, G. (1990) *The Post-Colonial Critic*. London: Routledge.

von Krafft-Ebing, R. (1886) *Psychopathia Sexualis*. New York: G.P. Putnam & Sons (1965 edition).

Weeks, J. (1979) *Coming Out*. London: Quartet.

Whisman, V. (1993) 'Identity crises: Who is a lesbian anyway?' In A. Stein (ed.) *Sisters, Sexperts, Queers*. New York: Penguin.

Part III

Women working with women

The common theme in this section is women working with women. Sherly Williams (Chapter 8) considers the influence of the reality of the analyst's gender and offers some thoughts on why it might be that women seek out a woman psychotherapist or analyst. She considers the unconscious hopes, conflicts and anxieties that this may reveal and her clinical examples reveal the transference implications of this initial search for a woman. Chapter 9 (Kavaler-Adler) and Chapter 10 (Springer) are unusual in that it is rare for women to write about long-term sustained erotic transferences of their women patients. Both authors return to themes addressed in their previous chapters in Part II. Chapter 9 by Susan Kavaler-Adler extends her idea of developmental mourning (Chapter 6) through the analysis of a female patient's deeply erotic transference. This lesbian erotic transference demonstrates the movement from the protosymbolic period in analysis, to developmental mourning and so to symbolisation. Significantly the patient's homoerotic desires are understood as part of her adult nature and not merely as regression. In Chapter 10 Anne Springer follows on from Chapter 4 in suggesting that perversion stands in the way of true object relating by giving a false sense of relatedness. She addresses the dislike of the term perversion in culture and suggests that this is because it has to do with things 'which are forbidden, hidden and embarrassing, frightening and which in a strange way are both attractive and repulsive' (p. 185). The single case study is a depth exploration of the erotic transference experience of a woman patient with a woman analyst. It is clear from both of these chapters that awareness of bodily countertransference is a factor in monitoring the erotic nature of the transference. This leads to Chapter 11, where Susie Orbach places her own bodily countertransference centre stage. Although this is not directly about the erotic transference, Orbach demonstrates how the analyst's attention to a variety of sense experiences may reveal unconscious elements of the patient's inner world. She makes the point that it is more common for bodily countertransferences to be understood in psychic terms but, in a reversal of the body–mind relationship, Orbach privileges thoughts about what the body does to the mind. Therefore she understands bodily countertransferences in terms of their physical meanings and shows how the therapist's body is an essential tool that can be tempered and sensitised.

Chapter 8

Women in search of women

Clinical issues that underlie a woman's search for a female therapist

Sherly Williams

In this chapter I wish to address an issue that has compelled my attention as a therapist since I joined the staff of a Women's Therapy Centre. Women often approach the centre seeking with unequivocal urgency a 'feminist therapist' (synonymous for most with a woman psychotherapist). They are specifying not the theoretical orientation of the therapist but another kind of orientation – one that I have come to see spells out fears and longings that will become central to the therapy and to the relationship between therapist and client.

Gender and analytic tradition

Analytic tradition has generally held that the genders of therapist and patient make little difference to transference phenomena. Although Freud in his essay on female sexuality (1931) indicated that female analysts might be better suited than male analysts to analyse the pre-Oedipal conflicts of women, the generally accepted view is that expressed by Fenichel (1945): 'both men and women patients can and do develop both father and mother transference toward the analyst, whether male or female' (p. 328). The concept of bisexuality with its implication that the analyst has access to male and female aspects of himself is also used to dismiss the role of gender in the unfolding of the therapist/patient, interaction (Lester 1990). Lasky (1989) in his survey of literature on gender issues in the analytic dyad, indicates that the views represented range from those authors who believe that the genders of therapist and patient make an absolutely critical difference to the outcome of treatment to those authors who simply point to the ways in which gender issues can affect the transference relationship.

The significance of gender

Gender is a powerful organiser of experience – inner and outer, past and present. From the time an individual's birth is announced – 'it is a boy/it is a girl' – issues of gender begin to influence the way he or she is perceived and related to. Gender structures his or her perception and experience of the world, and is present in the linguistic and symbolic structures developed in early childhood: 'gender ... remains a crucial modifier, a key element of patterned form in the continuous processing of perception throughout life' (Lester 1990: 435). Stoller (1968) sees an individual's 'core gender identity', that is, our sense of being male or female, developing out of parental attitudes and ascription of maleness and femaleness as well as the actual nature of genitalia. He demonstrates rather convincingly that 'core gender identity' is established between the ages of 18 months and 2 years and remains unaltered for life. 'Gender behaviour', that is, the behaviour one learns as appropriate to one's gender, is more susceptible to being altered or modified by later experience and education. Even so, gender behaviour is nonetheless a firm part of the child's identity and will influence all subsequent relationships with self and others. In this chapter, I shall take the term gender to include both biological sex (as determined by chromosomes, hormones and genitalia) and the more cultural and psychological notions of masculinity and femininity.

Gender and unconscious phantasy

Gender issues can be powerfully present in the relationship between patient and therapist. The nature of the unconscious phantasy that underlies the seeking out of a therapist of a particular gender will become evident in the transference conflicts and transference expressions that emerge in the therapy. In unconscious phantasy, maleness and femaleness are associated with the presence and image of the father and mother respectively. The fact that the gender of the therapist has become an issue at all for the patient implies a degree of differentiation between the images of father and mother. The early merged parental imago gradually gives place in normal development to the differentiated image of father and mother – moving, as it were, from 'twoness' to 'threeness', from dyadic interaction to the primal scene. Only two distinct separate parents may have intercourse. For the child, the move from the early dyadic relationship with mother to an intimation of intercourse between mother and father is full of potential disturbance and creativity (Samuels 1985). On the one hand, the child experiences envy and rage when 'confronted by a relationship and an image of a relationship he or she is not in' (Samuels 1985: 122); on the other hand, it is the basis for the child of the knowledge that she is created. This knowledge has potential to generate in the child an anticipatory excitement that she may in time be allowed to create something herself.

In seeking out a female therapist, a woman may be in flight from the agonising perception of the third person, the father, who challenged her early intense feeding dyad with mother. It could also be that she is looking for the experience of a dyadic relationship so that she may understand the nature of the intercourse that is possible between two persons: 'There are two primary images of twoness – mother and baby, and then the baby's image of his parents ... images of twoness create a climate in which images of threeness can exist and the paternal image emerge' (Samuels 1985: 114). The female therapist must foster not just mother–daughter identification with her female patients, but also mother–daughter differentiation. This she does by maintaining boundaries and by allowing conflict, aggression and autonomous strivings. Room can be made by the female therapist for father; father and daughter can relate to each other because of their common relation to mother. As Samuels points out in *The Plural Psyche* (1989), unlike the primal relationship between mother and infant, 'the father–child relation has to be declared' – only the mother can declare this with any authority.

The search by a woman for a female therapist is in itself an enactment of unconscious hopes, conflicts and anxieties that will gradually become externalised in the here and now of the transference relationship. In this chapter I intend to explore how the gender of the female therapist was used by female patients as raw material for unconscious phantasy concerning their relation to the world, to others and ultimately to themselves.

The search for a female therapist represents both expectation and avoidance. At times, women seek female therapists because they are actively seeking something. At other times, they may be actively avoiding what they may encounter in a male therapist. I intend to explore five areas which are marked by the patient's expectation of a female therapist and which relate closely to the experience of the early dyadic relationship with mother. I will conclude with a discussion of the avoidance of the father which relates to the Oedipal phase and primal scene phantasy.

Reaction to persecutory experience

There are naturally women who seek out female therapists because of fear, mistrust and anger towards men: women who have been physically and sexually abused by men; women who have had fathers hostile to their development as women; women who have been subjected to relentless pressures in a male-dominated world. The persecutory experiences these women have endured awaken, in relation to men, all the earliest anxieties about survival and loss of self that an infant feels in relation to the abusive or non-adaptive maternal environment. In a female therapist, women who have suffered at the hands of men hope to find an environment that is less dangerous, less abusive, more congruent with their own natures than has been their experience in childhood or in a society that, shaped by men, can be inimical to the lives of women. They hope to find in a female therapist what we have all hoped for as our starting point in life – an environment that is passionately disposed in our favour.

Search for transformation of gender experience

The active search by a woman for a female therapist is a search for a relationship which will impart meaning and value to her gender experience, what Christopher Bollas (1987) describes as 'the search for the transformational object in adult life' which springs from the memory of the early relationship with mother who transforms the infant's internal and external experience of the world in accordance with the infant's needs: thus hunger gets transformed into fullness, rage into contentment.

For many women, their experience of their own gender has been fraught with feelings of helplessness, inferiority and shame. In 1924 Freud wrote that 'anatomy is destiny'. What did not urgently concern him, however, was that the destiny attached to possessing female genitalia has been characterised by the history of the social and cultural oppression of women. When a woman seeks out a female therapist she hopes to find an experience of transformation of unsatisfying gender experience into the experience of self-esteem and wholeness.

Bernstein (1990) demonstrates that a girl's anxiety regarding her genitals is different from a boy's regarding his. While a boy's anxieties revolve around castration, a girl's revolve around issues specific to the nature of the female genital: issues around access, penetration and what she calls 'diffusivity', namely 'the spread of sensation . . . when the genital is touched from clitoris to vagina . . . to pelvis and to the urethral and anal passages which adds to the feeling of not being able to conceptualise clearly the nature of her genital' (1990: 153). Bernstein suggests that as a little girl becomes aware of her sexuality she suffers a temporary psychic disorganisation that threatens her sense of self and during which she turns to her mother to help her establish control and pleasure concerning her own body. In order for the girl to locate, understand and integrate what is mostly beyond her sight, touch and control, she has to turn to her mother for both support and identification (1990: 159):

> The girl must rely on her mother's reassurance that her genital is, indeed, inside . . . 'Seeing is believing' gives concrete reality to boys' definition whereas girls must integrate their genital on a sense of faith; she must 'know' it without evidence and trust her mother's explanation.

Far too often, however, the direct and indirect explanations regarding her sexuality given to the girl are coloured by the mother's own confusion, self-disparagement and disappointment at the role society has allocated her as a woman.

The search for a female therapist could, therefore, represent the search for a female parent who will give to the woman a more satisfying explanation of her sexuality. A girl child needs the help of her female parent to integrate her genital experience into a secure sense of body ego, so that she can inhabit her own body in a psyche-soma unity that is the basis for psychological well-being.

Thus, a woman who seeks out a female therapist in the hope of finding a transformational object for her gender experience is bound to make her approach with enormous expectation of almost magical transformation of need into satisfaction. Inevitably, unless the therapist herself overidentifies with the idealised projection, the woman's hope of finding a fairy godmother who transforms her and her gender experience into something beautiful and good comes up in the transference against the reality of the mother who originally failed in her function as transformational object.

Clinical example: disillusionment

Rachael was a 35-year-old woman who sought me out specifically because she wanted a woman therapist. She presented with unmanageable feelings of distress since her separation from her husband who four years ago had left her for another woman after ten years of marriage. She found herself still waiting for his return, unable to take an interest in other men, often breaking down in tears, having sleepless nights and many physical symptoms of stress.

Rachael came from an upper class background. When she was born, her mother employed 'a six-week nurse' to attend to the newborn baby and the nurse was subsequently replaced by a live-in nanny. Mother had a busy social life and Rachael did not see much of her, though mother's presence was always eagerly awaited. 'I always wanted a *real* mother,' she told me wistfully, and described how as child and in her teens she used to search out large, cuddly mother figures as 'aunts'.

It was this longing for a 'real mother' that had prompted her to go to some trouble to seek out a female therapist. Naturally, the stage was already set for disappointment – even my physique did not match her image of a real mother. At one point in the therapy she burst out, 'You're exactly the same size as my mother.' Her mother had been small, petite, protected by father and unwilling to offer the cuddly mothering Rachael needed. 'My mother never touched me,' she told me early on in the therapy, but in her ex-husband who had been physically very loving and tender with her she had found the kind of mothering she longed for. Perhaps he had even left because of the intensity of her demands for mothering. It was this touching, this physical holding and intimacy she missed with every fibre of her body which now screamed with pain. She developed various physically distressing conditions – her back ached from a slipped disc, she suffered from an irritable bowel, cystitis and post-viral fatigue.

While Rachael craved for the bodily holding that she had lost with her husband's departure, causing her to regress to the forlorn, unheld place she had inhabited as an infant, she did not seem to expect holding from me – only childminding such as the nurse and nanny had provided. She expected to engage only my head, not my heart, often posing me with psychologically framed dilemmas such as the problem of sleeplessness which she wanted analysed. She carefully arranged for male carers outside the therapy situation to provide care for her body's needs – a male homeopath and a male chiropracter. She had some memory of father bathing her and holding her on his lap; mother, on the other hand, had avoided all physical contact with her. I think she felt that her female body could therefore hold no meaning or delight for me, another woman.

Rachael's mother seemed not to have felt able and free to handle, gratify and enjoy her child's body as an object of love and pleasure. It is this sensual contact between mother and child which forms the basis for the child of all libidinal life. From birth, the infant, with increasing initiative, searches for and maintains bodily contact with mother. Rachael knew, from her mother's account, that her mother found it impossible to breastfeed her, actually fainting whenever the baby was put to her breast. Rachael's later experience even of being kissed on family occasions was of her mother always somehow managing to kiss without any physical contact: 'a kiss in mid-air', as Rachael described it.

Rachael began to show a dawning awareness that holding might be available with me. After a break in sessions she made oblique reference to her wish to be held by describing how she had seen her young daughter embrace someone 'in the way women sometimes greet each other, arms right around', a holding in which their bodies touch in unmistakable intimacy. However, if I interpreted such situations too directly she withdrew into the haughty aloofness of her mother: '*This* is different ... I'm used to professionals behaving professionally,' she would say, and then say no more. Yet she continued to present, in this ambivalent way, her wish to be held. She spoke of 'a desperate need to put (her) head down somewhere', but the thought of lying on the couch in my room appalled her. A little later on, she would say to me, 'You can't possibly want my dirty shoes on your couch.' A memory came back to her of how as a child her mother had allowed her to be in bed with her during a storm but had placed a big bolster down the middle of the bed between them so that there would be no physical contact.

Although Rachael had specifically sought out a female therapist in conscious recognition of her need to receive something she felt only a woman could give her, she told me repeatedly that if only I were a man I would be more useful to her. She would be able to weep more freely with me and feel me to be more interested in her. The relationship with a previous male therapist had mattered much more to her, she told me, than her present relationship to me. Mother had not been interested in her little daughter, accepting embraces from her two sons and pushing Rachael away. Rachael, in a vain attempt to engage her mother's love, had chosen whenever she could to wear boys' clothes – 'I preferred grey flannel shorts to dresses.' Although she now desperately hoped that I, as a woman therapist, would repair the narcissistic wound that had been dealt to her femaleness, she often disparaged my capacity to do so. By finding a woman therapist and then telling her she was useless because she was a woman, she was giving me in projective identification, the experience of her own narcissistic wound – the rejection of her femaleness, first by her mother and repeated in the rejection by her husband. 'Am I that unattractive?' she would ask me more than once.

Mirroring and 'erotic playback'

The woman first experiences herself in the intense reciprocity of the early relationship with mother. It is her mother's face which provides her first mirror and it is from the reflection of herself she finds on her mother's face that she constructs her self-image. She is 'given' her sense of self initially through the responses of her mother.

Winnicott (1971) writes of the baby's search for itself in the face of the mother. At the earliest stage, the baby finds satisfaction auto-erotically, that is, from within herself or from her mother's body which seems to be experienced by the baby as an extension of her own body. The baby then transfers this body satisfaction to a satisfying image of herself as seen in the eyes, face, responses of her mother. This must include a satisfying image of the baby's sexual identity. A girl child needs her sexuality to be supported and admired by her mother. Searles (1959), writing of Oedipal love, describes the importance of fathers to daughters in their growing up to be sexually confident women. Samuels (1989) writing on a similar theme recognises the importance of the father's 'erotic playback' in his relationship to his daughter. In my work with women, especially with those who have specifically sought me out as a female therapist, I have witnessed an equal longing for 'erotic playback' from the mother as the basis for daughters of a healthy narcissism about their bodies.

One woman whose mother had ignored her in many ways, including sexually, except to criticise her when she occasionally displayed her sexuality too overtly, was sure I would do the same. A year or so into the therapy, she told me she would like to come to a session dressed like the pop star Madonna in a defiant display of her sexuality that she thought I, like her mother, wanted her to repress. Yet what she wanted from me was both permission and admiration. She talked to me about her body, her anxiety about its ugliness and its hairiness. She sat in an upright position, afraid that if she stretched herself out in the chair she would become visible to me in a bodily way that I would not want to see. Then, in a recent session, she allowed herself to stretch; a button on her dress popped open; she giggled embarrassedly and apologised. She longed to be seen and admired, but feared I would see – only to disapprove.

A daughter needs a mother before whom she need not conceal her own eroticism. Often, however, mother has been experienced as disapproving, repressive or simply unerotic. Hence the despair and anger of a woman patient towards her mother who had over the years neglected her own appearance and whose only comment regarding sexual intercourse was 'Give me a box of chocolates instead any time.' Sex for this woman was, therefore, always a furtive activity and she was only able to experience orgasm when masturbating by herself. She sought out a female therapist in the hope of finding a mother who would recognise and mirror positively the surge of eroticism that she held repressed within herself. Her mother and her teachers, for instance, had always insisted she wore her long hair tied up in a tight braid. In the therapy, after struggling with many inhibitions, she began describing in one session a turbulent, exciting sexual encounter – and then suddenly stopped talking. A look of apprehension came over her face and she said she was afraid I was listening with increasing disapproval. I said in reply, 'Is it not possible that I might like seeing you with your hair flowing free?' She blushed and carried on with the exciting tale.

When the transference in the female patient/female therapist dyad becomes thus eroticised, it is important that the patient's erotic wishes be understood and mirrored positively. It is the patient's wish for total bodily acknowledgement that must be responded to, not simply the oral regressive elements that are also present within the transference. Eva Lester (1990) writes of possible neurotic countertransference reactions within the female therapist in response to the female patient's erotisation of the transference due to 'fears of using *her* own body to express concern and empathy [and this] may confuse the patient, arouse guilt and cause stalemate' (1990: 443). The therapist, she suggests, may withdraw in such instances into technical correctness or show an excessive 'maternal' concern for the patient which 'is directed at the most regressive and passive elements in the patient and not at the erotisation of the transference' (1990: 443). Yet what the patient may need is the knowledge that her femaleness, with all its bodily implications, is pleasing to her therapist/mother. In order to experience a whole-body eroticism rather than erotic connection based only upon the genitals, a woman needs to introject and identify with 'a satisfactory, satisfying woman's body which satisfied her and which she felt she satisfied when she was an infant' (Balint 1973: 343).

Fleeing the rivalrous mother

The pre-Oedipal sexual involvement with mother is what enables the girl to move into the Oedipal phase with a sense of being her mother's equal and a worthy object of her father's love. When, however, the girl in the Oedipal phase does choose her father as her love object, she experiences her mother both as rival and as the object of her jealousy. A mother who does not have sufficient narcissistic investment in, or identification with, her daughter can in fact become a terrifying rival to the daughter – much like Snow White's mother who tries to kill off her stepdaughter. Interestingly enough, as Bruno Bettelheim (1976) points out in his interpretation of the story of Snow White, when the stepmother finds Snow White alive in the home of the dwarfs, she tempts her with gifts that are addressed to her sexuality: the brightly coloured silk stay-laces in which the stepmother laces Snow White up too tightly; the poisoned comb that is supposed to make Snow White look more beautiful; the rosy red apple that is an appeal to her sensual appetite.

Many women feel that they have been left unaided by their mothers in their development. A common theme is the rage and sorrow women feel as they describe the insensitive and even cruel ways their passage into womanhood was treated by their mothers: the first period, the first bra, the first sexual experiences. The woman searching for a female therapist may be fleeing Snow White's stepmother and seeking instead a mother who, like Cinderella's fairy godmother, will give her all the gifts necessary for her to take her rightful place in the world as a beautiful, adult, sexual woman – a hope that is certainly not to be treated derisively, although the stepmother in the therapist will also have to be confronted.

Clinical example: breaking incestuous bond with father

Despite all the rivalry, jealousy and competition a girl in the Oedipal phase may feel towards her mother, she also needs her mother as the guardian of the incest taboo in relation to the father. Just as a daughter needs her father to free her from the early symbiotic dyadic relationship with the mother, she needs her mother's help to break away from the incestuous attachment to the father.

Joy was a Chinese woman who sought out a female therapist at a time when she was seeking courage to leave home and live with a man of whom her father strongly disapproved. She felt that her father's hold over her and his power to make her obey him was too great for her to defy on her own. Joy was 21 years old, but her father would tell her, 'You are not too old for me to put you over my knee.' He forbade her make-up or grown-up clothes, wanting to keep her his little girl so that he would not need to renounce his incestuous wishes towards her. He derided her attempts to be grown up with a mocking, 'So you think you are a big woman.' Her mother appeared to have abdicated, simply telling her, 'You know your father adores you and only wants the best for you.' Joy was terrified of her own longings for adult sexual relationship, feeling herself 'tainted' by the strong incestuous bond between her and father – in erotic dreams her fiancé would change into her father and back again. Part of what she needed from me was to discover an image of womanhood that would be powerful enough to break the incestuous spell in which she was held. As the therapy progressed, she began to search out older female relatives of her extended family who might become allies in her bid to leave her father and live with her fiancé. She succeeded in recruiting some support, but the breakthrough came when she eventually discovered that the name she had always imagined for herself was the name of a warrior woman in her culture. A female therapist was for her, perhaps, an equivalent figure.

Avoidance of the father

A female therapist could appear to offer to a woman all the safety of sameness. There can be for the patient an illusion of being totally 'at one' with the therapist simply because they are of the same sex. The sameness of bodies can blur the boundaries which signify the separate nature of 'the other'. It could seem to offer the possibility of regressing to the early oneness with mother. This need not necessarily be a bad thing in itself. Following Kris's aphorism 'regression of ego in the service of ego' (1952), the longing to regress into the fused state with mother may be a search for the matrix of one's being, a regenerative source of personality enhancement and enrichment. However, the search for a female therapist could also be an attempt to avoid the father and all the vicissitudes of the Oedipal phase. It could be a defensive move, an attempt to remain unaware of the existence of a third person, the father.

When the infant becomes aware of the existence of the father as separate from the mother, he or she is forced to give up the merged state with the mother and all the attendant blissful phantasies of fusion. Differentiating between mother and father brings in its wake the realisation of parental intercourse, and the infant's own sense of exclusion from the gratifications the parents are exchanging between themselves. Thus the seeking out by a woman of a female therapist could be an attempt to exclude the father, and a defence against the acute feelings of jealousy, envy and deprivation that the image of parental intercourse can bring. Segal (1973) writes of the moment when the infant becomes aware of the important link that exists between its mother and father: [the infant] 'phantasises his parents in almost uninterrupted intercourse ... as constantly giving one another precisely those gratifications which the infant wishes for himself' (p. 103).

Clinical example: avoidance of the father

Kay was an only child whose parents appear to have had a rather fused relationship. Mother had been dependent and depressed and father had lavished all his love and care on mother. Father, however, died when Kay was 10 years old. Kay had dealt with this by cutting off all memories of father, excluding him in the way she had felt excluded and regressing into a merged state with her mother, recovering thus the pre-Oedipal mother who had in fantasy belonged only to her. When her mother eventually moved to a retirement home in another town, she sought out the Women's Therapy Centre in some desperation, hoping to recapture with a female therapist the experience of fusion she had just lost. Her mother's move to another town must have indicated to Kay that mother had a separate life of her own. I think this must have recalled to her in quite an unbearable way the early loss of mother to father.

At the Women's Therapy Centre, she had six months therapy with a psychotherapist who worked in a humanistic way. This therapist then left the centre and Kay consented to continue therapy with me. At first she attempted simply to recreate with me the fused state she had achieved with her first therapist, denying that she found me any different and expressing her certainty that her relationship with me would be exactly the same as the one she had lost. She insisted, if ever I suggested otherwise, that we were perfectly in accord, especially as I was a therapist working in a Centre for women, and would therefore know and understand her experience as a woman.

However, as therapy progressed, she found that, unlike her previous therapist, I maintained time and touch boundaries that became for her increasingly difficult to tolerate as they disturbed the illusion of oneness with me. She began for the first time since her father died to have recurring dreams about him that brought back shatteringly vivid memories of being excluded from her parents' relationship. At one point I interpreted her growing discomfort with the therapeutic boundaries as her dismay and rage at re-encountering her strict father who had stopped her having ready access to mother. A few days after this session she left a stammered out message on my answerphone saying she felt she was breaking down and had to end therapy because she could no longer manage without her mother and was, in fact, that very day moving away to live with her. In a follow-up session we had a few months later when she felt able to return for a one-off session, she told me that her panic had been precipitated by my suggestion that she had encountered her father in me. The strict excluding father I had become in the transference induced in her the same feelings of rage, helplessness and threat of personal annihilation that had come in infancy when she had been deprived of her fused relationship with mother. In a similar way to her father, I must have seemed to exclude her from the warmth and safety of the fused relationship she had experienced with her previous therapist. It has been suggested that while the patiently containing attitude of the therapist is a maternal function, the therapist's limiting function in attending to the boundaries is a paternal one (Chasseguet-Smirgel 1984). In this way at least, even with a female therapist, father representing otherness cannot in the end be avoided. Nor should he be avoided, because it is only through negotiating the disappointments of the Oedipal phase that an individual can form relationships not on the basis of fusion but from a knowledge of personal autonomy and the autonomy of others.

Conclusion

Our identities have taken shape in a world that is biologically and culturally divided into two sexes. The realities of gender must therefore have at least some impact upon the therapist/patient relationship, organising the client's phantasies and giving particular form to transference expressions and conflicts. In this chapter, I have used clinical material where the starting point of therapy has been an urgent need for a therapist of a particular sex. In such instances, I would suggest that gender issues do markedly affect the transference, pointing to the central anxieties, conflicts and hopes of the client.

References

Balint, E. (1973) 'Technical problems found in the analysis of women by a woman analyst: a contribution to the question "What does a woman want?"'. In G. Kohon (ed.) *The British School of Psychoanalysis: The Independent Tradition.* London: Free Association Books (1986 edition).

Bernstein, D. (1990) 'Female genital anxieties, conflicts and typical mastery modes'. *International Journal of Psycho-Analysis* 71: 151–165.

Bettelheim, B. (1976) *The Uses of Enchantment.* London: Thames and Hudson.

Bollas, C. (1987) *The Shadow of the Object: Psychoanalysis of the Unthought Known.* London: Free Association Books.

Chasseguet-Smirgel, J. (1984) 'The femininity of the analyst in professional practice'. *International Journal of Psycho-Analysis* 65: 169–178.

Fenichel, O. (1945) *The Psychoanalytic Theory of Neurosis.* New York: Norton.

Freud, S. (1924) 'The dissolution of the Oedipus Complex'. *Standard Edition* Vol. 19: 178.

Freud, S. (1931) 'Female sexuality'. *Standard Edition* Vol. 21: 225–243. London: Hogarth Press.

Kris, E. (1952) *Explorations in Art.* New York: International Universities Press.

Lasky, R. (1989) 'Some determinants of the male analyst's capacity to identify with female patients'. *International Journal of Psycho-Analysis* 70: 405–418.

Lester, E. (1990) 'Gender and identity issues in the analytic process'. *International Journal of Psycho-Analysis* 71: 435–444.

Samuels, A. (1985) 'The image of the parents in bed'. In A. Samuels (ed.) *The Father: Contemporary Jungian Perspectives.* London: Free Association Books.

Samuels, A. (1989) *The Plural Psyche: Personality, Morality and the Father.* London: Routledge.

Searles, H. (1959) 'Oedipal love in the counter-transference'. In H. Searles (ed.) *Collected Papers on Schizophrenia and Related Subjects.* London: Hogarth Press (1968 edition).

Segal, H. (1973) *Introduction to the Work of Melanie Klein.* London: Hogarth Press.

Stoller, J. (1968) *Sex and Gender.* London: Hogarth Press.

Winnicott, D. (1971) *Playing and Reality.* London: Tavistock Publications.

Chapter 9

Lesbian homoerotic transference in dialectic with developmental mourning

On the way to symbolism from the protosymbolic

Susan Kavaler-Adler

This clinical study illustrates the developmental nature of homoerotic transference, when the psychoanalyst is attuned to the evolving dynamics of the mourning process, in this case with a lesbian analysand. The analysand's psychic fantasies of the female analyst as a muse and a demon lover figure are seen to transform into discrete mother and father transferences, as split off feminine and aggressive parts of the self are reintegrated along with heterosexual desires and Oedipal desires. Protosymbolic enactments in terms of romantic gift giving and other seductive overtures transform into symbolic expressions of love, concern, regret and tenderness. A lesbian marriage is preserved and the loss of intimacy with men is mourned so that desires for intimacy with men can be sublimated.

The case described here demonstrates how an attunement to object-related contact, within the course of psychoanalysis, allows a natural mourning process to unfold, thus contributing to an ongoing positive evolution in the use of the erotic transference in treatment. To understand the interaction of the erotic transference and the developmental mourning process, it is necessary to view erotic desires not merely as drive impulses, but also as expressions of object-related desires, with a full range of Oedipal and pre-Oedipal dimensions. The psychic fantasies that emerge within the erotic transference can in this context be seen to chart a developmental course, crystallizing the intense and multi-textured, object-related desires. Symbolizing these desires inevitably leads to loss and grief, as symbolization is a developmental separation process (Kavaler-Adler 1988, 1992, 1993a, 1993b, 1995, 1996, 1998, 2000, 2003a, 2003b, 2004, 2005a, 2006b). It is through the mourning of this loss and grief that psychic structure transformation becomes possible (as opposed to the 'symbolic equation', Segal 1986). Without this mourning process evolution, erotic transference can act as a resistance to psychic change, as Freud first warned in 1915.

'Potential space' (Winnicott 1971; Ogden 1986), or psychic space, opens as developmental mourning evolves out of the normal disillusionment created by the symbolic expression of erotic desires. There is a gradual relinquishing of the old object constellations that bind Oedipal and pre-Oedipal object longings within the framework of historically formed character structure. Where Fairbairn (1952) spoke of letting go of the bad object, I speak of letting go of the erotically desired Oedipal object through symbolizing desire and tolerating the affects of loss and grief that the inevitable disillusionment of desire demands. Symbolization, connecting to the affective engagement with longing and loss, culminates in the capacity for new external object relations – external in the sense that they exist beyond the internal world where the cherished Oedipal object and objects prevail. The Oedipal object then is not simply renounced, but relinquished with a transformational flourish, leading to renewed and evolving object relations engagement with the external world. This process does not simply involve saying goodbye to an incestuous object and hello to a non-incestuous object, for such an exchange would not transform initial psychic structure. Rather, it consists of relinquishing internal world ties and transferring affective links to these objects through symbolized psychic fantasies onto new external objects. Thus true intimacy can be achieved – intimacy at an adult level, colored and enhanced by the richness of childhood Oedipal wishes.

Such a journey is necessary for healthy heterosexual and healthy homosexual maturity to evolve. Homosexual erotic transference has the same power and intensity as heterosexual erotic transference. Like the heterosexual erotic transference, homosexual erotic transference is multi-layered and multi-textured with differentiated Oedipal desire genital intensities interacting with pre-Oedipal hungers. The Oedipal love object always causes the projections of an early breast mother as well as the more differentiated Oedipal object. Homoerotic transference occurs with heterosexual, homosexual and bisexual analysands. It is, therefore, of particular interest to study the nature of the erotic transference with homosexual and bisexual analysands in relation to a heterosexual analyst. Such cases, permitting us to see that the journey from protosymbolic enactment in the course of psychoanalytic regression to symbolic expression, punctuated by the affects and memories of mourning, offer a unique perspective on a developmental progression that also occurs in heterosexual analysands. The heterosexual can discover the homosexual energies in full object relations analysis, just as the homosexual can discover heterosexual energies in extensive analysis. The common denominator is mourning as a developmental process. The case vignette I describe here, from a longer case study, highlights the journey of mourning as developmental process. The subject is a lesbian who was in treatment with me, a female heterosexual analyst. In this treatment situation the intensity of the analysand's erotic transference held the potential of blossoming into a symbolic level where mourning could occur only through the transition of protosymbolic enactments expressed in the form of wooing and courting the analyst.

When I speak of the protosymbolic expression of erotic transference, I mean sensory and visceral experiences, with powerful pressures for behavioral enactment, but with little representational form in the patient's internal world or secondary process. By symbolic expression, I refer to vivid verbal descriptions of psychic fantasy constructed from differentiated whole object characters. The individual's vivid verbal descriptions gradually separate out from impulsive visceral and somatic reactions, gradually becoming an adequate container of transference longings in treatment sessions, without enactments by phone or concrete gifts (with unanalyzed motives) of the undefined visceral impulses outside the perimeter of analytic sessions.

'Pauline' is a middle-aged woman who had been living in a lesbian relationship for many years when she entered treatment. She was formerly married to a man for many years and left the former marriage due to the abusive behavior of her husband, as well as her interest in other men and women as romantic partners. She is a highly intelligent and intellectual woman of strong academic interests who had been a university professor, at the graduate level, for 16 years. She has a child from her former marriage who is grown up and lives in another state.

One of Pauline's presenting problems when beginning psychoanalysis with me was that of compulsions to fantasize having affairs with women other than her long-term partner and extreme terrors that she would act on these fantasies and lose the love and security of her lesbian marriage. She was also hidden behind the façade of a butch pseudomasculine identity when she began treatment. She dressed in a masculine manner and believed that she was 'in disguise', so that others would not suspect her extreme emotional vulnerability. It was during treatment that she came to discard her masculine mode of dress and to dress and groom herself in a distinctly feminine manner. She came to re-own the feminine side of herself so that she could integrate her masculine and feminine attributes in a true self that was vulnerable, receptive, and aggressive in a much less stereotyped manner than had been her practice.

The first three years of thrice-weekly analysis for Pauline involved an intense mourning process, which transformed the nature of her transference expressions, particularly her erotic transference expressions. To describe the varying forms of developmental evolution that open up naturally in an object relations psychoanalytic treatment, I call the mourning process a 'developmental mourning' process (see Kavaler-Adler, 1988, 1992, 1993a, 1993b) 1995, 1998, 2000, 2003a, 2003b, 2004, 2005, 2006a, 2006b). Such a developmental evolution involves the integration of self through abandonment-depression mourning related to pre-Oedipal separation-individuation loss and trauma, grief for narcissistic wounds, grief for unrequited love with its Oedipal disillusionments, mourning of actual object loss (as in the parents' death), depressive-position existential-mourning of grief related to hurting the love object, and mourning of depressive pain related to the relinquishment of omnipotence and the acceptance of existential limits. These modes of mourning characterized the developmental process in this analysand. Pauline's developmental mourning continued throughout her fourth and fifth years of treatment, but the first three years of mourning and its working through allowed significant transformations to become highlighted and defined during the fourth year.

Although traditionally the erotic transference has been viewed as a defense against remembering, I believe that from an object relations perspective the erotic transference provides a transitional object experience for the analysand. As such, it offers an avenue to consciousness for the deepest desires and conflicts of the internal world. In addition, erotic transference helps access memory despite inhibiting it by functioning as a protective screen against experiencing the links to differentiated recall. Why can erotic transference function in this seemingly contradictory manner? The most intense erotic desires always originate from early infant experience, as well as from every level of pre-Oedipal and Oedipal experience, and from all that experience derived from both the pre-Oedipal and Oedipal levels whose influence continues into adolescence and adulthood. Whether the erotic transference is a defense against or an avenue to the unconscious depends on its reaching the symbolic level of felt and then spoken psychic fantasy.

However, for this erotic transference to be contained and then transformed from the protosymbolic sensory and visceral level to a symbolic level of differentiated psychic fantasy and differentiated affects of love, lust, aggression, and tenderness, the developmental mourning process is essential. I first demonstrated this in 'Mourning and Erotic Transference' (Kavaler-Adler 1992, Chapter 6 in this book), describing the treatment of a male analysand. What I present here is an excerpt from a more recent case, in which I focus on the critical role of mourning and erotic transference in a lesbian (Kavaler-Adler 2003b).

Pauline's erotic and homoerotic transference

From the onset of treatment, Pauline's erotic transference was front-stage center, and Pauline herself was aware that from the beginning I was an object of desire. Through the emergence and expression of the erotic transference in treatment, Pauline gained insight into her primal yearnings for her mother that could compel her into perpetual enactments in her life, sabotaging her attempts to commit to a long-term, intimate relationship. But she was only able to relinquish the compulsion to enact this erotic transference in her outside life, through behavior that was potentially sabotaging to herself and her long-term monogamous and committed love relationship with a female partner, after she surrendered to repeated cycles of developmental mourning. In the process of this surrender, she let go of her primal mother and father. With developmental mourning, she opened up psychic space in which she could develop a new relationship with me as a transitional object. Then, using this relationship as a base, she was able to develop new psychic internalizations that could be carried to other relationships.

From the beginning of treatment, Pauline experienced me as her artist muse, a form of mother-muse-lover. Her mother had in fact been an artist.

Pauline both wished and feared that I would become her 'Demon Lover' (Kavaler-Adler 1993a, 1996), the dark and powerfully erotic side of this mother-muse-lover trinity. When she first asked to be in treatment with me she expected me to attract her and repel her simultaneously, just as her mother had. I embodied the transference displacement of her Oedipal fantasy mother, just as many other women had for her, particularly women writers and artists – both gay and straight – with whom she had fantasized having affairs. Pauline presented herself as agonizing over what she considered to be her sinful betrayal, not in her behavior but in her thoughts, of her steady live-in lover and partner, whom she 'loved more than life itself'. Pauline trod her course in her own words, like a 'hamster on a wheel', always turning her head toward some new female attraction, having let go of the idea of having male lovers following her divorce from her husband and prior to her long-term lesbian relationship. She reported experiencing her attraction to me as an 'ocean of longing'. This feeling was accompanied by repulsion and terror at entering a hopeless land of endless and unfulfilled desire, where she would suffer once again the agony of intense abandonment and self-annihilation, which for her were integral components of unrequited love. Entering my office, she had in her head the whole script of an anticipated romance based on sexualized needs for an early maternal responsiveness, as well as on profound and frustrated Oedipal desires, placed and displaced onto a woman. This script, which became a fantasy blueprint for her agenda within the psychoanalytic situation, had been developed and rewritten within her mind over several decades, the result of multiple forays and mishaps in matters of the heart. I fit vividly into Pauline's category of artist-muse-lover as I possessed, according to her, an 'erotic intellect' and a flamboyant personal style and language. I also fit into the category of artist – her mother's category, which made me a muse, because I had written two books and many articles about women writers and artists. So I presented a convenient target for her projections of (the muse-goddess-artist) an idealized fantasy of her mother as a narcissistic extension of herself. Pauline could cling to her fantasy ideal mother to buttress her own inadequate sense of self. Her higher level romantic desires overlapped with her pre-Oedipal hungers for a self-extension perceived as being outside of herself.

I became the target both for Pauline's self needs and her instinctual oral and genital desires. I also became a target for her projections of the dark side of that role, as the erotic demon lover, similar to Fairbairn's exciting and rejecting object. One of Pauline's initial fantasies of me was that I would stab her in the vagina with a knife while she was on the couch. I certainly was at first the phallic mother for her, reflected in her initial fears of my interpretations. Only erratically, with some trust in me developing during the first year of treatment, could Pauline take in and digest my interpretations. Initially threatened by them, she needed to understand their connection to her fantasies of me as a dangerous phallic mother. Pauline later told me that when I sat in a certain high-backed chair I had seemed like this awesome, omnipotent judge. She was too intimidated by this image of me to tell me how she felt at this time. Gradually she could experience the deep emotional connection between her internal phallic mother and its projection onto me by mourning her disillusionments in the transference. This mourning process brought Pauline's memories of her mother's cutting rejections and threatened abandonments alive in the moment.

But this lay ahead. During this early treatment stage, Pauline was quite emphatic in expressing her wish to turn the tables on me, placing me in the same vulnerable position of need and desire she so feared being in herself. She wanted me to want her from a helpless position of out-of-control desire. And she split off and projected onto me her own unconscious internal infant and child psychic states, which evolved into the open format of analysis though her expression of erotic transference fantasies whose meaning became increasingly clear with each phase of mourning during treatment. In the beginning of treatment, I felt the power of her affect in a highly visceral and sensory form, as described by her own phrase as an 'ocean of longing'. She idealized me. In one of her dreams during this period, I appeared as a huge female icon, floating high above her in the air, and then descending to her bed within a theater used for grand operas and stage productions, where she found herself. In this same dream, I had long flowing hair and wore a colorful silk gown. I also had an erect penis, despite my exaggerated female attire and my role as an icon.

Pauline's goddess image of me was accompanied by paranoid thoughts. She broadcast her general sense of distrust at the beginning of treatment via her description of the scene in another dream, which followed the other, and which directly preceded her first consultation with me. In this other dream she unzipped her chest, gave me her heart, and then experienced the terrible sense of a black hole of unrequited love, which she fantasized as having the huge enormity of the Grand Canyon.

Despite the terror that she exhibited during our first sessions, Pauline gradually began to trust me. This initial trust allowed her to share with me her first erotic transference fantasies. She was a brave soul from the start, and her courage extended to an acute curiosity about her own internal life. So she shared these fantasies as they arose during our sessions, along with intense feelings within her body, suggesting layers of unsymbolized somatic expressions of her most profound desires (protosymbolic) that accompanied the symbolic level of her fantasies and associations. On the level of conscious fantasy she reported visions of having an affair with me in my office, where she would order me: 'spread your legs', and would 'take your pearl in my mouth, drown in your come, and then wrap you in a blanket and feed you'.

This fantasy also included a negative Oedipal triangle, which revealed itself in her free associations to the fantasy. Pauline imagined meeting my husband after he banged on my office door, entering my office in an enraged state (one form of primal scene fantasy). She imagined engaging in an open skirmish with him as he jealously 'defended his territory'. Another frequent fantasy, with a multitude of variations, was of her being an audience of one, watching while a man – sometimes my husband – made love to me. In this fantasy, she cheered me on to orgasms as my male lover forced me into a state of submission by beating me – which she imagined I would love – or merely penetrated me, as I surrendered to him in a state of passionate and hungry lust, from a passive receptive position. She also imagined herself as the male lover, or as the other woman in a 'ménage à trois' with a male lover who appealed to both of us, providing each of us with pleasure.

Pauline revealed many levels of erotic fantasy during treatment. At first she longed to make love to me as one woman to another, wishing me to be in the more vulnerable and receptive position, while she was in the more active phallic role. Later, during the third year of treatment, Pauline went through a phase of picturing me as a phallic woman, as in her dream reported earlier, who penetrated her with my penis. This fantasy interacted with her father transference projections onto me, and with the full emergence of her identifications with her father as the seductive male among women, the 'cock of the walk'. Still later, during the fourth year, she imagined a triadic relationship, in which, in her male persona, she and another 'man' penetrated me, or, conversely, in her female persona, she was penetrated by me in my male persona and by another man in the same scene. The man was anonymous in the scene of her being penetrated along with me, but when she was the one penetrating me along with another man, her fantasy would sometimes portray this other man as my husband. Ultimately, Pauline reported an orgasm fantasy of being ravished anally by a group of male father figures, which she had reported within the first year of treatment, changing during the fifth year of treatment into the fantasy of a highly mutual and erotic intercourse with such father figures, with diminished sadomasochistic dynamics.

At times, throughout the first three years of her treatment in particular, Pauline also expressed her erotic negative transference in sadomasochistic wishes to throw me against the wall and 'fuck' me then and there in the treatment room. I interpreted the connection between her wish for love through anal submission and her wish to have me submit to her as she had me do in her fantasy of throwing me against the wall and fucking me. However, at the moment of rage and desire, I could not interpret this. It had to be 'strike when the iron is cold', as Fred Pine (1985) speaks of when addressing clinical work with those of primary developmental trauma and developmental arrest. At the moment of rage and desire, the compulsive urge toward exhibition was at its height. Only when Pauline was feeling loss and was therefore more in contact with her inner self could I ask her to define her anger, bringing the protosymbolic exhibitionism to a symbolic level. The intensity of both her rage and desire was at such moments palpable. Nevertheless, over time, her ability to entertain interpretations about the transference implications of these and other fantasies developed as she worked through her mourning process.

Although Pauline could express these psychic fantasies to me verbally during the first three years of treatment, she still had great difficulty coping with the highly visceral body experiences that accompanied her report of these fantasies to me. Sometimes Pauline stopped in the midst of describing such a fantasy, cutting off her verbal level of functioning, because she became overwhelmingly dizzy or felt suffocated as she literally felt as if she were choking on her emotions. Then, feeling it impossible to breathe lying down, she would sit up to feel she could breathe. She could not say the words of love to me at this earlier time, during the first two years of treatment. She could say the words of love by her third year, when she had mourned her primal mother loss, from pre-Oedipal separation – individuation stage trauma – and could differentiate her feelings, her thoughts, me, and her internal mother. Thus, her somatic discomfort lessened, and she felt a freedom to articulate her desires as she found the words to express her love and her wishes to be loved. She could say the words later, relieved of the former pain and of the tremendous backlash reactions of guilt and despair that came when she associated to fears of having betrayed her real-life lover by declaring her (transferential) love for me. When I interpreted Pauline's guilt and fear, it helped. Pauline's guilt could turn to concern as she realized, with my help, that she was afraid of hurting her lovers as she had been hurt by her mother's rejections. Pauline could then differentiate her transference love from her love for her real-life partner.

Pauline was still unconscious of the incestuous nature of her longings for me and the guilt and shame they invoked. Yet, during this period when her verbalization of her feelings was first becoming possible, during her second and third years of treatment, she would often leave her psychoanalytic session overwhelmed. Frequently unable to complete her sentences, she left at the end of a session only to discover that she often could not sustain the connection with me until the next session without calling me beforehand in a state of terror and despair at how she thought she had offended me. I interpreted Pauline's fears of me, as her transferential mother, retaliating. I also emphasized, however, Pauline's genuine desires to connect with me at the very primal level and her fear of losing that connection as she had lost her mother. This calmed her. Only later could true reparation be made, when she let go of me as her transferential mother and surrendered to the vivid experience of loss in developmental mourning. Her visceral intrusions and disruptions, as well as her guilt-ridden backlashes, changed as she traversed the stages of developmental mourning. This transition is encapsulated during the first three years of treatment in her using and then relinquishing a concrete romantic gift – a gift which condensed her longings in an inchoate, preverbal and protosymbolic form.

From the protosymbolic to the symbolic: giving the romantic gift

In the beginning of treatment Pauline attempted to enact a fantasized love affair, which she imagined taking place between us, by sending me beautiful long-stemmed red roses. Even after discussing with me her impulse to send them, she felt compelled at times to actually act it out. There were also many other times when she thought she would send them and restrained herself, but the impulse to call the flower shop was powerfully acute. On the occasions when she did send this romantic gift, she wanted the beauty of the flowers to speak their own symbolism. She reported that she imagined them opening to me with a full color and redolence that possibly represented the way she felt her mind and body opening to me. So in this action, as in her fantasies, Pauline was able to play a masculine and a feminine role. In courting me by sending flowers, she enacted her male persona, while in symbolizing her body opening to me through the opening of the blooming roses, she enacted her female persona. Pauline said later during her fourth and fifth years of analysis, that when she sent me flowers she was regressing to an early psychic place, a child's place, where words never adequately expressed feelings. Only an image or symbolic gift could.

It was through the mourning process that Pauline was able to move beyond the enactment of wooing me through actually sending flowers to using the flowers as a symbolic expression of her own feelings. Increasingly, she began to verbalize her flowering feelings. As psychic space opened within her, Pauline felt her feelings toward me while in the room with me at a level that grew increasingly tolerable for her. Through mourning a lifetime of losses, her psychic fantasies became better containers for her feelings, felt subjectively as unrequited love. In this process, Pauline opened to her primal longings for the first time. She offered them to me verbally. For example, she reported, 'I want you so much right now' or 'I'm feeling this feeling in my vagina, wanting you'. It was only at this point that she could describe her erotic transference fantasies without splitting them off into compulsive activities and obsessional thinking outside the sessions. It was important for me to receive these expressions of her feelings without interpreting at the time. She needed to feel that both her love and her aggression could be accepted by me. In Winnicott's terms, she needed to see that I could 'survive' her impulses and passions. She needed to know I heard her and was not rejecting her as she expected me to in her anticipatory script of unrequited love and repetition of the traumatic experience with her mother. However, because I was not responding to her expressions of love as a lover, she experienced me as rejecting her Oedipal wishes, which had served, in part, as a defense against pre-Oedipal rejection. Such disappointments, experienced at tolerable levels in treatment, led Pauline to a tolerance of loss and with its painful grief affect, evolving into an overall mourning process.

It was only at this stage of treatment that Pauline began to reveal the deeper longings that were now becoming differentiated from the diffuse ocean of desire within her. She expressed the heartfelt yearnings that had formerly been split off and projected onto the 'other'. She was able to own and articulate the wish to sit in my lap and for me to stroke her hair, as well as the wish to be held and comforted at my breast like an infant. Such moments of courageous revelation spoke volumes about the tender child within, but these wishes also revealed a dark side, resonating to the most primal terrors of the muse mother turned demonic. For example, when Pauline announced her core wish to inhabit a special place in my vagina, through phallic penetration (which would result in her living inside of my womb), the underbelly of her fantasy flipped dramatically into her consciousness. She reported a black, swirling terror erupting from within, a vortex comprised of an infinity of darkness. This was the visual representation of what she experienced as the impinging threat of her being suffocated and lost inside my womb, as it turned into an infinite black hole. The fantasy flipped to the dark side, repeatedly, each time I failed to instantly reciprocate her feelings. If I did not express feelings akin to her own (twinship transference), I became the sadistically withholding mother of 'unrequited love'. But with the container of the holding environment of psychoanalytic treatment, Pauline could feel rage and disappointment, ultimately surrendering to the grief of loss that opened a rebirth of connection to her inner self, her internal world, and to others in her interpersonal world.

Glimpses of developmental mourning in treatment

If mourning helps to create a safe analytic space to contain the erotic transference in treatment, disappointments in erotic transference wishes also open up grief and mourning. Cycles of mourning and erotic transference interact. As they do psychic fantasies become more refined and verbal, a new capacity for digesting transference interpretations emerges, and the nature of the erotic fantasies evolves from sadomasochistic to mutually interpenetrating dimensions.

Pauline showed all these trends as she navigated the many forms of mourning during analysis. With each transference disillusionment, she relived an experience of unrequited love. When she first felt unlovable and unwanted by me because in her mind I was not playing the role of the lover in her transference script, she experienced primitive abandonment and annihilation terrors. These terrors originated when she was 3 years old (perhaps even earlier), after her mother, angry at Pauline's father, threatened to leave him and therefore threatened to leave Pauline and her entire family. After recovering from the black hole sense of self-dissolution, Pauline was able, aided by my support and presence, during her second year of treatment, to recall her mother's dramatic displays of threatening departure – signaled by her putting on red lipstick.

This memory led to other memories of her mother periodically withdrawing to bed, leaving her feeling emotionally abandoned and devastated.

She remembered her mother's punitive cold rages whenever Pauline expressed either implicitly or explicitly her own needs. And she recalled now, too, her mother's total withdrawal when Pauline was 14 years old and first experienced erotic feelings for other females. The mother's extreme emotional withdrawal at this time was a retaliatory reaction to her daughter not fitting into the mother's beliefs concerning what she thought her daughter should be, as the mother wished to gratify her own narcissism. Pauline's sexual interest in girls and women threatened her mother's whole image system that supported her mother's narcissistic defenses. Feeling narcissistically affronted by Pauline being herself, which involved feeling attracted to females at camp, Pauline's mother withdrew all her warmth and proceeded vindictively to punish Pauline through her own form of narcissistic injury. Recalling this led Pauline to remember many incidents in which she had suffered narcissistic injury because of her mother's behavior. Her mother's favored weapons were contempt and sarcastic ridicule. More than once during Pauline's childhood and adolescence the mother had slapped the daughter when she dared to disagree with or express anger at her.

At other times, Pauline's transference disillusionments in relation to the analyst, which she experienced as unrequited love, brought up memories of acute and traumatic loss triggered by rejections from women who served as mother displacements. These other muse goddess experiences (occurring prior to my taking that projected role in the transference) ranged from a latency and teenage love for a girlfriend to many rejections by straight women who were threatened by her intensity when she claimed that she wanted to be friends only, and to her rejection by a bisexual woman, when Pauline was in her early thirties. This last rejection occurred after Pauline had been married for many years to the husband whom she soon separated from after this attempted affair. At this stage of her life, Pauline saw the artistic woman she was enamored with as potentially offering her the only chance to give and receive love, especially with a female. When such a hope was harshly repudiated, she fell apart, but with the support of her previous psychotherapy she established a lesbian identity and connected with a lesbian community. Specifically, Pauline was able to form a deep love attachment to a woman prior to her analysis with me, and with this growing and developing lesbian relationship she was supported in her attempts to assume an identification with other lesbians that she discovered in New York. Nevertheless, each of her losses still demanded grieving, which Pauline, with increasing depth, plunged into during our analysis. She mourned all her maternal abandonments and unrequited love affairs with women and then the grief of losing men as intimate and sexual partners. In addition, she mourned the split off, needy and dependent child part of her, as she reconnected with it through re-owning what she had projected onto me in her erotic fantasies.

A dream brought up an opportunity for interpreting her fear of her own needs. Pauline dreamed of throwing fish endlessly back into a boat. She associated this endless and fruitless task with trying to meet my needs. I interpreted her seeing me as an insatiable mother whose needs and demands overwhelmed her. However, I also interpreted that she was projecting her own overwhelming needs and demands into me as a transferential mother. She got angry. I was interfering with her script of repeating rage at an overly demanding, narcissistic mother. After her anger she found insight and began to understand my interpretations. She acknowledged her understanding by saying that she was afraid she would be too much for me. I then interpreted that her mother had seemed to experience Pauline as too much for her, leaving her feeling hopeless about having any needs at all. Seeing her needs as my needs, I continued, was a way of defending against her hopelessness and the related anxiety.

Following this Pauline mourned the latent feminine side of her personality that had been split off when she assumed a masculine persona in the world. Femininity and helpless dependence had been associated in her mind, so to not seem too needy she had rejected her feminine side. As she regained the split off parts of her psyche, such as her potential feminine self, Pauline felt more whole and better equipped to deal with other forms of mourning.

In order for Pauline to regain the split off feminine part of herself, I needed to interpret a whole line of projective identification. Through projective identification, Pauline had mentally 'put into' me her identity as a woman. She saw me as being her feminine self on a protosymbolic level or on the level of the paranoid-schizoid position. On the level of the depressive position, where she could experience symbolic meanings, she saw me as 'representing' her feminine self or identity. I addressed this with her, after the point of interpreting her distaste for feminine identity within herself as when she associated such femininity with neediness and helpless dependence on a narcissistic mother.

It was clear that her view of her defensive disowning of a feminine identity was ego syntonic. The dialog between us went something like this: I said that she was using me as her disowned feminine self. By being absorbed in me and all my feminine attributes, including my mode of dressing, she was avoiding her own need for a female identity and for the development of a potential authentic feminine side of her personality. I said this was a problem. She retorted, 'That's the solution.' She said she was quite content to use me as her feminine self. I reiterated that that was 'the problem'. She laughed and replied, 'No! That's the solution!' However, as Pauline entered the depressive position more and more through the mourning process, nature took its course, and she decided that she had needs for a feminine part of herself that she had denied. She realized that she wanted to be seen as beautiful, not just as handsome. Her lover balked at her wish to wear a dress and more feminine clothing in general. However, she was able to express to her lover the pain of always being in the position of the adoring lover who worshipped the beauty of the other woman. She exclaimed that she wanted to be seen as beautiful, even if she did not have the same form of beauty as her mother. She began to wear a brooch of her mother's and other items of jewelry that her mother might have worn. She could only do this when she had consciously processed her rage at her mother's rejections and thus could forgive her mother and re-own a wish to identify with her, while also retaining her lesbian object choice and her separate identity as a woman who could erotically love and adore other women.

The depressive position

The other forms of mourning seen in Pauline's process, as a form of therapeutic action in developmental terms, fall within Melanie Klein's depressive position – the mourning of guilt and loss related to hurting the person we love, as well as the grief of accepting the losses that come with acknowledging existential limits and our mortality. The latter was often experienced by Pauline as the relinquishment of certain aspects of heterosexual love and life. Pauline experienced the depressive pain in the transference with me. She felt the grief of regret after angry, negative transference projections, in which she accused me of being her cold, abandoning mother, or the 'Medusa', 'Gorgon head' mother of frigid rejection in her teenage years. At this time Pauline first indirectly revealed to her mother that she was homosexual by being attracted to girls at camp, which was reported to her mother by the camp director. Now Pauline yearned to repair her former relationship with her mother through her relationship with me. She tried to regain the sense of love she had formerly felt for her mother, prior to her mother's emotional withdrawal when Pauline was 14 years old and had revealed her lesbian proclivities. She sought to regain the love connection to her mother by relinquishing the defenses against the grief and loss she felt in having lost her mother, opening areas of psychic receptivity by accepting sadness and longing. She also faced a formerly unconscious guilt that followed her paranoid rage. After experiencing many cycles of mother loss and disruptions between us in the transitional object relationship, followed by reparation and a renewed love born out of her deep grief of mournful sadness, Pauline opened to new modes of interpersonal dialectic with me. She opened too to the dialectical understanding of self and other contained in my transference interpretations. In Thomas Ogden's (1986) words, she became by the fourth year of treatment an 'interpreting subject', with the capacity to reflect on her own experience from a more separate and dialectical perspective and to take in my interpretations as gifts of insight to digest and use. She had previously experienced such interpretations as assaults on her wishes to merge directly with me through sensory and visceral erotic overtures, as she had indeed attempted to do during the earlier stages of treatment. In this fourth year, however, Pauline reported that she felt sad about 'giving up the fantasy of being your lover' in her own mind. What led to this point was Pauline's relinquishing of her protosymbolic activity of sending me roses and calling me outside the perimeter of an analytic session. She had used the roses and calls as an attempt to repair what she experienced as a break between us during a session, at times when she would accuse me of being cold and rejecting, just like her mother.

Pauline's increasing use of her own symbolic fantasies to contain her affect, rather than employing them in an attempt to seduce me into an enactment of a wish for sexual merger with an idealized artist mother, was shown in how she greeted me on my return from a vacation during the fourth year of treatment. Her vivid words depicted me as a separate and erotically desired lover. But her meaning this time was clearly metaphorical and symbolical. She visualized entering me, upon my return, as a man penetrates a woman, but also as a woman penetrates a woman, 'with your beautiful vulva and clitoris opening like a flower, glowing, radiant and receptive'. She then expressed her joy in being with me in reality in a session in a sublimated way, surrendering her former attitude of pressuring me into responding to her erotic love overtures. Mourning disillusionments of the idealized mother in the transference, mourning unrequited love, and mourning the grief of hostile encounters with her internal cold mother, frequently projected onto me, all led to this point.

An example of mourning through reparative dialogue following depressive grief

How does the transference in this treatment expose the painful regret, highlighted in Melanie Klein's theory, of hurting the one you love? Pauline speaks to me through this aspect of her transference. Her own words illuminate how the process works. 'It was so heartbreaking after I left that other session, when I got so cold, I felt like all the warmth in the world was gone, like those days when my mother withdrew to her bed and it felt like the sun never would come out. That's why I had to call you afterwards!' The yearning for reconnection to a loving bond with me was unconscious at this point, but her fears of me retaliating were less conscious. Pauline acknowledged her own aggression, but could only see her fears of my aggression after her longing for a renewed bond of love was validated. In these remarks Pauline was exploring why she had called me after a session during which she was angry and accusatory toward me, just before I left for summer vacation. She was terrified I would leave without her being able to make reparations to me. She had tried to coerce me into apologizing to her during that session for something I had allegedly done during the previous session. After she left my office following this session, she grew concerned that she had hurt me. She had never seen herself as cold and accusatory – that had been primarily her experience of her mother whenever her mother was angry. But each time Pauline experienced the pain of her regret after expressing anger at me, she increasingly realized that she could act in the same cold, sarcastic and accusatory manner as her mother. This realization was partly prompted by my comments about her behavior, as I attempted to respond without submitting to her coercion. It was extremely difficult for Pauline to perceive her own coldness because, as she observed, it hadn't been part of her self-concept. Pauline found it painful to understand that she could be cold like her mother. Yet, she did (and does) know that she had hurt me and, once hit by the pain of this awareness, her sense of regret, as well as her fear of abandonment, compelled her to repair her connection with me as quickly as possible by apologizing. She imagined that I must have been bitterly disappointmented in her and personally hurt because, after all I had done for her, she had acted so ungratefully. Pauline's regret seemed to express genuine concern for me at this point, not merely a defensive fear of retaliation from me as the feared maternal object. Both this and her ability to reflect on her own self-concept in terms of how aggressive parts of herself (modeled on her mother) were left out of this self-concept signified that she was operating more within the depressive position than she had been formerly. Pauline was reflecting rather than reacting, increasingly over time, as she mourned her real childhood experiences with her mother, as well as her wishes inscribed in psychic fantasy. She began to see herself as well as her mother from a more separate and objective position.

She could not wait to tell me of these insights and to see my face and to hear my voice again. She was terrified that she had killed off all the warmth between us and all the warmth in me. She said that she was afraid I would never again show her approval or the warmth in my eyes or the warmth of my smile. In fact, she feared that I would never smile at her again. She feared I would freeze up and turn into the Gorgon's head, the head of Medusa – the image of the cold stone-faced mother she had seen at the dinner table when she was 14 years old.

Unlike earlier in her childhood, when Pauline turned 14 years old, she reciprocated her mother's rage. The ensuing coldness was bitter. Fearing that she would never regain her warm mother, Pauline fell into despair. Her relationship with her mother seemed over forever. Despite her own anger, she felt terribly guilty at seeing her mother's accusatory stare; she believed that she had stabbed her mother with her anger. This belief, however, was mixed in with the feeling that her mother had stabbed her. Perhaps to defend herself against total loss of love, Pauline transformed the terror of being stabbed in the heart to the castration of being stabbed in her vagina. This displacement captured her mother's rejection of her sexuality. When she entered treatment she feared that I would stab her in her vagina.

When I answered the phone during a session (a rare exception), Pauline experienced my action as if I had stabbed her, mistakenly believing that I was giving her less time than other patients, as if I had abandoned her. She came to the next session prepared to defend herself. But when she became aware of her cold and accusatory manner, and of her coercive insistence on receiving an apology from me, which cut off rather than facilitated communication and contact, she felt bereft with the depressive pain of regret. She felt she would die if she could not repair things and remembered back to the 14-year-old girl who had thoughts of killing herself. Like then, all the warmth had gone out of the world. Therefore, when she started to feel responsible for her part in precipitating the coldness she was experiencing, Pauline started to grieve. This followed my interpreting her coldness as a part of her she could not own because it was too much like her mother's coldness.

Pauline's grief hit her with the force of a huge weight, and she experienced a sadness that seemed infinitely thick and heavy. This sadness was a symptom of her love and need for the transferential mother and was as well grief and regret related to the real analyst she had hurt, which in her fantasy was a crime. Once discussing such a precipitating incident or action, we sought out together what I had actually done and not done. We also defined her own exaggerated fantasy of annihilating all my love for her by her retaliation. As she remembered her mother's behavior toward her when she was 14 years old, Pauline began to see how she was reliving her past with me. She became aware of how she had never fully mourned her grief over the loss of her relationship with her mother. But Pauline's regret over attacking me in the present was also real. She felt better when she was able to cry deep tears of sadness while with me – tears of regret and remorse. In doing so, Pauline began rebuilding the loving connection with me inside of herself – going back to the love in infancy with her mother – as I stayed present and empathized with her pain.

Pauline had not injured me the way she fantasized, but she had frustrated me by closing off any emotional connection to me, departing from me coldly before my summer vacation. She felt compelled to repair her connection to me before we actually separated. In apologizing, she needed to understand that her fantasy of keenly hurting me was, in part, a projection onto me of her mother's very real hurt and of her own pain when she was 14 years old. When Pauline said that she feared she deeply wounded me, I interpreted her fear of her own retaliatory impulse to get back at me as she could never get back at her mother, both because of her fear and because of her guilt. My interpretation helped her to become more in touch with how her aggressive impulses always brought up a devastating sense of mother loss.

All this sorting out of the past and present – of me as separate from her mother, and of her striking out to hurt, and of her retaliating when she was feeling hurt – was part of Pauline's mourning process. Her mourning involved processing the depressive pain and her fantasies of hurting the ones she loves – me as well as the internal mother I represented. Pauline's mother seemed to come alive in the room with us as Pauline mourned the loss of love her anger created.

Within this period of mourning, a dialectic developed between us in which I was able to freely apologize for an angry moment in which I seemed cold to her. My apology helped her to reconsider how I then appeared to her. She exclaimed that she had to remember that I had never previously acted coldly with her, even though she expected me to respond that way in response to the cold manner in which she expressed her anger toward me. Prior to my apology she had attacked herself for her coldness toward me, not only mentally, but somatically, stabbing herself viscerally in her own heart. After my apology she was able to associate to her somatic symptom and to realize that the anger she turned inward played a part in creating the symptom. As she said, 'I couldn't forgive myself for getting cold towards you,' I interpreted her somatic symptom as self-punishment for her rage, as she feared she had not sufficiently repaired her hurtful attack on me.

Although I chose to apologize to Pauline for speaking to her with some anger, the content of what I had been saying at that moment was important. I had been speaking of her projection onto me of her cold mother whenever I was not feeling her pain as mine, prompted by her wish that I be completely inside her pain with her. My apology for the touch of annoyance in my tone, which she accurately picked up as I interpreted her projection and the powerful longing for intimacy behind it, allowed Pauline to receive me as a loving presence through my reparative gesture. Consequently, Pauline began to show more self-reflective understanding of my interpretation than previously. In addition, her reception of my reparative gesture allowed Pauline to forgive herself. But this explanation leaves out one step in Pauline's process: she needed to mourn the loss of love that she had felt as she opened herself to receiving my apology. She did this by yielding to a deep sadness, combined with a sense of her own hurt, which yielded to a renewal of loving feelings toward me. I knew as she cried in response to my apology that she was receiving me and my apology as a whole constellation, which could be sustained as a psychic reparative element within. Such incidents occurred repeatedly in the interpersonal sphere of her mourning process. Both my apology, which acknowledged my role in provoking her anger (even though the anger was already there from the past), and my sharing my own reactions seem to have helped Pauline surrender to her natural developmental mourning process, and to thus surrender the paranoid stance that she would regress into within the transference. She needed feedback from me as a real, present and differentiated other in order to lessen her paranoid fears and to understand the nature of her paranoid expectations with their self-fulfilling prophesy script. Pauline could gradually differentiate me, as well as others who became mother displacements, from the true mother of her past who had genuinely betrayed her due to her mother's limitations.

Pauline's reception of my apology psychically interacted with the pain of her own regret about attacking me. This was repeated many times, permitting Pauline to move from the protosymbolic level of somatic and interpersonal enactment to interpersonal communication. My apology allowed her to listen as I interpreted her coldness as a reaction to her disappointed fantasy of my being fully inside her pain with her, not simply feeling empathy to her pain from a separate position. Given our dialogue, and her own processing of depressive pain she felt (pain containing grief and guilt), Pauline now understood the symbolic communication in my interpretation and so could associate freely to it on a symbolic level. Through our dialogue, Pauline came to understand the nature of her implicit, lifelong definition of love as being inside the other's pain. She formed this belief through her history of merging with her mother's pain as a way of reaching and loving her mother after her mother had withdrawn from Pauline. This understanding opened up the floodgates of earlier memories. Pauline vividly recalled how she sat in her mother's bedroom, listening to silence, which was finally broken by a storm of tears from her mother. Now she realized how her mother had withdrawn into emotional paralysis many times throughout her childhood, controlling all those around her in her family who felt punished by the silent and guilt-provoking accusations in her cold martyrdom. In the face of her mother's punitive coldness, Pauline would lose all sense of her own agency. Pauline now realized how she had relived this period many times in the transference with me. She had tried to cross the gap created by her mother's despair either through erotic overtures or angry accusations, both of which caused her much guilt and self-punishment until she understood the scenes she was reliving. Once Pauline remembered this terrible time when 'all the sun had gone out of the world', she could grieve the loss of her mother's love.

Countertransference and the analyst as the container for developmental mourning

In his article 'On Love and Lust in Erotic Transference', Glen O. Gabbard (1994) quoted Freud (1915/1958: 386) on 'forecasting grave consequences for gratifying the patient's sexual and romantic longings'. Sexual enactment forecloses memory. Yet as Gabbard (1994) articulated, Freud encouraged actual marriage between analysts and patients. He was inclined to concretize the longings by recommending marriage, not yet really believing that tendencies toward erotic enactment could transition into verbal symbolism for analytic work. Freud was concerned with finding memories rather than repeating unconsciously driven behavior, yet he did not see how an analyst could serve to facilitate the expression of erotic feeling through words and verbal communication. The expression of powerful feelings in the treatment room was not distinguished from action. I have found in my clinical work that with a focus on feelings that are intensely erotic, but which have another side of feared loss of the love object, an analyst can contain powerful affect states in the service of developmental mourning, resulting in memory rather than enactment. Can an analyst feel pleasure in this process and still serve as an adequate container for this developmental mourning process to unfold? I would say yes, particularly after my experience working with Pauline and her intense homoerotic transference. Melanie Klein's theory of development helps me to conceptualize this and to fill in gaps in Freud's view.

Freud lacked a developmental view of affect process although he had a developmental view of libidinal drive conflict and fixation. Melanie Klein's view of psychic movement from the paranoid schizoid to the depressive position allowed for an affect focus that has a developmental evolution. Following from her thinking, I speak of 'developmental mourning', which requires the analyst to serve as a container for powerful affect states in the patient as a means for progress in developmental affect terms.

Gabbard (1992) spoke of a case in which the erotic transference served mainly as a resistance. But he used interpretation to allow symbolization to unfold and to articulate the enacted sexual fantasies that went on through subtle power dynamics between analyst and analysand in the session. He spoke of unwittingly encouraging a sadistic attack, which gratified the analysand's wish for erotic masochistic submission by repeating interpretations in a forceful and penetrating way when the analysand resisted reflecting on his interpretations and resisted even hearing them. Then he interpreted his own countertransference interplay with the patient. Although intense grief for a lost paternal object emerged in Gabbard's psychoanalytic mode of practice, he did not focus on the mourning process in the treatment per se. He did not see himself as a psychic container for grief affect as I do in reviewing the case of Pauline, as well as in reviewing the case of a male analysand in an intense erotic transference (Kavaler-Adler 1992; see Chapter 6 in this book). Gabbard astutely noted the erotic transference as a resistance, but his focus was entirely upon interpretation by the analyst. This is where we differ because, following Klein's view of developmental movements toward increasing forays into the depressive position, I focus on a developmental mourning process as the major route to transforming erotic enactments into symbolic erotic fantasies. I see these erotic fantasies as carrying deeply repressed affect states, which can become alive as a dialogue for psychoanalytic work. Because Gabbard did not focus on mourning, he did not emphasize the affective aliveness that moves the erotic transference into a developmental process. My object relations viewpoint, which emphasizes the critical developmental role of mourning for psychic change, presents a different view of therapeutic action from that of classical theory, and it is in this respect that my view of the treatment process seems to differ somewhat from Gabbard's.

My clinical experience suggests that interpretation would not have been enough in the case of Pauline. Pauline needed me to provide a developmental function as a psychic container for her powerful erotic and grief states. I would speak of the 'container' both in terms of D. W. Winnicott's 'holding environment' and in terms of Wilfred Bion's (1959, 1988) view of the analyst as an active processor of all kinds of preverbal experience when in the room with a patient. When an erotic transference has a primary pre-Oedipal origin, as in the case of Pauline, despite the evolution of the erotic transference into Oedipal dynamics, the role of the analyst as a container for developmental mourning becomes essential in my opinion, along with the use of interpretation. The analyst needs to tolerate, contain, and bring to a symbolic level of understanding through his or her own affect experience in the session all the intense arousal of the analysand, especially when erotic intensity is mixed in with abandonment depression rage, void sensation, and a particularly powerful form of grief sadness. This allows for potential protosymbolic enactments to move to a level of symbolism, interpersonal communication, memory and to the opening of psychic space for new and whole object internalizations.

Perhaps reflective of the distinction between my way of viewing the process and that of Gabbard, Gabbard speaks of love being harder for an analyst to accept than sexual desires. This has not been the case for me, and was not in the case of Pauline. My technique involved a capacity to breathe deeply and to open my whole psychophysical being to the reception of feelings of love and intimacy that Pauline needed to express. This technique could be seen as countertransference reaction, but I believe it evolved naturally as I sensed the developmental process from my analysand on an affective level. My main goal was to help Pauline communicate. Whatever pleasure I felt in Pauline's expression of her feelings and fantasies about me (so idealized in the beginning) was in the background as I focused on allowing Pauline to full psychophysical expression of her feelings and wishes. This may not have been true at all times, but was true as a general rule. As Pauline expressed the feelings she felt so deeply in the moment, she was able to re-own split off parts of herself by tolerating the intense affect and by verbalizing the longings related to that affect. My capacity to allow this full affective emergence encouraged Pauline to surrender her tendencies to enact sexual overtures with wooing behavior, such as in the form of sending flowers, and encouraged her to tell me her sexual fantasies as they were repeated in states of both rage and desire. Pauline was able to feel the loss of the idealized primal object and of the romantic Oedipal love object as she opened to memories of rejection, and to memories of unrequited love with her mother and with other women. Being allowed to express her deep loving as well as erotic thoughts allowed Pauline to surrender to her dependent longings and to recall tender memories of her mother from when she was very young. Unlike Gabbard, I found the love in these wishes and fantasies to be quite moving. I felt a tenderness that was pleasurable and I could allow Pauline's experience, while needing only to interpret the link back to the precious few memories of her mother's tenderness toward her. I did not resist making such interpretations, but there were times in which I did not in order to avoid aborting Pauline's very personal sense of experience with me. Some might say that I was engaging in a countertransference enactment as I allowed myself to feel the full range of tenderness that was emerging in Pauline in the here-and-now moment, but the developmental process that unfolded testifies to the therapeutic action involved in my psychic holding and containing.

Burch (1996) differs from Gabbard in speaking of finding the hidden erotic desires behind a more benignly presented love transference. With Pauline, such desires were often out in the open, although she would close them off when she feared she was betraying her actual female lesbian lover and feared losing her real-life love relationship. Burch (1996: 475) emphasized the difficulties of the analyst in tolerating the emerging reliving of 'the erotic-romantic aspects of the early mother-daughter relationship'. Burch stated that there is a neglect of the female analyst and female patient experience of this mother–daughter romance in its sexual form in the literature. I found this mother–daughter romance to be there from the beginning with Pauline, but it was always expressed with a great deal of conflict, as Pauline started out predominantly in a paranoid-schizoid psychic state in which she was terrified of an attack from me following her open expression of desire for me. She feared being stabbed in her vagina (and later in her heart).

Pauline felt safer when she could encapsulate her longings to love me and to be loved by me in her scripted sexual fantasies. I did not need to do anything to stimulate such fantasy. I had no reciprocal countertransference fantasies, although I felt a general body excitement when Pauline expressed deep loving tenderness combined with erotic sexual desire. As Pauline differentiated through repeated cycles of mourning, in terms of loss, trauma, narcissistic injury, and regret over not being able to care more for her parents when they were old, the body feelings she could arouse in me became more distinct. Toward the end of her treatment (fifth year), I was aware of a distinct vaginal contraction in me as she expressed a fantasy, at an Oedipal erotic level, of taking me over to a bed and making love to me. This had never happened earlier in treatment, when I had experienced a general body excitement.

Also interesting, throughout the treatment, I never experienced homosexual erotic fantasies. I was curious as to whether I would. But I discovered that on a level of conscious cognitive fantasy, I still had ideation that was heterosexual, rather than homosexual in nature, despite my body sensations. Consequently, I did not experience what Gabbard's (1994) female colleague, in consultation with him on her countertransference, experienced in his article on erotic countertransference. Gabbard's consultation supervisee actively fantasized a romance with her male patient. She anticipated the excitement of the breakdown of boundaries, the reversal of the power dynamics in a sexual surrender to her patient. She relinquished this fantasy when her patient started to actively fantasize sexual lovemaking with her, allowing his repressed sexual desires to be expressed symbolically in the transference. My patient, Pauline, had active sexual ideation in the beginning, even when she was in a position of enactment through active wooing behavior. I received her feelings, opened myself to contain them, even focusing on deep breathing that allowed me to take in the impact of the affect in my body. Yet I never had homosexual fantasies on a cognitive and ideational level. My sexual fantasies remained heterosexual (see McDougall 1998 for comparison studies). On the other hand, I did feel narcissistic gratification in some of Pauline's expressions of fascination with me as an erotic and sexual figure. However, any pleasure I may have taken in her response to me was always modified, and increasingly so by my interest in helping Pauline mourn her transference love so she could invest both her love and sexuality in a real-life relationship. I therefore began to interpret Pauline's wishes toward me as wishes toward her mother, rather than just receiving them and containing them within the context of a holding environment. Once I was taken over by some anxiety that I had delayed interpreting and I began to interpret her maternal transference wishes a little too abruptly. Pauline reacted with shock and rage at this point. As I continued to make transference interpretations, Pauline's rage became an angry dynamic that she articulated. She told me that she felt I was taking something away from her. She told me that she feared she was just going to re-experience the sense of unrequited love, felt at a traumatic level, that she had felt when she tried to approach heterosexual women with her loving adoration of them during her twenties. Pauline then recalled the devastating rejection she had suffered at the hands of a bisexual woman that led to a deep depression and to the break-up of her marriage to a man. As she remembered the shocks of rejection she felt in response to this bisexual woman's seductive behavior, followed by belittling and distancing comments, she collapsed in the grief of emotional despair. For the first time Pauline tolerated the anguish of loss that she needed to feel whole again.

Ultimately Pauline's rage with me led to another phase of an active grieving process, in which the displacement of desire for her mother to another woman had brought renewed trauma. In my presence, with the containing of the session structure, and with my capacity to be with her in her pain, Pauline was able to actively mourn and to let go of the dejected self-image she had carried with her from this traumatic experience. Letting go of this allowed her to re-own a feminine side of herself that she would have felt too vulnerable to own before.

In contrast to Gabbard (1992) saying that he deflected his male patient's experience of love, I generally stayed directly with Pauline's expressions of love to me. However, I felt I had resisted relating these loving feelings, so filled with sexual desires, back to the longings for the mother. I believe that Pauline's mother's rejection of her in adolescence, due to her homosexual interests, had resulted in such a traumatic experience of abandonment and self-annihilation that Pauline lived in a constant fear in the transference that she would lose her basic and core maternal object. I came to understand increasingly how Pauline feared that her anger and desire would alienate me forever. Pauline was intensely vulnerable and needed a great deal of assurance. When I was not sensitive to Pauline's need for such reassurance, I became the cold, abandoning mother.

Surrendering the projected fantasy of an omnipotent bisexual muse mother and the reowning of the feminine self

In *The Bonds of Love*, Jessica Benjamin (1988) spoke of the need for recognition of self through recognition of desire. If this desire, which emanates from a core true self and its spontaneous gesture (Winnicott 1971), is not received by the parent, the desire must be split off or repressed, and it frequently gets projected into another. Pauline's core homoerotic sexual desire was not only not received or acknowledged in her adolescence, but it was also devastatingly rejected and denied. This could not have been anything less than traumatic, similar to Melanie Klein speaking of the child's trauma if reparative gestures toward the mother are not received by the real mother (see 'Envy and Gratitude', Klein 1957/1975a). When one's own desire is not validated, as stated by Benjamin, it is frequently hidden behind an identification with a man who is seen as a legitimate source of desire. This was true in Pauline's case. Pauline identified with her father as the parent who expressed open erotic desire, and whose behavior expressed his erotic desire as part of his identity, while her mother's eroticism was constantly disowned and expressed indirectly through her narcissism.

When Pauline saw me as a transferrential figure of both erotic desire (a female goddess with a penis) and as a muse offering creative and narcissistic modes of inspiration, she was combining her parents, as she saw them, in a combined transferential image. The transferential muse mother combined with the phallic desire of the father is symbolized by a female creature, with flowing long hair and flowing long gowns, who possesses a penis. Such a picture appears to be an archetypical combination, as well as a kind of intrapsychic psychic fantasy phenomenon, seen as innate and axiomatic by Melanie Klein (1940/1975b). As previously stated, Klein had noted in her clinical work with play therapy with children that mommy is perceived as having daddy's penis inside her body, before mommy and daddy are differentiated as two separate human beings. At the level of intrapsychic conflict that Pauline regressed to in her analysis, her internal parent was a combined mother–father, or mother with a penis of father inside of her. I have shown how Pauline's mourning process changed this internal constellation, so that I became a differentiated female figure. Her fantasy that she possessed a penis with which to penetrate me changed as well. Although defensively holding onto the illusion of having a penis, when Pauline surrendered to the loss of the mother as an idealized figure and faced the traumas, injuries, and disappointments that her actual relationship with her mother had entailed, she could re-own her feminine genitals as a conscious part of her constitution. She did so after having a dream in which she viewed me as walking away with her female genitals, lodged in a glass case for protection. She had given her feminine side away to me, as symbolized by the female genitals in the case and, after the anxiety aroused in the dream, she wanted to reclaim her feminine side. Facing the loss and the disillusionment related to her mother throughout the course of treatment allowed her to do this. Pauline no longer had to give everything up to her transferential mother to protect her from her anger and from her wishes to separate. Pauline proceeded to dress in a totally different style of dress. She began wearing female suits and dresses and wearing more feminine shoes. She grew her hair into a flowing style, where it had formerly been short and chopped off and clipped. She began wearing jewelry and earrings.

Pauline has sustained this new manner of dress, often alternating dresses with feminine pants suits. Her new identity appears consistent and firmly routed in identifications with her real mother as she remembers her, and with me as her transferential mother. She can now have her desire, while owning female rather than male genitals. She can more playfully entertain the illusion of having a penis now, without desperately needing to be an extension of a mother who is seen as a goddess who has everything, including a penis and without having to be a phallic woman. As Burch (1996) has noted, lesbians often have the benefits of a healthy fluidity in gender identity capacities, not only a pathological side. This has been true for Pauline. As she has become more solidly identified with female receptivity, female softness, and female desire, Pauline also retains a sense of phallic penetration in her intellectual pursuits and in her professional work as a teacher.

Burch (1996) has stated how rare it is in the literature to see any studies of erotic feelings in the transference in a female analysand with a female analyst. I have many female patients expressing such feelings, both heterosexual and homosexual patients. This case of the interaction of mourning with the full acknowledgement and symbolization of sexual feelings in a female analysand with a female analyst is all the more important in light of what Burch has cited as a lack of such discussions in the literature. Burch also speaks of a mother–daughter romance that continues beyond the pre-Oedipal period and which can interact with an Oedipal romance with a father figure for a little girl. This can be seen in the case of Pauline. During the fifth year of treatment, she developed a powerful Oedipal transference to a male colleague who she saw as a father figure. She had conscious fantasies of wishing to marry him and distinct erotic fantasies of having sex with him that interacted with her transformed masturbation fantasy, in which submission to men becomes a mutually pleasurable heterosexual intercourse. Yet, at the same time, she retained erotic longings for me that she felt she had to give up. These longings became displaced into a female friend, and were as intense as ever in their homoerotic nature, despite her heterosexual longings. She went through an extremely anguished mourning process in her fifth year of treatment to face the loss of her illusion that she could marry the man she had a romantic crush on. At the same time, Pauline had to face the loss of having a romance with a particular woman in her life. She had to face loss as unrequited love, but in a gentler form than earlier because, despite being a lesbian, this woman did not have the same Oedipal-level erotic desire for Pauline that she felt toward the woman. Pauline also needed to relinquish her wishes to act out a love affair with this woman due to her commitment to her long-term female lover, whom she still loved 'more than life itself'. Having developed a capacity to contain, face and process the anguish of grief, within her developmental mourning process in treatment, Pauline was able to mourn much more on her own during the termination phase of treatment and in the year following that termination. When we met again in a consultation, Pauline shared how she had tolerated the intense depressive feelings of loss and grief related to this last mourning process. Tolerating the grief allowed her to reflect on her life. She came to terms with relinquishing the chance to act out a heterosexual love affair at this time in her life, and she sublimated her wishes for me. This allowed Pauline to work with a male mentor in her professional work, and to thus grow from a mutually gratifying learning process between her and this male mentor. She also had to relinquish wishes for a new female love, which we analyzed as being, in part, a wish to displace longings for an erotic connection with me that now had to come to a definite end. She faced her losses and reinvested in her lesbian marriage of 16 years. She accepted a more feminine identity within a broader bisexual identity and a commitment to a lesbian relationship. She continued to feel the grief of surrendering her fantasy of emotionally merging with an idealized mother-lover who would serve as her inspirational muse as well as her erotic lover. In surrendering the enactment of such wishes she was left with the pain of loss, but she was able to re-own her own capacities to inspire herself and to enjoy erotic fantasies that could be part of her actual sex life with her lover, but which could not be fulfilled in reality. Simultaneously, she reopened areas of poetry and creative imagination within herself. My acceptance of her erotic wishes toward me helped Pauline to be less conflicted about these wishes, less scared of driving women away when she had such wishes toward them. As Burch (1996) has suggested, if I were not to accept these wishes from the analysand I would be repeating the mother's shame-inducing withdrawals from her to the extent that I failed to be open to the expression of such wishes at any one time. I would become the rejecting mother whom she pictured as a cold, stone goddess, self-contained, with a penis, but not showing warmth, interest, or engagement with her. Sometimes Pauline would see me as this cold mother at times of separations when she was particularly sensitive. But her later fantasies of our reuniting and having our bodies open to each other suggested a happier resolution of her separation anxieties.

To the degree that I could accept the full expression of Pauline's erotic longings, she avoided being retraumatized and came to accept these desires, in both their Oedipal and pre-Oedipal dimensions. It was important that I acknowledged her adult homoerotic nature and not just see the expression of her wishes as a regression, in keeping with Burch's (1996) comments. The wishes behind these fantasies could still be analyzed by Pauline and me together. For example, we analyzed how her fantasy of falling in love with and marrying her male colleague was a wish for a closeness with her father that she had never had, when her sister was her father's favorite and she remained in a special sadomasochistic connection with her mother.

References

Benjamin, J. (1988) *The Bonds of Love: Psychoanalysis, Feminism, and the Problem of Domination*. New York: Pantheon Books.

Bion, W. R. (1959) 'Attacks on linking'. *International Journal of Psycho-Analysis* 40: 308–315.

Bion, W. R. (1988) *Attention and Interpretation*. London: Karnac.

Burch, B. (1996) 'Between women: the mother–daughter romance and homoerotic transference in psychotherapy'. *Psychoanalytic Psychology* 13: 475–494.

Fairbairn, R. (1952) *Psychoanalytic Studies of the Personality*. London: Routledge.

Freud, S. (1957) 'Mourning and melancholia'. In J. Strachey (ed. & trans.) *The Standard Edition of the Complete Psychological Works of Sigmund Freud* (Vol. 14, pp. 237–258). London: Hogarth Press. (Original work published 1917).

Freud, S. (1958) 'Observations on transference love. Further recommendations on the technique of psychoanalysis'. In J. Strachey (ed. & trans.) *The Standard Edition of the Complete Psychological Works of Sigmund Freud* (Vol. 12, pp. 159–171). London: Hogarth Press. (Original work published 1915).

Gabbard, G. O. (1994a) 'On love and lust in erotic transference'. *Journal of the American Psychoanalytic Association* 42: 385–403.

Gabbard, G. O. (1994b) 'Sexual excitement and countertransference love in the analyst'. *Journal of the American Psychoanalytic Association* 42: 1083–1106.

Kavaler-Adler, S. (1988) 'Diane Arbus and the demon lover'. *American Journal of Psychoanalysis* 48(4): 366–370.

Kavaler-Adler, S. (1991) 'Emily Dickinson and the subject of seclusion'. *American Journal of Psychoanalysis* 51(1): 21–38.

Kavaler-Adler, S. (1992) 'Mourning and erotic transference'. *International Journal of Psycho-Analysis* 73: 527–539.

Kavaler-Adler, S. (1993a) *The Compulsion to Create: A Psychoanalytic Study of Women Artists*. New York and London: Routledge.

Kavaler-Adler, S. (1993b) 'Object relations issues in the treatment of the preoedipal character.' *American Journal of Psychoanalysis* 53(1): 19–34.

Kavaler-Adler, S. (1995) 'Opening up blocked mourning in the preoedipal character'. *American Journal of Psychoanalysis* 55(2): 145–168.

Kavaler-Adler, S. (1996) *The Creative Mystique: From Red Shoes Frenzy to Love and Creativity*. New York: Routledge.

Kavaler-Adler, S. (1998) 'Vaginal core or vampire mouth: visceral manifestation of envy in women: the protosymbolic politics of object relations'. In N. Burke (ed.) *Gender and Envy*. New York: Routledge.

Kavaler-Adler, S. (2000) *The Compulsion to Create: Women Writers and their Demon Lovers*. New York: Other Press.

Kavaler-Adler, S. (2003a) *Mourning, Spirituality and Psychic Change: A New Object Relations View of Psychoanalysis*. New York and London: Brunner-Routledge.

Kavaler-Adler, S. (2003b) 'Lesbian homoerotic transference in dialectic with developmental mourning: on the way to symbolism from the protosymbolic'. *Psychoanalytic Psychology* 20(1): 131–152.

Kavaler-Adler, S. (2004) 'Anatomy of regret: a developmental view of the depressive position and a critical turn toward love and creativity in the transforming schizoid personality'. *American Journal of Psychoanalysis* 64(1): 39–76.

Kavaler-Adler, S. (2005) 'From benign mirror to demon lover: an object relations view of compulsion versus desire'. *American Journal of Psychoanalysis* 65(1): 31–92.

Kavaler-Adler, S. (2006a) 'Pivotal moments of surrender to mourning the parental internal object'. *Psychoanalysis and Psychotherapy*, in press.

Kavaler-Adler, S. (2006b). 'My graduation is my mother's funeral: transformation from the paranoid-schizoid to the depressive position in fear of success, and the role of the internal saboteur'. *International Forum of Psychoanalysis* 15: 117–130.

Klein, M. (1975a) 'Envy and gratitude'. In M. Klein *Envy and Gratitude and Other Works, 1946–1963* (pp. 176–235). London: Hogarth Press. (Original work published 1957).

Klein, M. (1975b) 'Mourning and its relation to manic depressive states'. In M. Klein *Love, Guilt, Reparation and Other Works, 1921–1945* (pp. 344–469). London: Hogarth Press. (Original work published 1940).

McDougall, J. (1998) *The Many Faces of Eros*. New York: Norton.

Ogden, T. (1986) *Matrix of the Mind*. Northvale, NJ: Jason Aronson.

Pine, F. (1985) *Developmental Theory and Clinical Process*. New Haven, CT: Yale University Press.

Segal, H. (1986) 'Notes on symbol formation'. In *The Work of Hanna Segal*. Northvale, NJ: Jason Aronson.

Winnicott, D. W. (1965) *Maturational Processes and the Facilitating Environment*. New York: International Universities Press.

Winnicott, D. W. (1971) *Playing and Reality*. Harmondsworth: Penguin.

Chapter 10

Female perversion
Scenes and strategies in analysis and culture

Anne Springer

The author presents some ideas derived from observation in analysis about differing positions of Freud and Jung on perversion and probable differences in perverse structural elements of women in contrast to men. In general perversion is seen as a defensive way of achieving a false wholeness, a pseudo-androgyny. A case study describes the unfolding of a perverted transference. The importance of reaching the analyst and being understood by the analyst through projective identification is stressed. Quite often a sexually abusive mother seems to play an important role in generating female perversion; the implications in analysis are discussed as well as some ideas about culture and gender.

Jung on perversion

In the chapter of *Memories, Dreams, Reflections* devoted to Freud, Jung includes the following remarks:

> Incest and perversions were no remarkable novelties to me, and did not call for any explanation. Along with criminality, they formed part of the black lees that spoiled the taste of life by showing me only too plainly the ugliness and meaninglessness of human existence. That cabbages thrive in dung was something I had always taken for granted. In all honesty I could discover no helpful insight in such knowledge. 'It's just that all of those people are city folks who know nothing about nature and the human stable', I thought, sick and tired of these ugly matters.
>
> (Jung 1963: ch. V)

As a further introduction, I quote again from Jung, from his essay 'Concerning Mandala Symolism':

> An artistically gifted patient produced a typical tetradic mandala and stuck it on the sheet of thick paper. On the back there was a circle to match, filled with drawings of sexual perversion. This shadow aspect of

the mandala represented the disorderly, disruptive tendencies, the 'chaos' that hides behind the self and bursts out in a dangerous way as soon as the individuation process comes to a standstill, or when the self is not realized and so remains unconscious.

(Jung 1950: para 689)

Jung speaks then about the magical character of the image, but does not report what exactly the patient offers as an image which for her is positive. Nor does he specify in more detail the type of relationship between the good front side and the shadowy and chaotic reverse side. The two interrelated aspects of the patient are obviously in tension, and the patient probably wishes to be seen by the analyst with the tension and the links between the various parts which she has presented. I want to address the difficulties involved in grasping the relationship between the 'image' and the chaotic reverse in the analytical process. It may be obvious that cabbage grows well in dung, but how does that work?

The words 'perversion', 'perversity', 'perverse' give rise to unusually unsettling thoughts and feelings in very many people in our culture: they have to do with things which are forbidden and hidden, embarrassing, frightening, and which in a strange way are both attractive and repulsive. Moral value judgments are evoked which are supposed to work in opposition to this dark fascination, but which are unable to do so. Films like *Fatal Attraction* draw us inextricably into a scenario which grips us with a mixture of interest, horror and disgust. Female perversion, as portrayed by Glenn Close in *Fatal Attraction*, until recently appeared only as the exception in the psychoanalytic literature (apart from the Kleinian school); even then it did so usually in the description of special pathologies such as kleptomania, or as highly controversial classification of homosexuality. With the exception of Freud's 'Three Essays on the Theory of Sexuality' (1949), the widely expressed opinion was that men are perverse, if anyone is; women on the other hand are neurotic, psychotic or borderline cases. It is only recently that we have seen systematic consideration specifically of female perversion in the psycho-analytic field (Welldon 1988; Kaplan 1991; also Zavitzianos 1972). We are more likely to find accounts of female perversion in the forbidden libraries of pornography or in treatises on sexual science.

After his break with Freud, Jung no longer studied perversion system-atically. He referred to it in some cases as pathological (e.g. Jung 1928: para 337), but was not interested specifically in its genesis nor in its inner structure. We frequently find negative connotations when Jung speaks about the perverse in the context of his break with Freud. In his efforts to distance himself he used the term 'perversive' as an anti-psychoanalytic battlecry through the well-known outbursts of 1934 (Jung 1934: para 356). There he speaks of:

> The infantile-perverse jargon of certain neurotics who display all the peculiarities of a Freudian psychology. It is positively grotesque that the doctor should himself fall into a way of thinking which in others he rightly censures as infantile and wants to cure for that reason.
>
> (Jung 1934: para 356)

On the other hand Jung encourages the analyst to view the bizarre and strange in their extremities as possible elements and expressions of individuation (see also Guggenbühl-Craig 1976).

Almost as an aside, Jung provides comments which can contribute toward the comprehension of the perverse. I will return to this point later. Of course, more recent work, for example, by Kramaer et al. (1976), Storr (1957), Wyly (1989), Fordham (1988), Wisdom (1988) and Proner (1988), is also important for an understanding of the perverted person and relationship from a Jungian point of view.

I do not intend to deal here with perversion as a circumscribed syndrome and as a pathology which is explicitly expressed by the patient. I am interested in an examination of the perverse structural elements of women as I have encountered these in analysis.

I came to refer to the structural elements and their relationship presented in the analysis as being perverse only as a result of the learning process with these particular patients after lack of progress in the analysis, and counter-transference reactions which were highly confusing for me.

Definitions

At this point I shall explain some of the terms I shall be using, following my observations in analysis. As far as perversion is concerned, the perverse structural component is described thus by Kaplan:

> However, the sexual pervert behaves very differently from the countless men and women who evoke erotic fantasies, and sometimes enact them to heighten their sexual pleasure. The pervert is not making love; he is making hate. The pervert has no choice. His sexual performance is obligatory, compulsive, fixated, and rigid.
>
> (Kaplan 1991: 40)

Louise Kaplan, who has investigated female perversion very extensively, refers here to Stoller, who understands perversion as the erotic form of hate (Stoller 1975).

The main difference between male and female perverse phantasizing and actions lies in the direction in which they are aimed. Whereas men relate to external part objects, for women the site of perversion is their own body or another whole body which they unconsciously phantasize as part of their own body or as their own corporal product which belongs to them. Not a part of the body, as with male perversion, but the whole female body is involved.

Perversion and perverse structural elements represent an amazingly complex mental performance, like almost everything pathological. As Morgenthaler says (1988: 29), their inner psychic function is to protect against threatening disintegration through overwhelming excitation, which in its extreme form can lead to psychosis, or, if coupled with impulses to act, can result in suicide either directly or as a result of manipulation. The perverse is always to be seen as a defense of the self. In particular, with women, it stimulates in a defensive way a wholeness and completeness which is intended to eliminate the reality of the other sex (which is not-self) by means of the phantasy of always having had this as her own in herself: a sort of pseudo-androgyny, the hermaphrodite at the beginning of the opus. Here I make use of an idea of Fordham (1988).

A case study

I shall now turn to Frau L, one of four patients who all posed similar and comparable problems for me. At the start of the analysis, Frau L is 32 years old, a highly qualified and successful lawyer suffering from depressions, back pains and specific difficulties at work. She copes well with large tasks, but often only manages smaller tasks after overcoming considerable anxiety, involving an element of pleasure which I came to recognize only later. She is very thin (looking almost anorexic), is attractive and well mannered, wearing expensive clothes and fashionably styled. Despite being attractive, she seems to be strangely unerotic. She is carefully made up, and in her narrow face her eyes seem remarkably large, hungry and childlike. She has come to the analysis because of severe depression and because in the end all her relationships break down. She had lived in a series of heterosexual relationships, and had been left by her lover shortly before the analysis began. She speaks in staccato; her body emanates something of the quality of a marionette. In the preliminary consultation she says dryly, 'The analysis is the final attempt to make a go of my life.' Her facial expression switches confusingly between momentary petrification, which suggests profound desperation, and the charming beaming of an omnipotent maiden. We agree on a three-hour-per-week analysis: she will use the couch. She has saved a considerable sum of money which would cover the costs her health insurance would not meet.

The initial dream: the patient is given flowers by a female colleague who in reality is married with two children, and to whom the patient has an apparently negative attitude. In the dream the patient accepts the flowers. The acceptance seems to me to be condescending; the patient says that in the dream, and now when retelling it, she is moved by the friendly act. She is also condescending in the way she tells the dream to me, gives me the flowers. She says, 'I am being good, I will tell my dreams. I hope you can make something of it all.' The aggressive aspect is completely alien to her consciousness. The start of the analysis is determined by the patient clinging to the hope that her lover will come back. She stays by the phone, waiting in vain and suffering considerably. The analysis circles for some 150/160 hours around this relationship and two others, showing the following pattern. She meets a man who clearly treats her sadistically and aggressively. She is fascinated, plays with the idea of falling in love with him, and now phantasizes total closeness and fusion, while at the same time provoking him to hurtful words and deeds, which she recognizes rationally but is unable to resolve. In this phase of sadomasochistic entanglement she rejects genital sexuality, eagerly registering every small sign of tenderness from her partner, only to denounce it immediately as being insufficient; she masturbates at home alone for hours on end.

The tormenting process intensifies, accompanied by growing diffuse excitation. At the same time her already massive fear of people grows further. She appeals to herself that she must break with the man for her own self-esteem, but she is unable to. In the sessions, she eventually becomes completely unreachable, enclosed in herself. She also seems unreachable when dealing with family entanglements. Her parents are controlling but not caring; her brother marries and she feels deserted by him. However, she cannot separate from the family because of financial ties, though these are clearly maintained by the patient. The partner relationships end with her being left, after long tormenting scenes. A brief emerging anger with the partner is immediately withdrawn. At this point she says, 'Better this way than me becoming a *Megaera* ['fury'], then I could stand myself even less and would have to kill myself.' The patient has no female friends. She is ashamed, she could not display her misery to other women, they (I) did everything better than her anyway. The fear of the extent of her envy became very clear at this point, and is gradually becoming partially accessible to the patient.

She keeps her sexuality, her sexual phantasies, out of the sessions. It is noticeable that she never really loses her charm. She talks a lot, but the short periods of silence have a mute quality; it is as if she has disappeared. In particular when she is silent I am devoid of any ideas: she kills almost every idea and almost every feeling, i.e. a part of me inside. Her body, if she refers to it at all, is a thing, an assembled machine. Later, I recall the automata built to resemble people in the eighteenth and nineteenth centuries. Her body must be thin, otherwise it is objectionable. Her uterus is a burden. Children would make her swell up, and she says, 'I would not be good for children, I can't play.' Very frequently she enters the consulting room like a freshly washed and dressed baby doll, with arms slightly apart and a spring in her step, like a little girl who has just been told 'Don't go and get your nice clothes dirty'. When it comes to my holidays she briefly becomes an angry little princess. In turn, I feel like some servant maid who should not be making any fuss; after all I am getting paid. I increasingly feel the need to do something very tangible to liven myself up. In the sessions I become irritated and tired at the same time. But she is obviously trying hard to be a particularly good and productive patient. The irritability and the anger interchange with unspecific excitation which remains void, with no ideas, phantasies, or more precise feeling. On the other hand, I feel a growing need to enquire aggressively, inquisitively, invasively, and in a strangely excited way searching for a way of discharging tension and reviving myself. Outside the sessions, she occupies my thoughts to a considerable degree, but unproductively. In the sessions I increasingly feel that I do not understand her anyway.

With her mysteriousness and reserve there is an undertow dragging me into a game I do not know, and which I am not sure I wish to know. Something is permanently disturbing the possibility and potential of the reverie – I lose her through not reaching her. From the content of what she says, the dreams and the fragments of memories, and from the tranference/countertransference, I gradually form a fragmentary and highly confusing inner image of the mother: a large, thick-skinned woman, mostly silent but aggressive in bursts, who degraded the father in front of the patient but who felt extremely dependent on him, unpredictable; a mother who told her daughter with every new boyfriend 'He isn't good enough'. As a small child, and through into adolescence, the patient remembers herself to be very aggressive. As a child and teenager she almost always played alone, climbing daringly in the garden and house; 'I was never afraid there'. In addition to concern at this point, I also feel an aggressive indifference, 'Let her fall down out of the tree, I can't help it'; it was an aggressively tinted separation phantasy. After the patient has explained much about her childhood pastimes over a number of sessions, she comes to the next (181st) session and says, 'But in the evening I crept into bed with my mother, both of us in front of the television.' I feel some anxiety, then brief but intense sexual excitation – without phantasy or feeling. Then, strangely, a new man friend of the patient comes to my mind, about whom she has spoken in glowing tones. She is in love with him, but he does not sleep with her: he is a homosexual, a practising masochist, who fascinates the patient with stories about his 'Domina'; for the patient he is a tender friend, but acting out his sexuality in a sadomasochist hell.

For the first time in this analysis I have the impression at this point – at the moment of physical excitation – that I am able to reach a missing part of the patient. I comment, 'Who seduces whom?' The patient starts, then says, 'The door to my mother's bedroom had a translucent pain of glass, and through it you could see something of her, large, pink, always pink nightdresses. In bed I always slid up to the top where she lay. Then she scolded me and pulled me back down again. She always wanted me to sleep there. She had said: "Naughty girl but better than your brother, he's roaming around outside. You won't be like daddy, we don't need him here." She caressed me, but at night she stuck her finger into me down there, and I pretended to be asleep. I always thought "I am bad" because it had excited me so; she mustn't notice anything.

One time I crept away, she said I was bad. She always had chocolates in bed.' The voice has become that of a child. For the first time she cries, a confused, miserable, deserted child. In this scene the child is about 6 years old.

Later discussions between the patient and her brother, and diffuse memories which gradually come together, indicate that as a small child she was probably masturbated regularly by her mother if she did not go to sleep and was crying, just as she calmed herself with endless masturbation in the loneliness and torment of her relationships with men. In the subsequent sessions she cries a lot, with anger interchanging with sorrow. Then in the 200th sessions, the patient again speaks about the sexual scenarios of her homosexual boyfriend and his fears of AIDS. She still likes him, but is also annoyed that he keeps a part of his life inaccessible to her, just as she had kept a part of her life inaccessible to me. She says, 'I should stick with my phantasies, that way you can't get AIDS.' I say, 'When you masturbate, you enjoy without danger.' The patient: 'Since I was 15, I have had a phantasy which always does the trick. I imagine I am a great queen in a room with glass all the way round, and a ceiling and floor of glass too. Outside are people: men, women and children. The people can see me – otherwise they can't be there, if they can't see me. But they can only be there if they hurt themselves, have sex. Each one is there for me, I fetch one that I want into the room, but he can't do anything to me in the room, just look together with me at what they are doing outside'.

Shortly before developing this central masturbation phantasy in adolescence, the patient had experienced a double loss, and was very depressive and suicidal. Her dog, which she had loved but also tormented and sexually stimulated, had died, and she also lost the therapist her parents had engaged in view of her considerable aggressiveness and non-conformity, and with whom she had fallen in love. Once again, she was alone and lonesome, as she had been as a baby and small child, and from this time her personality developed as I came to know it: a princess-like femininity as masquerade (Riviere 1929/ 1993) for a child, deserted and constantly threatened by disintegration under the pressure of sorrow, anger and longing. The princess masquerade included the sexualized seduction, coupled with the desire for revenge, Her fear of disintegration in her solitude demonstrated itself as a fear of being overwhelmed by a diffuse sexualized excitation. The phantasy of the queen represented inversion and falsification. For the helpless baby there was nobody really and constantly there.

Subsequently in the analysis she naturally clung to the seductive entanglement which had served her so long as a necessary defence and which made living possible. Considerable aggression and devaluation were released, impulses to act out the sadism which was becoming clearer, and an immense wish for revenge, both in the analysis and at work.

The newly found injured baby began only very slowly to feel and let me feel in a more precise and related way, and to play in the analysis in a non-masturbatory way; for example, with ideas about how she would redesign my room together with me, safe in the knowledge that I would survive the destruction which this would involve. As a way of understanding this, I offered the interpretation that she wanted to go exploring in my body like that, looking to see which bits were where. And, she asked, could it really be that she did not have a very small penis inside herself? Ashamedly and triumphantly she disclosed that she had always assumed she really did have one. There were repeated setbacks due to severe feelings of guilt with which she responded to good experiences. Experiencing good meant being bad, and dependent through the wish for more. The feelings of guilt led to self-damage: a short anorexic phase, a disfiguring hairstyle, extreme self-doubt in her work, emptiness and inconsolable desperation after professional success. In the meantime the treatment has for the time being reached a conclusion (after 380 sessions). The patient lives free from symptoms in a relationship with a man who is probably somewhat soft; each has his/her own apartment. She finds it reassuring that she can return to the analysis when children become a topic in the relationship.

Transference–countertransference

Once the patient had finally been able to reach me in body by projective identification (the anxious and sexualized excitation I felt when she told me that she crept into bed with her mother), the transference and counter-transference could be identified much more clearly. The childhood fate of the patient as far back as the pre-Oedipal area and the world of her inner objects, and thus also of her real object relationships, was re-enacted in the here and now of the transference. The inner world of the patient was dominated and determined in the extreme by the experience of a dangerous and sexualizing mother, who regarded the child as an extension of herself and who arranged a perverse scenario with the child. Kramer said in 1980 about incestuous mothers: ' I speculate that they [incestuous mothers] could not enjoy their own genitals for sexual pleasure, but masturbated the genitals of their incompletely separated and individuated children as dehumanized extensions of the maternal body' (Kramer 1980: 330, cited by Welldon 1988: 98–99). This could be said about abusing female analysts too.

The child introjects the experience of this perverse mother and her own relationship with her. Like a transplant, the reversal of the mother, turning around maternal aggression into apparent love, was firmly fixed in her. She identified with it, and lived out the same scenario herself. At the same time, the perverse phantasies and relationship arrangements, as well as the perverted treatment of her own body, served as a defence against the diffuse anxiety, anger and sadness of a deserted child. In the central masturbation phantasy, she later turns the smallness and vulnerability of the baby daughter into apparent greatness and autonomy, perhaps following a phantasy of the mother that she is her devalued penis. Now she seduces instead of being seduced, and she can revenge herself. At the same time she can see and be seen, which was not possible then, and which was also impossible in her relationship in adult life, because good objects and good experiences would have rocked the stabilizing defences too much. As it turned out, she experienced coitus in adulthood – as well as analysis – as psychically empty, merely as a discharge of tension (that is frigidly) or as using a man to please herself (that is as masturbation). In the transference over a long period she enacted the mother–child pair who do not understand each other, in changing constellations, with the potentially over-reaching and stimulating mother, but also with her identification with the perverse mother. By means of the projective identification, mother and daughter confront each other in the transference from both sides in the bedroom. From this moment on, the patient is able rudimentarily to draw on good experiences with a woman (the paternal grandmother) in order to begin very carefully to allow an approach to a good object (the analyst). The central masturbation phantasy of the patient, however, characterizes the long period of abuse, i.e. the perversion of the analytic situation. The queen in the glass room wants to be seen, and left alone, wants to be understood but kills the thinking/feeling process. She denies her solitude and lack of happiness, and attacks the analytical process with unconscious pleasure. The analysis could become, in these circumstances, a masturbation for two.

How are we to understand what it is we do when, as Jung, so vividly described it in *The Psychology of the Transference*, we share as the analytical pair – the couple that wants to know – the bath which also contains the mud (Jung 1946)? Let me answer with the striking words of a non-Jungian, but which every one of us can second. Betty Joseph writes:

> By definition [transference] must include everything that the patient brings into the relationship. What he brings in can best be gauged by our focusing our attention on what is going on within the relationship, how he is using the analyst, alongside and beyond what he is saying. Much of our understanding of the transference comes through our understanding of how our patients act on us to feel things for many varied reasons; how they try to draw us into their defensive systems; how they unconsciously act out with us in the transference, trying to get us to act out with them; how they convey aspects of their inner world built up from infancy – elaborated in childhood and adulthood, experiences often beyond the use of words, which we can often only capture through the feelings aroused in us, through our counter-transference, used in the broad sense of the word.
> (Joseph 1983: 157)

In my interventions, then, I had to be very careful, including in my choice of words, not to get actively involved in the relationship entanglements and reversals, but to take these apart, that is to analyse them. Anything else would have meant getting involved in the reversed inner world of relationships described above, and at the archetypal level the world of the primitive androgyny, the primitive hermaphrodite. My task, therefore, was to make myself available as a sufficiently good object, in order to offer again the archetypally available images of a good mother and a mother–child relationship which makes separation possible, and then to help fill these out. This is the way from the constant object to the possibility of object constancy (see Plaut 1993: 135–144).

I was helped by the few publications available on the problem of perverted transference by Joseph (1969/1989), Meltzer (1973), Etchegoyen (1978), Malcolm (1988) and Steiner (1993). Steiner describes the perverse confusion in the world of inner objects as a result of incomplete inner separation and division into good and evil parts. This results in fragmentation, and the fragments group to form a sort of intrapsychic path which infiltrates the good parts, attacks them from within and dominates them – a sort of intrapsychic masked mafia. In opposition to this negative process, it was important in the regression in the analysis to initiate new and beneficial separation and differentiation processes.

Constructions of feminity

The question which the patient asked both explicitly in words and implicitly in the transference was threefold: Am I a woman? What sort of woman am I? How did I become a woman? This question, which the patient wanted answered but to which she feared the answer, concerned her own femininity. If I examine the history of this woman before and during the analysis in the light of this question, what do I find?

The mother could not provide adequate support for her daughter's efforts to achieve separation, but used her as a self-object, in the function of a transitional object. The daughter – stuck in her development in this mother – developed images of women in her own inner world, in her inner relationships, which largely fitted the negative mother complex: possessive, devouring, providing poorly. On the other hand, however, there were positive elements from the paternal grandmother. They probably allowed the mental survival of the patient (and possibly also physical survival), as well as a rudimentary ability to recognize in me a good object. Furthermore, the daughter identified with the projected image of the mother: the well-behaved daughter who did not rob and injure the mother by her own separation, but who remained dependent, the princess daughter who lets herself be worshipped. As an object for the daughter's immense anger, which was really aimed at the mother, the mother offered the men she had devalued, for two contradictory reasons: Don't become dependent on men like I am on your father, everything you need you get from me, and you are everything (that is, both sexes) for me. And a second message: Without a man you are nothing; I am also dependent on a man – your father; don't believe you can have more autonomy than me.

For this patient the image of the inner parental couple is sadomasochistic in structure. Good heterosexual and homosexual pair images are underdeveloped and filled with much less experience, and are thus fragile and threatened. In this inner chaos, the patient 'chose' a specific construction of femininity which I found with all four of the women patients considered here: A primitive androgyny (primitive because it remains concrete – 'I have a penis') guarantees staying with the mother ('You are everything for me' says the mother) and apparent independence in the world. As the personal counterpart, the father remains pale, impotent, a possession of the mother, only offering an opportunity for identification in terms of achievements. As a woman she sought in men the other and better mother, but repeatedly ended up in the internalized sadomasochistic pattern. Every attempt to achieve a good pair image was successfully attacked by the inner sadomasochistic parental pair, which was masked as a good pair – as part of the inner mafia – both intraphysically and in reality. A primitive androgyny (see Fordham 1988) had to be maintained against this in the sense of a holistic phantasy of autonomy which was supposed to offer salvation. This phantasy was staged in the enclosed worlds of perverse relationships, inner and outer, and in the transference. Such staging of a shuttered holistic phantasy, preventing separation, is described by Jung in the Children's Dream Seminars, and at one point clearly for a boy (Jung 1987: 47–48). There he speaks of people's bisexuality (what I have referred to here as primitive androgyny), referring to it as an archetypal fact. Here we find important components of modern psychoanalytical thought, such as Morgenthaler's on perversion and perversity, and of modern Jungian thought, particularly Fordham's, which are valid for both sexes but which, in my opinion, take on a particular complexity for women.

On the other hand, the female persona of these patients shows the partially unconscious primitive androgyny phantasy through clothes and hairstyles, but also through ideology formations. On the other hand, it consists of a façade, a secondary, constructed femininity. You may recall that Frau L seemed to me to be like a puppet on a string, a machine. Very late in their analyses, these patients (who incidentally had all been sexually attacked by their mother or nanny, cf. Welldon) reported extensively, in a shy but triumphant manner, how they had in part quite consciously decorated themselves as women with elements of fashion and items from the arsenal of socially recognized female gestures and movements. This 'womanliness as a masquerade', already described by Joan Riviere (1929/1993), serves in turn self-deception and self-protection, but also brings about the expression of the unconscious anger of these women by its triumphant deceptive character. The apparent craziness of the masquerade is in its message: I am only feminine, but in fact I am everything.

It is this craziness, in the sense of an inherent fragmentation and contradiction which cannot be resolved in this crazy cosmos, which inspires the search for an image capable of encompassing the whole of this tension, both as a way of bringing things to a head and as a means of defence against anxiety. It was in the course of this search that I finally thought of Lilith – with a feeling that I was realizing the obvious. Lilith is also threefold – the terrible, child-devouring, disappointed woman and mother, the vulnerable baby, and the glittering and exciting seductress, accompanied in the myths by unimportant, castrated, smaller male demons, which are perhaps to be thought of as triumphal compensation after the lost struggle with Adam, and as justification for the anxiety about challenging Adam at all – why should Lilith want to fight with a man who is already devalued (see Hurwitz 1980)?

Commenting on this type of construction of femininity – that a woman creates herself anew, and in addition as only-woman – Joan Riviere (1929/1993) writes: 'The reader may now ask how I define womanliness or where I draw the line between genuine womanliness and the "masquerade". My suggestion is not, however, that there is any such difference; whether radical or superficial, they are the same thing.' If this is true, it is unsettling.

Frau L and the other patients are therefore perhaps acting against a specific background of conflict and, with specific psychic functions, it may be something which women do in our culture when they use the typical features of 'normal femininity'. It is not a coincidence that the masquerade is such an important topic in Anglo-American feminist theory. It is deceptively easy for women to see the figure portrayed by Glenn Close in *Fatal Attraction* merely as the image of male phantasy. It is also caricatured by very concrete presentation of elements of 'normal femininity': she wants her lover for herself, and she wants to have his baby – whatever the cost. All her actions say: better to kill desperately and pleasurably for this purpose than to be alone. Are all women perhaps also Lilith? Why is the androgyne so modern? Are we part of a world becoming more perverse? Perhaps the disorientation of patients like Frau L will cause us to question our assumptions about the dichotomy of the sexes which we maintain with anxiety. There are innumerable constructions, some more male in identity, others more female. Our confrontations of masculinity and femininity, or of anima and animus, are still used much too often not as shorthand for a basic polarity; this dichotomy tends to have the function of protecting us against fear of variety. The formulation of the anima–animus pair is an important step in this context (see also Hultberg 1994; Kast 1994).

To be fascinated by identity means being fascinated by the idea of wholeness. Identity purports to bring together the split off parts of a life and to form a unity out of them, a whole life that makes sense. This may produce both a psychic and an aesthetic satisfaction. But – is there really nothing worse than a life that does not present itself as something that makes sense as a whole? These are the words not of an analyst but of a journalist, writing under the heading 'Against Identity' about the defensive search for identity and the false search for entirety (Wieseltier 1995, translated by the author).

Just as we can sit as men and women in the prison of a defensively determined identity which imprisons the opposite and keeps everything disquieting at a distance, then the defensive need for an unambivalent and false harmony and wholeness which has always contained and already knows everything can also come to dominate analysts and their schools, and this perhaps could then be perverse (see Meltzer 1973: 139; Khan 1974).

References

Etchegoyen, R. H. (1978) 'Some thoughts on transference perversion'. *International Journal of Psycho-Analysis* 59: 45–53.

Fordham, M. (1988) 'The androgyne: some inconclusive reflections'. *Journal of Analytical Psychology* 33(3): 217–228.

Freud, S. (1949) 'Three essays on the theory of sexuality'. *Standard Edition* Vol. VII. London: Hogarth Press.

Guggenbühl-Craig, A. (1976) 'Psychopathologia sexualis und Jungsche Psychologie' [Psychopathology sex and Jungian psychology]. *Zeitschrift für Analytische Psychologie* 7(2): 110–122.

Hultberg, P. (1994) 'Inspiriert zu neuer geschlechtlicher Identität' [Being inspired for a new sexual identity]. In H. Meesman and B. Sill (eds) *Androgyn*. Weinheim: Deutsche Studien Verlag.

Hurwitz, S. (1980) *Lilith: die erste Eva* [Lilith: the first Eve]. Zürich: Daimon.

Joseph, B. (1969) 'A clinical contribution to the analysis of a perversion'. In M. Feldman and E. B. Spillins (eds) *Psychic Equilibrium and Psychic Change: Selected Papers of Betty Joseph* London: Routledge (1989 edition).

Joseph, B. (1983) 'Transference: the total situation'. In M. Feldman and E. B. Spillins (eds) *Psychic Equilibrium and Psychic change: Selected Papers of Betty Joseph*s. London: Routledge (1989 edition).

Jung, C. G. (1928) 'The relations between the ego and the unconscious'. CW Vol. 7. London: Routledge & Kegan Paul.

Jung, C. G. (1934) 'The state of psychotherapy today'. CW Vol. 10. London: Routledge & Kegan Paul.

Jung, C. G. (1946) 'The psychology of the transference'. CW Vol. 16. London: Routledge & Kegan Paul.

Jung, C. G. (1950) 'Concerning mandala symbolism'. CW Vol. 9i. London: Routledge & Kegan Paul.

Jung, C. G. (1963) *Memories, Dreams, Reflections*. London: Collins and Routledge & Kegan Paul.

Jung, C. G. (1987) 'Kindertraumseminare' [Seminar on children's dreams]. 1st series. Olten: Walter Verlag.

Kaplan, L. J. (1992) *Female Perversions: The Temptations of Madame Bovary*. New York: Doubleday.

Kast, V. (1994) 'Fasziniert vom seelischen Bild des Paares' [On being fascinated by the pair image]. In H. Meesman and B. Sill (eds) *Androgyn*. Weinheim: Deutsche Studien Verlag.

Khan, M. M. (1974) 'The use and abuse of dream in psychic experience'. In M. M. Khan *The Privacy of the Self: Papers on Psychoanalytic Theory and Technique*. Madison, CT: International Universities Press.

Kraemer, W. et al. (eds) (1976) *The Forbidden Love*. London: Sheldon Press.

Kramer, S. (1980) 'Object-coercive doubting: a pathological defensive response to maternal incest'. *Journal of the American Psychoanalytical Association* 31: 325–351.

Malcolm, R. R. (1988) 'The mirror: a perverse sexual phantasy in a woman is seen as a defence against a psychotic breakdown'. In E. B. Spillius (ed.) *Melanie Klein Today*. London & New York: Routledge in association with the Institute of Psycho-Analysis.

Meltzer, D. (1973) *Sexual States of Mind*. Pitlochry: Clunie Press.

Morgenthaler, F. (1988) *Homosexuality, Heterosexuality, Perversion*, trans. A. Aebi, ed. P. Moor. Hillsdale, NJ: Analytic Press.

Plaut, F. (1993) *Analysis Analysed*. London: Routledge.

Proner, B. (1988) 'Comment on the paper by J. O. Wisdom'. *Journal of Analytical Psychology* 33(3): 249–251.

Riviere, J. (1929/1993) 'Womanliness as a masquerade'. *International Journal of Psycho-Analysis* 10: 303–313.

Steiner, J. (1993) 'Perverse relationships in pathological organizations'. In J. Steiner *Psychic Retreats*. London & New York: Routledge in association with the Institute of Psycho-Analysis.

Stoller, R. (1975) *Perversion: The Erotic Form of Hatred*. New York: Pantheon.

Storr, A. (1957) 'The psychopathology of fetishism and transvestism'. In A. Samuels (ed.) *Psychopathology: Contemporary Jungian Perspectives*. London: Karnac. (1991 edition).

Welldon, E. V. (1988) *Mother, Madonna, Whore: The Idealization and Degeneration of Motherhood*. London: Free Association Books; New York: Columbia University Press.

Wieseltier, L. (1994) 'Against identity'. *The New Republic* 8, 28 November.

Wisdom, J. O. (1988) 'The perversions: a philosopher reflects'. *Journal of Analytical Psychology* 33(3): 229–248.

Wyly, J. (1989) 'The perversions in analysis'. *Journal of Analytical Psychology* 34(4): 319–337.

Zavitzianos, G. (1972) 'Homeovestism: perverse forms of behaviour involving wearing clothes of the same sex', trans. R. Holmes. *International Journal of Psycho-Analysis* 53: 471–477.

Chapter 11

What can we learn from the therapist's body?

Susie Orbach

I suggest a re-theorisation of the relationship between psyche and soma in which the body is no longer seen as 'mere' receptacle for unwanted contents of the mind but in which a body subjectivity has a developmental history in its own right. I argue that the body has its own history arising out of the attachment nexus and the internalisation of the bodies of its caregivers and the bodies they are able to recognise in their infants and children. I illustrate the way developmental body issues appear in the clinical setting and how the therapist's body can be used to locate and identify the troubled bodies of our clients. A long history of work with women with eating problems and troubled bodies shows that bodies are not born but are acquired in relationship with key caregivers.

Introduction

- I close the outer door of my consulting room after letting my patient in. Before closing the inner one, I stick out my tongue between the two doors. I cross the room to sit down with my patient, wondering about this involuntary act.
- A supervisee tells me of having to interrupt a session because she smelt fire outside her consulting room. Her patient was at that moment discussing something inappropriate going on involving an American GI, an uncle when she was a child. The detail of the fire, which turned out to crystallise crucial aspects of the patient's tableau, was not something she had mentioned to the therapist until the therapist's nostrils compelled her to leave the room.
- I feel my body purring during a session. The feeling – an unexpected one – is of deep contentment. My patient has an extremely troubled experience of her body. It is a trouble to her, has always been so. It is forever ill, it hurts, ulcerates. I wonder where this perfectly contented purring body has come from.
- I referred a 50-year-old woman with vaginismus to a colleague of mine. Months into the therapy when he had been inclined to turn away from her

physically but had recognised that this was precisely what he needed not to do, he noticed a putrid smell in the room as though he were with an over-ripe mango.

- Professor Mavis Gallant, the Professor of Midwifery at Sheffield University reports that she has been able to calculate the number of centimetres of dilation of a woman in labour through changes in the bodily feelings in her own genital area. This is then confirmed through physical examination.

How are we to understand these kinaesthetic phenomena? What sense can we make of them? What is the use, the function, the meaning of the bodily feelings that are aroused in the psychotherapist during the course of a session?

History

The origins of psychoanalysis are situated firmly in the relationship between body and mind with Freud and Breuer's early work *Studies in Hysteria* examining the phenomenon of physical symptoms that had no organic basis. Since the Second World War, however, psychoanalysis has focused almost exclusively on the mind, translating whatever bodily responses the patient has as an expression of mental processes – the body seen alternately as a container or a dustbin for that which the psyche cannot handle (McDougall 1989). A physical complaint such as colitis is often taken as a sign of a patient's difficulties with absorption and digestion: the pain and gas, the ulcers on the colon representing the irritations caused by the difficulty in taking in and using what the emotional environment (the mother, the object) has to offer. The lesions in the colon, the abdominal pain, the bloody diarrhoea, the fatigue, are interpreted as the means by which the patient attempts to evacuate what she or he is unable to use. Nourishment, in this schema, is weaponised into searing pain or eliminated with bile. The physical symptom becomes a somatic symptom valuable for what it can reveal about the patient's mental state. Rarely is there a consideration of what the colitis and its symptoms might reveal about the patient's difficulties with their body qua body. Such a question or consideration fails to materialise in this hypermentalist period of psychoanalysis. If it did, we might discover that the colitis is also about a fragile and tender alimentary canal in which the literal feeding and sense of physical movement is blocked. The body as a body feels vulnerable and tense, nervous and fearful. The colitis body is revealed as unreliable and unpredictable and in need of particularly careful attention.

The body for itself

In our non-reflected-upon habit of endowing the superiority of the mind, we focus on what our minds are capable of doing to our bodies. We can unintentionally ignore what the body is capable of doing to the mind or what the body discloses about the body per se. The body of course is a crucial aspect of attachment, and body distress – imagined (as in dysmorphia) or physically based as in colitis, eczema, asthma and so on – may signal aspects of disorganised body attachment. Although attachment theory is unaccustomed to thinking of the body in attachment terms or recognising how the attachment system works at enabling a body to develop in the particular forms that it does, we can imagine quite easily how the avoidant, ambivalent, secure and insecure body are examples of how attachment dynamics play out at the physical level and what difficulties at that level mean in terms of the insecure, disorganised or secure sense of bodily self an individual develops. (Indeed a research project using Ainsworth's schema could be readily devised which would track the intersubjective body-to-body attachment matrices.)

It is not only psychoanalysis and the talking therapies that make immediate translation of bodily symptoms into dramas of the mind. Many of the body therapies do so too. One can frequently hear body therapists talk about that whatever is going on in the mind comes out in the body, emphasising the body as a vehicle rather than the body having a mentality of its own or a psychological life of its own.

I know the ideas that I am suggesting here can sound strange. What do I mean about the body having its own mentality? What is this false divide between the body and the mind? But I want to reverse a tendency that has made our conversations about the relationship between corporeality and psyche a one-way street and go the other way by privileging our thoughts about the body, difficult as that is, so that its neglect, its relegation to being the mind's dustbin, can be addressed.

Just as the patient's symptomatic body is dismissed or read in a limited way, so too, the physical sensations that a therapist experiences during the course of his or her work, the body countertransferences, are usually understood in psychic terms and not explored for the physical meanings that can be made of them. If the therapist is inclined to nod off (Field 1989), this is often understood as the patient boring the therapist or the patient's anxiety and fear of engagement which renders the therapy so tiring and dead that the therapist is lulled into not being interested. Now accurate as such kinds of interpretation might sometimes be, the interpretation of the physical entirely in terms of the mental can miss crucial dimensions of the patient's physicality and their experience of their body. In my own supervisory experience, I have observed that when a supervisee has wanted to nod off, to give one example, this has been what Racker (1968) would term a concordant counter-transference. The patient evokes in the therapist a sense of peace: a need to be with the patient in stillness and safety very much as Winnicott (1958) describes in his understanding of the baby's developing capacity to be alone in the presence of the available mother.

If we think about the examples I have given above of my and my colleagues' physical sensations in bodily terms, our understandings reach our patients at levels which, if left unaddressed, continue to trouble them. What can be going on when I stick out my tongue after letting my patient Jane into the room and before closing the second door? Where does such an impulse come from? Jane had a phobia around vomiting. Her sibling was disabled in a way that meant he was physically uncontrolled and his body and physical being were repulsive to her. If we were trying to understand my tongue motion purely in psychic terms we might think that the countertransference alerted me to a kind of childhood dynamic, a sort of 'I'm better than you' refrain, and yes I think that was being enunciated between us. But if as well I reflect on what I felt physically, if I actually repeat the gesture after Jane has left the session and stick out my tongue between the two doors, I find that I am not so much in the territory of the playground or sibling rivalry but I feel a certain physical revulsion for myself, a kind of disgust about my own body and my physicality that surprises me.

Tying this to Jane's experience I begin to wonder about how she feels in her own physicality. We have often talked of her phobias and her disgust at her brother's body. We have never come close to the possibility that she feels a physical disgust in her own body. I hold on to my experience. I have little choice. The compulsion to stick out my tongue carries on for months.

One day we come to talk about her difficulty in handling her 3-year-old daughter. She says that she is beginning to realise that she has never felt quite right around her. She has never liked her daughter's body. She had an easy time with her son. His body was one she could admire and cherish. She loved throwing him in the air, encouraging him to catch ball, suckle, cuddle, bathe him and help him climb the stairs. She's been wary with her daughter, tentative and inconsistent. Sometimes she has seen her as a fragile china doll while at other times she has been quite rough with her. We ponder this together. Such a response would be less surprising if her daughter had been her first child: a parent will often have hesitations about handling an infant. But her daughter is her second child. As we continue to talk, we see that whereas she feels she has been able to give her son a body, a sense of being rooted in his corporeal self, a sense that his body is where he lives and that it is robust and extendable, she sees in her daughter a fragility, a brittleness, a congenial, unlovable body. Her son by contrast had an 'imaginal' body for her (Samuels 1989). She could see it as she wished, as glorious and handsome and quite uncontaminated by her revulsion towards her brother's body which in a complicated manner had been absorbed into a personal, physical and mental self-hatred in part engendered by the guilt she felt for being 'perfect'. Further conversation with Jane reveals that she has always hated her body. Despite the fact that she has been a model and in that job represented something about beauty for other women, privately she has a basic instability and revulsion to her body. It has always been something she has been prepared to subject to extreme manipulation through drugs and food deprivation. Her physicality has always been a difficulty to her. In creating the conditions where my involuntary sticking out of my tongue induced a mild version of this body revulsion, we were eventually able to work on her fragile body and in time to institute some processes by which she felt more body integrity.

The patient, Herta, with whom I felt this extraordinary feeling of purring contentment was a woman similarly troubled by her body, although in her case it was something she brought into the therapy from the beginning. She had grown up in post-war Germany, amidst poverty. As a baby she had sicked up some of her feed. When Herta later developed a symptom of vomiting, she was taken to a behavioural psychologist and made to reimbibe her vomit. This cruel treatment stopped her vomiting but shortly after she became a bed wetter and by the time I met her she had suffered with ulcerated colitis for several years. (For a further discussion of this case see Orbach 1995.)

Herta's primary relationship to her body was that it was an object to her. It was a trouble to her. She had no experience of living in it per se but rather by being burdened by it. She always had to attend to it. By focusing on the body countertransference – the contented purring body feeling that I believe she evoked in me in the therapy – we were able to address the body per se. She needed to be able to enter into the hatred she had with her body directly so that she could be inside that feeling directly. Without confronting the fact that her body only existed for her as hated, she would not be able to relinquish or transform this subjective sense of her body. But the difficulty of course was that to acknowledge the hate and the ensuing fear that she was either a hated body or was without a body, she needed a stable, good enough body in the room to rely on while she went through this process.

In cueing me into the need for this provision, Herta enabled me to offer her my body much as I have been able to offer a therapeutic version of my psyche – one that is stimulated by the therapeutic relationship – as an auxiliary to her in a matter of fact way, during the course of practice, to my patients, over the years. Now it was my body's turn to become an auxiliary. And in the therapeutic space, I found that Herta had indeed invoked in me a body which was solid and sufficiently reliable. This co-created therapeutic endeavour allowed me to take on both her projections and fantasies about my relationship to my body without becoming damaged or harmed by either her poisonous feelings and utterances or flayed by her fears of a disintegrating body.

In the example which involved the smell of fire in the therapist's nostrils, we can see that a physical sensation aroused in the therapist was a way the patient found to bring up a deeply distressing episode involving the transgression of her body. The patient conveyed something, and we aren't sure how this is done, to the therapist. This then made it possible for the patient to free associate to the smell of fire, a smell the therapist believes was conveyed in this extraordinary form.

I've been interested in this issue of body countertransference for the last 20 years or so, and as I've talked about the issues that have intrigued me I've gathered many different examples from colleagues who themselves have been puzzled and interested in what we might do about these wildcat feelings in our body; what using them might add to our work both at the technical level and theoretically. How might we extend some of the taken for granted supremacy of the mind on the one hand and add meaning and substance to some of the assumptions we have about the psyche-soma on the other? Not least, of course, is how we might open up new ways of working with people who have troubled bodies.

In relation to the countertransferences, I have come to think of them as falling into three distinctive categories. The first example I mention – the tongue sticking out – seems to me to be an instance of something we are very accustomed to within the countertransference: a way in which the experience of distress an individual experiences is conveyed to the analyst. By experiencing an overwhelming physical sensation of disgust I am encouraged to think about the physical dis-ease of my patient in her body. I am enabled to think with her about the origins of her body hatred, not simply the psychological origins of her self-hatred but the ways in which her body is a central player in her experience. Surprisingly, we discover that this body of hers, which she has used to earn her living, has never existed as a reliable and alive home for her. It is not so much a hated body as a pretending to be body. Jane never felt her body had a beginning or an end, an inside and an outside. It was as though she weren't physically encased, and when she came to reproduce her body in the body of her daughter she found herself enacting a distress that emerged from not having a body.

With Herta, I see the countertransference as a demand for some provision. The patient desperately in need of a new body creates for us within the therapy a body that is deeply content. Although she cannot give this body to herself because that would feel inauthentic – you can't build a good body on rotten foundations – she can invoke in me, in our relationship, a body with which to identify which will, by alerting me to its appearance, show us both the necessity of her being able to accept the disturbed and distressed body she has.

Another example of provision which has been reported to me comes from a colleague in New Zealand who while working with a regressed patient felt the let-down reflex in her breasts that alerts a breastfeeding woman that her baby is ready for a feed. There was something quite literal and concrete about her patient's need for a physical feed that this stimulation of her reflex brought into the therapy.

The fire example is one that I would classify as a straightforward communication. This patient isn't conveying the idea that her body per se is a problem to her but that something has been done to or with it or it has been involved in something traumatic that has been dissociated until that time.

I've been led to think about the body's mentality and its development as an outcome of my work with women with troubled eating (Orbach 1986, 1993, 1998, 1999, 2006). All around us we see evidence that girls as young as 6 and women in old age homes exhibit an obsessive preoccupation and desire to change their bodies. This desire to change their bodies includes the literal size of their bodies – wanting them usually to be smaller or slimmer as well as wanting to change their body parts either through exercise and diet or through the more drastic, but ever more commercially available, route of plastic surgery.

We have bred into girls a profound insecurity about their bodies. So great is this insecurity that they are receptive to the blandishments of the style industries that encourage them to disparage their bodies and want to change them. How might we understand at a psychological level what is going on when so many people are able to override their physical appetites: to eat when they are not hungry on an almost continual basis, to not even know what physiological hunger feels like because one is so used to eating without regard to physical cues signalling hunger, or on the other hand recognising the feeling of hunger as in anorexia nervosa and consistently and deliberately not responding to it with food?

We have understood many of the social reasons of this epidemic. We know the power of visual imagery to construct and shape our desire in particular ways. We recognise that girls and women in the west and in those countries now entering modernity through globalism do actually transform their bodies to meet the current aesthetic (Becker 1995). In the latter part of the twentieth century, beauty has been democratised, homogenised and valorised into a passport for social acceptance (Orbach 1978). Marking, inscribing, and transforming the body are the ways in which the rules of a given culture are enunciated and displayed (Foucault 1978; Butler 1990; Grosz 1994).

Many different kinds of excellent explanations analyse social phenomena which occur habitually as generational transmissions or indeed as markers of generational differentiation. The question that intrigues me is how the destabilising of the body is achieved at a psychological level. Or to put it another way, what is the nature of our contemporary relationship to the body such that it can and does appear to require remapping constantly? Are there tools within attachment theory and psychoanalysis that can address the depth of instability of bodies in our time? Is there sufficient theory to enable us to understand what makes it possible for so many people to make their bodies so available for transformation?

Bowlby's work and attachment theory addresses itself to the issue of security. In optimum conditions, the baby reaches for its mother and finds her there reassuringly and calmly providing what the baby needs and requires for its growth and development. The mother's capacities to think and feel what the baby needs and to either provide it or find the means to soothe the baby when needs cannot be met immediately form a template of experience which will underpin the security of the baby. The mother does this through her attunement and through her sensitive handling, holding and feeding of the baby.

Babies and mothers who are misattuned develop, in Bowlby's and his collaborator Mary Ainsworth's schema, a set of behaviours – clinginess, avoidant, anxious and disorganised – indicating insecure attachment. These behaviours are thought to mirror in some form the mother's own attachment behaviours: the babies developing secure or insecure attachment styles as a response to what they are offered. When secure attachment is not available the child will internalise the caregiver's defences (Eichenbaum & Orbach 1982; Fonagy 1999). To relate this concept to Winnicott's idea of the false self, the baby takes on the mother's gestures and makes them her own and this forms a basis of the making of a self (albeit an unstable self). In this way, the baby not only internalises aspects of the mother but also confirms and legitimates her modes of relating.

If we return to the question of how bodies are destabilised (a phenomenon we see explicitly in clinical practice through body countertransferences), we can perhaps draw out the unwelcome idea that the bodies we meet in therapy are bodies that have not been securely received in the first place. It isn't so much that these bodies are now being destabilised by all the cultural pressures – that is certainly the case – but it is a cultural pressure that has already destabilised the maternal body which is the original body from which and to which a baby develops either a secure or insecure attachment. The cultural destabilisations then work on already insecurely attached bodies: bodies which have embedded anxiety and disorganisation in their origins.

We could call it misattunement and we could call it cultural patterning. These are two different ways of analysing the current phenomenon. But however we describe it, we need to factor into the developmental story the way an individual comes to regard its body's subjectivity and to experience her body as either inviolable or as potentially available for transformation. In crude terms, I suspect that a suitably adapted attachment interview research project looking at the body would discover many aspects of transgenerational transmission of insecure bodies, particularly from mothers to daughters (but also from mothers to sons). If a mother is insecure or disorganised or anxious – to use attachment terms – in her body, this is the body that she will bring to her baby and it will be the raw material from which the baby will create a body for itself. Even if the mother is not insecure in her own body, there are overarching cultural imperatives that quite consciously influence a mother's relationship to her child's body. A mother inevitably prepares a daughter for the malleability of biological change and transmits the cultural prohibitions and fears that still coalesce around female sexuality, for example. These obvious requirements of the conduction of femininity mark a girl's body and her sense of it in ways that make her available to manipulate it as she grows up.

Consider the most basic of issues, the feeding and holding of infants, the recognition of their physical needs. Cross-cultural research shows the stunning effects in the very early treatment of babies by gender (Brunet and Lezine

1966). Boys are breastfed for longer than girls, each feed lasts longer, boys are weaned more gradually, they are potty trained later, they are held more. In work with mothers specifically around gender and appetites we know that where mothers are gleeful about the appetites of their sons, they are wary of daughters with large ones. If we move from appetite to holding, we only have to observe parents or carers to see that boys' physicality is more easily embraced as they are encouraged to extend their body's potential by climbing ladders and stairs while girls' physical explorations tend to be treated with hesitancy and a tone of caution.

These differing attitudes towards feeding and the very differing emotional experiences of physical handling that girls and boys receive is worth commenting on when we are trying to understand the question of the malleability and instability of girls' and women's bodies. We can see from very early on that girls are subject to a truncated physical experience. Mothers breastfeed daughters less and wean them earlier, not because girls need less food but because they unconsciously project on to girl infants something about what they consider to be appropriate about physical appetites and physical desires. They treat their daughters' bodies as they treat themselves. They create in them the conditions for deprivation and denial. And in that unconscious transaction, they set out an agenda for the physicality of their daughters which marks the girl's future relationship to her body.

The body of a woman comes from the body of her mother, both literally and in terms of the psychic history, which bequeaths her relation to that body. (Of course women also give boys their bodies which raises very interesting questions about the nature of both female and male sexuality and the role of the mother in the development, acceptance and integration of that sexuality.) The mother's sense of her own body, secure and thus relatively stable, or insecure and thus related to anxiously and in a disorganised fashion, is passed on to her child. This is done in two ways: one comes from what a mother represents to her child about her own body, how she is in it, her confidence or preoccupation with it; two, what the mother imagines for the body of her child, the potentialities that she holds for it and that she introduces to the child.

Mothers who may be uneasy in their bodies, who treat their own bodies as emergencies, bring that uneasy crisis body to their babies who then, in my clinical experience, grow up to be women with a great instability in their bodies. For some, this is expressed as a kind of void, a not really knowing how one's body is plotted, where it begins and ends. For others it is experiencing the body as a hated attribute. For still others it means having this thing, the body, which is out of control. For others it is always just an elusive size away from contentment. Mothers of daughters today have been subject to the most massive onslaught and attack on their bodies. This attack has come from those industries breeding body insecurity which has intensified the kind of foreboding women have always carried in relation to their bodies in which femininity, particularly female sexuality, has been represented as being extremely dangerous and in need of containment and denial.

So much of what we see in our consulting rooms is not the body as a container for unmanageable or painful mental contents but a body that is literally in trouble, a body that is unstable, fragile, immobile and insecure; a body self that needs the same kind of attention in therapy that we give to the psychological self. If we focus on our patients' physical development via the body countertransference, we learn many interesting things which enhance our work. We can understand the ways in which some of our patients take their own bodies as their object. They become involved in a kind of physical obsession with self in the attempt to create a body object that didn't exist from the beginning. They try to fill the void by creating a body for themselves. By doing, touching, fretting, fussing, manipulating, abusing, caring and obsessing in one way or another over this body, they concretise for themselves something that has not felt alive and they provide soothing and attention towards a body that has felt insecure.

When we bring the body into the therapeutic relationship, we then have a chance to recognise and reverse the ravages of body hatred. As we can welcome first the hated body or the disintegrated-in-bits body, the body that is a void, the body that can only weep, scratch or scream, then we can help our patients build from what is and what was rather than fictionalising their experience of hated bodies. By providing a relationship which can receive a sense of a hated, disintegrated or voided bodies, we begin the processes that will not only address their pain but will deconstruct the defences that have developed to manage the chaotic, disorganised or insecure body that constitutes the body subjectivity of the patient. In deconstructing those defences we are enabling the patient to face the pain and fright that feeling rudderless within one's body provokes.

Deconstructing those defences is often contingent on making our bodies available to our patients in the therapeutic relationship in a way akin to the way we make our psyches available. Although we may often feel unaware of our own bodies or experience ourselves as more like a brain, a head or a heart as we do our work in the consulting room, the various body counter-transferences that I discussed in the early part of this chapter have forced me to confront how very significant, for some patients, my body has become.

At first, such a recognition can cause discomfort. One is not easy with the thought that one's body is being scrutinised or used. We may imagine, especially if we have had personal issues around our bodies, that our patients are viewing our bodies in a critical light or that they track the nuances of change which occur for all of us. Of course some patients do: they have an uncanny knack of keying into an individual's private experience of, for example, an as yet to be spoken about pregnancy. Then at a general level, most patients will notice how the body is decorated and if the style or colours of a psychotherapist change.

One may tend, initially, to forget the ways in which our bodies are also transference objects for our patients and thus realise that the body our patients see is of course a body that has in essence been created in the therapy relationship. It is a body that represents the imaginative and cross-transference needs of the patient and the therapist. It is not a 'natural' or 'neutral' body. It expresses the relational complexities between the two people in the room.

Reminding oneself of the intersubjective aspect of the therapist's body both lifts the pressure and difficulty one might first encounter when reflecting on the need to acknowledge that our bodies are of course being used by our patients in the work we do with them. But more importantly, it allows us to further the work so that we can use the powerful body countertransferences to help transform the very anguished bodies that are our patients experience of their corporeality.

Conclusion

Attachment theory with its notion of the human as essentially a social animal doing its learning in the context of attachment relationships is especially well placed to enhance our understanding of how the mentality and subjectivity of the body develops. Attachment theory may also provide a useful undergirding schema for making sense of the wildcat body countertransferences that can beset a therapist in practice. What I have been able to understand so far is that the body is made in relationship: to paraphrase Simone de Beauvoir, the body is made, not born. The details of how it is made and the ways in which it may need to be unmade and remade within the context of a therapy relationship are yielding interesting and challenging clinical material, which will in time rebalance the overemphasis I believe psychoanalysis has brought to the study of mental processes.

Acknowledgement

This piece originally appeared in *Attachment and Human Development* 6(2), June 2004.

References

Becker, A. (1995) *The Body, Self & Society: The View from Fiji*. Philadelphia: University of Pennsylvania Press.
Butler, J. (1990) *Gender Trouble: Feminism and the Subversion of Identity*. New York: Routledge.
Brunet, O. and Lezine, I. (1966) *I Primi Anni del Bambino*. Rome: Armando.
Eichenbaum, L. and Orbach, S. (1982) *Outside In, Inside Out*. Harmondsworth: Pelican.
Field, N. (1989) 'Listening with the body'. *British Journal of Psychotherapy* 5(4): 512–522.

Fonagy, P. (1999) 'Transgenerational consistencies of attachment: a new theory'. Paper to the Developmental and Psychoanalytic Discussion Group, American Psychoanalytic Association Meeting, Washington, DC, 13 May.

Foucault, M. (1978) *The History of Sexuality: An Introduction*. London: Allen Lane.

Grosz, E. (1994) *Volatile Bodies: Towards a Corporeal Feminism*. Indianapolis: Indiana University Press.

McDougall, J. (1989) *Theatres of the Body*. London: Free Association Books.

Orbach, S. (1978) *Fat is a Feminist Issue*. London: Arrow.

Orbach, S. (1986) *Hunger Strike*. Harmondsworth: Penguin.

Orbach, S. (1993) 'Working with the false body'. In A. Erskine and D. Judd (eds) *The Imaginative Body*. London: Whurr.

Orbach. S. (1995) 'Countertransference and the false body'. *Winnicott Studies* 10, London: Karnac.

Orbach, S. (1998) 'In Dialogue with Stephen Mitchell'. *British Journal of Psychotherapy* 15: 194–200.

Orbach, S. (1999) *The Impossibility of Sex*. Harmondsworth: Penguin.

Orbach, S. (2006) 'How can we have a body: desire and corporeality'. *Studies in Gender and Sexuality*.

Racker, H. (1968) *Transference and Countertransference*. New York: International Universities Press.

Samuels, A. (1989) *The Plural Psyche: Personality, Morality and the Father*. London and New York: Routledge.

Winnicott, D.W. (1958) 'The capacity to be alone'. *International Journal Psycho-Analysis* 39: 416–420.

Part IV

Historical perspectives on women working with men

The intention in this final historical section is to demonstrate how comparatively recently it is that women have begun to write about erotic transferences of their male patients. Twenty years ago this was quite exceptional and all the chapters included in this section were challenging and liberating for those reading them at the time. The relief that at last this was being discussed was considerable for a number of women analysts and psychotherapists. These chapters are included because they reveal the path that has been travelled and offer the background to some of the thinking in the earlier chapters.

Chapter 12, by Herta Guttman, is deceptively simple, delineating some common sexual themes encountered in the female analyst–male patient dyad. The chapter was first published in 1984 and it is evident that attitudes to gender and sexuality have changed and so it is not easy to realise how isolated a female practitioner could feel at that time. Guttman, a psychoanalyst, applies terminology familiar in analytical psychology when she writes of archetypal themes between the female therapist and male patient. The language might be different today but similar issues may still be encountered in clinical practice, with the associated potential for unconscious, culturally stereotyped behaviours. This calls for sensitive awareness of difference in the supervision of both female and male supervisees. Herta Guttman explains the history of her chapter and sets it in context:

> This article, along with three other papers, was first presented at a panel at a meeting in Toronto of the American Academy of Psychoanalysis and then published in the Academy's journal, in 1984. Those who presented belonged to a seven-member group of women psychiatrists, which I had formed several years before, because I felt isolated, as the only senior female staff member of the Department of Psychiatry of the Jewish General Hospital in Montreal and I wanted to have a venue to discuss gender issues with female colleagues. There were so few of us at that time. The group members were Louise Carignan, Herta Guttman, Marie-Rose Jodoin, Suzanne Lamarre, Catherine Laroche, Eva Lester and Vivan Zicherman. It was at the height of the Women's Movement and the

Quebec Separatist movement. We did not want to have a consciousness-raising group but a group that addressed professional issues. Discussion ranged from domestic violence, to the role of women in psychiatric departments, from the gender of the therapist to suitable clothes for the female professional. Of course, political and social issues inevitably came into the discussions. However, although we had lots of heated discussions, we always managed to contain them, perhaps because of our professional training.

Eva Lester had the idea of presenting a panel on gender issues between the female therapist and the male patient. Everybody participated in preparing the papers, either by writing or by affording constructive criticism. This was the final event in our life as a group; but it left us all a little bit freer and bolder to speak up when women's issues came to the fore in our respective workplaces.

Herta A. Guttman (personal communication, August 2005)

The three chapters that follow develop similar themes. It is hard to imagine now how innovative were these papers when they were first published in the early 1980s. Nancy Kulish (Chapter 13) discusses gender and transference, questioning how the analyst's gender might take a 'maternal or paternal cast' and how it might contribute to a highly eroticised transference. The concept of 'the phallic mother' is discussed critically and it is suggested that it might at times contribute to gender-related blind spots. She suggests that there are times when such a construct might mean that the female analyst misses the paternal transference. Today such observations have passed into the language of psychoanalysis as we saw in Covington's chapter (Chapter 5). Laila Karme (Chapter 14) discusses another technical issue: the negative Oedipal transference. Her single case example shows how this emerges, is analysed and resolved in the case of a male patient working with a female analyst. This too links with Covington (Chapter 5). The final chapter (Chapter 15) by Marianne Goldberger and Dorothy Evans Holmes was one of the first to address the topic of the erotic transference in the male patient/female analyst dyad. They propose a spectrum of transference manifestations in the psychoanalysis of male patients in analysis with female analysts. They demonstrate through five brief case examples, erotic and paternal transferences of male patients with female analysts linking the fear of the erotic to an unconscious fear of aggression.

These chapters remind us of the journey that has been travelled in the last 20 years and so conclude the book.

Chapter 12

Sexual issues in the transference and countertransference between female therapist and male patient

Herta A. Guttman

It is always difficult to describe a myth; it cannot be grasped or encompassed; it haunts the human consciousness without ever appearing before it in fixed form. The myth is so various, so contradictory, that at first its unity is not discerned: Delilah and Judith, Aspasia and Lucretia, Pandora and Athena – woman is at once Eve and the Virgin Mary. She is an idol, a servant, the source of life, a power of darkness; she is the elemental silence of truth, she is artifice, gossip and falsehood; she is healing presence and sorceress; she is a man's prey, his downfall, she is everything that he is not and that he longs for, his negation and his raison d'être.

Simone de Beauvoir (1953: 143)

Introduction

One aspect of belonging to one or the other of the two sexes is that this membership organizes our perception of ourselves and other people's perceptions of us. Every culture and society develops archetypal images of each sex, that is, generalized representations of qualities and attributes that are particularly connected with one sex or the other, and which are believed to be universally present in every member of a given sex. These images evoke rather predictable, almost stereotyped feelings and responses in other people, according to their sex. To say that such archetypal images are socially conditioned does not imply that they are any less general than if they were biologically determined: the universality of certain myths attests to our common humanity as much as does our common genetic structure.

It is my contention that transference and countertransference phenomena originate in idiosyncratic personal experiences and associations, but that these are embedded in and informed by the archetypes of the society in which we grow to perceive each sex in a certain way and to have certain commonly held beliefs and expectations concerning male and female attributes. The male patient arrives at the female therapist's office with some of these fundamental images of women. Those that are most personally meaningful will probably be those that best connect with his particular early experiences.

The female therapist, in turn, has certain fundamental images of men, some of which may inform her general attitude to male patients and some of which may be elicited by a specific patient's attitudes and behavior. I will consider only those fundamental, stereotyped positive and negative images, which relate specifically to the sexual transference and countertransference.

The male patient's transference images

Asexual images of the therapist

1. The nurturant mother, the 'good breast', the mirror, the asexual madonna

This is probably a primordial image, more or less damaged by our real life experiences, but nonetheless a fundamental symbol of basic trustworthiness and of the expectation of good things.

Very often, it is the nurturant image that is most quickly projected onto a female therapist by male patients, and the dreams in which the therapist first appears undisguised have as their underlying theme the wish for nurturance. It is probably not surprising that this often antedates more obviously sexualized transferences. What is more evocative of a fairly normative mother–child relationship than the therapeutic situation, in which the patient confides his innermost thoughts and feelings to a woman who is associated with acceptance and nurturance? Indeed, in our society, adult males do not generally easily confide in one another, presumably because they expect to experience competition and power struggles with one another.

The therapeutic relationship we are considering is one of the few male–female relationships in our society in which a woman is supposed to be more powerful and authoritative than a male. If it does not immediately become a power struggle, this is precisely because of the early, nurturant, asymmetrical mother–child relationship. However, it is culturally deviant to openly express one's sexual feelings to an asexual mother figure who is our authoritative confidante. Perhaps this accounts for the fact that male patients seem to report fewer overtly sexual dreams, associations and thoughts to their female therapists.

> A 32-year-old man in the course of therapy became aware that he had selected the one female on a list of possible therapists given to him by his family practitioner. He related this to his greater ease in confiding in women, be they friends or lovers. He connected this with his family of origin, in which he had great difficulty in relating to an impatient, critical father and turned to his mother for understanding. He had come to therapy because he was in a quandary about leaving his wife for his mistress. The sexual aspects of the transference were always muted, as he

had two readily available women with whom to act out his conflicts and desires.

2. The suffocating, merging, engulfing female

When pushed to the extreme, the image of the nurturant mother becomes that of the engulfing female who does not permit distantiation and differentiation. Fear of fusion with the mother is probably always present, to some extent, in every relationship with a female.

3. The withholding, inattentive mother, the 'bad breast', the self-sacrificing martyr

The converse of the good mother image is that of a woman who exacts a high price for her gifts. This image often (but not always) underlies the derogatory generalizations that male patients may make about woman in general, and the therapist in particular – about their stupidity, their avarice, their cupidity, their narcissism, their self-interestedness, and their manipulativeness (Woods 1976). This image is perhaps most obvious in the instant, strong negative transference of borderline patients, whose real experience of precarious mothering gives them the most reason to be suspicious.

These three asexual images can coexist or rapidly succeed one another in the transference. They are often combined with more sexualized feelings, because males have a tendency to deny their dependent feelings or their crises of trust, and to substitute sexual themes for them (Woods 1976).

> A single man of 35 alternately feels that the therapist is a wise, highly intuitive, strong and comforting figure and that she is like a mysterious siren, who knows everything he thinks and feels, and could influence him without his being aware of it. He is not sure he can trust this influence. Again, he sometimes feels that she is too close, too enveloping in her all-knowingness. He is reminded of his sporadic impotence; he feels suffocated by women in general and by the therapist in particular. At times when he feels very suffocated, he misses an appointment.

Sexual images of the therapist

The foregoing images of the therapist are essentially asexual. They are – in a sense – pre-Oedipal. The sexual images that are projected onto the therapist are of two kinds: the sexually pleasing, potentially gratifying sexual object; and conversely, the sexually tantalizing, frustrating, or devalued woman-object, the whore who can be dangerous and even lethal.

1. The therapist as a positive sexual object

Having a therapist they find attractive probably validates some patients and increases sexual confidences with a woman if they perceive her as being sexually knowledgeable. However, this image can be discomforting, for two reasons. First, it is not considered 'proper' to divulge one's sexual feelings to a 'lady'. Second, it is not congruent for a man to have sexual feelings in a situation in which the woman is dominant:

> A successful, professional, middle-aged man came for treatment because of feelings of failure and emptiness relating to repeated disappointing relationships with women. He described a pattern of 'falling in love, being on a high', followed by disenchantment, disappointment and emptiness. On the patient's return from his first vacation since therapy started, he arrived early but complained that he had rushed to the session without his morning coffee, and playfully asked what the therapist was going to do to make up for this deprivation? For the first time since therapy began, his tone was openly flirtatious. Later in the session, he said he felt as if he were on a 'first date' with the therapist, having to start all over again, not being sure of being accepted or interesting enough, and extra-attentive to what he related. His flirtatious, sexually provocative words seemed to express positive, possibly excited feelings about seeing the therapist again. However, the patient's behavior also reflected some disquiet at returning to therapy. It probably demonstrated his precarious relationship with a mother whom he perceived as having been distant, uninterested and somewhat rejecting.

As the patient's comfort with the therapist and with himself as a sexual being increases, veiled allusions to her positive sexuality may become more evident, often as teasing references to her dress or her putative sex life. He will rarely speak openly or directly about his fantasies. He will not recognize a sexualized symbol of the therapist in a dream. He will often express his feelings through acting them out – for instance, choosing a psychologist or a doctor as a new girlfriend.

It must be remembered that every male can just as easily feel himself a rapist as a sexually potent man, that he has been taught from early childhood to be vigilant concerning this putative potential. Just as the female patient will think twice about being blatantly sexy with a male therapist, for fear of being labeled a vamp or a whore, the male patient will be careful in expressing his sexual feelings, lest he be considered dangerous.

2. The therapist as a negative sexual object

The converse of the positive, sexually attractive image of the female therapist is that of the therapist-female as a sexually tantalizing, frustrating, potentially dangerous object. This image indubitably has deep roots in our psychology. It is related to such concepts as castration anxiety, womb envy, the fear of being sexually devoured (Horney 1932). Interestingly, most of these concepts originate in descriptions of male and not of female psychology. In a male-dominated society, moreover, this image is egosyntonic and consonant with the culture's stereotypes (Woods 1976), so that it is almost predictable and perhaps not unacceptable for male patients to express fear, contempt or loathing for women in a sexualized manner in certain situations of frustration, disappointment or anxiety. The difference is perhaps that with female therapists, because the listener and witness is a woman, male patients are not always as direct in sharing such thoughts and feelings. They will make indirect references: e.g., to a 'cold, Vogue-model type'; to a 'Women's Liberation type, screwing everyone in sight'; to a 'ball crusher'. Again, this transference is expressed as a displacement or generalization rather than as a direct statement.

The therapist's countertransference images

There are two possible sources of the therapist's countertransference feelings: either previous personal experiences and conflicts are projected onto the patient, or transference messages from the patient stimulate unconscious responses in the therapist (Heimann 1950; MacLaughlin 1981). Much as there is a stereotyped, archetypal quality to the patient's transference images, so do the therapist's corresponding contertransferential responses follow certain archetypal images of men.

Asexual images of the male patient

1. The needy child

This image is perhaps the one which is most commonly evoked in female therapists because it is culturally consonant with being a sympathetic, giving, nursing woman, sensitive to people's needs, accepting a man's confidences. It is probably the therapist's favorite retreat when she feels helpless in the face of the patient's dependent or aggressive demands. This countertransference can lead to passive and overly accepting behavior, if the therapist sacrifices the patient to her own need to be a 'good mother' at all costs, rather than fostering his autonomy and growth by making relevant interpretations and limiting his tendency to be dependent and demanding.

2. The provocative child

Feeling that the patient is an angry, untrusting, provocative child can make a female therapist placate him, avoid him, or get angry with him. Females easily become anxious and frightened by men's hostility because of the ever-dormant fear that violence could erupt. Needy, grasping and demanding men and children easily anger them. As women, female therapists tend to suppress their anger and irritation at being drained, exploited or blamed. They tend to placate or withdraw from the patient rather than confront him.

Sexual images of the male patient

1. The positive sexual male image

Any therapist, male or female, can react positively to a patient of the opposite sex, especially if the client is obviously enamoured of the therapist and goes to some lengths to let the therapist know about this attraction. As women, female therapists have been well trained to censor their sexual feelings, to suppress them – even to protest that they do not exist. Tower (1956) reports becoming aware of her Oedipal countertransference in a dream. This demonstrates the tendency of female therapists to suppress their conscious awareness of such dangerous feelings. Acknowledging sexual arousal evokes in female therapists, as in all women, images of the incestuous mother or of the whorish 'other woman'. Female therapists may also react in this way to the male patient's sexuality, pretending that he is not attractive, that he is not attracted, that he is not sexually arousing and he is not speaking in a way that is sexually arousing.

This reaction is reinforced by a culture which consistently tells women that it is their fault if a man is attracted to them, that they must have done something to be provocative. Marlaina Sacks Sniderman (1980) describes having been cautioned against dressing provocatively, and I have witnessed the discomfort of female therapists in training who cringe as they await some insinuation on the part of the supervisor that they are contributing to the patient's sexual reactions. Nobody seems truly to subscribe to Freud's dictum (1915) that the charms of the therapist's person are not the source of these feelings in the patient.

On the other hand, it can happen that a female therapist's positive sexual countertransference feelings come through in her dress, her smile and her general body language. These reactions should, of course, be within the therapist's awareness as much as possible, so that she has the freedom to express them in a therapeutic way, if at all.

> A therapist treating a recently separated man became aware of her strong feelings of attraction to him and of feeling somehow comforted and eased by his allusions to having had several affairs during his marriage, as if these experiences validated her desires. She connected her feelings to two sources: (1) an obvious Oedipal component, involving a kind of triumph over the man's estranged wife; (2) an attraction toward this patient's

behavior as a professional man, in that he tended to be protective and admiring of his female colleagues, a situation which the therapist felt was lacking in her own current relationship with her colleagues, and for which she yearned.

Positive sexual countertransference, well handled, can facilitate the patient's comfort with himself as a sexual person and in expressing feelings that he might not easily share. It may then allow the patient to express his sexuality more appropriately in the outside world. This, however, does not mean that the therapist should make prurient inquiries into the patient's sexual fantasies. Orr (1954) quotes Ferenczi and Rank, who caution against the narcissistic aspect of countertransference, which can lead the therapist to concentrate on those aspects of the patient's feelings which flatter him or her. Female therapists are not generally exhibitionistic in this regard: on the contrary, they are often overly prudent, avoiding opportunities to facilitate the expression of the sexual aspects of their patients' thoughts and fantasies because they fear appearing prurient or brazen. Abramowitz et al. (1976), studying the differences in length of time of psychotherapy with various patient–therapist pairs, hypothesize that it is this discomfort that makes female therapists less likely to prolong therapy with male than female patients.

2. The negative sexual male image

Archetypal negative sexual images of males relate to their sexually devaluing, degrading, or violent attitudes towards sex and women. The female therapist may react to a male patient with fear, anger, disgust, irritation, loathing or contempt. She may be fearful of a man who recounts his sadistic sexual exploits; she may be uncomfortable with a patient who delights in detailed descriptions of his experiences with oral sex; she may be contemptuous of a man who, in his love life, is a weak supplicant rather than a virile suitor. These are all rather common countertransference reactions, which must be recognized and dealt with by identifying them, connecting them with one's experiences, and using them empathically.

'Sexist' images of the male patient

Female therapists can also react negatively to the specifically male chauvinist traditions of our society (Woods 1976). They increasingly share women's emerging consciousness of themselves as respect-worthy persons who should not be belittled because of their sex, and particularly not in sexually demeaning ways (Nadelson et al. 1978). They are not willing any longer to attribute every derogatory remark or unfeeling act to a particular male patient's psychopathology, but rather recognize a more universal, damaging pattern.

A male patient may behave as if he is 'God's gift to women', a Don Juan who 'loves them and leaves them', sometimes using his social position or superficial tenderness to exploit and charm women. Such men are often completely unconscious of this aspect of their behavior, assuming it is natural for men to evaluate, choose, and discard females. A variant of this is the male patient who is withdrawn and does not socialize with women, claiming that none of them is sufficiently beautiful, clever, sexy, or intelligent. As a pastime, he spends time with 'the boys', with whom he bonds to make devaluing comments and jokes about women.

A male patient may use women in an inferior social position to serve or to service him. By being simultaneously charming and patronizing, he can keep his fundamental dependence on them out of his awareness. Or he may have aggressive, even sadistic, sexual feelings and fantasies but may rationalize his hostility toward his partners by espousing such 'liberated' practices as 'swinging'. He may adopt a master–slave relationship in his sexual practices because it is more exciting: 'S–m's an "in" thing to do.'

A man may deride Women's Liberation, opposing women's attempts at self-fulfillment by calling such women a variety of derogatory names. If the woman is his wife, he might be even more directly negative and oppositional (Gold and Gold 1981). A male patient can use the philosophy of Women's Liberation to emotionally or materially exploit his partner, in the guise of being avant-garde – for instance, having his wife or girlfriend pay more than her share of the bills, recreational expenses, etc.

Indeed, it is not clear whether the therapist's negative reaction should be called countertransference, in the strict sense of the word, since her feelings are usually conscious and founded in reality. Her dilemma is in deciding whether or not to address the patient's sexist assumptions within the therapeutic situation, as part of the field of psychotherapy. Therapists, in general, have tended to regard these attitudes as defensive rationalizations, which help the man to feel competent when he is really at his most dependent and incompetent. However, because they feel increasingly responsible toward the women in such men's lives, increasing numbers of therapists – perhaps particularly female therapists – are beginning to question the acceptance of these attitudes, arguing that the therapist's reactions should be used in a more feminist, albeit therapeutic manner.

Sexual countertransference in male and female therapists

A review of the literature (and particularly of the psychoanalytic literature) on countertransference reveals that, whereas male therapists more often report erotic transference in female patients, it is female therapists who more frequently report their own erotic countertransference (Heimann 1950; Tower 1956; Lester 1982). Does this observation imply that male analysts and therapists are less likely to acknowledge the self-generated aspect of their countertransference feelings and are more likely to attribute them entirely to the effect of the patient's sexual transference? Does it imply that male therapists find such feelings more acceptable and accepted, given that they are more socially congruent? Are female therapists more careful, because of their cultural conditioning as women, to scrutinize and repress their sexuality? Perhaps, in this instance, being female is advantageous. Female therapists, like all women, are not as committed to preserving the illusion of their power in relationships, therapeutic or otherwise. They may more easily admit the patient's reciprocal power over them.

Conclusion

In this chapter, I have surveyed some of the archetypal images, both positive and negative, that are carried by male patient and female therapist, and that conditions aspects of their interaction with respect to sexuality – how it is expressed or not expressed in therapeutic sessions. It is my impression that it is easier for male patients to be direct in expressing their dependency needs and that their sexual feelings for the therapist remain veiled and indirect, often finding expression in acting out or displacement. This is because everything in our social customs and taboos militates against the expression, to a female in a dominant position, of sexual fantasies and desires. Similarly, everything militates against the female therapist's reciprocal conscious recognition of the male patient's sexual wishes and of her own erotic countertransference. Therefore, the female therapist–male patient dyad must overcome many strictures in order to address sexual issues freely.

Acknowledgement

This chapter was first presented at a Special Panel, 'The Erotic Transference between the Female Therapist and the Male Patient', 26th annual meeting of the American Academy of Psychoanalysis, Toronto, 1982.

It was published in 1984 in the *Journal of the American Academy of Psychoanalysis* 12(2): 187–197.

References

Abramowitz, S. I., Abramowitz, C. V., Roback, H. W., Corney, R. T. and McKee, E. (1976) 'Sex-role related countertransference in psychotherapy'. *Archives of General Psychiatry* 33: 71–73.
De Beauvoir, S. (1953) *The Second Sex*. New York: Knopf.
Dinnerstein, D. (1976) *The Mermaid and the Minotaur*. New York: Harper.
Freud, S. (1915) 'Recommendations on the technique of psychoanalysis: observations on transference-love'. *The Collected Papers*. Vol. 2 (E. Jones) Ed. New York: Basic Books. (1959 edition, p. 379).
Gold, J. H. and Gold, E. (1981) 'The belittled wife: social, legal and psychotherapeutic considerations'. *Canadian Journal of Psychiatry* 26: 402–405.

Heimann, P. (1950) 'On countertransference'. *International Journal of Psycho-Analysis* 31: 81–84.

Horney, K. (1932) 'The dread of woman'. *International Journal of Psycho-Analysis* 13: 348–360.

Lester, E. P. (1982) 'The female analyst and the erotized transference'. Paper presented at the annual meeting of the American Academy of Psychoanalysis, Toronto, May.

MacLaughlin, J. (1981) 'Transference, psychic reality and countertransference'. *Psychoanalytic Quarterly* 50(4): 639–664.

Nadelson, C. C., Notman, M. T. and Bennett, M. B. (1978) 'Success or failure: psychotherapeutic considerations for women in conflict'. *American Journal of Psychiatry* 135: 1092–1096.

Orr, D. W. (1954) 'Transference and countertransference: a historical survey'. *Journal of the American Psychoanalytic Association* 2: 621–669.

Sniderman, M. S. (1980) 'A countertransference problem: the sexualizing patient'. *Canadian Journal of Psychiatry* 25: 303–307.

Tower, L. E. (1956) 'Countertransference'. *Journal of the American Psychoanalytic Association* 4: 224–265.

Woods, S. (1976) 'Some dynamics of male chauvinism'. *Archives of General Psychiatry* 33: 63–65.

Chapter 13

Gender and transference

The screen of the phallic mother

Nancy Mann Kulish

Introduction

Recently psychoanalytic writers, mostly women, have begun to focus on the question of how gender of the analyst or therapist might affect the transference in psychoanalysis or psychoanalytic psychotherapy. This question has also made its way into the popular literature in the best selling novel *August* by Judith Rossner (1983). The novel depicts the interfacing lives of a young woman and her female analyst in New York. The story, in which the girl had previously seen two male analysts, gives Rossner the opportunity to comment on the differences in the girl's treatment at the hands of a male versus a female therapist, largely in terms of her feminist concerns with a male's lack of empathy for and power over a female.

Indeed, it may have been at the nudging of feminists that psychoanalysis has turned its attention to the questions of gender-related differences in psychosexual development and how they impact on the psychotherapeutic process. The interest in the subject also reflects a general shift within psychoanalysis in the conceptualizations of transference. The classical view of transference stems from Freud's first writings on the subject. He pictured transference as a fixed disposition within the individual to repeat his or her infantile conflicts with the person of the analyst (Freud 1912, 1915). Later writers such as Blum (1971) and Sandler (1976) have encompassed Freud's later structural theories and emphasis on aggressive as well as libidinal drives into the understanding of transference. Such writers view transference as less fixed and more possibly influenced by present realities within the analytic situation, including the gender of the analyst. Other writers such as Gill (1982) or Langs (1973) have emphasized the importance of the interaction between patient and therapist in the unfolding of the transference. In this interaction, the actuality of the therapist's personality and the patient's view of it help to determine and define the transference. My own view of transference does take as its starting point an unconscious, genetically and internally based disposition, which is influenced by and influences the interpersonal process of which it becomes a dynamic part.

The current interest in gender and transference has generated much excitement and discussion as it touches upon important theoretical and clinical issues, such as the role of reality in the unfolding of transference or the selection of therapist by gender. Yet, a review of the literature on gender and transference (Kulish 1984) generates many questions but few substantial findings. There is general agreement on several points: one, that gender of the therapist can contribute to major resistances within the transference, especially early in the treatment; two, that gender influences or facilitates positive transferences that may help to launch an analysis; three, that gender shapes or colours the content of the clinical material; four, that gender may determine the order in which this material emerges. These latter two points were first mentioned by Freud (1931), who suggested that early, pre-Oedipal material relating to the mother might make itself known more readily in the transference to female analysts.

Two other intriguing but more controversial questions have been raised in the recent literature. The first is that gender of the analyst differentially determines whether the transference takes a 'maternal' or 'paternal' cast. The second concerns the question of strongly erotic or 'eroticized' transferences and how the gender of the analyst may contribute to such manifestations. In both of these questions the concept of 'the phallic mother' has frequently been advanced as an explanation of observed differences. It is my intention here to examine more closely the concept of the phallic mother as it appears in this context. It is not my purpose to focus on the concept in itself, but only to use it to illustrate how gender of the therapist might relate to the transference. It is my feeling that gender can be a major organizing factor both for the patient and for the analyst. A conceptual construction such as 'phallic mother' both conveys gender-related distortions and fantasies which make up transferences, and gender-related biases and blindspots which contribute to countertransferences. Before turning to the discussion of the 'phallic mother' as it relates to gender and transference, however, I will briefly review the usage of the concept of phallic mother more generally within psychoanalysis. Its usage demonstrates how an aspect of theory can serve both as a powerful explanatory device and as a limiting curb to our understanding of ourselves and our patients.

The concept of the phallic mother

Freud did not use the term phallic mother until late in his writings, although Little Hans' fantasy that his mother possessed a penis is clearly discernible in the material of the case published in 1909. In his writings on fetishism, Freud (1927, 1940) described how the little boy must construct a fantasy of a woman with a phallus to ward off the recognition of the threatening reality of a castrated, penisless creature, the woman, and the possibility of his own castration. In 1933, Freud referred to Abraham's discussion of the spider as a symbol of the mother. The sight of a spider evokes dread of incestuous wishes toward mother, and horror of the female genital. According to Freud, both little girls and little boys view mother as possessing a penis until the time they discover sexual differences.

Later writers have elaborated on the role of the fantasied phallic mother in defending against the boy's castration anxiety. Bak (1968) described the phallic woman as 'the ubiquitous fantasy in perversions'. Stoller's work (1975) emphasizes the importance of the fantasy for male homosexuals, transvestites and fetishists. In dressing up as a woman, for example, the transvestite acts out this unconscious fantasy of a woman with a penis. Greenacre (1968) also pointed to the underlying castration anxiety and fantasy of the phallic mother in understanding the meaning of the fetish in the male. Both Stoller and Greenacre stress the role of childhood trauma, such as an overly seductive mother, in the reinforcement of the fantasy in such male patients. Helene Deutsch (1965) felt that homosexuality in women also reveals the presence of this fantasy. A lesbian, in taking a masculine role or choosing a masculine lover, may be creating in fantasy such a phallic mother and denying her perception of being castrated.

While the concept has been seen primarily as a denial of castration anxiety of both the girl and the boy, the 'phallic mother' has also been understood as expressing earlier, more infantile fears. Ruth Mack Brunswick (1940) asserted that the concept is a regressive compensatory one. The phallic mother not only possesses a penis, she is 'all powerful'. The idea of a penis is projected back upon the image of the active mother and her breast, from the oral stages. Roheim (1945), in a fascinating essay on the phallic mother in mythology, focused on the images of witches in central European folklore. The witch with her broomstick, hairy chin and pointed hat is clearly the woman endowed with a phallus. The common folktale that a witch can be discerned through a hole in a piece of wood betrays the wish that the phallus may be spied through the female's hole or vagina. Thus, Roheim also suggested that the phallic mother defends not only against the threat of castration, but the recognition of the existence of the vagina. At the same time, mythological witches are frequently tied to or identified with images of cows and milk, especially ruined or poisoned milk. The phallic mother is really the oral mother, then, the witch who attacks the source of milk and embodies the infant's aggression against the mother. Here is the equation: 'penis equals breast'. Other authors (Evans 1972; Ewens 1976; Greenacre 1968; Hermann 1949) have stressed the pregenital underpinnings of the phallic mother. Chronologically, sexual differences come into focus during the anal phase, so she is also the sadistic anal mother (Chasseguet-Smirgel 1964).

In a similar vein, Chasseguet-Smirgel (1964) asserted that the image of the omnipotent mother survives in us all. The boy's desire to free himself from her domination and his guilt about his hostility and his triumph over her add power to the fantasy of the phallic mother. The sight of the female genital is frightening, not only because it arouses castration anxiety, but because it confirms the role of the father and his penis in sexual intercourse. The fantasy also expresses the boy's denial of the existence of the adult vagina and the feelings of inadequacy it evokes. The fantasy concerns both fears about differences in the sexes and differences in the generations.

Kubie (1974) explained the fantasy from a unique perspective: as a manifestation of the 'drive to become both sexes', with which, he suggested, everyone struggles. The phallic mother equals the man–woman both male and female patients would wish to become. Kubie believed that the inability to commit oneself to either gender and the desire to identify with both parents spring from a deep tendency of human nature. This wish can be traced in psychopathology, relationships between the sexes, works of art and literature, and in fantasy life.

This brief review of the literature on the concept of the phallic mother shows how it plays a role in many current theoretical controversies: the attack on the notion of the primacy of the phallus and penis envy in female psychosexual development; the meaning and timing of the child's recognition of sexual differences; the role of pre-Oedipal versus Oedipal factors in the genesis of neurosis; that is, how 'phallic' is the 'phallic mother'? While highlighting these controversies is not my aim, I will attempt to show that our theoretical concepts such as phallic mother, with all the weight that they carry, do shape our processing, understanding, and management of the transference and, particularly as it relates to our gender. The 'phallic mother' has been variously described as a projected image in the transference as maternal, paternal, bisexual, a ban against or an expression of erotic feelings toward the same or opposite sex.

The maternal versus the paternal transference

An obvious influence of therapist's gender on the transference may be its influence on whether the material has a 'maternal' versus 'paternal' cast. Theoretically, 'maternal' and 'paternal' transferences should be evoked freely by analysts or therapists of both sexes; certainly, we know this to be the case. Nevertheless, Freud (1931) was the first to point out that maternal transferences were less available to him and less understood by him than paternal transferences because of his sex. The minuscule bit of empirical data available on the question suggests that in therapies other than analysis images of therapists correlate with their manifest genders (Goldberg 1979). The psychoanalytic literature on the subject suggests a puzzling difference, however: that male analysts, since Freud, do report many instances in which they are seen as the mother in the transference, yet virtually no reports by female analysts of sustained paternal transferences are available.

Even in the novel *August*, this apparent difference is noted in a conversation between a female and male analyst at a cocktail party: ' "It's my experience," Seaver said, "that the analyst becomes both the mother and father." "It's not my experience," Lulu said' (Rossner 1983: 38). Does this difference reflect a clinical actuality, and if so why? In approaching this question, I have been speaking with female analysts from around the country to tap their clinical experiences. Several of these women felt there was no truth to the statement that paternal transferences are less common for female analysts and cited their clinical experience in observing paternal transferences. Some suggested that the presumed lack of paternal transferences to female analysts may be a function of referral patterns. Women analysts tend to see fewer men than women, and the men who seek them out, or are referred to them, tend to be more disturbed and hence more prone to pre-Oedipal maternal transferences. More of the women analysts, however, used such words as 'more subtle', 'less frequent', 'not sustained', to describe the incidences of paternal transferences. I am uncomfortable with this overly schematic terminology of 'maternal' versus 'paternal' transferences, as I view transferences as organized around affects or need-states. For the sake of argument, however, I will stick with this language. In my own clinical experience prior to beginning this research, I had only seen fleeting paternal images.

The difference, if real – fewer or weaker paternal transferences with female analysts – can be explained from the side of the patient, the analyst, or both. From the patient's side, several explanations have been advanced. These revolve mainly around developmental issues. Because early experiences with the mother form the basic matrix from which all object relations spring, maternal transferences are, in general, more prevalent or more central (Greenacre 1954; Zetzel 1966). A second argument suggests that our knowledge of 'maleness' comes developmentally later and is differentiated from our knowledge of 'femaleness'. Hence, 'maleness' is tied more to reality and less resistant to breakdown than the concept of 'femaleness'. Thus, paternal or masculine images are more tied to the reality of the therapist's gender and less likely to be superimposed on a female therapist (Zetzel 1966; Karme 1979, Chapter 14 in this book; Mason 1983).

From the side of the analyst, it is possible that an analyst might have difficulty, in general, in perceiving the transference in terms of images, roles or attitudes related to the opposite sex. This difficulty would, of course, hold true for male analysts as well as female analysts (Stein and Auchincloss 1984). It may be particularly difficult, however, for women to allow themselves to view or understand the transference in masculine or 'paternal' terms. Several writers have suggested, for example, that women analysts may be inclined to focus too readily on the early maternal material or interpret into the 'dyad' (Berstein 1984; Stein and Auchincloss 1984). Lerner (1974), in a thought-provoking paper about the depreciation of women in society in general and in psychoanalytic theory in particular, concludes that 'the character of the primitive maternal image and women's related fear of their castrating and destructive potential may be such that the female sex has relatively greater difficulty acknowledging and directly expressing aggressive, competitive and ambitious strivings' (1974: 551).

Kubie (1974) came to an opposite conclusion about how cultural attitudes may influence the expression of 'the drive to become both sexes'. He felt that in our culture the drive is tolerated or even encouraged in women, but almost totally repressed in men, except in cases of sexual deviation. While Kubie's premise of a primary, unconscious drive to be both sexes is debatable, his notion that the individual expresses or becomes aware of attitudes or attributes relative to both sexes as a function of differing environmental influences is relevant here.

Another explanation of the lack of reported paternal images is that paternal or masculine images in the transference are interpreted in terms of the 'phallic mother'. A search of the clinical literature reveals how a construct such as the 'phallic mother' can obscure the vision of the analyst to other paradigms in the transference. In a case of a male patient presented by Eva Lester (1982), the concept of the phallic mother figured predominantly. Within the transference the patient projected some masculine images, she felt, but a 'consolidating maternal image' arose – a feared phallic mother. In this case and elsewhere (Szmarag 1982), Lester asserted that in the male patient–female analyst dyad the paternal negative Oedipal transference is qualitatively indistinguishable from the maternal one to the phallic mother; that is, she felt that certain paternal images are indistinguishable from maternal ones. In her discussion of Lester's case, Marianne Goldberger (Lester 1982) pointed out that the manifestations Lester labelled as phallic mother could also be interpreted in terms of the paternal transference. Moreover, Goldberger suggested that phallic mother and penetrating father may be possible to distinguish.

Differentiating the 'phallic mother' from images of the father may, indeed, not be simple. As in all other matters, we must be guided by the context in which the clinical material appears, the accumulated clinical data about the patient, and not the manifest content of the associations. Very little help can be found in the literature on this question.

Bernstein and Warner (1984) summarized several cases of female patients seen by female analysts in which images of the analyst in the transference alternated at times between phallic mother and Oedipal father or became condensed into one intrusive figure. Since the cases are not reported in detail, it is not clear how these images were distinguished, except on the obvious grounds of whether pre-Oedipal or Oedipal concerns were reflected in the material. They suggest that the sexualized homosexual transference, which develops initially with certain of their female patients, is pre-Oedipal, as a defence against deep, early longings for the mother perceived as unavailable. The mother, in such cases, can also appear as phallic. Notably, Bernstein and Warner also observed that female analysts, including themselves, resist seeing themselves in masculine roles in the transference.

Male analysts as well as female encounter the issue of differentiating the penetrating father from the phallic mother in the transference. Shengold (1963), in a rich paper on the sphinx, whom he feels represents the primal parent and the phallic mother, described a clinical case in which he, as analyst, was used as the penetrative phallic mother. Other male writers (Finklestein 1975; Orgel 1965), however, described cases replete with genetic and fantasy material about 'phallic mothers' in which they do not report themselves in terms of this role in the transference.

In a clinical paper about a case of a man whose history revealed he had been used as and took on the role of his mother's phallus, Shevin (1963) briefly addressed this issue. In the transference, Shevin described how he became the patient's (phallic) mother for whom the patient performed and with whom the patient was regressively fused. At other times the patient took the role of the mother and treated the analyst as the phallic extension of himself. Later on in the treatment, the patient was able to identify with the analyst and other males by first acting as a phallus for a strong man. Shevin differentiated very similar paternal from maternal images partially on the basis of developmental lines: the analyst in the father role was viewed as more of a whole entity than in the mother role.

Chasseguet-Smirgel (1964) spoke directly to the differences and similarities between the images of the father and the phallic mother. Relationships to the father, for the little girl, often recapitulate the relationship to the mother, as 'penis envy' toward the male carries earlier conflicts toward the mother. In this sense, paternal images are really a double exposure of maternal ones and indistinguishable from them. Yet as it emerges in treatment, she asserts, the transference to the father is more idealized, with triadic dimensions, as compared with the maternal.

Whether or not images of phallic mother versus penetrating father are difficult or impossible to discern in the transference, and whether these or any other criteria for their differentiation can be useful, we cannot make a differentiation if we are not set to do so. It is my thesis that we as well as our patients can become tied up by our manifest sex so that we do not look beyond it. As I said before, until beginning this research, I had experienced only fleeting paternal transferences in my own clinical practice. Since that time, I have begun to see and recognize paternal transferences – some sustained – in many of my cases. The inference here is that my mind has been opened to new understandings and experiences, not that my clinical caseload or material has changed.

The erotic or eroticized transference

A second suggested difference in the transferences to male and female analysts is in the area of the strongly erotic or the 'eroticized' transference. It is striking that there are virtually no published reports of strongly and sustained erotic or eroticized transferences of male patients toward female analysts, in contrast to the common story of the female falling deeply in 'love' with her male analyst, or into a wildly unmanageable erotic transference. There is much more agreement in the literature and among the female analysts with whom I have spoken that this difference does indeed exist. Several female analysts, however, would contest this assertion by pointing to their clinical experiences with highly erotic transferences. If erotic transferences do occur, however, they are not written about. [Editor's note: This has changed since the time when this chapter was originally published; even so this is still an under-explored area.] Again, we must ask what factors – within the patient, or the analyst – might account for this supposed phenomenon, which flies in the face of our theory.

Before answering this question, I should distinguish the 'eroticized' transference from an erotic transference. The eroticized transference, as described in the literature (Blum 1973; Rappaport 1956), is characteristic of the borderline or more disturbed patient. In the eroticized transference, the patient exhibits excessive cravings to be loved by the analyst, often with overt demands for sexual gratification. Eroticized transference is thought to be a manifestation of pre-genital issues: underlying hostility, needs for control, and weaknesses in ego functioning. In contrast to the strongly erotic transference characterized by persistent erotic manifestations, the eroticized transference is characterized by the patient losing sight of the 'as-if' quality of the situation. I would also add by way of warning that male and female patients may express similar underlying psychopathology with different outward manifestations. Thus, trying to compare eroticized transferences of male and female patients can become very complicated if not misleading.

From within the patient, there are several inhibiting factors against the development of a strongly erotic transference. First, the incest taboo seems to operate more strongly against mother–son incest than father–daughter incest, against a male's erotic involvement with an older woman than a female's involvement with an older man. Second, the male patient may deeply fear and block the expression of erotic feelings toward a female analyst, which may represent merger with the pre-Oedipal mother, and loss of his masculine identity. Third, the type of male patients sent to or choosing female analysts may be more prone to passivity or to pre-Oedipal problems and skew the transferences away from Oedipal issues. Finally, the male patient may defend against erotic feelings because of feelings of shame, fear of erections on the couch, and castration anxiety. A common theme in the literature is that the male patient's castration anxiety is stirred by 'the spectre of the phallic mother' (Szmarag 1982).

Karme (1979, and Chapter 14) reported on her analysis of a male patient whose brief period of working out negative Oedipal feelings in the treatment prompted her to speculate on the differences in Oedipal and erotic transferences for male and female analysts. Throughout the analysis, and even during the phase when the patient was dealing with homosexual concerns around his father, Karme felt that she remained in the transference a maternal figure. Further, the fear of her as the phallic mother, she writes, constantly inhibited the patient in directly expressing his erotic feelings toward her in the transference. She asserted that fear of the phallic mother is a major determinant of the negative Oedipal complex.

In her case of a male patient, Lester (1982) reported that feared images of the powerful phallic mother overshadowed an erotic Oedipal transference. While Lester felt that this fantasy did indeed become a powerful inhibiting force for the patient, she candidly presented her own dream which revealed countertransference against letting the patient express erotic feelings and against presenting herself as an erotic female instead of a nurturing mother.

In a special panel on erotic transference and countertransference between the female therapist and the male patient (Szmarag 1982), several analysts again raised this spectre of the phallic mother as the impediment to erotic transferences for male patients. Yet it was the consensus of the panel that female therapists 'collude' with their male patients in avoiding a hotly sexual transference.

In an excellent article on countertransference, Lucia Tower (1956) pointed out that erotic countertransferences are in general taboo in psychoanalysis:

> Virtually every writer on the subject of countertransferences, for example, states unequivocally that no form of erotic reaction to a patient is to be tolerated. This would indicate that temptations in the area are great, and perhaps ubiquitous ... Other countertransference manifestations are not routinely condemned. Therefore I assume that erotic responses to some extent trouble nearly every analyst.
>
> (Tower 1956: 230)

I would suggest that erotic countertransference may be especially troubling and subject to inhibition for woman analysts. On the other hand, as we know, erotic countertransferences are more likely acted out overtly by male therapists (Feldman-Summers and Jones 1984).

Clinical material

The following brief clinical examples will be presented to illustrate the issues of how the transference may become organized around the gender of the analyst, how maternal and paternal images in the transference may become disguised or confused, and how erotic material may become inhibited in the therapeutic interaction. The 'phallic mother' plays various roles in the material, from lurking in the wings to appearing on centre stage.

Vignette 1

A young adolescent girl, Terry, sought treatment because of severe obsessive-compulsive rituals. In addition, she was distressed and depressed about current problems with her father. She lived with her mother and stepfather, as her parents were divorced when she was a toddler. Her father, who lived out of state, had recently begun to press for her to spend more time with him, which she said she was loath to do. She was very attached and loyal to her very competent and caring mother with whom she was also closely identified.

Because Terry was extremely bright, verbal and introspective, the treatment progressed well. At the end of the second year, however, she became painfully silent and blocked in the sessions. Her discomfort was so great that she said that she should quit. My attempts to interpret the resistance met with rejoinders that she simply had nothing to say. My suggestions as to her possible anger elicited polite denials that she had no reason to 'dislike me'. Knowing this was an obsessive-compulsive girl, I speculated that we had come to an anal struggle between the withholding, stubborn 2-year-old and her mother. I assumed underlying issues over control.

Indeed, she was touchy about times and scheduling. Several months before the impasse, she asked for a time change, which I was unable to meet. Shortly thereafter, she reported a dream in which her paternal grandmother, from whom she was estranged, appeared transformed: she was wearing tight slacks, high spiked heels and blonde dyed hair as she tauntingly held out two huge pointed pens. Here was the cruel, withholding anal/phallic mother, I thought, whom I must have become in the transference. I had this construct in my mind, as I struggled unsuccessfully to understand and break the impasse in the treatment which stretched into several months.

Finally Terry came into her session and spoke of how she had received a petulant note from her father complaining of her not writing to him. Then came another uncomfortable, long silence. I realized suddenly how blocked out I too felt and interpreted the silence as her attempting to push me out of her life as she does her father, that is, in terms of a paternal transference to me. This interpretation was greeted with a rush of words – a relieved, yet anxiety-ridden confession that she had been disturbed with me these last months because she felt that I was being critical of her mother. While these thoughts reflected the projection of Terry's emerging critical feeling toward her mother on to me, they contained a kernel of truth, as I had felt annoyed at the mother's subtle interference in the treatment and possessiveness toward the girl, who was having difficulty with the developmental task of separation in adolescence. Terry felt caught between me and her mother, as she must feel caught between her two parents and by her conflicts in regard to separating from her mother and her fear of Oedipal urges toward her father.

The point is that my predilection to process the material in terms of pre-Oedipal maternal images and my failure to recognize the paternal transference contributed to and prolonged the impasse we had come to in the treatment.

Vignette 2

A middle-aged woman, Mrs J, came into treatment with me after two previous therapies with males with whom she had sex. She was immediately caught up in a highly charged eroticized and idealized transference toward me that lasted several years. She was pulled by yearnings to suck on my breasts, or crawl into my vagina; she needed to hold my card inside her brassiere between sessions. Such symptoms revealed her severe difficulties with separation, object constancy, and early trauma. The idealized transference expressed her yearning for a wished-for mother and covered over her rage. Her own mother was a beautiful, extremely narcissistic and ungiving woman who left much of the girl's care to the father. The only time she remembered being touched by the mother was in the administration of enemas as she lay on the cold bathroom floor. After years of treatment, the maternal transference was worked through so that the sexualized narcissistic and oral material subsided and more phallic concerns emerged – in masturbation fantasies, competition and jealousy with me, etc. It is easy to make the transition in the transference to the mother as penetrator, the anal/phallic mother who administered the enemas. Yet, her father, who was the parent who bathed her as a toddler, had her stand in the tub while he sprayed her body with the hose attachment. Both parents apparently were penetrating and sexually exciting to this patient as a child. For patients with such early problems with separation/individuation and/or sexual identity, male and female images are indeed confused and confusing. Does it matter, therefore, and is the question an artificial one, whether we call the images in the transference maternal or paternal? In this case, I think sorting out paternal from maternal proved to be important. The patient's initial picture of the mother as all bad and the father as good, while a partial approximation of reality, was a result of defensive 'splitting' and distortion. The image which finally began to emerge in the transference of a sexually seductive father, who himself was ungiving and narcissistic, proved helpful to this patient in unravelling her competitiveness and realizing her more genuine loving feelings toward women and her sexual feelings toward men. For example, the patient struggled to understand why she could not have orgasm in intercourse while she could in other ways; that is, to allow herself to experience pleasure with a man via his penis she had to work out in the transference her feelings toward the male and not the phallic mother.

Vignette 3

A young, brilliant scientist, Dr G, came into treatment because his fiancée complained that his anxieties and preoccupation with work interfered with their relationship. He himself realized that because of his paralysing conflicts with authority, general anxiety, and sense of inferiority, he inhibited himself from further advancement in his career and from giving fully of himself otherwise. These problems appeared to stem from his relationship with his father who was an extremely critical, arbitrary and controlling man. In the first year and a half of his intensive treatment, the patient concentrated on and partially worked through these problems with his father and male figures of authority at work. Correspondingly, the transference over a year and a half took on a consistently paternal cast: he experienced me as a superego, as critical, arbitrary, and controlling, someone he wished to please and yet needed to defy and with whom he competed. These issues were of real importance to the patient and their elucidation brought progress. Yet, the paternal transference also became a resistance. Strikingly, he rarely spoke of women: not his fiancée, who presumably drove him to treatment, and whom he married in the meantime; not his mother whom he described initially as passive, but nice; not even in his dreams which were peopled wholly by males (with only two exceptions – a policewoman and a female barber). Finally, when he remarked that his relations with his boss seem to dictate his moods, I observed that he spoke of nothing else in the treatment.

The next session he reported a dream:

> A gun he has been holding accidentally goes off and kills a blond man. All the (male) friends present urge him to escape from the police, who will come to arrest him. He keeps procrastinating and finding impediments to his escape.

Later in his meagre associations, he said that the blond man in the dream is 'a composite', partially reminding him of a competitor at work. His only other association was to the movie *A Passage to India*, in which the character acts as if guilty about a crime of which he is accused and not necessarily guilty. I remembered that the character is a physician and the crime rape, although Dr G did not say so.

Thus, the first glimpse of manifestly sexual material – possible masturbation conflicts and wet dreams (the gun that went off in his lap) – appeared in a break from the material related to father. Subsequent dreams featured women and triangular interactions. In this case, the paternal transference, not a phallic mother, overshadowed sexual feelings in transference. The patient was not able to admit to himself that he enjoyed coming to the sessions and hence made our scheduling a matter of my coercion and control to which he reacted by complaining, trying to change the time, coming late, and getting me to argue with him, just as he behaved with his bosses in regard to obligations at work.

Vignette 4

Mr S was a married man who had struggled all his life against strong homosexual impulses. In the course of previous brief therapies with male therapists, his symptoms receded of themselves, to reappear after termination. In desperation, Mr S finally decided to seek treatment with a woman, in spite of his manifest terror. Issues of femininity and masculinity, both his and mine, which reflected his deep conflicts about sexual identity, dominated his treatment. In his dreams and fantasies, he produced an unending number of bewildering bisexual images: phallic shaped foods, phallic shaped yet vaginal containers such as cars, gloves, shoes, a phallic-shaped 'mummy', white substances he likened to milk and sperm, ambiguously marked rest-rooms, etc. He endowed the woman with a phallus in maternal images of buildings or mountains with peaks or towers, and a cat with claws, or with a hidden phallus, as symbolized by faecal-like objects contained in tunnels and giant tubes. The transference organized itself around such maternal images: first, a cold, rejecting, non-nurturing mother, unappreciative of his needs and his masculinity – the cold, hard mountain; then, the seductive, yet castrating mother who envied his phallus – the cruel cat or a greedy, voluptuous pig. I focused on his feelings of hatred, fear, awe, and jealousy toward me as a woman as they were projected in the transference.

In going over this case, which first stimulated my thoughts as to how gender might influence the transference (Kulish 1985), I was struck by how the preoccupation with the maternal transferences had made me miss the paternal transference. These potent, compelling images of the mother overshadowed more disguised and buried images of the father. I realized that the patient chose a female therapist, in spite of his fear of women, because of a deeper fear of discovering with intensive work with a male therapist the hate and disappointment he harboured toward his idealized and beloved father. Thus, via the transference, I began to question whether his wish and fear of the penetrating healer was inevitably the 'phallic mother' and to interpret certain negative feelings expressed toward me as referring to his father. The following dream illustrates this shift, and the patient's sense that I had been missing something:

> He is talking to his father who is large and vivid. He only comes up to his chest. His father admonishes him not to use the term 'Daddy'. He answers that it is a term of endearment, not a sign of disrespect. Then his father appears dressed like a clown, with a plastic bra and a peaked hat.

His associations are that 'Daddy' sounds like 'Nancy'. Further, he, like his father, is getting old, which may make him, like his father, an 'intimate' of his mother. The halter-like bra reminds him of blinders.

I ask the patient if he sees me as acting the fool with blinders to something. He replies that may be it is he himself that has the blinders. He goes on to a memory of how his father chastised him as a child for 'swirling' paints together and how controlling his father actually was. In contrast, he tries to let his children have a sense of autonomy. He even let his teenaged daughter go and visit her boyfriend alone. He agreed, reluctantly, to my observation that beneath his usually glorifying picture of his father were cutting impulses, coming out in the dream and toward me. Thus, both the patient and I were blinded by my manifest sex, as symbolized in the dream by the plastic brassiere.

While fears about the all-powerful mother inhibited the expression of sexual and positive feelings toward me and women in general, idealized fantasies about men pointed Mr S toward homosexual objects and obscured murderous and incestuous feelings toward the father. As the 'bad' aspects of himself which he projected onto women were reallotted to men and to himself, he became much more mellow and open toward sexual (perhaps Oedipal) feelings toward me.

In this period, seemingly disembodied from the current clinical material and my conscious feelings toward the patient, I experienced on several occasions sexual thoughts which intruded suddenly and surprisingly into my mind. I asked myself whether these intrusions marked a change in the quality of the transference and paralleled the threatening erotic feelings this patient attempted to stamp out throughout the course of his long, difficult treatment. Perhaps this sudden breakthrough of erotic countertransference resulted from the chronic inhibition of erotic feelings within the psychoanalytic setting, to which female therapists and male patients may be especially prone.

Discussion

It is my contention that therapist's gender does influence the process of psychoanalytic treatment, although this influence may work in unseen subtle ways, and it is, in any case, difficult to isolate. One way in which gender may operate is that it serves as an organizing, limiting factor both for the patient and for the therapist. The reality of gender may set certain limits to the patient's fantasies, just as the form of a Rorschach blot sets limits to the fantasies projected on to it. A good example of this organizing influence is furnished by the theoretical concept of the 'phallic mother'. Such a fantasy is often evoked in the relationship to a female therapist and can become a consolidating transference. Our manifest sex is often one of the few things our patients know about us, and fantasies, curiosities, and feelings revolve around it. The 'phallic mother' owes its ubiquitousness in mythology, dreams, and fantasy to the fact that sexual differences are of such great concern and fascination to us all, throughout the course of our development.

At the same time, the 'phallic mother' is a theoretical construct from psychoanalysis and as such enables the analyst to organize his or her own thoughts. As the confusing array of material emerges in the course of the treatment, we process it through the filter of our own feelings, past and present experiences, and our theoretical expectations which are partially determined by our gender. Thus, gender carries inevitable blind spots, biases, and countertransferences as well as special sensitivities, capacities, and understandings. Gender in interaction with our theoretical, intellectual ideas sets us to understand and react to clinical material in terms of a 'phallic mother' or 'punishing father', being penetrator or penetrated, etc. The patient projects the 'phallic mother' on to the 'blank screen' of the analyst. In another sense, the 'phallic mother' can act as a screen for the analyst's conceptions and misconceptions. The concept of the phallic mother has become institutionalized in psychoanalysis as a barrier to the full exploration of a male patient's erotic fantasies toward a female therapist. Paradoxically it can also stand in the way of a female therapist realizing her masculine role in the transference. At the same time, current emphasis in psychoanalysis on the early mother–child dyad may give males theoretical 'permission' to see themselves in terms of the maternal transference.

Chasseguet-Smirgel (1984) has spoken of both the feminine and the masculine attitudes as crucial to the analyst's functioning. She defines a patient, containing attitude as feminine and a penetrating curiosity as masculine. I would suggest that an openness and flexibility to experience oneself in roles or feelings of the opposite sex would help us realize our full potentials as clinicians and human beings as we help our patients realize theirs.

Summary

The question of how an analyst's gender might affect the transference has currently stirred the interest of psychoanalytic writers. Two questions have been raised in the literature: how analyst's gender might determine whether the transference takes a 'maternal' or 'paternal' cast, and how it might contribute to a highly eroticized transference. In both these questions, the concept of the 'phallic mother' has been raised in the explanation of the observed differences. The author critically examines the concept of phallic mother in this context. The concept is reviewed historically to demonstrate how it has reflected changes in psychoanalytic theory. Clinical examples are presented to illustrate how transference can become organized around analyst's gender, how maternal and paternal images in the transference can become confused, and how male patients' erotic fantasies may become inhibited by the female analyst. The fantasy of the phallic mother, which is prominent in the clinical material, is a projection of the patient, which can be centred upon the analyst's gender. Phallic mother as a concept can also contribute to gender-related blind spots and countertransferences. It is suggested that such theoretical constructs may become obstructions preventing analysts from perceiving themselves in the opposite-sexed roles within the transference.

References

Bak, R. C. (1968) 'The phallic woman: the ubiquitous fantasy in perversions'. *Psychoanalytic Study of the Child* 23: 15–16.

Bernstein, A. E. and Warner, G. M. (1984) *Women Treating Women*. New York: International Universities Press.

Berstein, D. (1984) 'The female-patient, female-analyst dyad'. Paper presented at the meeting of American Psychological Association, Toronto, 26 August.

Blum, H. P. (1971) 'On the conception and development of the transference neurosis'. *Journal of the American Psychoanalytic Association* 19: 41–53.

Blum, H. P. (1973) 'The concept of erotized transference'. *Journal of the American Psychoanalytic Association* 21: 61–76.

Brunswick, R. M. (1940) 'The preoedipal phase of the libido development'. *Psychoanalytic Quarterly* 9: 239–319.

Chasseguet-Smirgel L. J. (1964) 'Feminine guilt and the Oedipus complex'. In L. J. Chassegnet-Smirgel (ed.) *Female Sexuality*. Ann Arbor: University of Michigan Press.

Chasseguet-Smirgel, J. (1984) 'The femininity of the analyst in professional practice'. *International Journal of Psycho-Analysis* 65: 169–178.

Deutsch, H. (1965) *Neurosis and Character Types*. New York: International Universities Press.

Evans, W. M. (1972) 'The mother: image and reality'. *Psychoanalytic Review* 59: 183–199.

Ewens, T. (1976) 'Female sexuality and the role of the phallus'. *Psychoanalytic Review* 63: 615–637.

Feldman-Summers, S. and Jones, G. (1984) 'Psychological impacts of sexual contact between therapists or other health care professionals and their clients'. *Journal of Consulting and Clinical Psychology* 52: 1054–1061.

Finklestein, L. (1975) 'Awe and premature ejaculation'. *Psychoanalytic Quarterly* 44: 232–252.

Freud, S. (1909) 'Analysis of a phobia in a five year old boy'. *Standard Edition* Vol. X. London: Hogarth Press.

Freud, S. (1912) 'The dynamics of transference'. *Standard Edition* Vol. XII. London: Hogarth Press.

Freud, S. (1915) 'Observations on transference love'. *Standard Edition* Vol. XII. London: Hogarth Press.

Freud, S. (1927) 'Fetishism'. *Standard Edition* Vol. XXI. London: Hogarth Press.

Freud, S. (1931) 'Female sexuality'. *Standard Edition* Vol. XXI. London: Hogarth Press.

Freud, S. (1933) 'New introductory lectures'. *Standard Edition* Vol. XXIII. London: Hogarth Press.

Freud, S. (1940) 'Splitting of the ego in the process of defence'. *Standard Edition* Vol. XXIII. London: Hogarth Press.

Gill, M. M. (1982) *Analysis of Transference. Vol. 1: Theory and Technique* London: Hogarth Press. New York: International Universities Press.

Goldberg, J. (1979) 'Aggression and the female therapist'. *Modern Psychoanalysis* 4: 209–222.

Greenacre, P. (1954) 'The role of transference: practical considerations in relation to psychoanalytic therapy'. In *Emotional Growth*, Vol. 2. New York: International Universities Press, pp. 627–640.

Greenacre, P. (1968) 'Perversions: general consideration regarding their genetic and dynamic background'. In *Emotional Growth* Vol. 1. New York: International Universities Press, pp. 300–314.

Hermann, I. (1949) 'The giant mother, the phallic mother, obscenity'. *Psychoanalytic Review* 36: 302–306.

Karme, L. (1979) 'The analysis of a male patient by a female analyst: the problem of the negative oedipal transference'. *International Journal of Psycho-Analysis* 60: 253–261.

Kubie, L. (1974) 'The drive to become both sexes'. *Psychoanalytic Quarterly* 43: 349–426.

Kulish, N. M. (1984) 'The effect of the sex of the analyst on transference: a review of the literature'. *Bulletin of the Menninger Clinic* 48: 95–110.

Kulish, N. M. (1985) 'The effect of the therapist's gender on the transference'. *Yearbook of the Society of Psychoanalysts and Psychotherapists* 1: 17–31.

Langs, R. J. (1973) 'The patient's view of the therapist: reality or fantasy'. *International Journal of Psycho-Analysis* 2: 411–431.

Lerner, H. E. (1974) 'Early origins of envy and devaluation of women: implications for sex-role stereotypes'. *Bulletin of the Menninger Clinic* 38: 538–553.

Lester, E. (1982) 'The female analyst and the eroticized transference'. Paper presented at the meeting of the American Psychoanalytic Association, New York, December.

Mason, S. (1983) Personal communication, 23 July.

Orgel, S. (1965) 'On time and timelessness'. *Journal of the American Psychoanalytic Association* 13: 102–121.

Rappaport, E. (1956) 'The management of an erotized transference'. *Psychoanalytic Quarterly* 25: 515–529.

Roheim, G. (1945) 'Aphrodite or the woman with a penis'. *Psychoanalytic Quarterly* 14: 350–390.

Rossner, J. (1983) *August*. Boston: Houghton Mifflin.

Sandler, J. (1976) 'Countertransference and role-responsiveness'. *International Journal of Psycho-Analysis* 3: 43–48.

Shengold, L. (1963) 'Parent as sphinx'. *Journal of the American Psychoanalytic Association* 11: 725–751.

Shevin, F. F. (1963) 'Countertransference and identity phenomena manifested in the analysis of a case of phallus girl identity'. *Journal of the American Psychoanalytic Association* 11: 331–344.

Stein, G. J. and Auchincloss, E. (1984) 'The public and the private woman'. *Bulletin of the Association of Psychoanalytical Medicine* 24: 1–19.

Stoller, R. J. (1975) *Perversion*. New York: Random House.

Szmarag, R. (1982) 'Special panel A: erotic transference and countertransference between the female therapist and the male patient'. *Academy Forum* 26: 11–13.

Tower, L. E. (1956) 'Countertransference'. *Journal of the American Psychoanalytic Association* 4: 224–255.

Zetzel, E. R. (1966) 'The doctor–patient relationship in psychiatry' In *The Capacity for Emotional Growth*. New York: International Universities Press. 1970 pp. 139–155.

Chapter 14

The analysis of a male patient by a female analyst

The problem of the negative Oedipal transference

Laila Karme

Introduction

Freud describes the complete Oedipus complex as 'twofold, positive and negative ... a boy has not merely an ambivalent attitude towards his father and an affectionate object-choice towards his mother, but at the same time he also behaves like a girl and displays an affectionate feminine attitude to his father and a corresponding jealousy and hostility towards his mother' (Freud 1923: 33). An Oedipal transference – positive or negative – implies a triangular situation with the utilization of a third person outside the analytic situation (fantasied or real) as a mother or father substitute. In the negative Oedipal position, if the patient and the analyst are of the same sex, a homosexual transference develops. The question arises as to how the negative Oedipal position is manifested and worked through if the patient and the analyst are of opposite sexes.

This chapter will provide an account of the emergence, analysis, and resolution of the negative Oedipal position in the case of a male patient with a female analyst. It is of interest that he did not develop at any time during this analysis a paternal transference towards me. As it is well known that a maternal transference frequently develops in the analysis of female patients with male analysts, I had assumed there would be considerable literature reporting the development of the negative Oedipal transference in such situations. This is not the case. In fact, descriptions of maternal transferences seem almost exclusively pre-Oedipal although such a differentiation is not made in the literature.

Description

The patient is a 40-year-old, divorced, professional man. He is tall, well built, ruggedly handsome, and casually but impeccably dressed. He is intelligent, intellectual, articulate and comes across as impressive and confident. Despite these qualities, one detects a feeling of underlying sadness. He came to analysis because of difficulty expressing his feelings and recurrent difficulties in establishing lasting relationships with women. Despite his competency and appearance of confidence, he admitted to many self-doubts and a deep sense of inadequacy. The patient is the older of two children. He jealously recalls being abused by his father for the same behaviour that was regarded as 'cute' when exhibited by his six years younger sister. He also recalls that his mother worked early in his childhood but quit her job from the time his sister was born until she entered school at the age of six. His father, a retired engineer, has been partially paralyzed by polio since childhood. The patient remembers his pride in his father's success as an engineer. His mother, a retired schoolteacher, was described as the dominant person in the family. The patient's compulsive defences, intellectualization, and a rational, controlled, non-emotional approach to life fit in with his parents' system of values.

The patient met and married his wife while they were both 23-year-old students. They both worked and studied, living together like two college students sharing a house. His marriage became most unsatisfactory after the birth of their first child. At that time, he experienced his wife's involvement with their child as a rejection. He felt cheated and upset, angry, guilty, and they separated several times. He became involved with another woman and was on the verge of divorcing his wife when she unexpectedly became pregnant. The patient continued in his unhappy marriage for two more years. His two sons live with their mother.

The analysis

The patient rapidly developed a strong maternal transference. He reacted to me as the superior, giving and loving mother whom he strives to please, but more subtly as the castrating mother whom he envies, competes with, fears and to whom he dares not reveal his needs and weaknesses.

In the early phase of the analysis I dealt primarily with the patient's character defences against feeling. He dealt with my first vacation by ignoring it and feeling 'neutral'. By the time of the next interruption in the analysis, there had been considerable loosening of his character defences against experiencing affect directly and he felt vulnerable, abandoned, angry, helpless and needy.

Early in the analysis the patient expressed his envy and jealousy of women. He felt that his sister got special privileges because she was a girl. He expressed his hostile envy of women for having the caretaking and nurturing role which makes them powerful and dominant. There was a subtle undercurrent of mistrust, competitiveness, and envy of me almost from the start. He first denied having these feelings towards me, then admitted feeling so competitive with me that he was tempted to give me false leads and victoriously enjoy my blunders. He talked about his parents' marriage and how he saw his mother as the dominant force. He wondered if he had felt that his mother was responsible for his father's crippled condition and described his resistance to anything he perceives as domination by a woman.

The patient struggled between the passive dependent receptive role and his self-assertive genital drives. It became apparent, however, that the former was basically a regressive defence against his unresolved Oedipal conflict. As this was worked through in the analysis, his intense competitive strivings towards men became more open. He recalled that his mother had turned to him to do things his father could not do, and he acknowledged that his accomplishments in life have surpassed his father's. This acknowledgement led to Oedipal anxiety. As the patient resolved some of his anxiety and guilt over success, a typical Oedipal conflict emerged. He attended a professional meeting, felt successful, and for the first time permitted himself to have conscious erotic fantasies about me. Phallic dreams involving his car were prominent. In some of these dreams his car was missing, and its top was 'soft and flopping over'. He woke in a panic from a nightmare in which he had held hands with a woman (analyst) and was pushed off a cliff by a man. Triangular situations were prominent in his associations and dreams, and he had openly erotic dreams about me.

The patient's Oedipal anxiety mounted. His castration anxiety seemed more related to the fear of the phallic mother (the analyst in the transference) rather than to the rival father. This led to a negative Oedipal position where his father emerged as the protective, wished for, loved man. During this phase the maternal transference persisted.

Development and the analysis of the negative Oedipal phase

As the patient's fear of loving me (perceived as being castrated by a domineering phallic mother) increased, the wish for his father as a source of affection, love, comfort, and protection emerged. He lamented that in revealing his fear of me to me he gives me more power over him and puts me in a more controlling position. He remembered his initial fear about using the couch and wondered if he would have had the same fears if I were a male analyst. He recalled a dream in which there was the first allusion to homosexuality. It also portrayed his fear of me as the phallic, castrating woman.

> I was in a house. Two men came in, they wanted to spend the night. One of them smelled bad and I shot him. The other guy and I went to the bedroom and went to bed. Next morning we were running, trying to hide. Then I was in the lobby of this building, coming to see you. There was a kid in the lobby who had a small roll of movie film. He asked me if I would take it up to you. I called you on the phone and you said, 'Come on up.' Then you giggled and said, 'Excuse me, I had a few drinks.' There was a whole bunch of skis by your door. I said, 'Are these your skis?' You said, 'They're souvenirs.'

Skis are often phallic symbols to him. Skiing, at which he excels, is one of his favourite activities as it fits his super-masculine image. He contemplated that he wished to get rid of a stinking part of himself which he does not approve of. He associated to the roll of movie film. 'Exposed. I'm exposing parts of myself here.' He was completely oblivious to the homosexual aspects of the dream. I chose to interpret his sense of exposure to me, his fear of me and his defence against it by portraying me as silly.

He continued to struggle with his mistrust and fear of me and of women who are 'educated, intelligent and independent'. He recognized his 'macho image' as defensive. He had a dream which took place at a racetrack:

> He was not a driver, only a flagman. The person at the control point was a woman. In the dream he was concerned about being tangled up in the wire that went from the woman controller to his earphones. He identified the woman controller as the analyst.

This dream again portrays me as a controlling, phallic woman. Associations to his racing cars led to associations to his guns. He remembered at the age of 18 his mother took away his gun (the castrating mother). He then recalled how his father-in-law taught him to use guns. He associated to the 'sexual connotations' of guns.

His wish for a father to love and protect him (from the phallic mother) intensified and his anxiety about emerging homosexual wishes increased. He recalled his 'panic' at Christmas time and how he agonized obsessively that he might have mistakenly signed a Christmas card to a male friend 'love'. When I focused on his fear of signing the card 'love', he recalled receiving a 'warm' card from one of his male employees and his girlfriend warning, 'Watch out, he may be a homosexual.' This was the patient's first explicit reference to homosexuality in the analysis. It was at this point that I chose to interpret his wish to express his love to his friend and his fear that it would reveal homosexual feelings. I also interpreted his fear of my disapproval and scorn (like his girlfriend's).

Following my interpretation of his fear of homosexual feelings, he experienced a masculine identity crisis. He felt depressed and anxious, 'I didn't want to come back.' He related a dream he had the previous night reflecting his feelings that he was a woman and a member of a minority (different):

> I was in a hospital and had a male friend with me. A Mexican girl came in and begged to have an abortion. We were going to do it secretly. There was a tray in the room that had a wedge-shaped apparatus with a hole that went through the wedge. We figured that's what you need to do the operation. We slipped the wedge between her legs and slipped a sterile tubing in.

He associated to the Mexican girl as himself. 'In many ways I consider myself as a minority among people.' I connected his playing doctor and his fear and furtive feelings which he experienced in the dream, with his associations to himself as the Mexican girl who is not only a minority person, but also a woman. (The Mexican woman was also a reference to me, because of my dark features, and representative of his identification with me as mother.) I interpreted his wish to abort the feelings and conflicts he is experiencing in the analysis, and maybe the analysis itself, because of his non-acceptance of such feelings.

The patient recovered a series of memories centred around his mother's pregnancy and his very close relationship with one of the neighbour boys at that time. When the patient was 8 or 9 years old, he and his parents moved to another state, he was hurt by this enforced separation from his friend. He also recalled his swimming class in the ninth and tenth grades where the boys swam in the nude and how he avoided participating. He stated with intense emotion, 'I just remembered my comments to you in the past about not being able to play the guitar very well or sing. It may have something to do with my perception of what's manly and what is not, because I feel embarrassed and awkward when I do. I also flashed on my comments to you months ago about my difficulty producing free-flowing art. Most of the things I make or create are very geometric and also useful. This must be related to my feelings: Women create pretty things to look at, but men are builders, doers, engineers.' He then remembered how he hated his piano lessons 'because my friends were out doing something masculine or aggressive'. He added wistfully, 'Right now I wish I played the piano, and I wish I didn't impose all these inhibitions on myself.'

By incorporating my attitude of acceptance, some of these feelings became gradually more egosyntonic. He continued to work through his need for his 'macho image' (super-masculine protest against his isolated homosexual needs), and his now conscious wish to love and be loved by a man. He gradually recovered loving, warm, feelings for his father. A flood of memories about his father emerged. He recalled their playing with train sets, building crystal radios, and their experimenting together in their chemistry laboratory in the basement. He was able to feel more comfortable with his male friends. He experienced a sense of well being and stated, 'I want very much to have close, warm, relationships with men and women, something I have never found because of my own fear.'

Re-emergence of the positive Oedipal transference

As the patient started moving out of the negative Oedipal to the positive Oedipal position, his fear of me as the phallic, castrating mother intensified, and his identification with his 'crippled father' re-emerged. For several months he continued to experience and work through some of his fear of me. He has become increasingly aware of the many facets of his fear of women which determines his choice of weak, insecure, immature and dependent women with whom he feels more comfortable, but increasingly dissatisfied. This inevitably has led to his perpetual failure in interpersonal relationships, especially with women. One aspect of this fear was reflected in his need to split women, to relate to a woman either sexually or intellectually. Other facets of his fear – besides splitting himself, splitting women, and evoking women's empathy to feel somewhat in control – would include the following: (1) Choice of inferior women. (2) Strong need to do things for women, to please them and earn their love. (3) Manipulation of his relationships with women; the woman must need him, he cannot need her. (4) A need to make unilateral decisions to feel independent. (5) Perception of all interactions in terms of 'win–lose'. He has to feel he wins. (6) Feeling inferior and having nothing to offer to a 'complete woman', thus rules out or successfully suppresses his attraction to such a woman.

As the analytic work proceeded, his awareness of and desire for a different kind of relationship with a woman surfaced. He became more conscious of his loving feelings for me and he admitted to them. We struggled with his fears and conflicts around reciprocity and mutuality – an area that was most difficult for him. After a great deal of integrative work, the patient stopped splitting himself and women. He focused his dating on one woman who is a more mature choice, and is more able to permit mutuality with both his analyst and his girlfriend.

Discussion

This chapter focuses largely on the emergence, analysis and resolution of the negative Oedipal phase in the analysis of a male patient with a female analyst. The negative Oedipal phase in my female patients is typically manifested by a homosexual transference towards me. Similarly, in the case of male patients with a male analyst a homosexual transference occurs. A paternal homosexual transference did not develop in this case. The maternal transference persisted, and the patient's homosexual wishes and strivings were directed towards male objects (outside of the analytic situation) who functioned as father substitutes. Technically, there were two major areas of difficulty: (1) Since the patient placed great value on his super-masculine image, and since his sociocultural background is particularly adverse to any hint of homosexuality, bringing it into his conscious awareness was a matter of great delicacy. (2) The problem of bringing it into the analytic situation and analysing it within the transference, to avoid sterile intellectual speculations.

The negative Oedipal phase, as the dominant theme, encompassed only 30 sessions. While relatively brief, it was marked with very intense emotions and fraught with a great deal of anxiety. The patient experienced a masculine identity crisis and was tempted to flee the analysis. However, he did achieve a satisfactory resolution of this conflict and the gains have been sustained. He has neither repressed the experience nor has it re-emerged as a conflict. He continues to relate interactions with male friends and employees which exhibit openness and closeness without conflict or anxiety. He acknowledges this freedom and looks back with amusement on his previous rigidity. He also relates openly and warmly with his father, which is different from his previous guarded stance.

The question arises as to how this patient worked through this conflict in such a short time. One can partially answer this question by speculating that he incorporated the analyst's accepting attitude. The careful timing of the depth of interpretations and the consistent interpretations of his depreciatory projections and self-criticism also contributed. However, these are unsatisfactorily incomplete answers. Freud (1937) stated that the most difficult aspect to analyse in men was their fear of a passive homosexual attitude to men. Greenson (1967: 255) states that a great source of resistance is the fear of passive homosexual strivings: 'In patients of the same sex as the analyst, a persistent hostile transference may be used to defend against homosexual feelings.' Glover (1955: 101) in commenting on the transference resistance evoked by the negative Oedipal situation states:

> This ... factor in transference resistance is most easily observed by a male analyst during the analysis of a male patient or by a woman analyst during the analysis of a woman patient, but of course transference repetitions are not limited by the sex of the analyst, and the repetition of the complete Oedipus complex is an essential part of all analyses.

I agree with Glover that transference repetitions are not limited by the sex of the analyst. However, the form of such repetitions may be influenced by such reality, which I think is implied in Glover's statement. So the brevity of this period might have been – at least in part – related to the fact that the analyst is a woman and that the patient did not develop a paternal homosexual transference. This might have facilitated the patient's incorporation of the analyst's attitude of acceptance, which he could not misconstrue as a homosexual seduction. Also, this incorporation did not represent a passive homosexual submission.

An added factor might have been the freedom of the analyst from the possibility of a homosexual countertransference. As Glover (1955: 101) states: 'In fact, the analyst's homosexual countertransferences are a much commoner source of counter-resistance than his hetero-sexual countertransferences.' The negative Oedipal position in a male is multidetermined: (1) Identification with the pre-Oedipal mother. (2) Fear of the phallic mother. (3) Fear of castration by father. The male child, in order to attain a healthy sense of maleness, must replace the primary object of his identification, the mother, and must identify instead with the father. Greenson (1968: 373) poses some cogent questions as to what happens to the original identification with the mother: 'Does the identification with mother disappear, its place taken by the new identification? Does it remain but become latent?'

The fear of castration by the rival father as a determinant of the negative Oedipal complex is the one most elaborated, and is the one most evident in the analysis of men by male analysts. Freud (1925) noted that to escape castration the boy may abandon his aggressive Oedipal rivalry and develop a negative Oedipus complex. This is obviously a reaction formation. This point needs no further elaboration here as it is prevalent in the literature. The fear of the phallic mother has not received sufficient consideration as a determinant of the negative Oedipus complex. With the patient presented in this chapter there was some sexual rivalry and fear of castration by father. However, the prominent determinant was his fear of the analyst as the phallic mother. Was this fear intensified because the analyst was a woman? Was the fear of the phallic mother predominant because of this patient's own genetics and psychodynamics, and would it have appeared with the same intensity even with a male analyst? Although such questions cannot be answered with certainty, I feel they should be raised.

The transference and the sex of the analyst

Our main heritage from Freud lies in his creative and revolutionary discovery that the transference which at first seemed an insurmountable obstacle to analysis is in fact its most powerful ally. He realized that many of the patient's reactions towards the analyst are repetitions of, and have roots in, the past history and the primary object relationships of the patient. Freud termed the crystallization of transference expressions in the patient's relationship with the analyst the transference neurosis.

He considered that the psychoanalytic resolution of the transference neurosis was the means of the intrapsychic resolution of the patient's illness. However, Freud used the term transference to refer to the patient's unconscious fantasies about the analyst, to direct references to the analyst, and to the relationship of the patient to the analyst in its totality. He did not carefully establish criteria for the detection of transference manifestations and for the distinction between such manifestations and other aspects of the patient's relationship to the analyst. This inevitably led to conceptual and technical difficulties. Freud's main writings on this subject occurred before 1917 and he did not revise his conceptualization of the transference in view of his structural theory. This led to a relative neglect of the role of current realities, including the personality of the analyst. Freud stressed the use of genetic interpretations and reconstruction of genetic roots as a means of resolving the transference neurosis, at the expense of the interactional component of the patient's transference expressions. There has been an increasing recognition of the role of the analyst and of the analytic interaction in such expressions. The term transference, however, remains unclear. Failure to arrive at a clear consensus about a definition leads to a most fundamental and clinically crucial problem.

Transference as a universal mental function which may well be the basis of all human relationships has to be distinguished from the unique phenomenon as it occurs in the analytic situation – the transference neurosis. Brian Bird (1972: 280) states:

> Although things may not have gone quite this far, I do believe they have reached a point where most analysts nowadays work only with transference feelings. They either ignore the transference neurosis or believe ... that there are no significant differences between a transference neurosis and other transference reactions.

The latter are feelings, reactions, and automatic repetitions of past events, whereas the former is 'a creation of the analytic work done by analyst and patient, in which the old illness loses its autonomous and automatic character and becomes reactivated and comprehensible as a live responsive process and, as such, changing and changeable' (Loewald 1971: 62).

One of my patients whose father is a psychoanalyst came to the analysis with preformed automatic transference feelings toward me as the father. As soon as the transference neurosis developed, it was clearly a strong maternal one in which mental representations of her mother were replaced by mental representations of me. (There were also amalgamations of her mental representations of her mother and me, and of herself and me.) I became an intricate part of her neurosis and of her conflicts – old and new. Blum (1971) recognized the need to explore the transference neurosis from the vantage of ego psychology. He emphasized that transference depends on object representations, and that differentiation, constancy of self and object representations, and symbolic capacity are necessary for nonpsychotic transference. The urges and defences, the underlying neurotic symptoms and character, reappear in renewed analytic conflicts. The transference neurosis is a neurosis and should be understood in terms of structure and character. In his view, the transference neurosis has both defensive and adaptive aspects. It is transitional between past and present, repetition and organization. He states:

> Transference distortion, realistic perception of the analyst, therapeutic alliance, and the analyst as a new object and developmental reorganizer are overlapping dimensions of the analytic relationship ... the transference is probably influenced by variables in the therapist such as age, style, sex, and character traits ... With a female analyst ... the paternal transference may appear in fantasies about her husband, or be displaced onto paternal figures outside the analysis.
>
> (Blum 1971: 48, 50–51)

There has been a tendency in the analytic literature to deny any essential differences in the transference developed towards male and female analysts. Representative of this view is Fenichel (1945: 328): 'Both men and women patients can and do develop both father and mother transferences toward their analyst, whether male or female.' This seems obvious and true. Over the years I have read numerous clinical cases and have listened to many case presentations in which both the maternal and paternal transferences were convincingly demonstrated towards male analysts. In my own personal analysis I had developed both paternal and maternal transferences towards my male analyst. The fact that my patients did not seem convincingly to develop paternal transference neurosis towards me was puzzling. Transient paternal transference feelings – like the example I gave earlier in the discussion – are abundant. These are feelings determined by personal and sociocultural attitudes, not by the analytic situation. 'As the unconscious image of the psychiatrist is so definitely a father figure, female psychiatrists are probably conceived in the same role' (Redlich 1950: 569–570).

In reviewing the literature, in an attempt to learn about the development and analysis of the negative Oedipal transference in the case of female patients with male analysts, it became clear to me that the maternal transferences towards male analysts are almost exclusively pre-genital. In fact, pre-genital productions and the maternal transference are automatically equated. When the patient deals with pre-genital material, the male analyst (and the reader or the audience) immediately assumes a maternal transference. With a male analyst the patient develops a maternal transference in the pre-genital phase, but whenever Oedipal strivings or longings erupt they are directed towards the rival or the loved father-analyst depending on whether the patient is male or female (the reverse occurs in the negative Oedipal situation). With a female analyst it is not different, i.e. pre-genitally there is a maternal transference, and Oedipally she is either the loved or the rival mother-analyst. In other words, during the Oedipal phase the patient's transference is maternal or paternal according to the analyst's sex. This should not be too surprising if we understand the transference neurosis in view of the structural hypothesis, adaptation, and ego psychology. In the pre-genital phase, before the recognition of sex differences and before the development of gender identity, it is to be expected that the sex of the analyst would not interfere with the illusion necessary for the development of a mother transference. However, a child in the Oedipal phase has a much more developed ego, is capable of sex differentiation, and gender identity is established.

One would require a delusion, not an illusion, to blur or confuse these differences. I believe that there are two main reasons for the resistance to acknowledging that the sex of the analyst may influence the transference. Many analysts believe that this might diminish or invalidate the concept of the transference. As I have already stated, this is a consequence of not updating the concept of the transference neurosis in view of new developments. The second major problem is an apprehension that such an acknowledgement would imply that an analyst of a specific sex may be better or worse as an analyst. This is not necessarily the case. The pre-genital maternal transference occurs regardless of the sex of the analyst. On the other hand, the analysis of the Oedipal complex does not require any specific role, as long as the analyst is included as one of the parents in this triangular drama.

Analysts have struggled for years to reconcile some clinical observations with the theoretical notion that the sex of the analyst does not influence the transference. The sex of the analyst is carefully noted in evaluating suitability for referral. It is maintained that this may be important only in the early phase of the analysis or in specific situations, i.e. strong unrecognized homosexual tendencies with latent possibilities of panic. It is also maintained that it is not the reality of the sex per se but rather that it is the conveyor of some other less apparent reality which is more important!

There are obvious paradoxes in the literature, for example, Greenacre (1959: 494), after asserting that the sex per se is not what is important, added that in making referrals she treats with respect and compliance the patient's attitude towards the sex of the analyst, if such an attitude is definitely established, 'since I recognize that such a patient really would find it difficult, if not impossible, to work with an analyst of the undesired sex. But I also know that in a number of these cases, a change in the analyst to one of the opposite sex may be desirable later.' Why would that be desirable? It is my impression that there are misinterpretations in the literature which would account for reported paternal transferences with female analysts. Transference feelings are confused with transference neuroses. The analyst as phallic mother is sometimes misconstrued as the father in a paternal transference. Sociocultural prejudices further confuse achievement and success with masculinity. 'Undoubtedly what is considered "masculine" and what "feminine" is not so much biologically determined as culturally' (Fenichel 1945: 505).

Summary

The clinical work in this chapter is focused on the analysis of the negative Oedipal phase of a male patient with a female analyst. Determinants of this phase are discussed. Theoretical questions are raised and propositions advanced. Transference phenomena are differentiated from the transference neurosis and the types of transferences formed according to the sex of the analyst are discussed. It is proposed that patients develop maternal transferences to analysts of both sexes, but that such transferences are limited to pre-Oedipal phases for patients with male analysts. During the analysis of the Oedipal phase, both positive and negative, the patient's transference is to the analyst according to the analyst's sex. A true paternal transference neurosis to a female analyst ordinarily does not occur.

References

Bird, B. (1972) 'Notes on transference: universal phenomenon and hardest part of analysis'. *Journal of the American Psychoanalytic Association* 20: 267–01.

Blum, H. P. (1971) 'On the conception and development of the transference neurosis'. *Journal of the American Psychoanalytic Association* 19: 41–53.

Fenichel, O. (1945) *The Psychoanalytic Theory of Neurosis*. New York: Norton.

Freud, S. (1923) 'The ego and the id'. *Standard Edition* Vol. XIX. London: Hogarth Press.

Freud, S. (1925) 'Some psychical consequences of the anatomical distinction between the sexes'. *Standard Edition* Vol. XIX. London: Hogarth Press.

Freud, S. (1937) 'Analysis terminable and interminable'. *Standard Edition* Vol. XXIII. London: Hogarth Press.

Glover, E. (1955) *The Technique of Psychoanalysis*. New York: International Universities Press.

Greenacre, P. (1959) 'Certain technical problems in the transference relationship'. *Journal of the American Psychoanalytic Association* 7: 484–502.

Greenson, R. R. (1967) *The Technique and Practice of Psychoanalysis*. New York: International Universities Press.

Greenson, R. R. (1968) 'Dis-identifying from the mother: its special importance for the boy.' *International Journal of Psycho-Analysis* 49: 370–374.

Loewald, H. W. (1971) Panel Report. 'The transference neurosis: comments on the concept and the phenomena'. *Journal of the American Psychoanalytic Association* 19: 54–66.

Redlich, F. (1950) 'The psychiatrist in caricature: an analysis of unconscious attitudes toward psychiatry'. *American Journal of Orthopsychiatry* 20: 560–571.

Chapter 15

On transference manifestations in male patients with female analysts

Marianne Goldberger and Dorothy Evans Holmes

This chapter concerns certain issues arising in the analytic situation of a male patient with a female analyst. The analytic literature is relatively sparse on this gender combination. It has been suggested that full erotic transference manifestations do not occur in male patients with female analysts and that so-called erotized transferences hardly, if ever, occur. In addition, there has been some question as to whether a significant paternal transference to a female analyst develops. In this chapter we discuss both of these issues, as well as some other features of the transference in this therapeutic dyad, such as the difficulty that the male patient has in permitting himself to identify with his female analyst, and how his fear of aggression may influence the unfolding of erotic transference manifestations. We approach these issues by exploring clinical examples from the psychoanalysis of five patients.

In a review of the literature, Kulish (1984) referred to a prevalent opinion that male patients do not develop strong 'erotic transferences' toward female analysts. Lester (1982), in one of the few case reports on the subject, said that in her own practice she encountered 'only mild, transient, muted and unstable erotic transferences from male patients' (1982: 3). She herself questioned the validity of this observation and wondered whether it was corroborated by other women analysts. Szmarag (1982), reporting on a panel on 'Erotic Transference and Countertransference between the Female Therapist and the Male Patient', stated the panel's consensus 'that female therapists collude with their male patients in fostering the expression of their dependency feelings rather than confronting the more psychologically-forbidden and socially-awkward ones' (1982: 12). It is noteworthy that 'several female analysts disagreed with the panel's findings and reported that the majority of their male patients express erotic feelings toward them' (1982: 12). However, Bibring's famous case (Bibring-Lehner 1936) is the only example in the literature we know of that describes an 'erotized' transference with a female analyst.

In regard to paternal transferences to female analysts, the literature reflects varying points of view. In her review article, Kulish (1984) states that 'sustained paternal transferences have not been reported in the literature' (1984: 105) and Karme (1979), in another rare case report, avers that paternal transferences are not prevalent with female analysts. On the other hand, Chasseguet-Smirgel (1984), in an aside while writing on a related subject says, 'it is such a common experience that analysands can establish ... a paternal transference to a woman, that I will not dwell on this point' (1984: 173). (She does not specify the gender of the patient.) Fenichel (1945) states that 'a patient's ... father transference to a woman analyst, is a frequent occurrence in analytic practice' (1945: 328). He goes on to say:

> For the majority of patients, the sex of the analyst is not very important. Both men and women patients can and do develop both father and mother transferences towards their analyst, whether male or female. However, a minority of patients may have a completely different reaction toward men and toward women analysts.
>
> (Fenichel 1945: 328)

In a discussion of 'Contra-indications to analysis with a particular analyst', Fenichel says that the general rule that the sex of the analyst makes little difference '*has frequent exceptions*' (1945: 579, our italics). It is regrettable that he did not elaborate on what those exceptions are.

Before proceeding to the case material, some definitions are in order. Brenner (1982) has clarified the language referring to transference manifestations, pointing out that 'every transference manifestation expresses, in however distorted or disguised a way, childhood sexual wishes, i.e., childhood drive derivatives. *Every transference is erotic*' (1982: 205, our italics). Because the term erotic transference has been used to refer to so many disparate phenomena, we will use the term erotic transference manifestations in this chapter to refer to consciously available erotic elements that directly involve the analyst. Thus, we distinguish the erotic components of the transference that are not yet conscious, although they may be evident in the form of derivatives – for example, an erotic fantasy displaced from the analyst. Transference feelings that are not overtly erotic are described in terms of the manifest feeling. The phrase erotized transference is also used in literature, though we will question the usefulness of this concept in the Discussion. Most descriptions of the erotized transference have referred to the male analyst–female patient dyad (Blum 1973; Rappaport 1956; Swartz 1967). Blum (1973) defined the eroticized transference as:

> a particular species of erotic transference, an extreme sector of a spectrum. It is an intense, vivid, irrational, erotic preoccupation with the analyst ... The focus may not always be exclusively on the psychoanalytic situation. The eroticization may be intermittent, eclipsed by silence, sleep, resentment, or numerous other detours and defensive reactions.
>
> (Blum 1973: 63)

Thus, Blum includes conscious erotic preoccupations and unconscious erotic fantasies displayed through a variety of manifestations that vary with the defences utilized. For the sake of clarity, we describe intense erotic (conscious) transference manifestations and, in addition, indicate when and how strong erotic elements in the transference were defended against by our patients. We do not discuss the defensive function of erotic preoccupation (discussed by Coen 1981), though such functions were operative at times in all our cases.

The experience of these authors, as well as of colleagues with whom we have discussed the question, suggests that well-developed erotic transference manifestations do indeed regularly occur with male patients. Furthermore, our experience in the cases reported here demonstrates that the so-called eroticized transference is not the oddity that the dearth of reports might indicate, though it may be less frequent than in female patients with male analysts. In addition, we regularly observe paternal transference manifestations, although at times it is difficult to differentiate them until many details are known well into an analysis.

The following clinical examples from the authors' psychoanalytic experience were selected to illustrate only the specific issues of this chapter. Other aspects of the cases are omitted, such as the many varieties of maternal transference manifestations that are invariably seen in male patients with female analysts.

Clinical Examples

Case 1

Mr A was a 30-year-old married professional man of Italian extraction who sought analysis because of dissatisfactions with himself, his family, and his work. He felt intensely self-conscious in many situations and wanted relief from this problem in particular. He was dissatisfied with his professional achievements and doubted whether he had chosen the right career. As analysis progressed, problems in his relationships, with his wife, children, and co-workers emerged.

The early part of the analysis centred around the patient's concern about his looking at women 'too much' and having sexual thoughts about them. At other times, he spoke about his fears of being homosexual. He disliked in himself the ease of copying others' ways of talking and their mannerisms, feeling that he could not define his real self. His feeling of inadequacy in his work was also a major issue that occupied many of the early analytic hours.

Only after some time in analysis did it become clear that the patient had to ward off his awareness of the presence of the analyst. When the analyst spoke, he treated it as a bothersome interruption; after a brief pause he would try to pick up where he had left off. Soon, he began to fall asleep during the analytic hours. After a long time it emerged that sexual thoughts about the analyst or about his mother had preceded the sleep. Evidently, it was too dangerously stimulating for him to be aware of the presence of the analyst. He feared that she might be seductive. In this connexion, he spoke of the seductive behaviour of his mother, always kissing him on the mouth in greeting, taking naps with him until young adulthood, and going about in scant clothing. During his college years he would come home after classes and lie in bed with his mother for naps during which he struggled with sexual fantasies about her and about other women. His mother was upset when the patient made plans to marry. Although he had always felt himself to be her favourite up to that time, as soon as he got married, it seemed, his mother switched her intense affections to his younger brother. In connexion with speaking about his struggle with sexual thoughts about his mother, he spoke of his dismay any time he found a trait in himself that resembled his mother. 'Like my mother, I don't see things.' He was greatly distressed when he thought that his voice sounded like his mother's at times.

Mr A's reaction to the analyst's voice became an important and ongoing issue. Often, he reacted as if to a sudden shock when the analyst spoke, and he registered nothing of the content of what had been said. He asked for it to be repeated and tried to ward off his affective response. His reaction was often to the tone of voice, not to what had been said. He would wonder, 'Why are you using that voice?' His predominant fantasy was that it was a fake voice and he suggested various motives for the fakery, such as the analyst wanting to sound good, to maintain a superior position, or always to be right. Sometimes his associations to the use of a fake voice were to his mother and he seemed aware that something was being repeated in the analysis. As the analysis continued, he heard several different 'tones' in the analyst's voice – condescension, scoffing, stuffiness. His consistent preoccupation with the tone protected him from awareness of the content of what was said.

While Mr A was able to deal with very complex concepts in his daily work, he could not comprehend a sentence of more than a very few words when it came from his analyst. This massive inhibition defended globally against a variety of transference manifestations with the result that only very slowly was it possible to separate out specific constellations. A general issue of which he became aware was his fear of criticism and anticipation of attack. A more specific aspect was his view of the analytic situation as a game in which each person was sparring for position, requiring Mr A to take time to consider what position to adopt. This need was all the stronger since he viewed the analyst as greatly interested in maintaining her position. At other times, he treated the analyst as someone to whom everything needs to be explained and who remembers nothing of what has been said before.

While trying to ward off his awareness of the analyst's presence, Mr A also showed a certain demandingness that became progressively more insistent and indignant. His wishes to borrow magazines from the waiting room and to use the analyst's telephone were egosyntonic. When the analyst was not able to schedule a more convenient hour, he insisted upon knowing why. He felt that if he could not have what he wanted, he was at least entitled to know the reason. He believed it was simply a part of the analyst's 'front' that the reason was not given. When the attempt was made to analyse the meaning of his taking magazines from the waiting room, the patient focused on whether or not the analyst would give permission for it. Side by side with the demandingness was a strong need to please. He watched the analyst's face as he entered and left the sessions to assess signs of acceptance or rejection. He hated himself for this wish for praise and support, considering it a weakness that a man should not have, especially in regard to a woman. For this reason he was able to reveal such thoughts only well into the treatment, and then only with shame.

The conscious erotic thoughts about the analyst that appeared early in the treatment were brought up in a typically obsessional manner – isolated and without affect. Similarly, he spoke a good deal about being angry about many things but he very rarely experienced the feeling in the analytic hour. In addition to the prevalence of obsessional defences, a problem for the analysis was Mr A's defensive use of discharge outside the analytical situation. The insistent demandingness described above was an example of his propensity for immediate discharge. As the erotic transference manifestations intensified, he had an extramarital affair, something he had often fantasized but never before carried out. One result of putting his fantasies into action was his realization that his fantasies went on unabated. His longings persisted, unfulfilled, so that he developed some motivation to try to understand them. He was able to permit himself to perceive the analyst as two different women: one, old, fat and dumpy; the other, young and attractive. To the old one, he associated smelly genitals, a woman using the toilet, and heavy legs. Thoughts about the younger one led to erotic fantasies. Either train of thought often resulted in his falling asleep on the couch. Since he had shared a bedroom with his grandmother as a child, a working hypothesis was that the older woman stood for his grandmother, suggesting a specific genetic meaning for his falling asleep.

After four years of analysis, Mr A was offered an excellent job opportunity in another city that led to an interruption of his analysis. He planned to resume analysis, which he did several years later with a male analyst. During the five years of Mr A's second analysis, many of the same features were present. The problem of the patient's dozing during the analytic hours continued and was at times interpreted as a defence against erotic transference manifestations. However, the strong reaction to the analyst's voice was not present in the later analysis.

Discussion of Case 1

The case of Mr A illustrates the development of erotic transference manifestations as they are commonly observed. The frequency of Mr A's erotic thoughts and fantasies about the analyst increased during the analysis and included thoughts about her appearance, details about her body and manner of dress, and questions about sexual aspects of her life (such as whether she had a husband and what she did with her husband). These erotic transference manifestations are familiar to women analysts. However, some aspects of this case are also characteristic of an erotized transference as described by Blum (1973), Swartz (1967), and Rappaport (1956). The continued strong impact of the analyst's voice on the patient was evidence for the presence of an underlying erotization. It seemed that every time the analyst spoke, the patient's resources were taken up with coping with the tensions stirred in him by the sound, leaving him unable to deal with the content. The patient's history shows the genetic features Blum (1973) cited as common in cases of erotized transference:

> Sexual seduction in childhood ... instinctual overstimulation with deprivation of parental, phase-appropriate protection and support ... family toleration of incestuous or homosexual behaviour in the bedroom, bathroom, etc; revival and repetition of precocious and incestuous sexual activity in adolescence.
>
> (Blum 1973: 67)

This patient's exposure to primal scenes could be inferred from the frequency with which he exposed his own children to such scenes. In contrast to Blum's cases (1973), this patient did not show exaggerated transference love and admiration nor was he seductive with the analyst. The patient did show some features of the erotized transference emphasized by Swartz (1967) 'in which the patient places excessive and inappropriate and unrealistic demands upon the analyst' (1967: 317). He also illustrates Rappaport's observation (1956) that such patients are 'alternately ingratiating and obnoxious' (1956: 517). This last feature would be present regardless of the gender of the analyst, but it is mentioned here because the ingratiating aspect had for this patient the specific hazard of a feminine identification which is discussed next.

An important factor in Mr A's fear of being close to his analyst was his fear of identifying too much with her. This fear is frequently seen in men in analysis with women and was especially strong in this case. Mr A repudiated the similarities he perceived between himself and his mother not only because he disliked his mother's character traits but also because it made him doubt his masculinity and strength. Greenson (1968) has stressed the special problem that the early identification with his mother presents for a boy's development of gender identity. Mr A certainly exemplifies this problem, both in his early development during which he was very close to his mother and, of course, again, as he struggled against closeness with his analyst. The patient's unconscious identification with the analyst was confirmed by his idea that he and the analyst were 'good enough for each other' – that is, both were less than first rate. This idea arose whenever he spoke of the (older) male analyst he had originally consulted and whom he considered a better analyst. He feared he might not have 'made it' with this better analyst, and it was a male analyst with whom he later resumed analytic work.

Mr A intermittently demonstrated a paternal transference. When he experienced the analyst as superior, condescending, critical, and having to be right, it was clearly a repetition of his experiences with his father. This was not a 'sustained' picture of the analyst, but it emerged repeatedly and with conviction.

Case 2

Mr B was a married teacher of disturbed children whose analysis with a woman was supervised by one of the authors. He sought treatment because of work inhibitions, problems in his marriage, and premature ejaculation, and because he thought a personal analysis was important for his own work. He was the oldest of three, with a brother and a sister younger by three and six years, respectively. He had always been very close to his mother, felt himself to be her favourite as a child, and continued to have a warm, close relationship with her as an adult. He liked his mother very much for her sociability and generosity and also because of shared interests. By contrast, he had always had difficulty with his father; he had feared and disliked him as a child and had little in common with him as an adult. He was a very co-operative, well-motivated patient who defended against erotic transference manifestations mostly by obsessional mechanisms. As these defences were analysed over the course of a six-year analysis, a full expression of erotic feelings and fantasies emerged. Only two features of this man's analysis will be discussed in detail here: an example of paternal transference and the anxiety he experienced about identifying with a woman.

From time to time, Mr B described a particular kind of interaction with his wife which troubled him. He would make what seemed to him to be an innocuous remark or ask a 'simple' question and his wife would become very irritated with him. Soon the friction would escalate into an angry battle during which his wife would become quite irrational and the patient would end up trying to be helpful in calming her down. Since the sequence was manifested specifically with his wife, he assumed it had mostly to do with his difficulty with women. As he tried to engage the analyst in a similar kind of exchange, it was possible to get a better understanding of his behaviour with his wife. It emerged from associations to such an interaction with the analyst that the patient was enacting an old pattern of subtly provoking his father to an outburst of uncontrollable temper. As a boy, he had been very frightened by these outbursts but, at the same time, had felt that being able to elicit them gave him power over his father. An added bonus was his mother stepping in to stop the fight, since Mr B then felt protected by her. In the analysis it became clear that one way of dealing with the analyst as a frightening authority was to try to provoke her to be bad in some way so that he could then feel strong and superior. This paternal transference had been enacted with his wife for a long time but the specific nature of it could not be elucidated until it was experienced in the analytic transference.

The problem of identifying with a woman became especially conspicuous in this case since the patient was in a profession allied to that of his analyst. Conflicts about learning from one's analyst and about wanting to be like one's analyst are certainly common. Yet the literature is sparse concerning male patients' identification with their female analysts. In this case, the conflict gave the opportunity of bringing into the analysis Mr B's intense fear both of his longings to be female and his envy of women. Some of the early strong identification with his mother was well integrated and comfortably expressed in his life, as in his pleasure in being nurturing and helpful to family, friends and colleagues. However, other strivings to be like her were conflicted, as evidenced by rising anxiety during analytic hours when he expressed his wishes to be like his analyst. His associations led to various frightening fantasies about his body being like that of a woman, without a penis, with his 'opening' being stimulated. At times, he pictured himself being pregnant. One way of defending against such fantasies was to emphasize the real differences between himself and the analyst, dwelling on aspects of his own masculinity. Another way was to fantasize the analyst as having a penis.

Discussion of Case 2

Passive feminine fantasies such as those of Mr B are, of course, not unusual. What we wish to stress is the importance of a man's fear of identifying with a woman that emerges in the course of his analysis with a female analyst. We relate this fear to Greenson's description (1968) of the issues a boy faces in 'dis-identifying' with his mother. Stoller (1976), Tyson (1982), and Wagonfeld (1982) recognize the significance of this fear in the development of a boy's identity. The male patient has an opportunity to experience this fear of his feminine self in the transference with his female analyst, an opportunity that arises in the homosexual transference with a male analyst.

This case also illustrates the not infrequent elusiveness of the paternal transference to a woman. Some analysts have stressed the male patient's fear of the 'phallic' woman as the central inhibiting force in the analysis of a man by a woman analyst. However, our analytic experience suggests that some of that fear is due to paternal transference – that is, the so-called phallic woman is a man – and some of it is due to the dread of identifying with a woman. The concept of a phallic woman may be called forth, by both patient and analyst, because of the difficulty in recognizing the presence of paternal transferences when the analyst is a woman. This demonstrates that the reality of the analyst's gender can interfere with more specific understanding.

Case 3

Mr C was a 24-year-old unmarried student when he sought analysis because of procrastination in finishing his undergraduate studies in radio and television broadcasting. In addition, he was very distressed over erratic and unfulfilling efforts in work, friendships and love relationships. The patient grew up in a strict religious family; he was the second of four sons, the youngest of whom was six years younger than the patient and mentally ill. The defective son was viewed as a mystery or special blessing requiring worshipful attention. It appeared to the patient that the more erratic and difficult this brother was, the more frequently his mother demonstrated her affection for him. At the same time, she demanded that the other children grow up as fast as possible in deference to the youngest brother's special needs. His father, an architect, appears to have kept himself isolated from this turmoil by working on household tasks, most of which were assigned by his mother. Mr C identified with his youngest brother; like him, Mr C demanded attention through non-conformity. Erratic school performance began early in his life and during adolescence he was episodically delinquent. He hoped that his irregularity and unpredictability would win from his mother the same love and corrective influence she directed to his youngest brother. From early childhood, the patient consciously repudiated his father. He mocked his handiwork, calling it dull and overly routinized.

In latency and adolescence, Mr C identified with his mother in her dedicated attempts to salvage the youngest brother. Identifying also with his father's capacity for handiwork, he rummaged among discarded parts at auto and electrical repair stores, imagining himself able to reconstruct to wholeness even the most damaged items, and actually trying to do so. His career aspirations in the news media also reflected his identification with his mother, who used her writing skills in her role as advocate for her youngest son by writing local newspaper stories about deficiencies in educational programmes for emotionally handicapped children.

Mr C's most dramatic appeal for his mother's attention came when he was 15 years old. He hid in a store with a plan to pilfer it. He panicked and before stealing anything fled in fear of violent attack from the police. He fell down a flight of stairs and injured his leg. As he lay in the hospital emergency room, he thought of his mother, wishing that she would understand how much he needed her to protect him.

Mr C stated that as he grew up anything sexual was strictly forbidden by his mother. However, in analysis he came to realize that his mother had accused him of impulses against which she was struggling in herself, as revealed in her harsh and repeated condemnation of anything even vaguely sexual (commercials on television; pictures in news magazines). She scrupulously monitored television watching and conversations among the brothers. On many occasions, she would spring from the kitchen, turn off the television, stand in front of it and lecture them on the evils of sex. At the same time his mother was 'very physical with us . . . She slapped us as punishment until one time when I was 13, I slapped her back, whereupon she exclaimed, "I knew it! I just wondered which one of you would do it to be first!!" ' Mr C's associations revealed his unconscious fantasy that this retort was a provocation from his mother to attack her sexually and aggressively.

For the first year and a half of analysis, Mr C turned to the analyst as a mother from whom he demanded nurturant attention. The aggressive flavour of his demandingness was at first hidden by a reaction formation in which he treated the analyst with undue deference and politeness; later it emerged in undisguised form. He presented his increasingly frequent lateness (to analytic sessions and in payment of fees) and his erratic attendance at analytic hours as aspects of a pitiable self for which he pleadingly sought the analyst's help. As the analysis progressed, his demanding wish for the analyst to be his all-encompassing guardian became more explicit and urgent, albeit at times displaced to his live-in girlfriend. He frequently called other women from their shared home. When his girlfriend became enraged and threatened him with physical harm, he was incredulous and referred to his behaviour as innocent 'kid's play'. It was pointed out to him that he was displacing away from the analyst his very strong, anger-laden and long-held wish for an indulgent, protective mother who would welcome his 'adventure' as she had those of his defective brother. The analyst asked him if this involvement in danger was reminiscent of any other times in his life. He recalled the store incident and emergency room scene from the age of 15. The analyst indicated to him that he wished her to be his protector as he so futilely had wanted his mother to be.

As Mr C struggled with his feelings of disillusionment about the unavailability of his analyst as a guardian, he gradually made a shift away from the maternal transference in which he insisted on the analyst's protection. A paternal transference then began to emerge. He began to complain of feeling ill-equipped to work, including analytic work. He reported a lifelong tendency to quit that was correlated with feelings of being little and fraudulent. He came to see this tendency as a retreat from competition with his father whom he viewed as grumpy, demanding, critical, and never to be pleased. During this period, he 'quit' analysis again, with lateness and absences. He also began to experience the analyst's interventions as criticisms; with thinly veiled spite, he would respond, 'Oh, so I didn't do that right again!' These trends were interpreted as paternal transference reactions to the analyst which led him to criticize more openly his father and his analyst as uninspired, dull, and rule bound. These appraisals were explored in various ways, especially as defences against feared competition in the 'world of men'. Progress in analysis led to emergence of a capacity to observe and admire his father's steady, productive work. He came to feel that it was important for him to acquire these traits of his father's.

As the patient became more assertive and productive, he began to dread the analyst as one who, like his father, would resent and humiliate him for his manly sexual and aggressive strivings. He dreaded his mother's and the analyst's scorn for the same urges. As his vivid castration fears abated, he began to reveal his sexual longings for the analyst. He did so directly and intensely in periodic bursts over the last six months of his analysis. At first, Mr C expressed these feelings with much trepidation. On occasion they were accompanied by fleeting ego regressions, such as the use of projection, saying to the analyst, for example, 'You're stuffing these interpretations down my throat!' The patient's perception that the analyst was aggressively and orally attacking him became the transference ground on which to approach the patient's fused sexual and aggressive feelings for his mother. Suddenly, there was a burst of cancelled hours and unlike his previous deferential attitude, he was indifferent. The same casualness was manifested in regard to giving the analyst several bad cheques. He came to realize that he was trying to elicit an excited and angry attack from the analyst which he could then counter. After some months he recognized this as an effort to repeat the slapping exchange with his mother, and it then emerged that his reluctance to be aware of sexual longings was partly due to their fusion with aggressive feelings. His fear that the analyst would stuff erotic transference interpretations down his throat was then reworked as a projection and displacement of his sexual-aggressive urges towards the analyst.

After three years of analysis, Mr C began to realize that his attachment to his work situation reflected his wish that his employer grant him favours and let him continue in a status beneath his capabilities, as he had wanted his mother to do. He realized that he would have to leave 'home', perhaps including analysis, to find a meaningful job. This insight enriched his analytic pursuit of masterliness in work and in sexually intimate relationships. He finally received a very good offer in another city; he left analysis after four years to accept it.

Discussion of Case 3

Mr C showed scant evidence of erotic transference manifestations early in his analysis. Contrary to what some of the literature suggests, however, this limitation was only temporary and was a function of his need first to work through fears of his aggression and early identifications. Specifically, Mr C was inhibited from experiencing sexual longings for the analyst because they were fused with aggressive feelings of which he was very frightened. He began with deferential expressions of longing for the analyst's protection and nurturant love. The more these wishes were frustrated in the analysis, the more his deference turned to demandingness through which he revealed a complex identification with his defective youngest brother. Within this identification, he felt weak and ineffectual and he angrily demanded his analyst's protection and caring. Mr C came to understand that he clung to this identification as a defensive retreat from Oedipal issues. He recognized that the sense of weakness he felt in his work and with women was a feature of this identification with his brother and that it interfered with effective utilization of his identification with his mother's career interests.

As Mr C needed less to seek safety in identifying with his brother and his mother, he began to consider more of his conflicted view of his father, particularly his disdain for his father's steady application of assertive energy in his work. He came to understand the disdain as defensive against his fear of assertiveness, partly based in his identification with his weak, defective brother. It was here that Mr C showed paternal transference manifestations in which he likened the analyst's investment in work to his father's work style, both of which at first he spurned. It is important to note that this patient showed little anxiety in experiencing the analyst as father in the transference. One possible factor is that he could find the father in the analyst with relative ease because he had developed strong, albeit warded off, identifications with his father. In some other male patients with female analysts, the paternal transference manifestations may be more limited or more difficult to experience consciously if there have been faults in the patients' identification with their fathers (see discussion of Cases 2 and 4, pp. 259–260, 266–267). Later in analysis, the patient was able to explore his aggressively tinged sexual wishes for the analyst.

Case 4

Mr D, a 41-year-old married, childless political columnist sought analysis because of depression during an impending separation from his second wife. He expressed anguish and perplexity over his incapacity to maintain a marriage, and he dreaded the prospect that he would never become a father.

Born to a European father and an American mother, he was reared as an only child by his mother and maternal grandparents. Mr D's mother left his father in Europe at the behest of her parents when she was six months pregnant with Mr D. He did not see his father until he was 6 years old, and then only briefly, when his father visited. For several months after his father's visit, Mr D was ill with a sleep disturbance and anorexia. Throughout his childhood, he was plagued by recurrent nightmares of coffins and of hybrid creatures who impaled one another.

Twice in young adulthood, Mr D sought out his father. The visits were very amicable. Three months after the second visit, his father died. Mr D regarded his father as a war hero but also as 'gutless' for never claiming him.

Mr D's mother was a noted writer. She never remarried, though she had many lovers. Mr D considered her extremely strong-willed (except in relation to her parents) and domineering towards him; she never let him win an argument. He travelled extensively with her in his youth. He reported that she was very seductive with him, bathing him until he ended it in mid-latency. One of his vivid memories was from the age of 12 when she asked him to advise her on the sex appeal of a blouse with a plunging neckline. After the age of 9, he was placed in various military boarding schools in which he fared poorly because of breaking rules.

Mr D admired his maternal grandfather, but often tried to undo his reserve and make him more available emotionally by bucking his coolly administered authority. The grandfather died when Mr D was 14 years old. The patient had a largely unambivalent and very warm relationship with his maternal grandmother. However, he was anxious about this bond because he felt his mother was envious of it.

Mr D's first marriage failed after several years when his wife eloped with another man. In both marriages, he struggled between trying to dominate his wives and demanding that they control and nurture him. The demands for their mothering were expressed in covert ways, as by presenting numerous social and personal ineptitudes to them, requiring them to take over. This tendency included sexual impotence in the last two years of his second marriage.

The first evidences of erotic transference manifestations came a year into the analysis after a long period in which Mr D 'courted' the analyst with an elegant display of his verbal ability. He rendered richly textured, elaborate dreams and relished interpreting them. He was eager to consider all issues from multiple vantage points. Clearly, he wanted very much to be strong, forceful and potent with words. The narcissistic aim of his efforts was apparent from his consistent displeasure with any intervention made by the analyst other than an acknowledging statement. Any attempt at clarification was met with expressions of defeat and hurt. He would say that the analyst's comments caused him to 'lose his point'. Through multiple interpretations, the patient came to understand that it was important to him to win the analyst's favour through elegant oratory and that he was afraid her comments might reflect a rejection of his ideas. This approach helped the patient to rework his identification with his mother and his wish to have a mother who could accept his mastery of the same verbal skill. Erotic transference reactions followed closely once Mr D became more sure of his own verbal capacities. He spoke of the analyst's attractiveness and her physical likeness to his first wife with whom he had been fully and enjoyably potent sexually. He wondered if going to a restaurant for dinner in the neighbourhood of the analyst's office after his evening appointment for several consecutive weeks indicated his attraction to the analyst. He then wondered what kind of men the analyst liked. He concluded that they had to be macho, super-aggressive, streetwise, and smart. The patient grew increasingly uncomfortable in these musings and began to report that he had reached a stalemate at work and that he was having a recurrence of terrifying dreams about death and sex. Furthermore, he was impotent in his renewed relationship with his second wife.

Mr D saw no acceptable solution in either positive or negative Oedipal positions. He lamented the unavailability of a man in his childhood from whom he could have gained a sense of manly strength, confidence, and affection. He often wept with anger and fright that he had not received sustained affection from anyone except his maternal grandmother, yet he felt reproached by his mother for this relationship. He became furious with his mother, though he quickly rationalized it away. He began to deny less his feelings of abandonment by his father and became aware of his tendency toward reaction formations with men who disappointed him. Specifically, he tended to search these men out and take upon his own shoulders responsibility for whatever wrong he believed they had done him. When he angrily pledged to break this pattern, several paternal transference manifestations came into evidence. He began to view the analyst as unworthy of his respect, just as he viewed his father, and demonstrated the disrespect by keeping the analyst waiting repeatedly and by paying his bills late.

Within the period in which Mr D was struggling with and defending against his anger towards his mother and his search for a loving father, he expressed intense feelings of longing for an anchor or mooring post. He felt again the sense of utter dependence on his mother and her surrogates (his second wife and his analyst) to interpret reality for him. This tendency towards denying his ability to judge reality was enacted by his need to experience every self-perception in terms of his analyst's or his wife's view of him. In the midst of feeling that his grip on reality was tenuous, he went on a weekend visit to his mother and grandmother whom he regularly referred to as 'parents'. He found the visit very difficult and more keenly than ever felt his mother's rivalry with his grandmother. Mr D returned from the trip and was immediately shaken by news that his wife had been assaulted by a colleague of hers. He aided her appropriately during that day. However, on the pretext of a work overload he cancelled that evening's analytic session, sought out the wife's assailant and got into a fight with him. He knew all the while that his behaviour was driven but his judgement gave way temporarily to his consciously felt need to redeem his wife's honour by directly confronting her attacker. In analytic sessions, he referred to him affectionately by his first name, with no sense of the peril in which he had placed himself. Clarification of the familiarity with which he referred to his opponent led to the uncovering of a renewed search for the affectionate father who would understand his complaints about the ungiving mother (and analyst with whom he had cancelled his hour).

Mr D's enactments outside the analytic hours provided fertile material for analytic work leading to clarification of his complex identifications, principally with his mother. His dread of becoming a woman diminished and through analysis of distinctly paternal transference reactions, he came to accept the 'masculine' attributes he gleaned from his analyst – that is, what he called incisiveness, scrappiness, and assertiveness. Of note during this work on the paternal phase of the transference was the shift in the patient's attitude to the analyst's interventions. He began to reject her comments by engaging in stereotyped repetitions of previous sessions, as if nothing had been said to him. When this was brought to his attention, he recognized that he was disregarding the analyst on the grounds of thinking that she, like his father, was not an adequate caretaker and, therefore, unworthy of his regard. As he needed less to fend off the analyst during his sessions, Mr D was less driven to impulsive action and was able to work in a more committed way in the analysis.

Mr D began to view the night search for his wife's assailant as a re-enactment of his childhood night terrors, especially when travelling abroad with his mother. Going over the incident and its sequelae repeatedly provided an opportunity to review his demandingness toward his mother, his search for a nurturant father and his Oedipal searches, both positive and negative.

Discussion of Case 4

One of the major obstacles to the development of Mr D's transference, both maternal and paternal, was the threat he felt from the ways he had identified with his mother. The development of these transference manifestations also depended on his learning about the ways in which he had adapted to the profound emptiness and longing that he felt over the unavailability of a father with whom to identify.

Approaching the analyst as a positive Oedipal object was difficult because he concurrently viewed his mother as phallic and castrating and, likening himself to her, as one with a hole that could be penetrated. Thus, to approach the analyst was to risk being vulnerable, like her – that is, having a penetrable hole – and subject to her attack. He also feared attack from his father. Both fears served to diminish his positive Oedipal strivings.

As Mr D began to work through his identification with his mother in which he felt so weak, he began to search for male strength. This search was especially painful for him because he had attained only frail identifications with his father who had been absent most of his life. He learned to recognize certain strengths of his analyst as masculine even though he found them in a female. That is, he did gradually begin to show paternal transference manifestations. To do so was threatening because his underlying sense of himself as masculine was weak. Therefore, at first the concrete reality of the analyst's gender limited his imagination about where he could find the strength he was seeking. For example, when he 'discovered' that both his analyst and his mother shared a masculine characteristic he admired – that is, scrappiness – he said he was confused because he had never thought of it as female. For him, females were defined by their threatening, castrating qualities, and their vulnerabilities. His analysis enabled him to identify with women more fully, including with some of their masculine attributes. Other male patients who have had more consistent fathering may not find paternal transference reactions so difficult to express (for example, Case 3).

This case illustrates the complexity in the fluctuations between maternal and paternal transference manifestations, and the complexities within each manifestation. Thus, it is hardly surprising that it is frequently difficult to distinguish between them.

Case 5

Mr E was a separated professional man in his thirties who sought analysis because of his inability to be faithful to one woman. In addition, he was markedly dissatisfied with his work performance and suffered chronic anxiety. He had heard about his prospective analyst, was adamant that no one but she could help him, and was willing to wait until she had time.

During the initial phase of the treatment, the patient felt uniquely well understood. He was the oldest son in a large family in which the father was weak and largely absent. His mother was described as seductive, intimate with the patient, yet critical of him. All through his childhood, he spent much time alone with her. His earliest memories included repeatedly overhearing primal scene events. He was considered a very bright child but he had problems in school which he later attributed to his inability to concentrate.

The patient's concentration problem manifested itself in his current adult life as frequent preoccupation with erotic fantasies. He spoke with both amusement and annoyance about the chronic criticisms women in his life had about him – that he was cold, distant and inaccessible. In the analytic situation he tried to ward off awareness of the analyst's presence, yet he had vivid erotic fantasies about her. He tried to legislate when she would speak to him, and if she spoke unexpectedly his immediate anger made it difficult to explore the underlying anxiety. An example of his anxiety during analytic hours was his expressed fear that he would turn to jelly – 'no matter what you put jelly in, that's its shape'. He once called the analyst at home and a young woman answered. The next day the patient critically related the details of the telephone conversation and suggested that the analyst was trying to get him sexually involved with another woman. When the analyst wondered whether his discomfort might have to do with his fears of sexual thoughts, he became enraged and silent.

Despite his difficulty in dealing with the presence of the analyst, Mr E came to his sessions regularly and felt that his chronic and pervasive anxiety was diminishing. However, he increasingly began to fall asleep during analytic hours and to have long silences. He alternated between viewing his analyst as too formal and distant and as too friendly and seductive. At times, it was clear to the analyst that the patient had an erection while on the couch, a fact he was never able to mention.

After a few months, Mr E broke off the analysis and arranged treatment with a male analyst. He later telephoned the woman analyst to let her know that his treatment was now proceeding satisfactorily.

Discussion of Case 5

This patient's transference was so burdened by aggressive and erotic drive derivatives that he could not maintain an analytic situation with a woman. Quite possibly his ego pathology would also prevent his being able to do analytic work with a man. Although little information became available, it did seem that being alone in a room with a woman was over-stimulating for him. This case can be viewed as illustrating 'the extreme sector of a spectrum' described by Blum (1973), so much so that the whole treatment was aborted. Mr E's early history does contain elements characteristic of this group: sexual seduction in childhood, primal scene experiences, and instinctual over-stimulation with deprivation of parental protection and support.

The case of Mr E also demonstrates another problem common for men in analysis with women – that is, fear of having an erection on the couch. The fear of having strong erotic feelings is increased when a man starts to fear that he cannot prevent his feelings from showing.

Discussion

Some of the recent literature suggests strongly that when the analyst is female and the patient is male, both erotic and paternal transference manifestations will be poorly or fleetingly developed. Our experience is not in keeping with this suggestion. We will first discuss the question of the expression of erotic transference manifestations and then the development of paternal transferences in this analytic dyad.

Our experience, as illustrated by the five cases presented, suggests that there is a spectrum of erotic transference manifestations in the psychoanalysis of male patients with female analysts, ranging from the very constricted and inhibited at one end to the very intense and florid at the other. This spectrum is certainly well known to analysts in regard to other gender combinations. Some authors (cited in Kulish 1984) claim that all men in analysis with women will be on the constricted end of the spectrum, with only very muted expressions of erotic feelings and fantasies. Even the small sample we have selected from among our cases demonstrates that this is not so; men in analysis with women are not exclusively on the constricted, muted end of the spectrum. Examples in the literature of the florid extreme in the male patient–female analyst dyad are notably absent. Two of our cases (Cases 1 and 5) suggest that there are more examples in the unconstricted sector than previously thought, though it may be true that men in analysis with women tend to be in the more constricted range of the spectrum.

We believe that the spectrum should be viewed in a more general way – that is, to include aggressive as well as erotic transference manifestations. Our cases suggest that singling out the erotic components obscures rather than clarifies the clinical situation. We have found that just as the expression of erotic transference manifestations is often muted in men with women analysts, so is the expression of aggressive ones. The specific fear of aggression in the transference of male patients with female analysts has occasionally been alluded to in the literature. In an article about analytic patients' reactions to the analyst's pregnancy, Lax mentions fear of the patients' aggression by both patients and analysts (Lax 1969: 370–371). Tower (1956), in an article on countertransference, described a patient whose transference was so aggressive that she doubted his analysability by her or possibly any female analyst. She suggested that his problem 'might be worked through with a male analyst whom he would perceive as a person able to control him' (1956: 251).

Using the case material presented, we explored some specific dynamic factors that were important determinants of each patient's defences against both erotic and aggressive transference manifestations. This emphasis on specific factors is not meant to exclude the idea that general factors contribute to the phenomenon that men in analysis with women are more constricted in their expression of drive derivatives in the transference than are female patients with male analysts. However, it is beyond the scope of this chapter to discuss the important cultural factors that influence these constrictions in both patients and analysts, and the effects of the greater prevalence of obsessional character traits in men.

Some authors have called the more florid extreme of the spectrum, the erotized transference. We would like to question the usefulness of this concept. Freud did not use the term erotized, but he alluded to the particular kind of patient under discussion when he described 'women of elemental passionate-ness who tolerate no surrogates. They are children of nature who refuse to accept the psychical in place of the material' (Freud 1915: 166–167). Blum (1973), Swartz (1967), and Rappaport (1956) all emphasize the demanding quality of patients with an erotized transference. In fact, with some of these patients the aggressive components seemed to be more in the forefront. It would thus seem more useful to view this group as individuals who have difficulties with impulse control and hence have overly instinctualized transferences, rather than create a category called erotized. These are patients who have great difficulty in keeping within the boundaries of the analytic situation. The transference is similar to that of the patients described in the book by Abend et al. (1984) on borderline patients: 'A tendency toward action was noticed from the start ... there was an inability to accept the "as if" quality of the transference, with an insistence upon literal gratification from the analyst ...' (Abend et al. 1984: 176). The authors emphasize the quantitative difference of this transference, though qualitatively it occurs during periods of intense transference in any analysis. Our experience with patients who have overly instinctualized transferences – for example, Cases 1 and 5 – suggests that they have serious ego defects, even if they might not all be diagnosed as 'borderline'. Perhaps one important reason that some of these patients cannot remain in analysis with a woman is that the aggressive drive component in their transference is even more threatening (perhaps to both patient and analyst) than is the erotic.

In the discussions following each case report, we described the presence of paternal transference manifestations as well as some of the specific defences against it. We indicated that paternal transference manifestations occur regularly with a woman analyst. However, in considering this phenomenon, it may be important to note whether the analyst is looking for a 'sustained' transference, or whether she believes, as Greenacre (1959) does, that 'there is a constant panoramic procession of transference pictures merging into each other or momentarily separating out with special clarity' (1959: 652). The authors' experience is consistent with the latter view. Furthermore, we believe that the differentiation of transference neurosis from transference manifestations is not helpful. For this reason wc refer to the full spectrum of more or less richly elaborated transference manifestations.

There are some general factors which might interfere with the full development of paternal transferences. The reality of the analyst's gender interferes more in some patients with their capacity to fantasize the analyst as a man. Chasseguet-Smirgel (personal communication) has suggested that more disturbed patients – that is, those more uncertain of their own identity – cling more strongly to the reality gender of the analyst, while neurotic patients with pathology derived primarily from Oedipal conflicts can more easily fantasize their analysts as belonging to either gender. Another possible source of interference in the development of a paternal transference with a woman is the analyst herself. If there is an assumption of the need for extra-transference displacement of the paternal transference, or if a woman is reluctant to imagine herself pictured with a variety of masculine attributes, then it might be more difficult to hear the derivatives of the patient's associations that refer to the analyst as a man. In Case 2, for example, one might have assumed that the patient was referring to a 'phallic woman' as the paternal transference was developing. That is not to say that the patient did not also have fantasies of a phallic woman (which indeed he did at times); rather, we suggest that if one's prepared position is to think in terms of a 'woman with a penis', then the paternal transference could be missed. Much has been said about a man's fear in the transference of the 'phallic woman', and the issue of the male patient's anxiety in the maternal transference will be discussed shortly. Perhaps it is easier for a woman analyst to think of herself being pictured as a 'phallic woman' than as a father. Here patient and analyst alike are subject to a limitation in their imaginative repertoire. We suspect that the concept of phallic woman is sometimes invoked because of this limitation of imagination.

Despite the frequent presence of paternal transference manifestations with a woman analyst, the limit on a male patient's opportunity to experience his passive-homosexual conflicts with a woman analyst is still a reality. It is exactly when a patient becomes anxious, as he would when he approaches his passive feminine conflicts, that he is likely to cling to the actual gender of the analyst. This is one reason for the displacement outside the analysis of a male patient's homosexual conflicts. However, one opportunity for observing the passive feminine anxiety within the transference situation is when a male patient is struggling with his identifications with his woman analyst. As observed in Cases 2 and 4 (in which there were early strong feminine identifications), when the patients identified vividly with their analysts, they feared the loss of their solid sense of themselves as males. Stoller (1976) suggests that because of the early intimate relationship with his mother, a man's sense of maleness is more vulnerable than is a woman's sense of femaleness. Stoller views homosexuality as a 'threat to one's sense of core gender identity, of existence, of being' (1976: 296). This threat appears in the transference in a special way when a man's analyst is female. It also provides the patient in this therapeutic dyad with an opportunity to rework early conflicted identifications.

Summary

The transference issues that are specific to the psychoanalysis of male patients by female analysts have not been widely discussed in the literature. Most of the literature on this subject has indicated, contrary to the findings reported here, that full and intense erotic transference manifestations are rarely if ever seen in this therapeutic dyad. In order to clarify the issues, we have offered some definitions that may serve as a framework for future discussions.

We have utilized clinical examples from the psychoanalyses of five patients to illustrate certain aspects of the transference. We have demonstrated that male patients display a full range of erotic transference phenomena with female analysts and have focused attention on certain special features of these transferences. For example, in some cases it was only after considerable analysis of defences against aggression that the erotic transference manifestations emerged fully. We have also shown that paternal transferences occur regularly, though they may be difficult to elucidate until the later stages of analysis. We have paid special attention to the feared loss of maleness that attends male patients' identification with their female analysts.

References

Abend, S., Porder, M. S. and Willick, M. S. (1984) *Borderline Patients: Psychoanalytic Perspectives*. New York: International Universities Press.
Bibring-Lehner, G. (1936) 'A contribution to the subject of transference resistance'. *International Journal of Psycho-Analysis* 17: 181–189.
Blum, H. (1973) 'The concept of the erotized transference'. *Journal of the American Psychoanalytic Association* 21: 61–76.
Brenner, C. (1982) *The Mind in Conflict*. New York: International Universities Press.
Chasseguet-Smirgel, J. (1984) 'The femininity of the analyst in professional practice'. *International Journal of Psycho-Analysis* 65: 169–178.

Coen, S. J. (1981) 'Sexualization as a predominant mode of defense'. *Journal of the American Psychoanalytic Association* 29: 893–920.

Fenichel, O. (1945) *The Psychoanalytic Theory of Neurosis*. New York: Norton.

Freud, S. (1915) 'Observations on transference love'. *Standard Edition* Vol. XII. London: Hogarth Press.

Greenacre, P. (1959) 'Certain technical problems in the transference relationship'. In *Emotional Growth*, Vol. 2. New York: International Universities Press, 1971, pp. 651–669.

Greenson, R. R. (1968) 'Disidentifying from mother: its special importance for the boy'. *International Journal of Psycho-Analysis* 49: 370–374.

Karme, L. (1979) 'The analysis of a male patient by a female analyst: the problem of the negative oedipal transference'. *International Journal of Psycho-Analysis* 60: 253–261.

Kulish, N. M. (1984) 'The effect of the sex of the analyst on the transference'. *Bulletin of the Menninger Clinic* 48: 95–110.

Lax, R. F. (1969) 'Some considerations about transference and countertransference manifestations evoked by the analyst's pregnancy'. *International Journal of Psycho-Analysis* 50: 363–372.

Lester, E. (1982) 'The female analyst and the erotized transference.' Paper presented at the meeting of the American Psychoanalytic Association, New York, December.

Rappaport, E. (1956) 'The management of an erotized transference'. *Psychoanalytic Quarterly* 25: 515–529.

Stoller, R. J. (1976) *Sex and Gender*, Vol. II. New York: Jason Aronson.

Swartz, J. (1967) 'The erotized transference and other transference problems'. *Psychoanalytic Forum* 3: 307–318.

Szmarag, R. (1982) 'Special Panel A: erotic transference and countertransference between the female therapist and the male patient'. *Academy Forum* 26: 11–13.

Tower, L. E. (1956) 'Countertransference'. *Journal of the American Psychoanalytic Association* 4: 224–255.

Tyson, P. (1982) 'A developmental line of gender identity, gender role, and choice of love object'. *Journal of the American Psychoanalytic Association* 30: 61–86.

Wagonfeld, S. (1982) 'Panel on gender and gender role'. *Journal of the American Psychoanalytic Association* 30: 185–196.

Index

Morgenthaler, F. 81, 86
mother: and baby 204–5; body 206;
    coldness 171, 172, 174; controlling
    94–5; criticism of 206–7; and daughter
    identity 151–3; dependence on 265;
    emotional bond 41, 169; and fantasy
    146–7; and gender experience 148–9;
    and gender identity 257; idealised 39;
    identified with 266; impersonated 86;
    incestuous 184, 191; and infant bond
    23; and infants' gender 205–6; internal
    116; and lack of intimacy 22–3, 106;
    narcissistic 167; nurturant 214; and
    perversion 81, 82, 189–90; phallic see
    phallic mother; and physical contact
    26–7, 96, 149–50; power 19–20,
    111–12; rejecting 178; role in
    development 18, 97; search for 97;
    seductive 255; and sexual acting out
    87; sexually abusive 184, 191; as
    suffocating 133, 215; as terrifying
    figure 21; and transference 21;
    withdrawal 166–7; withholding 215
mothering, demands for 264
mourning 13, 72, 104–22, 157; analyst as
    container 174, 175–6; of analysts 114;
    and anger 172; as developmental
    process 158, 159–60, 174–8; and
    dreams 109–11; and erotic
    transference 160, 166, 175; and
    homoerotic transference 158;
    interpersonal 173; and loss tolerance
    165; and new life 113–14; of Oedipal
    object 113–16, 120; as positive force
    104–5; of pre-Oedipal object 106–11;
    resistance aspects 116; and separation
    107; stages 106, 166–9

narcissism 167; as compensation 118; in
    countertransference 74–5, 219; as
    defense 100, 102; in transference 74–5
neurosis, as infantile sexuality 56–7

O'Connor, Noreen 123–4
Oedipal anxiety 242
Oedipal complex 90, 102; defined 240;
    negative 230–1, 240, 245, 246–7
Oedipal conflict 123, 242
Oedipal father 228
Oedipal object: letting go of 120, 158;
    mourning of 113–16; wished for 120
Oedipal phase 249, 250; disappointments
    of 155

Oedipal transference 42–3, 180, 231;
    negative 100–1, 249; from negative to
    positive 244–5

paranoia 162
paranoid-schizoid position 120–1, 177
parents: empathy with 109; exclude child
    154, 155; and revenge 41, 108
paternal function 5–6, 41
paternal transference see transference,
    paternal
patient: attempts to control analyst 95,
    96, 97; blackmail 94; demanding 96,
    255–6, 261, 264; depends on analyst
    94; dying 13; fear of warmth 94;
    images of therapist 214–17; improved
    relations with women 245; in love with
    analyst 98; and mutuality 245;
    negative sexual image 219–20; and
    paternal v. maternal transference 227,
    233, 234, 235; positive sexual image
    218–19; and previous analysts 102;
    'wild side' 137–8
perversion 80–3, 143; acting out 82–4; and
    child development 81–2;
    contemporary thoughts on 81; female
    184–97 (as defense 187; definitions
    186–7; literature 185, 186; and
    relationships 187–8; site of 186–7)
phallic mother 93, 161–2, 179, 224–6;
    analyst seen as 98, 100, 179, 237; and
    castration anxiety 225; fears of 230–1,
    247; Freud's view 224–5; and infantile
    fears 225; and paternal images 228–9,
    232; as symbolic barrier 236–7; and
    theoretic controversies 226; and
    witches 225
phallic woman 163, 259, 270
phantasy: and gender 146–7; of
    masturbation 190; unconscious 146–7
political context 124, 126
power balance 19–20; and dying patient
    34
pre-genital stage 249
premature termination of analysis 61–2
pre-Oedipal stage 90, 180, 228, 250
professional ethics 73, 74, 75–80, 83–4
psychoanalysis: history 199; schools 4–5
psychoanalysis theory: and heterosexual
    identity 129; on homosexuality 127
psychoanalysts see analysts
psychological opposites 3–4
psychotherapist see analyst